THE ACCOMPLISHT COOK,
OR
THE ART & MYSTERY OF COOKERY

LECTOR HOUSE PUBLIC DOMAIN WORKS

THE ACCOMPLISHT COOK,
OR THE ART & MYSTERY OF COOKERY

ROBERT MAY

ISBN:978-93-5342-621-7

First Published: 1685

LECTOR HOUSE LLP
E-MAIL: lectorpublishing@gmail.com

THE
ACCOMPLISHT COOK,
OR
THE
ART & MYSTERY
OF
COOKERY.

Wherein the whole A R T is revealed in a
more easie and perfect Method, than hath
been publisht in any language.

Expert and ready Ways for the Dressing of all Sorts of FLESH, FOWL, and
FISH, with variety of SAUCES proper for each of them; and how to raise
all manner of *Pastes*; the best Directions for all sorts of *Kickshaws*, also the
Terms of C A R V I N G and S E W I N G .

An exact account of all *Dishes* for all *Seasons* of the Year, with
other *A-la-mode Curiosities.*

The Fifth Edition, with large Additions throughout the whole work: be-
sides two hundred Figures of several Forms for all manner of bak'd Meats,
(either Flesh, or Fish) as, Pyes Tarts, Custards; Cheesecakes, and Florentines, placed in Tables, and directed to the Pages they appertain to.

Approved by the fifty five Years Experience and Industry of
R O B E R T   M A Y ; in his Attendance on several Persons of great
Honour.

1685.

To the Right Honourable my Lord Montague,
My Lord Lumley, and my Lord Dormer; and to
the Right worshipful Sir Kenelme Digby, so well
known to this Nation for their Admired Hospitalities.

Right Honourable, and Right Worshipful,

HE is an Alien, a meer Stranger in *England*, that hath not been acquainted with your generous House-keepings; for my own part my more particular tyes of service to you my Honoured Lords, have built me up to the height of this Experience, for which this Book now at last dares appear to the World; those times which I tended upon your Honours were those Golden Days of Peace and Hospitality when you enjoyed your own, so as to entertain and releive others.

Right Honourable, and Right Worshipful, I have not only been an eye-witness, but interested by my attendance; so as that I may justly acknowledge those Triumphs and magnificent Trophies of Cookery that have adorned your Tables; nor can I but confess to the world, except I should be Guilty of the highest Ingratitude, that the only structure of this my Art and knowledge, I owed to your costs, generous and inimitable Epences; thus not only I have derived my experience, but your Country hath reapt the Plenty of your Humanity and charitable Bounties.

Right Honourable, and Right Worshipful, Hospitality which was once a Relique of the Gentry, and a known Cognizance to all ancient Houses, hath lost her Title through the unhappy and Cruel Disturbances of these Times, she is now reposing of her lately so alarmed Head on your beds of Honour: In the mean space that our English World may know the *Mecæna*'s and Patrons of this Generous Art, I have exposed this Volume to the Publick, under the Tuition of your Names; at whose Feet I prostrate these Endeavours, and shall for ever remain

Your most humble
devoted Servant.
ROBERT MAY.

From Soleby in
Leicestershire,

September 29. 1684.

To the Master Cooks, and to such young Practitioners of the Art of Cookery, to whom this Book may be useful.

T O you first, most worthy Artists, I acknowledg one of the chief Motives that made me to adventure this Volume to your Censures, hath been to testifie my gratitude to your experienced Society; nor could I omit to direct it to you, as it hath been my ambition, that you should be sensible of my Proficiency of Endeavours in this Art. To all honest well intending Men of our Profession, or others, this Book cannot but be acceptable, as it plainly and profitably discovers the *Mystery* of the *whole Art*; for which, though I may be *envied by some that only value their private Interests above Posterity, and the publick good*, yet God and my own Conscience would not permit me *to bury these my Experiences with my Silver Hairs in the Grave*: and that more especially, as the advantages of my Education hath raised me above the *Ambitions* of others, in the converse I have had with other *Nations*, who in this *Art* fall short of what I *have known experimented by you my worthy Country men*. Howsoever, the *French by their Insinuations, not without enough of Ignorance*, have bewitcht some of the *Gallants of our Nation* with Epigram Dishes, smoakt rather than drest, so strangely to captivate the *Gusto*, their *Mushroom'd Experiences* for *Sauce* rather than *Diet*, for the generality howsoever called *A-la-mode*, not worthy of being taken notice on. As I live in *France*, and had the Language and have been an eye-witness of their *Cookeries* as well, as a Peruser of their Manuscripts, and Printed *Authors* whatsoever I found good in them, I have inserted in this *Volume*. I do acknowledg my self not to be a little beholding to the *Italian* and *Spanish* Treatises; though without my fosterage, and bringing up under the *Generosities* and *Bounties of my Noble Patrons and Masters*, I could never have arrived to this *Experience*. To be confined and limited to the narrowness of a Purse, is to want the *Materials* from which the *Artist* must gain his knowledge. Those *Honourable Persons, my Lord* Lumley, and others, with whom I have spent a part of my time, were such whose generous cost never weighed the Expence, so that they might arrive to that right and high esteem they had of their *Gusto's*. Whosoever peruses this *Volume* shall find it amply exemplified in *Dishes* of such high prices, which only these *Noblesses Hospitalities* did reach to: I should have sinned against their (to be perpetuated) Bounties, if I had not set down their several varieties, that the *Reader* might be as well acquainted with what is extraordinary, as what is ordinary in this *Art*; as I am truly sensible, that some of those things that I have set down will amaze a not thorow-paced *Reader* in the *Art of Cookery*, as they are Delicates, never till this time made known to the World.

Fellow Cooks, that I might give a testimony to my *Countrey* of the *laudableness of our Profession*, that I might encourage young Undertakers to make a Progress in the *Practice of this Art,* I have laid open these Experiences, as I was most unwilling to hide my Talent, but have ever endeavoured to do good to others; I acknowledge that there hath already been *several Books publisht,* and amongst the rest some out of the *French,* for ought I could perceive to very little purpose, *empty and unprofitable Treatises,* of as little use as some *Niggards Kitchens,* which the *Reader* in respect of the confusion of the Method, or barrenness of those *Authors* experience, hath rather been puzled then profited by; as those already extant Authors have trac't but one common beaten Road, repeating for the main what others have in the same homely manner done before them: It hath been my task to denote some *new Faculty or Science,* that others have not yet discovered; this the *Reader* will quickly discern by those *new Terms of Art* which he shall meet withal throughout this *whole Volume.* Some things I have inserted of *Carving and Sewing* that I might demonstrate the whole Art. In the contrivance of these my labours, I have so managed them for the general good, that those whose Purses cannot reach to the cost of rich Dishes, I have descended to their meaner Expences, that they may give, though upon a sudden Treatment, to their Kindred, Friends, Allies and Acquaintance, a handsome and relishing entertainment in all seasons of the year, though at some distance from Towns or Villages. Nor have my serious considerations been wanting amongst direction for Diet how to order what belongs to the sick, as well as to those that are in health; and withal my care hath been such, that in this Book as in a Closet, is contained all such Secrets as relate to *Preserving, Conserving, Candying, Distilling,* and such rare varieties as they are most concern'd in the *best husbandring and huswifering* of them. Nor is there any Book except that of the *Queens Closet,* which was so *enricht with Receipts* presented to her *Majesty,* as yet that I ever saw in any *Language,* that ever contained so many *profitable Experiences, as in this Volume*: in all which the *Reader* shall find most of the *Compositions,* and mixtures easie to be prepared, most pleasing to the Palate, and not too chargeable to the Purse; since you are at liberty to employ as much or as little therein as you please.

In this Edition I have enlarged the whole Work; and there is added two hundred several Figures of all sorts of Pies, Tarts, Custards, Cheesecakes, &c. more than was in the former: You will find them in Tables directed to the *Folio* they have relation to; there being such variety of Forms, the Artists may use which of them they please.

It is impossible for any *Author* to please all People, no more than the best Cook can fancy their Palats whose Mouths are always out of taste. As for those who make it their business to hide their Candle under a Bushel, to do only good to themselves, and not to others, such as will curse me for revealing the Secrets of this Art, I value the discharge of my own Conscience, in doing Good, above all their malice; protesting to the whole world, that I have not *concealed any material Secret* of above my *fifty and five years Experience*; my Father *being a Cook* under whom in my Child-hood I was bred up in this Art.

To conclude, the diligent Peruser of this *Volume* gains that in a small time (as to the *Theory*) which an *Apprenticeship* with some *Masters* could never have taught them. I have no more to do, but to desire of God a blessing upon these my Endeavours; and remain.

Yours in the most ingenious
ways of Friendship,

Sholeby in
Leicestershire,
Sept. 30. 1664.

ROBERT MAY.

A short Narrative of some Passages of the Authors Life.

FOR the better knowledge of the worth of this Book, though it be not usual, the *Author* being living, it will not be amiss to acquaint the *Reader* with a breif account of some passages of his Life, as also the eminent Persons (renowned for their House-keeping) whom he hath served through the whole series of his Life; for as the growth of Children argue the strength of the Parents, so doth the judgment and abilities of the Artist conduce to the making and goodness of the Work: now that such great knowledge in this commendable Art was not gained but by long experience, practise, and converse with the most able men in their times, the *Reader* in this breif Narrative may be informed by what steps and degrees he ascended to the same.

He was born in the year of our Lord 1588. His Father being one of the ablest *Cooks* in his time, and his first Tutor in the knowledge and practice of Cookery; under whom having attained to some perfection in this Art, the old Lady *Dormer* sent him over into *France*, where he continued five years, being in the Family of a noble Peer, and first President of *Paris*; where he gained not only the *French* Tongue but also bettered his Knowledge in his *Cookery*, and returning again into *England*, was bound an Apprentice in *London* to Mr. *Arthur Hollinsworth* in *Newgate Market*, one of the ablest Work-men in *London*, Cook to the *Grocers Hall and Star Chamber*. His Apprentiship being out, the Lady *Dormer* sent for him to be her Cook under Father (who then served that Honourable Lady) where were four Cooks more, such Noble Houses were then kept, the glory of that, and the shame of this present Age; then were those Golden Days wherein were practised the *Triumphs and Trophies of Cookery*; then was Hospitality esteemed, Neighbourhood preserved, the Poor cherished, and God honoured; then was Religion less talkt on, and more practised; then was Atheism & Schism less in fashion: then did men strive to be good, rather then to seem so. Here he continued till the Lady *Dormer* died, and then went again to *London*, and served the Lord *Castlehaven*, after that the Lord *Lumley*, that great lover and knower of Art, who wanted no knowledge in the discerning this mystery; next the Lord *Montague* in *Sussex*; and at the beginning of these wars, the Countess of *Kent*, then Mr. *Nevel* of *Crissen Temple* in *Essex*, whose Ancestors the *Smiths* (of whom he is descended) were the greatest maintainers of Hospitality in all those parts; nor doth the present M. *Nevel* degenerate from their laudable examples. Divers other Persons of like esteem and quality hath he served; as the Lord *Rivers*, Mr. *John Ashburnam* of the Bed-Chambers, Dr. *Steed* in *Kent*, Sir *Thomas Stiles* of *Drury Lane* in *London*, Sir *Marmaduke Constable* in *York-shire*, Sir *Charles*

Lucas; and lastly the Right Honourable the Lady *Englefield*, where he now liveth.

Thus have I given you a breif account of his Life, I shall next tell you in what high esteem this noble Art was with the Ancient Romans: *Plutarch* reports, that *Lucullus* his ordinary diet was fine dainty dishes, with works of pastry, banketting dishes, and fruit curiously wrought and prepared; that, his Table might be furnished with choice of varieties, (as the noble Lord *Lumley* did) that he kept and nourished all manner of Fowl all the year long. To this purpose he telleth us a story how *Pompey* being sick, the Physitians willed him to eat a Thrush, and it being said there was none to be had; because it was then Summer; it was answered they might have them at *Lucullus*'s house who kept both Thrushes and all manner of Fowl, all the year long. This *Lucullus* was for his Hospitality so esteemed in *Rome*, that there was no talk, but of his Noble House-keeping. The said *Plutarch* reports how *Cicero* and *Pompey* inviting themselves to sup with him, they would not let him speak with his men to provide any thing more then ordinary; but he telling them he would sup in *Apollo*, (a Chamber so named, and every Chamber proportioned their expences) he by this wile beguil'd them, and a supper was made ready estimated at fifty thousand pence, every *Roman* penny being seven pence half penny *English* money; a vast sum for that Age, before the *Indies* had overflowed *Europe*. But I have too far digressed from the Author of whom I might speak much more as in relation to his Person and abilities, but who will cry out the Sun shines? this already said is enough to satisfie any but the malicious, who are the greatest enemies to all honest endeavours. *Homer* had his *Zoilus*, and *Virgil* his *Bavius*; the best Wits have had their detractors, and the greatest Artists have been maligned; the best on't is, such Works as these outlive their *Authors* with an honurable respect of Posterity, whilst envious Criticks never survive their own happiness, their Lives going out like the snuff of a Candle.

W. W.

Triumphs and Trophies in Cookery, to be used at Festival Times, as Twelfth-day, &c.

Make the likeness of a Ship in Paste-board, with Flags and Streamers, the Guns belonging to it of Kickses, bind them about with packthread, and cover them with close paste proportionable to the fashion of a Cannon with Carriages, lay them in places convenient as you see them in Ships of war, with such holes and trains of powder that they may all take Fire; Place your Ship firm in the great Charger; then make a salt round about it, and stick therein egg-shells full of sweet water, you may by a great Pin take all the meat out of the egg by blowing, and then fill it up with the rose-water, then in another Charger have the proportion of a Stag made of course paste, with a broad Arrow in the side of him, and his body filled up with claret-wine; in another Charger at the end of the Stag have the proportion of a Castle with Battlements, Portcullices, Gates and Draw-Bridges made of Past-board, the Guns and Kickses, and covered with course paste as the former; place it at a distance from the ship to fire at each other. The Stag being placed betwixt them with egg shells full of sweet water (as before) placed in salt. At each side of the Charger wherein is the Stag, place a Pye made of course paste, in one of which let there be some live Frogs, in each other some live Birds; make these Pyes of course Paste filled with bran, and yellowed over with saffron or the yolks of eggs, guild them over in spots, as also the Stag, the Ship, and Castle; bake them, and place them with guilt bay-leaves on turrets and tunnels of the Castle and Pyes; being baked, make a hole in the bottom of your pyes, take out the bran, put in your Frogs, and Birds, and close up the holes with the same course paste, then cut the Lids neatly up; To be taken off the Tunnels; being all placed in order upon the Table, before you fire the trains of powder, order it so that some of the Ladies may be perswaded to pluck the Arrow out of the Stag, then will the Claret-wine follow, as blood that runneth out of a wound. This being done with admiration to the beholders, after some short pause, fire the train of the Castle, that the pieces all of one side may go off, then fire the Trains, of one side of the Ship as in a battel; next turn the Chargers; and by degrees fire the trains of each other side as before. This done to sweeten the stink of powder, let the Ladies take the egg-shells full of sweet waters and throw them at each other. All dangers being seemingly over, by this time you may suppose they will desire to see what is in the pyes; where lifting first the lid off one pye, out skip some Frogs, which make the Ladies to skip and shreek; next after the other pye, whence come out the Birds, who by a natural instinct flying in the light, will put out the Candles; so that what with the flying Birds and skipping Frogs, the one above, the other beneath, will cause much delight and pleasure to the whole company: at length the Candles are lighted, and a banquet brought in, the Musick sounds, and every one with much delight and content rehearses their actions in the former passages. These were formerly the delight of the Nobility, before good House-keeping had left *England*, and the Sword really acted that which was only counterfeited in such honest and laudable Exercises as these.

On the Unparalell'd Piece of Mr. May His Cookery.

SEe here a work set forth of such perfection,
Will praise it self, and doth not beg protection
From flatter'd greatness. Industry and pains
For gen'ral good, his aim, his Countrey gains;
Which ought respect him. A good *English* Cook,
Excellent Modish Monsieurs, and that Book
Call'd *Perfect Cook*, *Merete's* Pastery
Translated, looks like old hang'd Tapistry,
The wrong side outwards: so Monsieur adieu,
I'm for our Native *Mays* Works rare and new,
Who with Antique could have prepar'd and drest
The Nations *quondam* grand Imperial Feast,
Which that thrice Crown'd Third *Edward* did ordain
For his high Order, and their Noble Train,
Whereon St. *George* his famous Day was seen,
A Court on Earth that did all Courts out-shine.

And how all Rarities and Cates might be
Order'd for a Renown'd Solemnity,
Learn of this Cook, who with judgment, and reason,
Teacheth for every Time, each thing its true Season;
Making his Compounds with such harmony,
Taste shall not charge with superiority
Of Pepper, Salt, or Spice, by the best Pallat,
Or any one Herb in his broths or Sallat.
Where Temperance and Discretion guides his deeds;
Satis his Motto, where nothing exceeds.
Or ought to wast, for there's good Husbandry
To be observ'd, as Art in Cookery.
Which of the Mathematicks doth pertake,
Geometry proportions when they bake.
Who can in paste erect (of finest flour)
A compleat Fort, a Castle, or a Tower.
A City Custard doth so subtly wind,

That should Truth seek, she'd scarce all corners find;
Platform of Sconces, that might Souldiers teach,
To fortifie by works as well as Preach.
I'le say no more; for as I am a sinner,
I've wrought my self a stomach to a dinner.
Inviting Poets not to tantalize,
But feast, (not surfeit) here their Fantasies.

James Parry.

To the Reader of (my very loving Friend) Mr. Robert May *his incomparable Book of Cookery.*

S Ee here's a Book set forth with such things in't,
As former Ages never saw in Print;
Something I'de write in praise on't, but the Pen,
Of Famous *Cleaveland,* or renowned *Ben,*
If unintomb'd might give this Book its due,
By their high strains, and keep it always new.
But I whose ruder Stile could never clime,
Or step beyond a home-bred Country Rhime,
Must not attempt it: only this I'le say,
Cato's Res Rustica's far short of *May.*
Here's taught to keep all sorts of flesh in date,
All sorts of Fish, if you will marinate;
To candy, to preserve, to souce, to pickle,
To make rare Sauces, both to please, and tickle
The pretty Ladies palats with delight;
Both how to glut, and gain an Appetite.
The Fritter, Pancake, Mushroom; with all these,
The curious Caudle made of Ambergriese.
He is so universal, he'l not miss,
The Pudding, nor Bolonian Sausages.
Italian, Spaniard, French, he all out-goes,
Refines their Kickshaws, and their Olio's,
The rarest use of Sweet-meats, Spicery,
And all things else belong to Cookery:
Not only this, but to give all content,
Here's all the Forms of every Implement
To work or carve with, so he makes the able
To deck the Dresser, and adorn the Table.
What dish goes first of every kind of Meat,
And so ye're welcom, pray fall too, and eat.
Reader, read on, for I have done; farewell,
The Book's so good, it cannot chuse but sell.

Thy well-wishing Friend,
John Town.

The most Exact, or A-la-mode Ways
of Carving and Sewing.

Terms of Carving.

Break that deer, leach that brawn, rear that goose, lift that swan, sauce that capon, spoil that hen, frust that chicken, unbrace that mallard, unlace that coney, dismember that hern, display that crane, disfigure that peacock, unjoynt that bittern, untach that curlew, allay that pheasant, wing that partridge, wing that quail, mince that plover, thigh that pidgeon, border that pasty, thigh that woodcock; thigh all manner of small birds.

Timber the fire, tire that egg, chine that salmon, string that lamprey, splat that pike, souce that plaice, sauce that tench, splay that bream, side that haddock, tusk that barbel, culpon that trout, fin that chivin, transon that eel, tranch that sturgeon, undertranch that porpus, tame that crab, barb that lobster.

Service.

First, set forth mustard and brawn, pottage, beef, mutton, stewed pheasant, swan, capon, pig, venison, hake, custard, leach, lombard, blanchmanger, and jelly; for standard, venison, roast kid, fawn, and coney, bustard, stork, crane, peacock with his tail, hern-shaw, bittern, woodcock, partridge, plovers, rabbits, great birds, larks, doucers, pampuff, white leach, amber-jelly, cream of almonds, curlew, brew, snite, quail, sparrow, martinet, pearch in jelly, petty pervis, quince baked, leach, dewgard, fruter fage, blandrells or pippins with caraways in comfits, wafers, and Ipocras.

Sauce for all manner of Fowls.

Mustard is good with brawn, Beef, Chine of Bacon, and Mutton, Verjuyce good to boil'd Chickens and Capons; Swan with Chaldrons, Ribs of Beef with Garlick, mustard, pepper, verjuyce, ginger; sauce of lamb, pig and fawn, mustard, and sugar; to pheasant, partridge, and coney, sauce gamelin; to hern-shaw, egrypt, plover, and crane, brew, and curlew, salt, and sugar, and water of Camot, bustard, shovilland, and bittern, sauce gamelin; woodcock, lapwhing, lark, quail, martinet, venison and snite with white salt; sparrows and thrushes with salt, and cinamon. Thus with all meats sauce shall have the operation.

Directions for the order of

carving Fowl.

Lift that Swan.

The manner of cutting up a Swan must be to slit her right down in the middle of the breast, and so clean thorow the back from the neck to the rump, so part her in two halves cleanly and handsomly, that you break not nor tear the meat, lay the two halves in a fair charger with the slit sides downwards, throw salt about it, and let it again on the Table. Let your sauce be chaldron for a Swan, and serve it in saucers.

Rear the Goose.

You must break a goose contrary to the former way. Take a goose[1] being roasted, and take off both his legs fair like a shoulder of Lamb, take him quite from the body then cut off the belly piece round close to the lower end of the breast: lace her down with your knife clean through the breast on each side your thumbs bredth for the bone in the middle of the breast; then take off the pinion of each side, and the flesh which you first lac't with your knife, raise it up clear from the bone, and take it from the carcase with the pinion; then cut up the bone which lieth before in the breast (which is commonly call'd the merry thought) the skin and the flesh being upon it; then cut from the brest-bone, another slice of flesh clean thorow, & take it clean from the bone, turn your carcase, and cut it asunder the back-bone above the loin-bones: then take the rump-end of the back-bone, and lay it in a fair dish with the skinny-side upwards, lay at the fore-end of that the merry-thought with the skin side upward, and before that the apron of the goose; then lay your pinions on each side contrary, set your legs on each side contrary behind them, that the bone end of the legs may stand up cross in the middle of the dish, & the wing pinions on the outside of them; put under the wing pinions on each side the long slices of flesh which you cut from the breast bone, and let the ends meet under the leg bones, let the other ends lie cut in the dish betwixt the leg and the pinion; then pour your sauce into the dish under your meat, throw on salt, and set it on the table.

To cut up a Turkey or Bustard.

Raise up the leg very fair, and open the joynt with the point of your knife, but take not off the leg; then lace down the breast with your knife on both sides, & open the breast pinion with the knife, but take not the pinion off; then raise up the merry-thought betwixt the breast bone, and the top of the merry-thought, lace down the flesh on both sides of the breast-bone, and raise up the flesh called the brawn, turn it outward upon both sides, but break it not, nor cut it not off; then cut off the wing pinion at the joynt next to the body, and stick on each side the pinion in the place where ye turned out the brawn, but cut off the sharp end of the Pinion, take the middle piece, and that will just fit the place.

You may cut up a capon or pheasant the same way, but of your capon cut not off the pinion, but in the place where you put the pinion of the turkey, you must put the gizard of your capon on each side half.

---

[1]   You must break a goose contrary to the former way. Take a goose being roasted...

Dismember that Hern.

Take off both the legs, and lace it down to the breast with your knife on both sides, raise up the flesh, and take it clean off with the pinion; then stick the head in the breast, set the pinion on the contrary side of the carcase, and the leg on the other side, so that the bones ends may meet cross over the carcase, and the other wings cross over upon the top of the carcase.

Unbrace that Mallard.

Raise up the pinion and the leg, but take them not off, raise the merry-thought from the breast, and lace it down on each side of the breast with your knife, bending to and fro like ways.

Unlace that Coney.

Turn the back downwards, & cut the belly flaps clean off from the kidney, but take heed you cut not the kidney nor the flesh, then put in the point of your knife between the kidneys, and loosen the flesh from each side the bone then turn up the back of the rabbit, and cut it cross between the wings, and lace it down close by the bone with your knife on both sides, then open the flesh of the rabbit from the bone, with the point of your knife against the kidney, and pull the leg open softly with your hand, but pluck it not off, then thrust in your knife betwixt the ribs and the kidney, slit it out, and lay the legs close together.

Sauce that Capon.

Lift up the right leg and wing, and so array forth, and lay him in the platter as he should fly, and so serve him. Know that capons or chickens be arrayed after one sauce; the chickens shall be sauced with green sauce or veriuyce.

Allay that Pheasant.

Take a pheasant, raise his legs and wings as it were a hen and no sauce but only salt.

Wing that Partridg.

Raise his legs, and his wing as a hen, if you mince him sauce him with wine, powder of ginger, and salt, and set him upon a chafing dish of coals to warm and serve.

Wing that Quail.

Take a quail and raise his legs and his wings as an hen, and no sauce but salt.

Display that Crane.

Unfold his Legs, and cut off his wings by the joynts, then take up his wings and his legs, and sauce them with powder of ginger, mustard, vinegar, and salt.

Dismember that Hern.

Raise his legs and his wings as a crane, and sauce him with vinegar, mustard, powder of ginger and salt.

Unjoynt that Bittern.

Raise his legs & wings as a heron & no sauce but salt.

Break that Egript.

Take an egript, and raise his legs and his wings as a heron, and no sauce but salt.

Untach that Curlew.

Raise his legs and wings as a hen, & no sauce but salt.

Untach that brew.

Raise his legs and his wings in the same manner, and no sauce but only salt.

Unlace that Coney.

Lay him on the back, and cut away the vents, then raise the wings and the sides, and lay bulk, chine, and sides together, sauce them with vinegar and powder of ginger.

Break that Sarcel.

Take a sarcel or teal, and raise his wings and his legs, and no sauce but only salt.

Mince that Plover.

Raise his leg and wings as a hen, and no sauce but only salt.

A Snite.

Raise his legs, wings and his shoulders as a plover, and no sauce but salt.

Thigh that Woodcock.

Raise his legs as a hen, and dight his brain.

The Sewing of Fish.
The First Course.

To go to the sewing of Fish. Musculade, Minews in few of porpos or of salmon, bak'd herring with sugar, green fish pike, lamprey, salent, porpos roasted, bak'd gurnet and baked lamprey.

The Second Course.

Jelly white and red, dates in confect, conger, salmon, birt, dorey, turbut holibut for standard, bace, trout, mullet, chevin, soles, lamprey roast, and tench in jelly.

The Third Course.

Fresh sturgeon, bream, pearch in jelly, a jole of salmon sturgeon, welks, apples and pears roasted; with sugar candy, figs of molisk, raisins, dates, capt with minced ginger, wafers, and Ipocras.

The Carving of Fish.

The carver of fish must see to peason and furmety, the tail and the liver; you must look if there be a salt porpos or sole, turrentine, and do after the form of venison; *baked herring*, lay it whole on the trencher, then white herring in a dish, open it by the back, pick out the bones and the row, and see there be mustard. Of salt fish, green-fish, salt salmon, and conger, pare away the skin; salt fish, stock fish, marling, mackrel, and hake with butter, and take away the bones & skins; *A Pike*, lay the womb upon a trencher, with pike sauce enough, *A salt Lamprey*, gobbin it in seven or eight pieces, and so present it, *A Plaice*, put out the water, then cross him with your knife, and cast on salt, wine, or ale. *Bace, Gurnet, Rochet, Bream, Chevin, Mullet, Roch, Pearch, Sole, Mackrel, Whiting, Haddock,* and *Codling*, raise them by the back, pick out the bones, and cleanse the rest in the belly. *Carp Bream, Sole,* and *Trout*, back and belly together. *Salmon, Conger, Sturgeon, Turbut, Thornback, Houndfish,* and *Holibut,* cut them in the dishes; the *Porpos* about, *Tench* in his sauce; cut two *Eels,* and *Lampreys* roast, pull off the skin, and pick out the bones, put thereto vinegar, and powder. A *Crab*, break him asunder, in a dish make the shell clean, & put in the stuff again, temper it with vinegar, and powder them, cover it with bread and heat it; a *Crevis* dight him thus, part him asunder, slit the belly, and take out the fish, pare away the red skin, mince it thin, put vinegar in the dish, and set it on the Table without heating. *A Jole of Sturgeon,* cut it into thin morsels, and lay it round about the dish, *Fresh Lamprey bak'd*, open the pasty, then take white bread, and cut it thin, lay it in a dish, & with a spoon take out Galentine, & lay it upon the bread with red wine and powder of Cinamon; then cut a gobbin of Lamprey, mince it thin, and lay it in the Gallentine, and set it on the fire to heat. *Fresh herring*, with salt and wine, *Shrimps* well pickled, *Flounders, Gudgeons, Minews,* and Muskles, Eels, and Lampreys, Sprats is good in few, musculade in worts, oysters in few, oysters in gravy, minews in porpus, salmon in jelly white and red, cream of almonds, dates in comfits, pears and quinces in sirrup, with parsley roots, mortus of hound fish raise standing.

Sauces for Fish.

Mustard is good for salt herring, salt fish, salt conger, salmon, sparling, salt eel and ling; vinegar is good with salt porpus, turrentine, salt sturgeon, salt thirlepole, and salt whale, lamprey with gallentine; verjuyce to roach, dace, bream, mullet, flounders, salt crab and chevin with powder of cinamon and ginger; green sauce is good with green fish and hollibut, cottel, and fresh turbut; put not your green sauce away for it is good with mustard.

Bills of F A R E *for every Season in the Year; also how to set forth the* M E A T *in order for that Service, as it was used before Hospitality left this Nation.*

A Bill of Fare for All-Saints-Day, *being* Novemb. 1.

Oysters.

1 A Collar of brawn and mustard.
2 A Capon in stewed broth with marrow-bones.
3 A Goose in stoffado, or two Ducks.
4 A grand Sallet.
5 A Shoulder of Mutton with oysters.
6 A bisk dish baked.
7 A roast chine of beef.
8 Minced pies or chewits of capon, tongue, or of veal.
9 A chine of Pork.
10 A pasty of venison.
11 A swan, or 2 geese roast.
12 A loyn of veal.
13 A French Pie of divers compounds.
14 A roast turkey.
15 A pig roast.
16 A farc't dish baked.
17 Two brangeese roasted, one larded.
18 Souc't Veal.
19 Two Capons roasted, one larded.
20 A double bordered Custard.

A Second Course for the same Mess.

Oranges and lemons.

1 A souc't pig.
2 A young lamb or kid roast.
3 Two Shovelers.
4 Two Herns, one larded.
5 A Potatoe-Pye.
6 A duck and mallard, one larded.
7 A souc't Turbut.
8 A couple of pheasants, one larded.
9 Marinated Carp, or Pike, or Bream.
10 Three brace of partridg, three larded.
11 Made Dish of Spinage cream baked.
12 A roll of beef.
13 Two teels roasted, one larded.
14 A cold goose pie.
15 A souc't mullet and bace.
16 A quince pye.
17 Four curlews, 2 larded.
18 A dried neats tongue.
19 A dish of anchoves.
20 A jole of Sturgeon.
Jellies and Tarts Royal, and Ginger bread, and other Fruits.

*A Bill of Fare for Christmas Day, and
how to set the Meat in order.*

Oysters.

1 A collar of brawn.
2 Stewed Broth of Mutton marrow
bones.
3 A grand Sallet.
4 A pottage of caponets.
5 A breast of veal in stoffado.
6 A boil'd partridge.
7 A chine of beef, or surloin roast.
8 Minced pies.
9 A Jegote of mutton with anchove
sauce.
10 A made dish of sweet-bread.
11 A swan roast.
12 A pasty of venison.
13 A kid with a pudding in his belly.
14 A steak pie.
15 A hanch of venison roasted.
16 A turkey roast and stuck with
cloves.
17 A made dish of chickens in puff
paste.
18 Two bran geese roasted, one larded.
19 Two large capons, one larded.
20 A Custard.

The second course for the same Mess.

Oranges and Lemons.

1 A young lamb or kid.
2 Two couple of rabbits, two larded.
3 A pig souc't with tongues.
4 Three ducks, one larded.
5 Three pheasants, 1 larded
6 A Swan Pye.
7 Three brace of partridge, three larded.
8 Made dish in puff paste.
9 Bolonia sausages, and anchoves,
mushrooms, and Cavieate, and
pickled oysters in a dish.
10 Six teels, three larded.
11 A Gammon of Westphalia Bacon.
12 Ten plovers, five larded.
13 A quince pye, or warden pie.
14 Six woodcocks, 3 larded.
15 A standing Tart in puff-paste, preserved fruits, Pippins, &c.
16 A dish of Larks.
17 Six dried neats tongues.
18 Sturgeon.
19 Powdered Geese.
Jellies.

A Bill of Fare for new-years Day.

Oysters.

1 Brawn and Mustard.
2 Two boil'd Capons in stewed Broth, or white Broth.
3 Two Turkies in stoffado.
4 A Hash of twelve Partridges, or a shoulder of mutton.
5 Two bran Geese boil'd.
6 A farc't boil'd meat with snites or ducks.
7 A marrow pudding bak't
8 A surloin of roast beef.
9 Minced pies, ten in a dish, or what number you please
10 A Loin of Veal.
11 A pasty of Venison.
12 A Pig roast.
13 Two geese roast.
14 Two capons, one larded.
15 Custards.

A Bill of Fare for February.

1 Eggs and Collops.
2 Brawn and Mustard.
3 A hash of Rabbits four.
4 A grand Fricase.
5 A grand Sallet.
6 A Chine of roast Pork.

A Bill of fare for March.

Oysters.

1 Brawn and Mustard.
2 A fresh Neats Tongue and Udder in stoffado.
3 Three Ducks in stoffado.
4 A roast Loin of Pork.
5 A pasty of Venison.
6 A Steak Pye.

A second Course for the same Mess.

Oranges and Lemons.

1 A side of Lamb
2 A souc't Pig.
3 Two couple of rabbits, two larded.
4 A duck and mallard, one larded.
5 Six teels, three larded.
6 A made dish, or Batalia-Pye.
7 Six woodcocks, 3 larded.
8 A warden pie, or a dish of quails.
9 Dried Neats tongues.
10 Six tame Pigeons, three larded.
11 A souc't Capon.
12 Pickled mushrooms, pickled Oysters, and Anchoves in a dish.
13 Twelve snites, six larded
14 Orangado Pye, or a Tart Royal of dried and wet suckets.
15 Sturgeon.
16 Turkey or goose pye.
Jelly of five or six sorts, Lay Tarts of divers colours and ginger-bread, and other Sweet-meats.

A second Course.

1 A whole Lamb roast.
2 Three Widgeons.
3 A Pippin Pye.
4 A Jole of Sturgeon.
5 A Bacon Tart.
6 A cold Turkey Pye.
Jellies and Ginger-bread, and Tarts Royal.

A second Course.

1 A side of Lamb.
2 Six Teels, three larded.
3 A Lamb-stone Pye.
4 200 of Asparagus.
5 A Warden-Pye.
6 Marinate Flounders.
Jellies and Ginger-bread, and Tarts Royal.

A Bill of fare for April.

Oysters.

1 A Bisk.
2 Cold Lamb.
3 A haunch of venison roast.
4 Four Goslings.
5 A Turkey Chicken.
6 Custards of Almonds.

A Bill of Fare for May.

1 Scotch Pottage or Skink.
2 Scotch collops of mutton
3 A Loin of Veal.
4 An oline, or a Pallat pye.
5 Three Capons, 1 larded.
6 Custards.

A bill of Fare for June.

1 A shoulder of mutton hasht
2 A Chine of Beef.
3 Pasty of Venison, a cold Hash.
4 A Leg of Mutton roast.
5 Four Turkey Chickens.
6 A Steak Pye.

A bill of Fare for July.

Muskmelons.

1 Pottage of Capon.
2 Boil'd Pigeons.
3 A hash of Caponets.
4 A Grand Sallet.
5 A Fawn.
6 A Custard.

A Bill of Fare for August.

Muskmelons.

1 Scotch collops of Veal.
2 Boil'd Breast of Mutton.
3 A Fricase of Pigeons.
4 A stewed Calves head.
5 Four Goslings.
6 Four Caponets.

A second Course.

1 Lamb, a side in joynts.
2 Turtle Doves eight.
3 Cold Neats-tongue pye.
4 8 Pidgeons, four larded.
5 Lobsters.
6 A Collar of Beef.
Tansies.

A Second Course.

1 Lamb.
2 A Tart Royal, or Quince Pye
3 A Gammon of Bacon Pie.
4 A Jole of Sturgeon.
5 Artichock Pie hot.
6 Bolonia Sausage.
Tansies.

A Second Course.

1 Jane or Kid.
2 Rabbits.
3 Shovelers.
4 Sweet-bread Pye.
5 Olines, or pewit.
6 Pigeons.

A Second Course.

1 Pease, of French Beans.
2 Gulls four, two larded.
3 Pewits eight, four larded.
4 A quodling Tart green.
5 Portugal eggs, two sorts.
6 Buttered Brawn.
Selsey Cockles broil'd.

A Second Course.

1 Dotterel twelve, six larded
2 Tarts Royal of Fruit.
3 Wheat-ears.
4 A Pye of Heath-Pouts.
5 Marinate Smelts.
6 Gammon of Bacon.
Selsey Cockles.

A Bill of Fare for September.

Oysters.

1 An Olio.
2 A Breast of Veal in stoffado.
3 twelve Partridg hashed.
4 A Grand Sallet.
5 Chaldron Pye.
6 Custard.

A bill of Fare for October.

Oysters.

1 Boil'd Ducks.
2 A hash of a loin of veal.
3 Roast Veal.
4 Two bran-geese roasted.
5 Tart Royal.
6 Custard.

A second Course.

1 Rabbits
2 Two herns, one larded.
3 Florentine of tongues.
4 8 Pigeons roast, 4 larded.
5 Pheasant pouts, 2 larded.
6 A cold hare pye.
Selsey cockles broil'd after.

A second Course.

1 Pheasant, pouts, pigeons.
2 Knots twelve.
3 Twelve quails, six larded.
4 Potato pye.
5 Sparrows roast.
6 Turbut.
Selsey Cockles.

A bill of Fare formerly used in Fasting days, and in Lent.

The first Course.

Oysters if in season.

1 Butter and eggs.
2 Barley pottage, or Rice pottage.
3 Stewed Oysters.
4 Buttered eggs on toasts.
5 Spinage Sallet boil'd.
6 Boil'd Rochet or gurnet.
7 A jole of Ling.
8 Stewed Carp.
9 Oyster Chewits.
10 Boil'd Pike.
11 Roast Eels.
12 Haddocks, fresh Cod, or Whitings.
13 Eel or Carp Pye.
14 Made dish of spinage.
15 Salt Eels.
16 Souc't Turbut.

A second Course.

1 Fried Soals.
2 Stewed oysters in scollop shells.
3 Fried Smelts.
4 Congers head broil'd.
5 Baked dish of Potatoes, or Oyster pye.
6 A spitchcock of Eels.
7 Quince pie or tarts royal.
8 Buttered Crabs.
9 Fried Flounders.
10 Jole of fresh Salmon.
11 Fried Turbut.
12 Cold Salmon pye.
13 Fried skirrets.
14 Souc't Conger.
15 Lobsters.
16 Sturgeon.

CONTENTS

SECTION IX.

SECTION XXI.

CONTENTS

THE
ACCOMPLISHT COOK,
OR,
THE WHOLE ART AND MYSTERY OF
COOKERY, FITTED FOR ALL
DEGREES AND QUALITIES.

SECTION I.

Perfect Directions for the A-la-mode Ways of dressing all manner of Boyled Meats, with their several sauces, &c.

To make an Olio Podrida.

Take a Pipkin or Pot of some three Gallons, fill it with fair water, and set it over a Fire of Charcoals, and put in first your hardest meats, a rump of Beef, *Bolonia* sausages, neats tongues two dry, and two green, boiled and larded, about two hours after the Pot is boil'd and scummed: but put in more presently after your Beef is scum'd, Mutton, Venison, Pork, Bacon, all the aforesaid in Gubbins, as big as a Ducks Egg, in equal pieces; put in also Carrots, Turnips, Onions, Cabbidge, in good big pieces, as big as your meat, a faggot of sweet herbs, well bound up, and some whole Spinage, Sorrel, Burrage, Endive, Marigolds, and other good Pot-Herbs a little chopped; and sometimes *French* Barley, or Lupins green or dry.

Then a little before you dish out your Olio; put to your pot, Cloves, Mace, Saffron, &c.

Then next have divers Fowls; as first

A Goose, or Turkey, two Capons, two Ducks, two Pheasants, two Widgeons, four Partridges, four stock Doves, four Teals, eight Snites, twenty four Quails, forty eight Larks.

Boil these foresaid Fowls in water and salt in a pan, pipkin, or pot, &c.

Then have *Bread, Marrow, Bottoms of Artichocks, Yolks of hard Eggs, Large Mace, Chesnuts boil'd and blancht, two Colliflowers, Saffron.*

And stew these in a pipkin together, being ready clenged with some good sweet butter, a little white wine and strong broth.

Some other times for variety you may use Beets, Potato's, Skirrets, Pistaches, PineApple seed, or Almonds, Poungarnet, and Lemons.

Now to dish your Olio, dish first your Beef, Veal or Pork; then your Venison, and Mutton, Tongues, Sausage, and Roots over all.

Then next your largest Fowl, Land-Fowl, or Sea-Fowl, as first, a Goose, or Turkey, two Capons, two Pheasants, four Ducks, four Widgeons, four Stock-Doves, four Partridges, eight Teals, twelve Snites, twenty four Quailes, forty eight Larks, &c.

Then broth it, and put on your pipkin of Colliflowers Artichocks, Chesnuts, some sweet-breads fried, Yolks of hard Eggs, then Marrow boil'd in strong broth or water, large Mace, Saffron, Pistaches, and all the aforesaid things being finely stewed up, and some red Beets over all, slic't Lemons, and Lemon peels whole, and run it over with beaten butter.

Marrow Pies.

For the garnish of the dish, make marrow pies made like round Chewets but not so high altogether, then have sweet-breads of veal cut like small dice, some pistaches, and Marrow, some Potato's, or Artichocks cut like Sweetbreads: as also some enterlarded Bacon; Yolks of hard Eggs, Nutmeg, Salt, Goosberries, Grapes, or Barberries, and some minced Veal in the bottom of the Pie minced with some Bacon or Beef-suit, Sparagus and Chesnuts, with a little musk; close them up, and bast them with saffron water, bake them, and liquor it with beaten butter, and set them about the dish side or brims, with some bottoms of Artichocks, and yolks of hard Eggs, Lemons in quarters, Poungarnets and red Beets boil'd, and carved.

Other Marrow Pies.

Otherways for variety, you may make other Marrow Pies of minced Veal and Beef-suit, seasoned with Pepper, Salt, Nutmegs and boiled Sparagus, cut half an inch long, yolks of hard Eggs cut in quarters, and mingled with the meat and marrow: fill your Pies, bake them not too hard, musk them, &c.

Other Marrow Pies.

Otherways, Marrow Pies of bottoms of little Artichocks, Suckers, yolks of hard eggs, Chesnuts, Marrow, and interlarded Bacon cut like dice, some Veal sweetbreads cut also, or Lamb-stones, Potato's, or Skirrets, and Sparagus, or none; season them lightly with Nutmeg, Pepper and Salt, close your Pies, and bake them.

Olio, Marrow Pies.

Butter three pound, Flower one quart, Lamb-Stones three pair, Sweet-Breads six, Marrow-bones eight, large Mace, Cock-stones twenty, interlarded Bacon one pound, knots of Eggs twelve, Artichocks twelve, Sparagus one hundred, Cocks-Combs twenty, Pistaches one pound, Nutmegs, Pepper, and Salt.

Season the aforesaid lightly, and lay them in the Pie upon some minced veal or mutton, your interlarded Bacon in thin slices of half an inch long, mingled among the rest, fill the Pie, and put in some Grapes, and slic't Lemon, Barberries or Goos-berries.

1. Pies of Marrow.

Flower, Sweet bread, Marrow, Artichocks, Pistaches, Nutmegs, Eggs, Bacon, Veal, Suit, Sparagus, Chesnuts; Musk, Saffron, Butter.

2. Marrow Pies.

Flower, Butter, Veal, Suet, Pepper, Salt, Nutmeg, Sparagus, Eggs, Grapes, Marrow, Saffron.

3. Marrow Pies.

Flower, Butter, Eggs, Artichocks, Sweet-bread, Lamb-stones, Potato's, Nutmegs, Pepper, Salt, Skirrets, Grapes, Bacon.

To the garnish of an extraordinary Olio: as followeth.

Two Collers of Pigbrawn, two Marrow Pies, twelve roste Turtle Doves in a Pie, four Pies, eighteen Quails in a Pie, four Pies, two Sallets, two Jelleys of two colours, two forc't meats, two Tarts.

Thus for an extraordinary Olio, or Olio Royal.

To make a Bisk divers ways.

Take a wrack of Mutton, and a Knuckle of Veal, put them a boiling in a Pipkin of a Gallon, with some fair water, and when it boils, scum it, and put to it some salt, two or three blades of large Mace, and a Clove or two; boil it to three pints, and strain the meat, save the broth for your use and take off the fat clean.

Then boil twelve Pigeon-Peepers, and eight Chicken Peepers, in a Pipkin with fair water, salt, and a piece of interlarded Bacon, scum them clean, and boil them fine, white and quick.

Then have a rost Capon minced, and put to it some Gravy, Nutmegs, and Salt, and stew it together; then put to it the juyce of two or three Oranges, and beaten Butter, &c.

Then have ten sweet breads, and ten pallets fried, and the same number of lips and noses being first tender boil'd and blanched, cut them like lard, and fry them, put away the butter, and put to them gravy, a little anchove, nutmeg, and a little garlick, or none, the juyce of two or three Oranges, and Marrow fried in Butter with Sage-leaves, and some beaten Butter.

Then again have some boil'd Marrow and twelve Artichocks, Suckers, and Peeches finely boil'd and put into beaten Butter, some Pistaches boiled also in some wine and Gravy, eight Sheeps tongues larded and boiled, and one hundred Sparagus boiled, and put into beaten Butter, or Skirrets.

Then have Lemons carved, and some cut like little dice.

Again fry some Spinage and Parsley, &c.

These forefaid materials being ready, have some *French* bread in the bottom of your dish.

Then dish on it your Chickens, and Pidgeons, broth it; next your Quaile, then Sweet breads, then your Pullets, then your Artichocks or Sparagus, and Pistaches, then your Lemon, Poungarnet, or Grapes, Spinage, and fryed Marrow; and if yellow Saffron or fried Sage, then round the center of your boiled meat put your minced Capon, then run all over with beaten butter, &c.

1. For variety, Clary fryed with yolks of Eggs.

2. Knots of Eggs.

3. Cocks Stones.

4. Cocks Combs.

5. If white, strained Almonds, with some of the broth.

6. Goosberries or Barberries.

7. Minced meat in Balls.

8. If green, Juyce of Spinage stamped with manchet, and strained with some of the broth, and give it a warm.

9. Garnish with boiled Spinage.

10. If yellow, yolks of hard Eggs strained with some Broth and Saffron.

And many other varieties.

A Bisk otherways.

Take a Leg of Beef, cut it into two peices, and boil it in a gallon or five quarts of water, scum it, and about half an hour after put in a knuckle of Veal, and scum it also, boil it from five quarts to two quarts or less; and being three quarters boil'd, put in some Salt, and some Cloves, and Mace, being through boil'd, strain it from the meat, and keep the broth for your use in a pipkin.

Then have eight Marrow bones clean scraped from the flesh, and finely cracked over the middle, boil in water and salt three of them, and the other leave for garnish, to be boil'd in strong broth; and laid on the top of the Bisk when it is dished.

Again boil your Fowl in water and Salt, Teals, Partridges, Pidgeons, Plovers, Quails, Larks.

Then have a Joint of Mutton made into balls with sweet Herbs, Salt, Nutmeggs, grated Bread, Eggs, Suit, a Clove or two of Garlick, and Pistaches, boil'd in Broth, with some interlarded Bacon, Sheeps tongues, larded and stewed, as also some Artichocks, Marrow, Pistaches, Sweet-Breads and Lambs-stones in strong broth, and Mace a Clove or two, some white-wine and strained almonds, or with the yolk of an Egg, Verjuyce, beaten butter, and slic't Lemon, or Grapes whole.

Then have fryed Clary, and fryed Pistaches in Yolks of Eggs.

Then Carved Lemons over all.

To make another curious boil'd meat, much like a Bisk.

Take a Rack of Mutton, cut it in four peices, and boil it in three quarts of fair Water in a Pipkin, with a faggot of sweet Herbs very hard and close bound up from end to end, scum your broth and put in some salt: Then about half an hour after put in thre chickens finely scalded and trust, three Patridges boiled in water, the blood being well soaked out of them, and put to them also three or four blades of large Mace.

Then have all manner of sweet herbs, as Parsley, Time, Savory, Marjorim, Sorrel, Sage; these being finely picked, bruise them with the back of a ladle, and a little before you dish up your boil'd meat, put them to your broth, and give them a walm or two.

Again, for the top of your boil'd meat or garnish, have a pound of interlarded Bacon in thin slices, put them in a pipkin with six marrow-bones, and twelve bottoms of yong Artichocks, and some six sweet-breads of veal, strong broth, Mace, Nutmeg, some Goosberries or Barberries, some Butter and Pistaches.

These things aforesaid being ready, and dinner called for, take a fine clean scoured dish and garnish it with Pistaches and Artichocks, carved Lemon, Grapes, and large Mace.

Then have sippets finely carved, and some slices of *French* bread in the bottom of the dish, dish three pieces of Mutton, and one in the middle, and between the mutton three Chickens, and up in the middle, the Partridge, and pour on the broth with your herbs, then put on your pipkin over all, of Marrow, Artichocks, and the other materials, then Carved Lemon, Barberries and beaten Butter over all, your carved sippets round the dish.

Another made Dish in the French Fashion, called an Entre de Table, *Entrance to the Table.*

Take the bottoms of boil'd Artichocks, the yolks of hard Eggs, yong Chicken-peepers, or Pidgeon-peepers, finely trust, Sweetbreads of Veal, Lamb-stones, blanched, and put them in a Pipkin, with Cockstones, and combs, and knots of Eggs; then put to them some strong broth, white-wine, large Mace, Nutmeg, Pepper, Butter, Salt, and Marrow, and stew them softly together.

Then have Goosberries or Grapes perboil'd, or Barberries, and put to them some beaten Butter; and Potato's, Skirrets or Sparagus boil'd, and put in beaten butter, and some boil'd Pistaches.

These being finely stewed, dish your fowls on fine carved sippets, and pour on your Sweet-Breads, Artichocks, and Sparagus on them, Grapes, and slic't Lemon, and run all over with beaten butter, &c.

Somtimes for variety, you may put some boil'd Cabbidge, Lettice, Colliflowers, Balls of minced meat, or Sausages without skins, fryed Almonds, Calves Udder.

Another French boil'd meat of Pine-molet.

Take a manchet of *French* bread of a day old, chip it and cut a round hole in the top, save the peice whole, and take out the crumb, then make a composition of a boild or a rost Capon, minced and stampt with Almond past, muskefied bisket bread, yolks of hard Eggs, and some sweet Herbs chopped fine, some yolks of raw Eggs and Saffron, Cinamon, Nutmeg, Currans, Sugar, Salt, Marrow and Pistaches; fill the Loaf, and stop the hole with the piece, and boil it in a clean cloth in a pipkin, or bake it in an oven.

Then have some forc't Chickens flead, save the skin, wings, legs, and neck whole, and mince the meat, two Pigeons also forc't, two Chickens, two boned of each, and filled with some minced veal or mutton, with some interlarded Bacon, or Beef-suet, and season it with Cloves, Mace, Pepper, Salt, and some grated parmison or none, grated bread, sweet Herbs chopped small, yolks of Eggs, and Grapes, fill the skins, and stitch up the back of the skin, then put them in a deep dish, with some Sugar, strong broth, Artichocks, Marrow, Saffron, Sparrows, or Quails, and some boiled Sparagus.

For the garnish of the aforesaid dish, rost Turneps and rost Onions, Grapes, Cordons, and Mace.

Dish the forced loaf in the midst of the dish, the Chickens, and Pigeons round about it, and the Quails or small birds over all, with marrow, Cordons, Artichoks or Sparagus, Pine apple-seed, or Pistaches, Grapes, and Sweet-breads, and broth it on sippets.

To boil a Chine of Veal, whole, or in peices.

Boil it in water, salt, or in strong broth with a faggot of sweet Herbs, Capers, Mace, Salt, and interlarded Bacon in thin slices, and some Oyster liquor.

Your Chines being finely boiled, have some stewed Oysters by themselves with some Mace and fine onions whole, some vinegar, butter, and pepper &c.

Then have Cucumbers boiled by themselves in water and salt, or pickled Cucumbers boiled in water, and put in beaten Butter, and Cabbidge-lettice, boiled also in fair water, and put in beaten Butter.

Then dish your Chines on sippits, broth them, and put on your stewed Oysters, Cucumbers, Lettice, and parboil'd Grapes, Boclites, or slic't lemon, and run it over with beaten Butter.

Chines of Veal otherways, whole, or in pieces.

Stew them, being first almost rosted, put them into a deep Dish, with some Gravy, some strong broth, white Wine, Mace, Nutmeg, and some Oyster Liquor, two or three slices of lemon and salt, and being finely stewed serve them on sippits, with that broth and slic't Lemon, Goosberries, and beaten Butter, boil'd Marrow, fried Spinage, &c. For variety Capers, or Sampier.

Chines of Veal boiled with fruit, whole.

Put it in a stewing pan or deep dish, with some strong Broth, large Mace, a little White Wine, and when it boils scum it, then put some dates to, being half boil'd and Salt, some white Endive, Sugar, and Marrow.

Then boil some fruit by it self, your meat and broth being finely boil'd, Prunes and Raisons of the Sun, strain some six yolks of Eggs, with a little Cream, and put it in your broth, then dish it on sippets, your Chine, and garnish your dish with Fruit, Mace, Dates Sugar, slic't Lemon, and Barberries, &c.

Chines of Veal otherways.

Stew the whole with some strong broth, White-wine, and Caper-Liquor, slices of interlarded Bacon, Gravy, Cloves, Mace, whole Pepper, Sausages of minced Meat, without skins, or little Balls, some Marrow, Salt, and some sweet Herbs picked of all sorts, and bruised with the back of a Ladle; put them to your broth, a quarter of an hour before you dish your Chines, and give them a warm, and dish up your Chine on *French* Bread, or sippits, broth it, and run it over with beaten butter, Grapes or slic't Lemon, &c.

Chines of Mutton boil'd whole, or Loins, or any Joint whole.

Boil it in a long stewing-pan or deep dish with fair water as much as will cover it, and when it boils cover it, being scumm'd first, and put to it some Salt, White-wine, and some Carrots cut like dice; your broth being half boil'd, strain it, blow off the fat, and wash away the dregs from your Mutton, wash also your pipkin, or stewing pan, and put in again your broth, with some Capers, and large Mace: stew your broth and materials together softly, and lay your Mutton by in some warm broth or dish, then put in also some sweet Herbs, chopped with Onions, boil'd among your broth.

Then have Colliflowers ready boil'd in water and salt, and put in beaten butter, with some boil'd marrow, then the Mutton and Broth being ready, dissolve two or three yolks of Eggs with White-Wine, Verjuyce or Sack; give it a walm, and dish up your meat on sippets finely carved, or *French* bread in slices, and broth it; then lay on your Colliflowers, Marrow, Carrots, and Gooseberries, Barberries or Grapes, and run it over with beaten Butter.

Sometimes for variety, according to the seasons, you may use Turnips, Parsnips, Artichocks, Sparagus, Hopbuds or Colliflowers, boild in water and salt, and put in beaten Butter, Cabbidge sprouts, or Cabbidge, Lettice, and Chesnuts.

And for the thickning of this broth sometimes, take strained Almonds, with strong broth, and Saffron, or none.

Other-while grated bread, Yolks of hard Eggs, and Verjuyce, &c.

To boil a Chine, Rack, or Loin, of Mutton, otherways, whole, or in pieces.

Boil it in a stewing-pan or deep dish, with fair water as much as will cover it, and when it boils scum it, and put to it some salt; then being half boil'd, take up the meat, strain the broth, and blow off the fat, wash the stewing-pan and meat, then put in again the crag end of the Mutton, to make the broth good, and put to it some Mace.

Then a little before you take up your mutton, a handful of picked Parsley, chopped small, put it in the broth, with some whole marigold flowers, and your whole chine of mutton give a walm or two, then dish it up on sippets and broth it. Then have Raisins of the Sun and Currans boiled tender, lay on it, and garnish your Dish with Prunes, Marigold-flowers, Mace, Lemons, and Barberries, &c.

Otherways without Fruit, boil it with Capers; and all manner of sweet herbs stripped, some Spinage, and Parsley bruised with the back of a Ladle, Mace, and Salt, &c.

To boil a Chine of Mutton, whole or in peices, or any other Joint.

Boil it in a fair glazed pipkin, being well scummed, put in a faggot of sweet herbs, as Time, Parsly, Sweet Marjoram, bound hard and stripped with your Knife, and put some Carrots cut like small dice, or cut like Lard, some Raisins, Prunes, Marigold-flowers, and salt, and being finely boiled down, serve it on sippits, garnish your dish with Raisins, Mace, Prunes, Marigold-flowers, Carrots, Lemons, boil'd Marrow, &c.

Sometimes for change leave out Carrots and Fruit.

Use all as beforesaid, and add white Endive, Capers, Samphire, run it over with beaten Butter and Lemons.

Barley Broth.

Chine of Mutton or Veal in Barley Broth, Rack, or any Joynt.

Take a Chine or Knuckle, and joynt it, put it in a Pipkin with some strong broth, and when it boils, scum it, and put in some French Barley, being first boiled in two or three waters, with some large Mace, and a faggot of sweet herbs bound up, and close hard tied, some Raisins, Damask Prunes, and Currans, or no Prunes, and Marigold-flowers; boil it to an indifferent thickness, and serve it on sippets.

Barley Broth otherwise.

Boil the Barley first in two waters, and then put it to a Knuckle of Veal, and to the Broth, Salt, Raisins, sweet Herbs a faggot, large Mace, and the quantity of a fine Manchet slic't together.

Otherwise.

Otherways without Fruit: put some good Mutton-gravy, Saffron, and sometimes Raisins only.

Chine or any Joint.

Otherways stew them with strong broth and White-Wine, put it in a Pipkin to them, scum it, and put to it some Oyster-Liquor, Salt, whole peper, and a bundle of sweet herbs well bound up, some Mace, two or three great Onions, some interlarded Bacon cut like dice, and Chesnuts, or blanched Almonds and Capers.

Then stew your Oysters by themselves with Mace, Butter, Time and two or three great Onions; sometimes Grapes.

Garnish your dish with Lemon-Peel, Oysters, Mace, Capers, and Chesnuts, &c.

Stewed Broth.

To make stewd Broth, the Meat most proper for it is.

A Leg of Beef, Marrow-Bones, Capon, or a Loin or Rack of Mutton or a knuckle of Veal.

Take a Knuckle of Veal, a Joynt of Mutton, two Marrow bones, a Capon, boil them in fresh water, and scum them; then put in a bundle of sweet herbs well bound up or none, large Mace, whole Cinamon, and Ginger bruised, and put in a littlerag, the spice being a little bruised also. Then beat some Oatmeale, strain it, and put it to your broth, then have boil'd Prunes and Currans strained also and put it to your broth, with some whole raisons and currans; and boil not your fruit too much: then about half an hour before you dish your meat, put in a pint of Claret Wine and Sugar, then dish up your meat on fine sippits, and broth it.

Garnish your dish with Lemons, Prunes, Mace, Raisins, Currans, and Sugar.

You may add to the former Broth, Fennel-roots and Parsley roots tied up in a bundle.

Stewed Broth new Fashion.

Otherways for change; take two Joints of Mutton, Rack and Loin, being half boiled and scummed, take up the Mutton, and wash away the dregs from it, strain the broth, and blow away the fat, then put to the broth in a pipkin a bundle of sweet Herbs bound up hard, and some Mace, and boil in it also a pound of Raisins of the Sun being strained, a pound of Prunes whole, with Cloves, Pepper, Saffron, Salt, Claret, and Sugar: stew all well together, a little before you dish out your broth, put in your meat again, give it a warm, and serve it on fine carved sippets.

To stew a Loin or Rack of Mutton, or any Joint otherways.

I.

Chop a Loin into steaks, lay it in a deep dish or stewing pan, and put to it half a pint of Claret or White-Wine, as much water, some Salt and pepper, three or four whole Onions, a faggot of sweet Herbs bound up hard, and some large Mace; cover them close, and stew them leisurely the space of two hours, turn them now and then, and serve them on sippets.

II.

Otherways for change, being half boiled, chop some sweet Herbs and put to them, give them a walm, and serve them on sippets with scalded Goosberries, Barberries, Grapes, or Lemon.

III.

Otherways for variety, put Raisins, Prunes, Currans, Dates, and serve them with slic't Lemon and beaten butter.

IV.

Sometimes you may alter the Spice, and put Nutmeg, Cloves, and Ginger.

V.

Sometimes to the first plain way, put Capers, pickled Cucumbers, Samphire, &c.

VI.

Otherways, stew it between two dishes with fair water, and when it boils, scum it, and put three or four blades of large Mace, gross Pepper, Salt, and Cloves, and stew them close covered two hours; then have Parsley picked, and some stripped Time, spinage, sorrel, savoury, and sweet Marjoram, chopped with some onions, put them to your meat, and give it a walm, with some grated bread amongst, dish them on carved sippets, and blow off the fat on the broth, and broth it: lay Lemon on it, and beaten butter, or stew it thus whole.

Before you put on your Herbs blow off the fat.

To boil a Leg of Mutton divers ways.

I.

Stuff a Legg of Mutton with Parsley being finely picked, boil it in water and salt, and serve it in a fair dish with Parsley, and verjuyce in sawcers.

II.

Otherways: boil it in water and salt, not stuffed, and being boiled stuff it with Lemon in bits like square dice, and serve it also with the peels square, cut round about it make sauce with the Gravy and beaten butter, with Lemon and grated Nutmeg.

III.

Otherways, boil it in water and salt, being stuffed with parsley, and make sauce with large mace, gravy, chopped parsley, butter, vinegar, juice of orange, gooseberries, barberries, or grapes and sugar: serve it on sippets.

IV. To boil a Leg of Mutton otherways.

Take a good leg of Mutton, and boil it in water and salt, being stuffed with sweet herbs chopped with some beef-suet, some salt and nutmeg.

Then being almost boiled, take up some of the broth into a Pipkin, and put to it some large mace, a few currans; a handful of French Capers, and a little sack, the yolks of three or four hard eggs, minced small, and some lemon cut like square dice; and being finely boil'd, dish it on carved sippets, broth it, and run it over with beaten butter, and lemon shred small.

V. Otherways.

Take a fair leg of mutton, boil it in water and salt, and make sauce with gravy, some wine vinegar, salt-butter, and strong broth, being well stewed together with nutmeg.

Then dish up the leg of mutton on fine carved sippets, and pour on your broth.

Garnish your dish with barberries, capers, and slic't lemon.

Garnish the leg of mutton with the same garnish, and run it over with beaten butter, slic't lemon, and grated nutmeg.

To boil a leg of Veal.

1. Stuff it with beef-suet, and sweet herbs chopped, nutmeg, salt, and boil it in fair water and salt.

Then take some of the broth, and put to some capers, currans, large mace, a piece of interlarded Bacon, two or three whole Cloves, pieces of pears, and some artichock-suckers boil'd and put in beaten butter, boil'd marrow and mace. Then before you dish it up, have sorrel, sage, parsley, time, sweet marjoram coursely minced, with two or three cuts of a knife, and bruised with the back of a ladle on a clean board, put it to your broth to make it green, and give it a warm or two. Then dish up the leg of veal on fine carved sippets, pour on the broth, and then your other materials, some Goosberries, or Barberries, beaten butter and lemon.

2. To boil a Leg of Veal otherways.

Stuff it with beef-suet, nutmeg, and salt, boil it in a pipkin, and when it boils, scum it, and put into it some salt, parsley, and fennel roots in a bundle close bound up; then being almost boil'd, take up some of the broth in a pipkin, and put to it some Mace, Raisins of the sun, gravy; stew them well together, and thicken it with grated bread strained with hard Eggs: before you dish up your broth have parsley, time, sweet marjoram stript, marigold flowers, sorrel, and spinage picked: bruise it with the back of a ladle, give it a warm and dish up your leg of veal on fine carved sippets: pour on the broth and run it over with beaten Butter.

3. To boil a Leg of Veal otherwise with rice, or a Knuckle.

Boil it in a pipkin, put some salt to it, and scum it; then put to it some mace and some rice finely picked and washed, some raisins of the sun and gravy; and being fine and tender boil'd, put in some saffron and serve it on fine carved sippets, with the rice over all.

4. Otherways with past cut like small lard, boil it in thin broth and saffron.

5. Otherways in white broth, and with fruit, spinage, sweet herbs and goose-berries, &c.

To make all manner of forc't meats, or stuffings for any kind of Meats; as Leggs, Breasts, Shoulders, Loins or Racks; or for any Poultry or Fowl whatsoever, boil'd, rost, stewed, or baked; or boil'd in bags, round like a quaking Pudding in a napkin.

To force a Leg of Veal in the French Fashion, in a Feast for Dinner or Supper.

T Ake a leg of Veal, and take out the meat, but leave the skin and knuckle whole together, then mince the meat that came out of the leg with some beef-suet or lard, and some sweet herbs minced also; then season it with pepper, nutmeg, ginger, cloves, salt, a clove or two of garlic, and some three or four yolks of hard eggs whole or in quarters, pine apple-seed, two or three raw eggs, pistaches, chesnuts, pieces of artichocks, and fill the leg, sow it up and boil it in a pipkin with two gallons of fair water, and some white wine, being scummed and almost boil'd take up some broth into a dish or pipkin, and put to it some chesnuts, pistaches, pine-apple-seed, marrow, large mace, and artichocks bottoms, and stew them well together; then have some fried tost of manchet or roles finely carv'd. The leg being finely boil'd, dish it on French bread, and fried tost and sippets round about it, broth it and put on marrow, and your other materials, with sliced lemon and lemon peel, run it over with beaten butter, and thicken your broth sometimes with strained almonds; sometimes yolks of eggs and saffron, or saffron onely.

You may add sometimes balls of the same meat.

Garnish.

For your Garnish you may use Chesnuts, Artichock, pistaches, pine-apple-seed and yolks of hard eggs in halves or potato's.

Otherwhiles: Quinces in quarters, or pears, pippins gooseberries, grapes, or barberries.

To force a breast of Veal.

Mince some Veal or Mutton with some beef-suet or fat bacon, and some sweet herbs minced also, and seasoned with some cloves, mace, nutmeg, pepper, two or three raw eggs and salt: then prick it up, the breast being filled at the lower end, and stew it between two dishes with some strong broth, white wine, and large mace, then an hour after have sweet herbs picked and stripped, time, sorrel, parsley, sweet Marjoram bruised with the back of a ladle, and put it into your broth with some beef-marrow, and give it a warm; then dish up your breast of Veal, on fine sippets finely carved, broth it, and lay on slic't lemons, marrow, mace and barberries, and run it over with beaten butter.

If you will have the broth yellow, put saffron into it.

To boil a breast of Veal otherwise.

Make a Pudding of grated manchet, minced suet, and minced Veal, season it with nutmeg, pepper, and salt, three or four eggs, cinamon, dates, currans, raisins of the Sun, some grapes, sugar, and cream, mingle them all together, and fill the breast; prick it up, and stew it between two dishes, with white wine and strong broth, mace dates, marrow, and being finely stewed, serve it on sippets, and run it over with beaten butter, lemon, Barberries, or grapes.

Sometimes thick it with some almond milk, sugar, and cream.

To Boil a breast of Veal in another manner.

Joint it well, and perboil it a little, then put it in a stewing pan or deep dish with some strong broth; and a bundle of sweet herbs well bound up, some large mace, and some slices of interlarded bacon, two or three cloves, some capers, samphire, salt, some yolks of hard eggs, and white-wine; stew all these well together, and being boil'd and tender, serve it on fine carved sippets, and broth it. Then have some fried sweetbreads, sausages of veal or pork, garlick or none, and run all over with beaten butter, lemon, and fried parsley.

Thus you may boil a Rack or Loin.

To make several sorts of Puddings.

1. *Bread Puddings yellow or Green.*

Grate four penny loaves, and fearce them through a cullender, put them in a deep dish, and put to them four eggs, two quarts of cream, cloves, mace, and some saffron, salt, rose-water, sugar, currans, a pound of beef-suet minced, and a pound of dates.

If green, juyces of spinage, and all manner of sweet herbs stamped amongst the spinage, and strain the juyce; sweet herbs chopped very small, cream, cinamon, nutmeg, salt, and all other things, as is next before laid: your herbs must be time stripped, savoury, sweet marjoram, rosemarry, parsley, pennyroyal, dates; in these seven or eight yolks of eggs.

Another Pudding, called Cinamon-Pudding

Take five penny loaves, and fearce them through a cullender, put them in a deep dish or tray, and put to them five pints of cream, cinamon six ounces, suet one pound minced, eggs six yolks, four whites, sugar, salt, slic't dates, stamped almonds, or none, rose-water.

To make Rice Puddings

Boil your Rice with Cream, strain it, and put to it two penny loaves grated, eight yolks of eggs, and three whites, beef suet, one pound of Sugar, Salt, Rose-water, Nutmeg, Coriander beaten, &c.

Other Rice Puddings.

Steep your rice in milk over night, and next morning drain it, and boil it with cream, season it with sugar being cold, and eggs, beef-suet, salt, nutmegs, cloves, mace, currans, dates, &c.

To mak Oatmeal puddings, called Isings.

Take a quart of whole oatmeal, being picked, steep it in warm milk over night, next morning drain it, and boil it in a quart of sweet cream; and being cold put to it six eggs, of them but three whites, cloves, mace, saffron, pepper, suet, dates, currans, salt, sugar. This put in bags, guts, or fowls, as capon, &c.

If green, good store of herbs chopped small.

To make blood Puddings

Take the blood of a hog, while it is warm, and steep in it a quart or more of great oatmeal groats, at the end of three days take the groats out and drain them clean; then put to these groats more then a quart of the best cream warmed on the fire; then take some mother of time, spinage, parsley, savory, endive, sweet marjoram, sorrel, strawberry leaves, succory, of each a few chopped very small and mix them with the groats, with a little fennel seed finely beaten, some peper, cloves, mace salt, and some beef-suet, or flakes of the hog cut small.

Otherways, you may steep your oatmeal in warm mutton broth, or scalding milk, or boil it in a bag.

To make Andolians.

Soak the hogs guts, and turn them, scour them, and steep them in water a day and a night, then take them and wipe them dry, and turn the fat side outermost.

Then have pepper, chopped sage, a little cloves and mace, beaten corian-der-seed, & salt; mingle all together, and season the fat side of the guts, then turn that side inward again, and draw one gut over another to what bigness you please: thus of a whole belly of a fat hog. Then boil them in a pot or pan of fair water, with a piece of interlarded bacon, some spices and salt; tye them fast at both ends, and make them of what length you please.

Sometimes for variety you may leave out some of the foresaid herbs, and put pennyroyal, savory, leeks, a good big onion or two, marjoram, time, rosemary, sage, nutmeg, ginger, pepper, salt, &c.

To make other Blood Puddings.

Steep great oatmeal in eight pints of warm goose blood, sheeps blood, calves, or lambs, or fawns blood, and drain it, as is aforesaid, after three days put to it in every pint as before.

Other Blood Puddings.

Take blood and strain it, put in three pints of the blood, and two of cream, three penny manchets grated, and beef-suet cut square like small dice or hogs flakes, yolks of eight eggs, salt, sweet herbs, nutmeg, cloves, mace and pepper.

Sometimes for variety, Sugar, Currans, &c.

To make a most rare excellent Marrow Pudding in a dish baked, and garnish the Dish brims with Puff past.

Take the marrow of four marrow bones, two pinemolets or french bread, half a pound of raisins of the Sun, ready boil'd and cold, cinamon a quarter of an ounce finely beaten, two grated nutmegs, sugar a quarter of a pound, dates a quarter of a pound, sack half a pint, rose-water a quarter of a pint, ten eggs, two grains of ambergreese, and two of musk dissolved: now have a fine clean deep large dish, then have a slice of french bread, and lay a lay of sliced bread in the dish, and stew it with cinamon, nutmeg, and sugar mingled together, and also sprinkle the slices of bread with sack and rose-water, & then some raisins of the sun, and some sliced dates and good big peices of marrow; and thus make two or three lays of the aforesaid ingredients, with four ounces of musk, ambergreece, and most marrow on the top, then take two quarts of cream, and strain it with half a quarter of fine sugar, and a little salt, (about a spoonful) and twelve eggs, six of the whites taken away: then set the dish into the oven, temperate, and not too hot, and bake it very fair and white, and fill it at two several times, and being baked, scrape fine sugar on it, and serve it hot.

To make marrow Puddings of Rice and grated Bread.

Steep half a pound of rice in milk all night, then drain it from the milk, and boil it in a quart of cream; being boild strain it and put it to half a pound of sugar, beaten nutmeg and mace steeped in rose water, and put to the foresaid materials eight yolks of eggs, and five grated manchets, put to it also half a pound of mar-row, cut like dice, and salt; mingle all together, and fill your bag or napkin, and serve it with beaten butter, being boiled and stuck with almonds.

If in guts, being boild, tost them before the fire in a silver dish or tosting pan.

To make other Puddings of Turkie or Capon in bags, guts, or for any kind of stuffing, or forcing, or in Cauls

Take a rost Turky, mince it very small, and stamp it with some almond past, then put some coriander-seed beaten, salt, sugar, rose-water, yolks of eggs raw, and marrow stamped also with it, and put some cream, mace, soked in sack and whitewine, rose-water and sack, strain it into the materials, and make not your stuff to thin, then fill either gut or napkin, or any fouls boil'd, bak'd or rost, or legs of veal or mutton, or breasts, or kid, or fawn, whole lambs, suckers, &c.

Sheeps Haggas Puddings.

To make a Haggas Pudding in a Sheeps Paunch.

Take good store of Parsley, savory, time, onions, oatmeal groats chopped together, and mingled with some beef or mutton-suet minced together, and some cloves, mace, pepper, and salt; fill the paunch, sow it up, and boil it. Then being boiled, serve it in a dish, and cut a hole in the top of it, and put in some beaten butter with two or three yolks of eggs dissolved in the butter or none.

Thus one may do for a Fasting day, and put no suet in it, and put it in a napkin or bag, and being well boiled, butter it, and dish it in a dish, and serve it with sippets.

A Haggas otherways.

Steep the oatmeal over night in warm milk, next morning boil it in cream, and being fine and thick boil'd, put beef-suet to it in a dish or tray, some cloves, mace, nutmeg, salt, and some raisins of the sun, or none, and an onion, somtimes savory, parsley, and sweet marjoram, and fill the panch, &c.

Other Haggas Puddings.

Calves panch, calves chaldrons; or muggets being clenged, boil it tender and mince it very small, put to it grated bread, eight yolks of eggs, two or three whites, cream, some sweet herbs, spinage, succory, sorrel, strawberry leaves very small minced; bits of butter, pepper, cloves, mace, cinnamon, ginger, currans, sugar, salt, dates, and boil it in a napkin or calves panch, or bake it: and being boiled, put it in a dish, trim the dish with scraped sugar, and stick it with slic't Almonds, and run it over with beaten butter, &c.

To make liver Puddings.

Take a good hogs, calves, or lambs liver, and boil it: being cold, mince it very small, or grate it, and fearce it through a meal-sieve or cullender, put to it some grated manchet, two penny loaves, some three pints of cream, four eggs, cloves, mace, currans, salt, dates, sugar, cinamon, ginger, nutmegs, one pound of beef-suet minced very small: being mixt all together, fill a wet napkin, and bind it in fashion of a ball, and serve it with beaten butter and sugar being boil'd.

Other Liver Puddings.

For variety, sometimes sweet herbs, and sometimes flakes of the hog in place of beef-suet, fennil-seed, carraway seed, or any other seed, and keep the order as is abovesaid.

To make Puddings of blood after the Italian fashion.

Take three pints of hogs blood, strain it, and put to it half a pound of grated cheese, a penny manchet grated, sweet herbs chopped very small, a pound of beef-suet minced small, nutmeg, pepper, sugar, ginger, cloves, mace, cinamon, sugar, currans, eggs, &c.

To make Puddings of a Heifers Udder.

Take an heifers udder, and boil it; being cold, mince it small, and put to it a pound of almond paste, some grated manchet, three or four eggs, a quart of cream, one pound of beef-suet minced small, sweet herbs chopped small also, currans, cinamon, salt, one pound of sugar, nutmeg, saffron, yolks of hard eggs in quarters, preserved pears in form of square dice; bits of marrow; mingle all together, and put it in a clean napkin dipped in warm liquor, bind it up round like a ball, and boil it.

Being boil'd dish it in a clean scoured dish, scrape sugar, and run it over with beaten butter, stick it with slic't almonds, or slic't dates, canded lemon peel, orange, or citrons, juyce of orange over all.

Thus also lamb-stones, sweet-breads, turkey, capon, or any poultrey.

Forcing for any roots; as mellons, Cucumbers, Colliflowers, Cabbidge, Pompions, Gourds, great Onions, Parsnips, Turnips or Carrots.

Take a Musk Mellon, take out the seed, cut it round the mellon two fingers deep, then make a forcing of grated bread, beaten almonds, rose-water and sugar, some musk-mellon stamped small with it, also bisket bread beaten to powder, some coriander-seed, canded lemon minced small, some beaten mace and marrow minced small, beaten cinamon, yolks of raw eggs, sweet herbs, saffron, and musk a grain; then fill your rounds of mellons, and put them in a flat bottom'd dish, or earthen pan, with butter in the bottom, and bake them in a dish.

Then have sauce made with white-wine and strong broth strained with beaten almonds, sugar and cinamon; serve them on sippets finely carved, give this broth a warm, and pour it on your mellons, with some fine scraped sugar, dry them in the oven, and so serve them.

Or you may do these whole; mellons, cucumbers, lemons or turnips, and serve them with any boil'd fowl.

Other forcing, or Pudding, or stuffing for Birds or any Fowl, or any Joint of Meat.

Take veal or mutton, mince it, and put to it some grated bread, yolks of eggs, cream, currans, dates, sugar, nutmeg, cinamon, ginger, mace, juyce of Spinage, sweet Herbs, salt and mingle all together, with some whole marrow amongst. If yellow, use Saffron.

Other forcing for Fowls or any Joint of meat.

Mince a leg of mutton or veal and some beef-suet, or venison, with sweet herbs, grated bread, eggs, nutmeg, pepper, ginger, salt, dates, currans, raisins, some dry canded oranges, coriander seed, and a little cream; bake them or boil them, and stew them in white wine, grapes, marrow, and give them a walm or two, thick it with two or three yolks of eggs, sugar, verjuyce, and serve these puddings on sippets, pour on the broth, and strew on sugar and slic't lemon.

Other forcing of Veal or Pork, Mutton, Lamb, Venison, Land, or Sea Foul.

Mince them with beef-suet or lard, and season them with pepper, cloves, mace, and some sweet herbs grated, Bolonia sausages, yolks of eggs, grated cheese, salt, &c.

Other stuffings or forcings of grated cheese, calves brains, or any brains, as pork, goat, Kid or Lamb, or any venison, or pigs brains, with some beaten nutmeg, pepper, salt, ginger, cloves, saffron, sweet herbs, eggs, Gooseberries, or grapes.

Other forcing of calves udder boiled and cold, and stamped with almond past, cheese-curds, sugar, cinamon, ginger, mace cream, salt, raw eggs, and some marrow or butter, &c.

Other Stuffings of Puddings.

Take rice flower, strain it with Goats milk or cream, and the brawn of a poultry rosted, minced and stamped, boil them to a good thickness, with some marrow, sugar, rosewater and some salt; and being cold, fill your poultry, either in cauls of veal or other Joynts of meat, and bake them or boil them in bags or guts, put in some nutmeg, almond past, and some beaten mace.

Other stuffings of the brawn of a Capon, Chickens, Pigeons, or any tender Sea Foul.

Take out the meat, and save the skins whole, leave on the legs and wings to the skin, and also the necks and heads, and mince the meat raw with some interlarded bacon, or beef-suet, season it with cloves, mace, sugar, salt, and sweet herbs chopped small, yolks of eggs grated, parmisan or none, fill the body, legs, and neck, prick up the back, and stew them between two dishes with strong broth as much as will cover them, and put some bottoms of artichocks, cordons, or boil'd sparagus, goosberries, Barberries, or grapes being boil'd, put in some grated permisan, large mace, and saffron, and serve them on fine carved sippets, garnish the dish with roast turnips, or roast onions, cardons, and mace, &c.

Other forcing of Livers of Poultry, or Kid or Lambs.

Take the Liver raw, and cut it into little bits like dice, and as much interlarded bacon cut in the same form, some sweet herbs chopped small amongst; also some raw yolks of eggs, and some beaten cloves and mace, pepper, and salt, a few prunes or raisins, or no fruit, but grapes or gooseberries, a little grated permisan, a clove or two of garlick; and fill your poultry, either boild or rost, &c.

Other forcing for any dainty Foul; as Turkie, Chickens, or Pheasants, or the like boil'd or rost.

Take minced veal raw, and bacon or beef-suet minc't with it; being finely minced, season it with cloves and mace, a few currans salt, and some boiled bottoms of artichocks cut in form of dice small, and mingle amongst the forcing, with pine-apple-seeds, pistaches, chesnuts and some raw eggs, and fill your poultry, &c.

Other fillings or forcings of parboild Veal or Mutton.

Mince the Meat with beef-suet or interlarded Bacon, and some cloves, mace, pepper, salt, eggs, sugar, and some quartered pears, damsons, or prunes, and fill your fowls, &c.

Other fillings of raw Capons.

Mince it with fat bacon and grated cheese, or permisan, sweet herbs, cheese curd, currans, cinamon, ginger, nutmeg, pepper, salt, and some pieces of artichocks like small dice, sugar, saffron, and some mushrooms.

Otherways.

Grated liver of veal, minced lard, fennel-seed, whole raw eggs, sugar, sweet herbs, salt, grated cheese, a clove or two of garlick, cloves, mace, cinamon and ginger, &c.

Otherways.

For a leg of mutton, grated bread, yolks of raw eggs, beef-suet, salt, nutmeg, sweet herbs, juyce of spinage; cream, cinamon, and sugar; if yellow, saffron.

Other forcing, for Land or Sea fowl boiled or baked, or a Leg of Mutton.

Take the meat out of the leg, leave the skin whole, and mince the meat with beef-suet and sweet herbs; and put to it, being finely minced, grated bread, dates, currans, raisins, orange minced small, ginger, pepper, nutmeg, cream, and eggs; being boiled or baked, make a sauce with marrow, strong broth, white-wine, verjuyce, mace, sugar, and yolks of eggs, strained with verjuyce; serve it on fine carved sippets, and slic'd lemon, grapes or gooseberries: and thus you may do it in cauls of veal, lamb, or kid.

Legs of Mutton forc't, either rost or boil'd.

Mince the meat with beef-suet or bacon, sweet herbs, pepper, salt, cloves and mace, and two or three cloves of garlick, raw eggs, two or three chesnuts, & work up altogether, fill the leg, and prick it up, then rost it or boil it: make sauce with the remainder of the meat, & stew it on the fire with gravy, chesnuts, pistaches, or pine apple seed, bits of artichocks, pears, grapes, or pippins, and serve it hot on this sauce, or with gravy that drops from it only, and stew it between two dishes.

Other forcing of Veal.

Mince the veal and cut the lard like dice, and put to it, with some minced Pennyroyall, sweet marjoram, winter savory, nutmeg, a little cammomile, pepper, salt, ginger, cinamon, sugar, and work all together; then fill it into beef guts of some three inches long, and stew them in a pipkin with claret wine, large mace, capers and marrow; being finely stewed, serve them on fine carved sippets, slic'd lemon and barberries, and run them over with beaten butter and scraped sugar.

Other forcing for Veal, Mutton, or Lamb.

Either of these minced with beef-suet, parsley, time, savory, marigolds, endive and spinage; mince all together, and put some grated bread, grated nutmeg, currans, five dates, sugar, yolks of eggs, rose-water, and verjuyce; of this forcing you may make birds, fishes, beasts, pears, balls or what you will, and stew them, or fry them, or bake them and serve them on sippets with verjuyce, sugar and butter, either dinner or supper.

Other forcing for breast, Legs, or Loyns of Beef, Mutton, Veal, or any Venison, or Fowl, rosted, baked, or stewed.

Mince any meat, and put to it beef-suet or lard, dates, raisins, grated bread, nutmeg, pepper and salt, and two or three eggs, &c.

Otherways.

Mince some mutton with beef-suet, some orange-peel, grated nutmeg, grated bread, coriander-seed, pepper, salt, and yolks of eggs, mingle all together, and fill any breast, or leg, or any Joynt of sweet, and make sauce with gravy, strong broth, dates, currans, sugar, salt, lemons, and barberries. &c.

Other forcing for rost or boil'd, or baked Legs of any meat, or any other Joint or Fowl.

Mince a Leg of Mutton with beef-suet, season it with cloves, mace, pepper, salt, nutmeg, rose-water, currans, raisins, carraway-seeds and eggs; and fill your leg of Mutton, &c.

Then for sauce for the aforesaid, if baked, bake it in an earthen pan or deep dish, and being baked, blow away the fat, and serve it with the gravy.

If rost, save the gravy that drops from it, and put to it slic't lemon or orange.

If boil'd, put capers, barberries, white-wine, hard eggs minced, beaten Butter, gravy, verjuyce and sugar, &c.

Other forcing.

Mince a leg of mutton or lamb with beef-suet, and all manner of sweet herbs minced, cloves, mace, salt, currans, sugar, and fill the leg with half the meat: than make the rest into little cakes as broad as a shilling, and put them in a pipkin, with strong mutton broth, cloves, mace, vinegar, and boil the leg, or bake it, or rost it.

Forcing in the Spanish Fashion in balls.

Mince a leg of mutton with beef suet and some marrow cut like square dice, put amongst some yolks of eggs, and some salt and nutmeg; make this stuff as big as a tennis ball, and stew them with strong broth the space of two hours; turn them and serve them on toasts of fine manchet, and serve them with the palest of the balls.

Other manner of Balls.

Mince a leg of Veal very small, yolks of hard eggs, and the yolks of seven or eight raw eggs, some salt, make them into balls as big as a walnut, and stew them in a pipkin with some mutton broth, mace, cloves, and slic't ginger, stew them an hour, and put some marrow to them, and serve them on sippets, &c.

Other grand or forc't Dish.

Take hard eggs, and part the yolks and whites in halves, then take the yolks and mince them, or stamp them in a Mortar, with marchpane stuff, and sweet herbs chopped very small, and put amongst the eggs or past, with sugar and cinamon fine beaten, put some currans also to them, and mingle all together with salt, fill the whites, and set them by.

Then have preserved oranges canded, and fill them with marchpane paste and sugar, and set them by also.

Then have the tops of sparagus boil'd, and mixed with butter, a little sack, and set them by also.

Then have boild chesnuts peeled and pistaches, and set them by also.

Then have marrow steeped first in rose-water, then fried in Butter, set that by also.

Then have green quodlings slic't, mixt with bisket bread & egg, and fried in little cakes, and set that by also.

Then have sweet-breads, or lamb-stones, and yolks of hard eggs fryed, &c. and dipped in Butter.

Then have small turtle doves, and pigeon peepers and chicken-peepers fried, or finely rosted or boiled, and set them by, or any small birds, and some artichocks, and potato's boil'd and fried in Butter, and some balls as big as a walnut, or less, made of parmisan, and dipped in butter, and fried.

Then last of all, put them all in a great charger, the chickens or fowls in the middle, then lay a lay of sweetbreads, then a lay of bottoms of artichocks, and the marrow; on them some preserved oranges.

Then next some hard eggs round that, fried sparagus, yolks of eggs, chesnuts, and pistaches, then your green quodlings stuffed: the charger being full, put to them marrow all over the meat, and juyce of orange, and make a sauce of strained almonds, grapes, and verjuyce; and being a little stewed in the oven, dry it, &c.

The dish.

Sweetbreads, Lambstones, Chickens, Marrow, Almonds, Eggs, Oranges, Bisket, Sparagus, Artichocks, Musk, Saffron, Butter, Potato's, Pistaches, Chesnuts, Verjuyce, Sugar, Flower, Parmisan, Cinamon.

To force a French Bread called Pine-molet, or three of them.

Take a manchet, and make a hole in the top of it, take out the crum, and make a composition of the brawn of a capon rost or boil'd; mince it, and stamp it in a mortar, with marchpane past, cream, yolks of hard eggs, muskefied bisket bread, the crum of very fine manchet, sugar, marrow, musk, and some sweet herbs chopped small, beaten cinamon, saffron, some raw yolks of eggs, and currans: fill the bread, and boil them in napkins in capon broth, but first stop the top with the pieces you took off. Then stew or fry some sweetbreads of veal and forced chickens between two dishes, or Lamb-stones, fried with some mace, marrow, and grapes, sparagus, or artichocks, and skirrets, the manchets being well boil'd, and your chickens finely stewed, serve them in a fine dish, the manchets in the middle, and the sweetbreads, chickens, and carved sippets round about the dish; being finely dished, thicken the chicken broth with strained almonds, creams, sugar, and beaten butter.

Garnish your dish with marrow, pistaches, artichocks, puff paste, mace, dates, pomegranats, or barberries, and slic't lemon.

Another forc't dish.

Take two pound of beef-marrow, and cut it as big as great dice, and a pound of Dates, cut as big as small Dice; then have a pound of prunes, and take away the out-side from the stones with your knife, and a pound of Currans, and put these aforesaid in a Platter, twenty yolks of eggs, and a pound of sugar, an ounce of cinamon, and mingle all together.

Then have the yolks of twenty eggs more, strain them with Rose-water, a little musk and sugar, fry them in two pancakes with a little sweet butter fine and yellow, and being fried, put one of them in a fair dish, and lay the former materials on it spread all over; then take the other, and cut it in long slices as broad as your little finger, and lay it over the dishes like a lattice window, set it in the Oven, and bake it a little, then fry it, &c. Bake it leisurely.

Another forc't fryed Dish.

Make a little past with yolks of eggs, flower, and boiling liquor.

Then take a quarter of a pound of sugar, a pound of marrow, half an ounce of cinamon, and a little ginger. Then have some yolks of Eggs, and mash your marrow, and a little Rose-water, musk or amber, and a few currans or none, with a little suet, and make little pasties, fry them with clarified butter, and serve them with scraped sugar, and juyce of orange.

Otherways.

Take good fresh water Eels, flay and mince them small with a warden or two, and season it with pepper, cloves, mace, saffron: then put currans, dates, and prunes, small minced amongst, and a little verjuyce, and fry it in little pasties; bake it in the oven, or stew it in a pan in past of divers forms, or pasties or stars, &c.

To make any kind of sausages.

First, Bolonia Sausages.

T He best way and time of the year is to make them in *September*.

Take four stone of pork, of the legs the leanest, and take away all the skins, sinews, and fat from it; mince it fine and stamp it: then add to it three ounces of whole pepper, two ounces of pepper more grosly cracked or beaten, whole cloves an ounce, nutmegs an ounce finely beaten, salt, spanish, or peter-salt, an ounce of coriander-seed finely beaten, or carraway-seed, cinamon an ounce fine beaten, lard cut an inch long, as big as your little finger, and clean without rust; mingle all the foresaid together; and fill beef guts as full as you can possibly, and as the wind gathers in the gut, prick them with a pin, and shake them well down with your hands; for if they be not well filled, they will be rusty.

These aforesaid Bolonia Sausages are most excellent of pork only: but some use buttock beef, with pork, half one and as much of the other. Beef and pork are very good.

Some do use pork of a weeks powder for this use beforesaid, and no more salt at all.

Some put a little sack in the beating of these sausages, and put in place of co-riander-seed, carraway-seed.

This is the most excellent way to make Bolonia Sausages, being carefully filled, and tied fast with a packthred, and smoaked or smothered three or four days, that will turn them red; then hang them in some cool cellar or higher room to take the air.

Other Sausages.

Sausages of pork with some of the fat of a chine of bacon or pork, some sage chopped fine and small, salt, and pepper: and fill them into porkets guts, or hogs, or sheeps guts, or no guts, and let them dry in the chimney leisurely, &c.

Otherways.

Mince pork with beef-suet, and mince some sage, and put to it some pepper, salt, cloves, and mace; make it into balls, and keep it for your use, or roll them into little sausages some four or five inches long as big as your finger; fry six or seven of them, and serve them in a dish with vinegar or juyce of orange.

Thus you may do of a leg of veal, and put nothing but salt and suet; and being fried, serve it with gravy and juyce of orange or butter and vinegar; and before you fry them flower them. And thus mutton or any meat.

Or you may add sweet Herbs or Nutmeg: and thus Mutton.

Other Sausages.

Mince some Buttock-Beef with Beef suet, beat them well together, and season it with cloves, mace, pepper, and salt: fill the guts, or fry it as before; if in guts, boil them and serve them as puddings.

Otherways for change.

If without guts, fry them and serve them with gravy, juyce of orange or vine-gar, &c.

To make Links.

Take the raring pieces of pork or hog bacon, or fillets, or legs, cut the lean into bits as big as great dice square, and the fleak in the same form, half as much;

and season them with good store of chopped sage chopt very small and fine; and season it also with some pepper, nutmeg, cloves, and mace also very small beaten, and salt, and fill porkets guts, or Beef-guts: being well filled, hang them up and dry them till the salt shine through them; and when you will spend them, boil them and broil them.

To make all manner of Hashes.

First, of raw Beef.

Mince it very small with some Beef-suet or lard, some sweet herbs, pepper, salt, some cloves, and mace, blanched chesnuts, or almonds blanched, and put in whole, some nutmeg, and a whole onion or two, and stew it finely in a pipkin with some strong broth the space of two hours, put a little claret to it, and serve it on sippets finely carved, with some grapes or lemon in it also, or barberries, and blow off the fat.

Otherways.

Stew it in Beef gobbets, and cut some fat and lean together as big as a good pullets egg, and put them into a pot or pipkin with some Carrots cut in pieces as big as a walnut, some whole onions, some parsnips, large mace, faggot of sweet herbs, salt, pepper, cloves, and as much water and wine as will cover them, and stew it the space of three hours.

2. Beef hashed otherways, of the Buttock.

Cut it into thin slices, and hack them with the back of your knife, then fry them with sweet butter; and being fried put them in a pipkin with some claret, strong broth, or gravy, cloves, mace, pepper, salt, and sweet-butter; being tender stewed the space of an hour, serve them on fine sippets, with slic't lemon, gooseberries, barberries, or grapes, and some beaten butter.

3. Beef hashed otherways.

Cut some buttock-beef into fine thin slices, and half as many slices of fine interlarded Bacon, stew it very well and tender, with some claret and strong Broth, cloves, mace, pepper, and salt; being tender stewed the space of two hours, serve them on fine carved sippets, &c.

4. A Hash of Bullocks Cheeks.

Take the flesh from the bones, then with a sharp knife slice them in thin slices like Scotch collops, and fry them in sweet butter a little; then put them into a Pipkin with gravy or strong broth and claret, and salt, chopped sage, and nutmeg, stew them the space of two hours, or till they be tender, then serve them on fine carved sippets, &c.

Hashes of Neats Feet, or any Feet; as Calves, Sheeps, Dears, Hogs, Lambs, Pigs, Fawns, or the like, many of the ways following.

Boil them very tender, and being cold, mince them small, then put currans to them, beaten cinamon, hard eggs minced, capers, sweet herbs minced small, cloves, mace, sugar, white-wine, butter, slic't lemon or orange, slic't almonds, grated bread, saffron, sugar, gooseberries, barberries or grapes; and being finely stewed down, serve them on fine carved sippets.

2. *Neats Feet hashed otherwise.*

Cut them in peices, being tender boild, and put to them some chopped onions, parsly, time butter, mace, pepper, vinegar, salt, and sugar: being finely stewed serve them on fine carved sippets, barberries, and sugar; sometimes thicken the broth with yolks of raw eggs and verjuice, run it over with beaten butter, and sometimes no sugar.

3. *Hashing otherways of any Feet.*

Mince them small, and stew them with white wine, butter, currans, raisins, marrow, sugar, prunes, dates, cinamon, mace, ginger, pepper, and serve them on tosts of fried manchet.

Sometimes dissolve the yolks of eggs.

4. *Neats Feet, or any Feet otherways*

Being tender boil'd and soused, part them and fry them in sweet butter fine and brown; dish them in a clean dish with some mustard and sweet Butter, and fry some slic't onions, and lay them all over the top; run them over with beaten Butter.

5. *Neats-feet, or other Feet otherways sliced, or in pieces stewed.*

Take boil'd onions, and put your feet in a pipkin with the onions aforesaid being sliced, and cloves, mace, white wine, and some strong broth and salt, being almost stewed or boil'd, put to it some butter and verjuyce, and sugar, give it a warm or two more, serve it on fine sippets, and run it over with sweet Butter.

6. *Neats-feet otherways, or any Feet fricassed, or Trotters.*

Being boil'd tender and cold, take out the hair or wool between the toes, part them in halves, and fry them in butter; being fryed, put away the Butter, and put to them grated nutmeg, salt, and strong Broth.

Then being fine and tender, have some yolks of eggs dissolved with vinegar or verjuyce, some nutmeg in the eggs also, and into the eggs put a piece of Fresh Butter, and put away the frying: and when you are ready to dish up your meat, put in the eggs, and give it a toss or two in the pan, and pour it in a clean dish.

1. *To hash Neats-tongues, or any Tongues.*

Being fresh and tender boil'd, and cold, cut them into thin slices, fry them in sweet butter, and put to them some strong broth, cloves, mace, saffron, salt, nutmegs grated, yolks of eggs, grapes, verjuyce: and the tongue being fine and thick, with a toss or two in the pan, dish it on fine sippets.

Sometimes you may leave out cloves and mace; and for variety put beaten cinamon, sugar, and saffron, and make it more brothy.

2. *To hash a Neats-Tongue otherways.*

Slice it into thin slices, no broader than a three pence, and stew it in a dish or pipkin with some strong broth, a little sliced onion of the same bigness of the tongue, and some salt, put to some mushrooms, and nutmeg, or mace, and serve it on fine sippets, being well stewed; rub the bottom of the dish with a clove or two of garlick or mince a raw onion very small and put in the bottom of the dish, and beaten butter run over the tops of your dish of meat, with lemon cut small.

3. *To hash a Tongue otherwise, either whole or in slices.*

Boil it tender, and blanch it; and being cold, slice it in thin slices, and put to it boil'd chesnuts or roste, some strong broth, a bundle of sweet herbs, large mace, white endive, pepper, wine, a few cloves, some capers, marrow or butter, and some salt; stew it well together, and serve it on fine carved sippets, garnish it on the meat, with gooseberries, barberries, or lemon.

4. *To hash a Tongue otherways.*

Being boil'd tender, blanch it, and let it cool, then slice it in thin slices, and put it in a pipkin with some mace and raisins, slic't dates, some blanched almonds; pistaches, claret or white whine, butter, verjuyce, sugar, and strong broth; being well stewed, strain in six eggs, the yolks being boil'd hard, or raw, give it a warm, and dish up the tongue on fine sippets.

Garnish the dish with fine sugar, or fine searced manchet, lay lemon on your meat slic't, run it over with beaten butter, &c.

5. *To hash a Neats Tongue otherways.*

Being boil'd tender, slice it in thin slices, and put it in a pipkin with some currans, dates, cinamon, pepper, marrow, whole mace, verjuyce, eggs, butter, bread, wine, and being finely stewed, serve it on fine sippets, with beaten butter, sugar, strained eggs, verjuyce, &c.

6. *To stew a Neats Tongue whole.*

Take a fresh neats tongue raw, make a hole in the lower end, and take out some of the meat, mince it with some Bacon or Beef suet, and some sweet herbs, and put in the yolks of an egg or two, some nutmeg, salt, and some grated parmisan or fat cheese, pepper, and ginger; mingle all together, and fill the hole in the tongue, then rap a caul or skin of mutton about it, and bind it about the end of the tongue, boil it till it will blanch: and being blanched, wrap about it the caul of veal with some of the forcing, roast it a little brown, and put it in a pipkin, and stew it with some claret and strong broth, cloves, mace, salt, pepper, some strained bread, or grated manchet, some sweet herbs chopped small, marrow, fried onions and apples amongst; and being finely stewed down, serve it on fine carved sippets, with barberries and slic't lemon, and run it over with beaten Butter. Garnish the dish with grated or searced manchet.

7. *To stew a Neats Tongue otherways, whole, or in pieces, boiled, blanch it, or not.*

Take a tongue and put it a stewing between two dishes being raw, & fresh, put some strong broth to it and white wine, with some whole cloves, mace, and pepper whole, some capers, salt, turnips cut like lard, or carrots, or any roots, and stew all together the space of two or three hours leisurely, then blanch it, and put some marrow to it, give it a warm or two, and serve it on sippets finely carved, and strow on some minced lemon and barberies or grapes, and run all over with beaten Butter.

Garnish your dish with fine grated manchet finely searced.

8. To boil a Tongue otherways.

Salt a tongue twelve hours, or boil it in water & salt till it be tender, blanch it, and being finely boil'd, dish it in a clean dish, and stuff it with minced lemon, mince the rind, and strow over all, and serve it with some of the Gallendines, or some of the Italian sauces, as you may see in the book of sauces.

To boil a Neats Tongue otherways, of three or four days powder.

Boil it in fair water, and serve it on brewice, with boiled turnips and onions, run it over with beaten Butter, and serve it on fine carved sippets, some barberries, goosberries, or grapes, and serve it with some of the sauces, as you may see in the book of all manner of sauces.

To Fricas a Neats Tongue, or any Tongue.

Being tender boil'd, slice it into thin slices, and fry it with sweet Butter, then put away your Butter, and put some strong broth, nutmeg, pepper, and sweet herbs chopped small, some grapes or barberries picked, and some yolks of eggs, or verjuyce, grated bread, or stamped Almonds and strained.

Somtimes you may add some Saffron.

Thus udders may be dressed in any of the ways of the Neats-Tongues before-said.

To hash any Land-Fowl, as Turky, Capon, Pheasant, or Partridges, or any Fowls being roasted and cold. Roast the Fowls for Hashes.

Take a capon, hash the wings, and slice into thin slices, but leave the rump and the legs whole; mince the wings into very thin slices, no bigger then a *three pence* in breadth, and put it in a pipkin with a little strong broth, nutmeg, some slic't mushroms, or pickled mushroms, & an onion very thin slic't no bigger than the *minced capon* being well stew'd down with a little butter & gravy, dish it on fine sippets, & lay the rump or rumps whole on the minced meat, also the legs whole, and run it over with beaten Butter, slices of lemon, and lemon peel whole.

Collops or hashed Veal.

Take a leg of Veal, and cut it into slices as thin as an half crown piece, and as broad as your hand, and hack them with the back of a knife, then lard them with small lard good and thick, and fry them with sweet butter; being fryed, make sauce with butter, vinegar, some chopped time amongst, and yolks of eggs dissolved with juice of oranges; give them a toss or two in the pan, and so put them in a dish with a little gravy, &c.

Or you may make other sauce of mutton gravy, juyce of lemon and grated nutmeg.

A Hash of any Tongues, Neats Tongues, Sheeps Tongues, or any great or small Tongues.

Being tender boil'd and cold, cut them in thin slices, and fry them in sweet butter; then put them in a pipkin with a pint of Claret wine, and some beaten cinamon, ginger, sugar, salt, some capers, or samphire, and some sweet butter; stir it well down till the liquor be half wasted, and now and then stir it: being finely and leisurely stewed, serve it on fine carved sippets, and wring on the juyce of a lemon, and marrow, &c.

Or sometimes lard them whole, tost them, and stew them as before, and put a few carraways, and large mace, sugar, marrow, chestnuts: serve them on fried tosts, &c.

To make other Hashes of Veal.

Take a fillet of Veal with the udder, rost it; and being rosted, cut away the frothy flap; and cut it into thin slices; then mince it very fine with 2 handfuls of french capers, & currans one handful; and season it with a little beaten nutmeg, ginger, mace, cinamon, and a handful of sugar, and stew these with a pound of butter, a quarter of a pint of vinegar, as much caper liquor, a faggot of sweet herbs, and little salt; Let all these boil softly the space of two hours, now and then stirring it; being finely stewed, dish it up, and stick about it fried tost, or stock fritters, &c.

Or to this foresaid Hash, you may add some yolks of hard eggs minced among the meat, or minced and mingled, and put whole currans, whole capers, and some white wine.

Or to this foresaid Hash, you may, being hashed, put nothing but beaten Butter only with lemon, and the meat cut like square dice, and serve it with beaten butter and lemon on fine carved sippets.

To Hash a Hare.

Cut it in two pieces, and wash off the hairs in water and wine, strain the liquor, and parboil the quarters; then take them and put them into a dish with the legs, shoulders, and head whole, and the chine cut in two or three pieces, and put to it two or three grate onions whole, and some of the liquor where it was parboil'd: stew it between two dishes till it be tender, then put to it some pepper, mace, nutmeg, and serve it on fine carved sippets, and run it over with beaten butter, lemon, some marrow, and barberries.

To hash or boil Rabits divers ways, either in quarters or slices cut like small dice, or whole or minced.

Take a rabit being flayed, and wiped clean, cut off the legs, thighs, wings, and head, and part the chine into four pieces or six; put all into a dish, and put to it a pint of white wine, as much fair water, and gross pepper, slic'd ginger, some salt butter, a little time and other sweet herbs finely minced, and two or three blades of mace, stew it the space of two hours leisurely; and a little before you dish it, take the yolks of six new laid eggs and dissolve them with some grapes, verjuyce, or wine vinegar, give it a warm or two on the fire, till the broth be somewhat thick, then put it in a clean dish, with salt about the dish, and serve it hot.

A Rabit hashed otherways.

Stew it between two dishes in quarters, as the former, or in peices as long as your finger, with some strong broth, mace, a bundle of sweet herbs, and salt; Being well stewed, strain the yolks of two hard eggs with some of the broth, and put it into the broth where the Rabit stews, then have some cabbidge lettice boiled in water; and being boild squeeze away the water, and put them in beaten Butter, with a few raisins of the Sun boiled in water also by themselves; or in place of lettice use white endive. Then being finely stewed, dish up the rabit on fine carved sippets, and lay on it mace, lettice in quarters, raisins, grapes, lemons, sugar, gooseberries, or barberries, and broth it with the former Broth.

Thus chickens, or capons, or partridg, and strained almonds in this Broth for change.

To hash a Rabit otherways, with a forcing in his belly of minced sweet herbs, yolks of hard eggs, parsley, pepper, and currants, and fill his belly.

To hash Rabits, Chickens, or Pigeon, either in peices; or whole, with Turnips.

Boil either the rabits or fowls in water and salt, or strained oatmeal and salt.

Take turnips, cut them in slices, and after cut them like small lard an inch long, the quantity of a quart, and put them in a pipkin with a pound of Butter, three or four spoonfulls of strong Broth, and a quarter of a pint of wine vinegar, some pepper and ginger, sugar and salt; and let them stew leisurely with some mace the space of 2 hours being very finely stewed, put them into beaten Butter, beaten with cream and yolks of eggs, then serve them upon fine thin toasts of French Bread.

Or otherways, being stewed as aforesaid without eggs, cream, or butter, serve them as formerly. And these will serve for boil'd Chickens, or any kind of fowl for garnish.

To make a Bisk the best way.

Take a leg of Beef and a Knuckle of veal, boil them in two gallons of fair water, scum them clean, and put to them some cloves, and mace, then boil them from two gallons to three quarts of Broth; being boil'd strain it and put it in a pipkin, when it is cold, take off the fat and bottom, clear it into another clean pipkin; and keep it warm till the Bisk be ready.

Boil the Fowl in the liquor of the Marrow-Bones of six peeping chickens, and six peeping pigeons in a clean pipkin, either in some Broth, or in water and salt. Boil the marrow by it self in a pipkin in the same broth with some salt.

Then have pallats, noses, lips, boil'd tender, blancht and cut into bits as big as sixpence; also some sheeps tongues boil'd, blancht, larded, fryed, and stewed in gravy, with some chesnuts blanched; also some cocks combs boil'd and blanched, and some knots of Eggs, or yolks of hard eggs. Stew all the aforesaid in some rost mutton, or beef gravy, with some pistaches, large mace, a good big onion or two, and some salt.

Then have lamb stones blancht and slic't, also sweet-breads of veal, and sweet-breads of lamb slit, some great oysters parboil'd, and some cock stones. Fry the foresaid materials in clarified butter, some fryed spinage, or Alexander leaves, & keep them warm in an oven, with some fried sausages made of minced bacon, veal, yolks of eggs, nutmegs, sweet herbs, salt and pistaches; bake it in an oven in cauls of veal, and being baked and cold, slice it round, fry it, and keep it warm in the oven with the foresaid fried things.

To make little Pies for the Bisk.

Mince a leg of Veal, or a leg of Mutton with some interlarded bacon raw and seasoned with a little salt, nutmeg, pepper, some sweet herbs, pistaches, grapes, gooseberries, barberries, and yolks of hard eggs, in quarters; mingle all together, fill them, and close them up; and being baked liquor them with gravy, and beaten butter, or mutton broth. Make the past of a pottle of flower, half a pound of butter, six yolks of eggs, and boil the liquor and butter together.

To make gravy for the Bisk.

Roast eight pound of buttock beef, and two legs of mutton, being throughly roasted, press out the gravy, and wash them with some mutton broth, and when you have done, strain it, and keep it warm in a clean pipkin for your present use.

To dish the Bisk.

Take a great eight pound dish, and a six penny french pinemolet or bread; chip it and slice it into large slices, and cover all the bottom of the dish; scald it or steep it well with your strong broth, and upon that some mutton or beef gravy; then dish up the fowl on the dish, and round the dish the fried tongues in gravy with the lips, pallats, pistaches, eggs, noses, chesnuts, and cocks combs, and run them over the fowls with some of the gravy, and large mace.

Then again run it over with fried sweetbread, sausage, lamb-stones, cock-stones, fried spinage, or alexander leaves, then the marrow over all; next the carved lemons upon the meat, and run it over with the beaten butter, yolks of eggs, and gravy beat up together till it is thick; then garnish the dish with the little pies, Dolphins of puff-paste, chesnuts, boiled and fried oysters, and yolks of hard eggs.

To Boil Chines of Veal.

First, stew them in a stewing pan or between two dishes, with some strong broth of either veal or mutton, some white wine, and some sausages made of minced veal or pork, boil up the chines, scum them, and put in two or three blades of large mace, a few cloves, oyster or caper liquor with a little salt; and being finely boil'd down put in some good mutton or beef-gravy; and a quarter of an hour before you dish them, have all manner of sweet herbs pickt and stript, as tyme, sweet marjoram, savory, parsley, bruised with the back of a ladle, and give them two or three walms on the fire in the broth; then dish the chines in thin slices of fine French bread, broth them, and lay on them some boiled beef-marrow, boil'd in strong broth, some slic't lemon, and run all over with a lear made of beaten butter, the yolk of an egg or two, the juyce of two or three oranges, and some gravy, &c.

To boil or stew any Joynt of Mutton.

Take a whole loin of mutton being jointed, put it into a long stewing pan or large dish, in as much fair water as will more than half cover it, and when it is scum'd cover it; but first put in some salt, white wine, and carrots cut into dice-work, and when the broth is half boiled strain it, blow off the fat, and wash away the dregs from the mutton, wash also the stew-pan or pipkin very clean, and put in again the broth into the pan or pipkin, with some capers, large mace, and carrots; being washed, put them in again, and stew them softly, lay the mutton by in some warm place, or broth, in a pipkin; then put in some sweet herbs chopped with an onion, and put it to your broth also, then have colliflowers ready boild in water and salt, put them into beaten butter with some boil'd marrow: then the mutton and broth being ready, dissolve two or three yolks of eggs, with white wine, verjuyce, or sack, and give it a walm or two; then dish up the meat, and lay on the colliflowers, gooseberries, capers, marrow, carrots, and grapes or barberries, and run it over with beaten butter.

For the garnish according to the season of the year, sparagus, artichocks, parsnips, turnips, hopbuds, coleworts, cabbidge-lettice, chestnuts, cabbidge-sprouts.

Sometimes for more variety, for thickning of this broth, strained almonds, with strong mutton broth.

To boil a Rack, Chine, or Loin of Mutton a most excellent way, either whole or in pieces.

Boil it either in a flat large pipkin or stewing pan, with as much fair water as will cover the meat, and when it boils scum it, and put thereto some salt; and being half boiled take up the meat, and strain the Broth, blow off the fat, and wash the stewing-pan and the meat from the dregs, then again put in the crag end of the rack of mutton to make the Broth good, with some mace; then a little before you take it up, take a handful of picked parsley, chop it very small, and put it in the Broth, with some whole marigold flowers; put in the chine again, and give it a walm or two, then dish it on fine sippets, and broth it, then add thereto raisins of the sun, and currans ready boil'd and warm, lay them over the chine of mutton, then garnish the dish with marigold-flowers, mace, lemon, and barberries.

Other ways for change without fruit.

To boil a Chine of Mutton in Barley broth; or Chines, Racks, and Knuckles of Veal.

Take a chine of veal or mutton and joynt it, put it in a pipkin with some strong mutton broth, and when it boils and is scummed, put in some french barley, being first boiled in fair water, put into the broth some large mace and some sweet herbs bound up in a bundle, a little rosemary, tyme, winter-savory, salt, and sweet marjoram, bind them up very hard; and put in some raisins of the sun, some good pruens, currans, and marigold-flowers; boil it up to an indifferent thickness, and serve it on fine sippets; garnish the dish with fruit and marigold-flowers, mace, lemon, and boil'd marrow.

Otherways without fruit, put some good mutton gravy, and sometimes raisins only.

To stew a Chine of Mutton or Veal.

Put it in a pipkin with strong broth and white wine; and when it boils scum it, and put to some oyster-liquor, salt, whole pepper, a bundle of sweet herbs well bound up, two or three blades of large mace, a whole onion, with some interlarded bacon cut into dice work, some chesnuts, and some capers, then have some stewed oysters by themselves, as you may see in the Book of Oysters. The chines being ready, garnish the dish with great oysters fried and stewed, mace, chesnuts, and lemon peel; dish up the chines in a fair dish on fine sippets; broth it, and garnish the chines with stewed oysters; chesnuts, mace, slic't lemon and some fried oysters.

To make a dish of Steaks, stewed in a Frying pan.

Take them and fry them in sweet butter; being half fried, put out the butter, & put to them some good strong ale, pepper, salt, a shred onion, and nutmeg; stew them well together, and dish them on sippets, serve them and pour on the sauce with some beaten butter, &c.

To make stewd Broth.

Take a knuckle of veal, a joint of mutton, loin or rack, two marrow-bones, a capon, and boil them in fair water, scum them when they boil, and put to them a bundle of sweet herbs bound up hard and close; then add some large mace, whole cinamon, and some ginger, bruised and put in a fine clean cloth bound up fast, and a few whole cloves, some strained manchet, or beaten oatmeal strained and put to the broth; then have prunes and currans boil'd and strain'd; then put in some whole raisins, currans, some good damask prunes, and boil not the fruit too much, about half an hour before you dish your meat, put into the broth a pint of claret wine, and some sugar; dish up the meat on fine sippets, broth it, and garnish the dish with slic't Lemons, prunes, mace, raisins, currans, scraped sugar, and barberries; garnish the meat in the dish also.

Stewed Broth in the new Mode or Fashion.

Take a joynt of mutton, rack, or loin, and boil them in pieces or whole in fair water, scum them, and being scummed and half boil'd, take up the mutton, and wash away the dregs from the meat; strain the broth, and blow away the fat; then put the broth into a clean pipkin, with a bundle of sweet herbs bound up hard; then put thereto some large mace, raisins of the sun boil'd and strain'd, with half as many prunes; also some saffron, a few whole cloves, pepper, salt, claret wine, and sugar; and being finely stewed together, a little before you dish it up, put in the meat, and give it a walm or two; dish it up, and serve it on fine carved sippets.

To stew a Loin, Rack, or any Joynt of Mutton otherways.

Chop a loin into steaks, lay it in a deep dish or stewing pan, and put to it half a pint of claret, and as much water, salt, and pepper, three or four whole onions, a faggot of sweet herbs bound up hard, and some large mace, cover them close, and stew them leisurely the space of two hours, turn them now & then, and serve them on sippets.

Otherways for change, being half boiled, put to them some sweet herbs chopped, give them a walm, and serve them on sippets with scalded gooseberies, barberries, grapes, or lemon.

Sometimes for variety put Raisins, Prunes, Currans, Dates, and serve them with slic't lemon, beaten butter.

Othertimes you may alter the spices, and put nutmeg, cloves, ginger, &c.

Sometimes to the first plain way put capers, pickled cucumbers, samphire, &c.

Otherwayes.

Stew it between two dishes with fair water, and when it boils, scum it, and put in three or four blades of large mace, gross pepper, cloves, and salt; stew them close covered two hours, then have parsley picked, and some stript, fine spinage, sorrel, savory, and sweet marjoram chopped with some onions, put them to your meat, and give it a walm, with some grated bread amongst them; then dish them on carved sippets, blow off the fat on the broth, and broth it, lay a lemon on it and beaten butter, and stew it thus whole.

To dress or force a Leg of Veal a singular good way, in the newest Mode.

Take a leg of veal, take out the meat, and leave the skin and the shape of the leg whole together, mince the meat that came out of the leg with some beef-suet or lard, and some sweet herbs minced; then season it with pepper, nutmeg, ginger, and cloves, all being fine beaten, with some salt, a clove or two of garlick, three or four yolks of hard eggs in quarters, pine-apple seed, two or three raw eggs, also pistaches, chesnuts, & some quarters of boil'd artichocks bottoms, fill the leg and sowe it up, boil it in a pipkin with two gallons of fair water and some white wine; being scumm'd and almost boil'd, take up some broth into a dish or pipkin, and put to it some chesnuts, pistaches, pine-apple-seed, some large mace, marrow, and artichocks bottoms boil'd and cut into quarters, stew all the foresaid well together; then have some fried tost of manchet or rowls finely carved. The leg being well boil'd, (dainty and tender) dish it on French bread, fry some toast of it, and sippets round about it, broth it, and put on it marrow, and your other materials, a slic't lemon, and lemon peel, and run it over with beaten butter.

Thicken the broth sometimes with almond paste strained with some of the broth, or for variety, yolks of eggs and saffron strained with some of the broth, or saffron only. One may add sometimes some of the minced meat made up into balls, and stewed amongst the broth, &c.

To boil a Leg or Knuckle of Veal with Rice.

Boil it in a pipkin, put some salt to it, and scum it, then put to some mace and some rice finely picked and washed, some raisins of the sun and gravy; being fine and tender boil'd put in some saffron, and serve on fine carved sippets, with the rice over all.

Otherwayes with paste cut like small lard, and boil it in thin broth and saffron.

Or otherways in white broth, with fruit, sweet herbs, white wine and goose-berries.

To boil a Breast of Veal.

Jonyt it well and parboil it a little, then put it in a stewing pan or deep dish with some strong broth and a bundle of sweet herbs well bound up, some large mace, and some slices of interlarded bacon, two or three cloves, some capers, samphire, salt, spinage, yolks of hard eggs, and white wine; stew all these well together, being tender boil'd, serve it on fine carved sippets, and broth it; then have some fried sweetbreads, sausages of veal or pork, garlick or none, and run all over with beaten butter, lemon, and fried parsley over all. Thus you may boil a rack loin of Veal.

To boil a Breast of Veal otherways.

Make a pudding of grated manchet, minced suet, and minced veal, season it with nutmeg, pepper, salt, three or four eggs, cinamon, dates, currans, raisins of the sun, some grapes, sugar, and cream; mingle all together, fill the breast, prick it up, and stew it between two dishes with white wine, strong broth, mace, dates, and marrow, being finely stewed serve it on sippets, and run it over with beaten butter, lemon, barberries or grapes.

Sometimes thick it with some almond-milk, sugar, and cream.

To force a Breast of Veal.

Mince some veal or mutton with some beef-suet or fat bacon, some sweet herbs minced, & seasoned with some cloves, mace, nutmeg, pepper, two or three raw eggs, and salt; then prick it up: the breast being filled at the lower end stew it between two dishes, with some strong broth, white wine, and large mace; then an hour after have sweet herbs pickt and stript, as tyme, sorrel, parsley, and sweet marjoram, bruised with the back of a ladle, put it into your broth with some marrow, and give them a warm; then dish up your breast of veal on sippets finely carved, broth it, and lay on slic't lemon, marrow, mace and barberries, and run it over with beaten butter.

If you will have the broth yellow put thereto saffron, &c.

To boil a Leg of Veal.

Stuff it with beef-suet, sweet herbs chopped, nutmeg and salt, and boil it in fair water and salt; then take some of the broth, and put thereto some capers, currans, large mace, a piece of interlarded bacon, two or three whole cloves, pieces of pears, some boil'd artichocks suckers, some beaten butter, boil'd marrow, and mace; then before you dish it up, have sorrel, sage, parsley, time, sweet marjoram, coursly minced with two or three cuts of a knife, and bruised with the back of a ladle on a clean board; put them into your broth to make it green, & give it a walm or two, then dish it up on fine carved sippets, pour on the broth, and then your other materials, some gooseberries, barberries, beaten butter and lemon.

To boil a Leg of Mutton.

Take a fair leg of mutton, boil it in water and salt, make sauce with gravy, wine vinegar, white wine, salt, butter, nutmeg, and strong broth; and being well stewed together, dish it up on fine carved sippets, and pour on your broth.

Garnish your dish with barberries, capers, and slic't lemon, and garnish the leg of mutton with the same garnish and run it over with beaten butter, slic't lemon, and grated nutmeg.

To boil a Leg of Mutton otherways.

Take a good leg of mutton, and boil it in water and salt, being stuffed with sweet herbs chopped with beef-suet, some salt and nutmeg; then being almost boil'd take up some of the broth into a pipkin, and put to it some large mace, a few currans, a handful of French capers, a little sack, the yolks of three or four hard eggs minced small, and some lemon cut like square dice; being finely boil'd, dish it on carved sippets, broth it and run it over with beaten batter, and lemon shred small.

Otherways.

Stuff a leg of mutton with parsley being finely picked, boil it in water and salt, and serve it on a fair dish with parsley and verjuyce in saucers.

Otherways.

Boil it in water and salt not stuffed, and being boiled, stuff it with lemon in bits like square dice, and serve it with the peel cut square round about it; make sauce with the gravy, beaten butter, lemon, and grated nutmeg.

Otherways.

Boil it in water and salt, being stuffed with parsley, make sauce for it with large mace, gravy, chopped parsley, butter, vinegar, juyce of orange, gooseberries, barberries, grapes, and sugar, serve it on sippets.

To boil peeping Chickens, the best and rarest way, alamode.

Take three or four *French* manchets, & being chipped, cut a round hole in the top of them, take out the crum, and make a composition of the brawn of a roast capon, mince it very fine, and stamp it in a mortar with marchpane paste, the yolks of hard eggs, mukefied bisket bread, and the crum of the manchet of one of the breads, some sugar & sweet herbs chopped small, beaten cinamon, cream, marrow, saffron, yolks of eggs, and some currans; fill the breads, and boil them in a napkin in some good mutton or capon broth; but first stop the holes in the tops of the breads, then stew some sweet-breads of veal, and six peeping chickens between two dishes, or a pipkin with some mace, then fry some lamb-stones slic't in batter made of flower, cream, two or three eggs, and salt; put to it some juyce of spinage, then have some boil'd sparagus, or bottoms of artichocks boil'd and beat up in beaten butter and gravy. The materials being well boil'd and stewed up, dish the boil'd breads in a fair dish with the chickens round about the breads, then the sweetbreads, and round the dish some fine carved sippets; then lay on the marrow, fried lamb-stones, and some grapes; then thicken the broth with strained almonds, some Cream and Sugar, give them a warm, and broth the meat, garnish it with canded pistaches, artichocks, grapes, mace, some poungarnet, and slic't lemon.

To hash a Shoulder of Mutton.

Take a Shoulder of Mutton, roast it, and save the gravy, slice one half, and mince the other, and put it into a pipkin with the shoulder blade, put to it some strong broth of good mutton or beef-gravy, large mace, some pepper, salt, and a big onion or two, a faggot of sweet herbs, and a pint of white wine; stew them well together close covered, and being tender stewed, put away the fat, and put some oyster-liquor to the meat, and give it a warm: Then have three pints of great oysters parboil'd in their own liquor, and bearded; stew them in a pipkin with large mace, two great whole onions, a little salt, vinegar, butter, some white-wine, pepper, and stript tyme; the materials being well stewed down, dish up the shoulder of mutton on a fine clean dish, and pour on the materials or hashed mutton, then the stewed oysters over all; with slic't lemon and fine carved sippets round the dish.

To hash a Shoulder of Mutton otherways.

Stew it with claret-wine, only adding these few varieties more than the other; *viz.* two or three anchoves, olives, capers, samphire, barberries, grapes, or gooseberries, and in all points else as the former. But then the shoulder being rosted, take off the skin of the upper side whole, and when the meat is dished, lay on the upper skin whole, and cox it.

To hash a Shoulder of Mutton the French way.

Take a shoulder of mutton, roast it thorowly, and save the gravy; being well roasted, cut it in fine thin slices into a stewing pan, or dish; leave the shoulder bones with some meat on them, and hack them with your knife; then blow off the fat from the gravy you saved, and put it to your meat with a quarter of a pint of claret wine, some salt, and a grated nutmeg; stew all the foresaid things together a quarter of an hour, and serve it in a fine clean dish with sippets of French bread; then rub the dish bottom with a clove of garlick, or an onion, as you please; dish up the shoulder bones first, and then the meat on that; then have a good lemon cut into dice work, as square as small dice, and peel all together, and strew it on the meat; then run it over with beaten butter, and gravy of Mutton.

Scotch Collops of Mutton.

Take a leg of mutton, and take out the bone, leave the leg whole, and cut large collops round the leg as thin as a half-crown piece; hack them, then salt and broil them on a clear charcoal fire, broil them up quick, and the blood will rise on the upper side; then take them up plum off the fire, and turn the gravy into a dish, this done, broil the other side, but have a care you broil them not too dry; then make sauce with the gravy, a little claret wine, and nutmeg; give the collops a turn or two in the gravy, and dish them one by one, or two, one upon another; then run them over with the juyce of orange or lemon.

Scotch Collops of a Leg or Loin of Mutton otherways.

Bone a leg of mutton, and cut it cross the grain of the meat, slice it into very thin slices, & hack them with the back of a knife, then fry them in the best butter you can get, but first salt them a little before they be fried; or being not too much fried, pour away the butter, and put to them some mutton broth or gravy only, give them a walm in the pan, and dish them hot.

Sometimes for change put to them grated nutmeg, gravy, juyce of orange, and a little claret wine; and being fried as the former, give it a walm, run it over with beaten butter, and serve it up hot.

Otherways for more variety, add some capers, oysters, and lemon.

To make a Hash of Partridges or Capons.

Take twelve partridges and roast them, and being cold mince them very fine, the brawns or wings, and leave the legs and rumps whole; then put some strong mutton broth to them, or good mutton gravy, grated nutmeg, a great onion or two, some pistaches, chesnuts, and salt; then stew them in a large earthen pipkin or sauce-pan; stew the rumps and legs by themselves in strong broth in another pipkin; then have a fine clean dish, and take a *French* six penny bread, chip it, and cover the bottom of the dish, and when you go to dish the Hash steep the bread with some good mutton broth, or good mutton gravy; then pour the Hash on the steeped bread, lay the legs and the rumps on the Hash, with some fried oysters, pistaches, chesnuts, slic't lemon, and lemon-peel, yolks of eggs strained with juyce of orange and beaten butter beat together, and run over all; garnish the dish with carved oranges, lemons, fried oysters, chesnuts, and pistaches. Thus you may hash any kind of Fowl, whether Water or Land-Fowl.

To hash a Hare.

Flay it and draw it, then cut it into pieces, and wash it in claret wine and water very clean, strain the liquor, and parboil the quarters; then take them and slice them, and put them into a dish with the legs, wings, or shoulders and head whole; cut the chine into two or three pieces, and put to it two or three great onions, and some of the liquor where it was parboil'd, stew it between two dishes close covered till it be tender, and put to it some mace, pepper, and nutmeg; serve it on fine carved sippets, and run it over with beaten butter, lemon, marrow and barberries.

To hash a Rabit.

Take a Rabit being flayed and wiped clean; then cut off the thighs, legs, wings, and head, and part the chine into four pieces, put all into a dish or pipkin, and put to it a pint of white wine, and as much fair water, gross pepper, slic't ginger, salt, tyme, and some other sweet herbs being finely minced, and two or three blades of mace; stew it the space of two hours, and a little before you dish it take the yolks of six new laid eggs, dissolve them with some grape verjuyce, give it a walm or two on the fire, and serve it up hot.

To stew or hash Rabits otherways.

Stew them between two dishes as the former, in quarter or pieces as long as your fingar, with some broth, mace, a bundle of sweet herbs, salt, and a little white wine, being well stewed down, strain the yolks of two or three hard eggs with some of the broth, and thicken the broth where the rabit stews; then have some cabbidg-lettice boil'd in fair water, and being boil'd tender, put them in beaten butter with a few boiled raisins of the sun; or in place of lettice you may use white endive: then the rabits being finely stewed, dish them upon carved sippets, and lay on the garnish of lettice, mace, raisins of the sun, grapes, slic't lemon or barberries, broth it, and scrape on sugar. Thus chickens, pigeons, or partridges.

To hash Rabits otherwayes.

Make a forcing or stuffing in the belly of the Rabits, with some sweet herbs, yolks of hard eggs, parsley, sage, currans, pepper and salt, and boil them as the former.

To hash any Land Fowl.

Take a capon, and hash the wings in fine thin slices, leave the rumps and legs whole, put them into a pipkin with a little strong broth, nutmeg, some stewed or pickled mushrooms, and an onion very small slic't, or as the capon is slic't about the bigness of a three pence; stew it down with a little butter and gravy, and then dish it on fine sippets, lay the rumps and legs on the meat, and run it over with beaten butter, beaten with slices of lemon-peel.

To boil Woodcocks or Snipes.

Boil them either in strong broth, or in water and salt, and being boiled, take out the guts, and chop them small with the liver, put to it some crumbs of grated white-bread, a little of the broth of the Cock, and some large mace; stew them together with some gravy, then dissolve the yolks of two eggs with some wine vinegar, and a little grated nutmeg, and when you are ready to dish it, put the eggs to it, and stir it among the sauce with a little butter; dish them on sippets, and run the sauce over them with some beaten butter and capers, or lemon minced small, barberries, or whole pickled grapes.

Sometimes with this sauce boil some slic't onions, and currans boil'd in a broth by it self; when you boil it with onions, rub the bottom of the dish with garlick.

Boil'd Cocks or Larks otherways.

Boil them with the guts in them, in strong broth, or fair water, and three or four whole onions, large mace, and salt, the cocks being boil'd, make sauce with some thin slices of manchet or grated bread in another pipkin, and some of the broth where the fowl or cocks boil, then put to it some butter, and the guts and liver minced, then have some yolks of eggs dissolved with some vinegar and some grated nutmeg, put it to the other ingredients; stir them together, and dish the fowl on fine sippets; pour on the sauce with some slic't lemon, grapes, or barberries, and run it over with beaten butter.

To boil any Land Fowl, as Turkey, Bustard, Pheasant, Peacock, Partridge, or the like.

Take a Turkey and flay off the skin, leave the legs and rumps whole, then mince the flesh raw with some beef-suet or lard, season it with nutmeg, pepper, salt, and some minced sweet herbs, then put to it some yolks of raw eggs, and mingle all together, with two bottoms of boil'd artichocks, roasted chesnuts blanched, some marrow, and some boil'd skirrets or parsnips cut like dice, or some pleasant pears, and yolks of hard eggs in quarters, some gooseberries, grapes, or barberries; fill the skin and prick it up in the back, stew it in a stewing-pan or deep dish, and cover it with another; but first put some strong broth to it, some marrow artichocks boil'd and quartered, large mace, white wine, chesnuts, quarters of pears, salt, grapes, barberries, and some of the meat made up in balls stewed with the Turkey being finely boil'd or stewed, serve it on fine carved sippets, broth it, and lay on the garnish with slices of lemon, and whole lemon-peel, run it over with beaten butter, and garnish the dish with chesnuts, yolks of hard eggs, and large mace.

For the lears of thickening, yolks of hard eggs strained with some of the broth, or strained almond past with some of the broth, or else strained bread and sorrel.

Otherways you may boil the former fowls either bon'd and trust up with a farsing of some minc'd veal or mutton, and seasoned as the former in all points, with those materials, or boil it with the bones in being trust up. A turkey to bake, and break the bones.

Otherways bone the fowl, and fill the body with the foresaid farsing, or make a pudding of grated bread, minced suet of beef or veal, seasoned with cloves, mace, pepper, salt, and grapes, fill the body, and prick up the back, and stew it as is aforesaid.

Or make the pudding of grated bread beef-suet minc'd some currans, nutmegs, cloves, sugar, sweet herbs, salt, juyce of spinage; if yellow, saffron, some minced meat, cream, eggs, and barberries: fill the fowl and stew it in mutton broth & white wine, with the gizzard, liver, and bones, stew it down well, then have some artichock bottoms boil'd and quarter'd, some potatoes boil'd and blanch'd, and some dates quarter'd, and some marrow boil'd in water and salt; for the garnish some boil'd skirret or pleasant pears. Then make a lear of almond paste strained with mutton broth, for the thickning of the former broth.

Otherways simple, being stuffed with parsley, serve it in with butter, vinegar, and parsley, boil'd and minced; as also bacon boil'd on it, or about it, in two pieces; and two saucers of green sauce.

Or otherways for variety, boil your fowl in water and salt, then take strong broth, and put in a faggot of sweet herbs, mace, marrow, cucumber slic't, and thin slices of interlarded bacon, and salt, &c.

To boil Capons, Pullets, Chickens, Pigeons, Pheasants or Partridges.

Searce them either with the bone or boned, then take off the skin whole, with the legs, wings, neck, and head on, mince the body with some bacon or beef suet, season it with nutmeg, pepper, cloves, beaten ginger, salt, and a few sweet herbs finely minced and mingled amongst some three or four yolks of eggs, some sugar, whole grapes, gooseberries, barberries, and pistaches; fill the skins, and prick them up in the back, then stew them between two dishes, with some strong broth, white-wine, butter, some large mace, marrow, gooseberries and sweet herbs, being stewed, serve them on sippets, with some marrow and slic't lemon; in winter, currans.

To boil a Capon or Chicken in white Broth.

First boil the Capon in water and salt, then take three pints of strong broth, and a quart of white-wine, and stew it in a pipkin with a quarter of a pound of dates, half a pound of fine sugar, four or five blades of large mace, the marrow of three marrow bones, a handful of white endive; stew these in a pipkin very leisurely, that it may but only simmer; then being finely stewed, and the broth well tasted, strain the yolks of ten eggs with some of the broth. Before you dish up the capon or chickens, put in the eggs into the broth, and keep it stirring, that it may not curdle, give it a warm, and set it from the fire: the fowls being dished up put on the broth, and garnish the meat with dates, marrow, large mace, endive, preserved barberries, and oranges, boil'd skirrets, poungarnet, and kernels. Make a lear of almond paste and grape verjuice.

To boil a Capon in the Italian Fashion with Ransoles, a very excellent way.

Take a young Capon, draw it and truss it to boil, pick it very clean, and lay it in fair water, and parboil it a little, then boil it in strong broth till it be enough, but first prepare your Ransoles as followeth: Take a good quantity of beet leaves, and boil them in fair water very tender, and press out the water clean from them, then take six sweetbreads of veal, boil and mince them very small and the herbs also, the marrow of four or five marrow-bones, and the smallest of the marrow keep, and put it to your minced sweetbreads and herbs, and keep bigger pieces, and boil them in water by it self, to lay on the Capon, and upon the top of the dish, then take raisons of the sun ston'd, and mince them small with half a pound of dates, and a quarter of a pound of pomecitron minced small, and a pound of Naples-bisket grated, and put all these together into a great, large dish or charger, with half a pound of sweet butter, and work it with your hands into a peice of paste, and season it with a little nutmeg, cinamon, ginger, and salt, and some parmisan grated and some fine sugar also and mingle them well, then make a peice of paste of the finest flower, six yolks of raw eggs, a little saffron beaten small, half a pound of butter and a little salt, with some fair water hot, (not boiling) and make up the paste, then drive out a long sheet with a rowling pin as thin as you can possible, and lay the ingredients in small heaps, round or long on the paste, then cover them with the paste, and cut them off with a jag asunder, and make two hundred or more, and boil them in a broad kettle of strong broth, half full of liquor; and when it boils put the Ransols in one by one and let them boil a quarter of an hour; then take up the Capon into a fair large dish, and lay on the Ransoles, and stew on them grated cheese or parmisan, and Naples-bisket grated, cinamon and sugar; and thus between every lay till you have filled the dish, and pour on melted butter with a little strong broath, then the marrow, pomecitron, lemons slic't, and serve it up; or you may fry half the Ransoles in clarified butter, &c.

A rare Fricase.

Take six pigeon and six chicken-peepers, scald and truss them being drawn clean, head and all on, then set them, and have some lamb-stones and sweet-breads blanch'd, parboild and slic't, fry most of the sweet-breads flowred; have also some asparagus ready, cut off the tops an inch long, the yolk of two hard eggs, pistaches, the marrow of six marrow-bones, half the marrow fried green, & white butter, let it be kept warm till it be almost dinner time; then have a clean frying-pan, and fry the fowl with good sweet butter, being finely fryed put out the butter, & put to them some roast mutton gravy, some large fried oysters and some salt; then put in the hard yolks of eggs, and the rest of the sweet-breads that are not fried, the pistaches, asparagus, and half the marrow: then stew them well in the frying-pan with some grated nutmeg, pepper, a clove or two of garlick if you please, a little white-wine, and let them be well stew'd. Then have ten yolks of eggs dissolved in a dish with grape-verjuice or wine-vinegar, and a little beaten mace, and put it to the frycase, then have a French six penny loaf slic't into a fair larg dish set on coals, with some good mutton gravy, then give the frycase two or three warms on the fire, and pour it on the sops in the dish; garnish it with fried sweet-breads, fried oysters, fried marrow, pistaches, slic't almonds and the juyce of two or three oranges.

Capons in Pottage in the French Fashion.

Draw and truss the Capons, set them, & fill their bellies with marrow; then put them in a pipkin with a knuckle of veal, a neck of mutton, a marrow bone, and some sweet breads of veal, season the broth with cloves mace, and a little salt, and set it to the fire; let it boil gently till the capons be enough, but have a care you boil them not too much; as your capons boil, make ready the bottoms and tops of eight or ten rowls of French bread, put them dried into a fair silver dish, wherein you serve the capons; set it on the fire, and put to the bread two ladle-full of broth wherein the capons are boil'd, & a ladlefull of mutton gravy; cover the dish and let it stand till you dish up the capons; if need require, add now and then a ladle-full of broth and gravy: when you are ready to serve it, first lay on the marrow-bone, then the capons on each side; then fill up the dish with gravy of mutton, and wring on the juyce of a lemon or two; then with a spoon take off all the fat that swimmeth on the pottage; garnish the capons with the sweetbreads, and some carved lemon, and serve it hot.

To boil a Capon, Pullet, or Chicken.

Boil them in good mutton broth, white mace, a faggot of sweet herbs, sage, spinage, marigold leaves and flowers, white or green endive, borrage, bugloss, parsley, and sorrel, and serve it on sippets.

To boil Capons or Chickens with Sage and Parsley.

First boil them in water and salt, then boil some parsley, sage, two or three eggs hard, chop them; then have a few thin slices of fine manchet, and stew all to-gether, but break not the slices of bread; stew them with some of the broth wherein the chickens boil, some large mace, butter, a little white-wine or vinegar, with a few barberries or grapes; dish up the chickens on the sauce, and run them over with sweet butter and lemon cut like dice, the peel cut like small lard, and boil a little peel with the chickens.

To boil a Capon or Chicken with divers compositions.

Take off the skin whole, but leave on the legs, wings, and head; mince the body with some beef suet or lard, put to it some sweet herbs minced, and season it with cloves, mace, pepper, salt, two or three eggs, grapes, gooseberries, or barberries, bits of potato or mushroms. In the winter with sugar, currans, and prunes, fill the skin, prick it up, and stew it between two dishes with large mace and strong broth, peices of artichocks, cardones, or asparagus, and marrow: being finely stewed, serve it on carved sippets, and run it over with beaten butter, lemon slic't, and scrape on sugar.

To boil a Capon or Chicken with Cardones, Mushroms, Artichocks, or Oysters.

The foresaid Fowls being parboil'd, and cleansed from the grounds, stew them finely; then take your Cardones being cleansed and peeled into water, have a skillet of fair water boiling hot, and put them therein; being tender boil'd, take them up and fry them in chopt lard or sweet butter, pour away the butter, and put them into a pipkin, with strong broth, pepper, mace, ginger, verjuyce, and juyce of orange; stew all together, with some strained almonds, and some sweet herbs chopped, give them a warm, and serve your capon or chicken on sippets.

Let them be fearsed, as you may see in the book of fearst meats, and wrap your fearst fowl in cauls of veal, half roast them, then stew them in a pipkin with the foresaid Cardones and broth.

To boil a Capon or Chicken in the French Fashion, with Skirrets or French Beans.

Take a capon and boil it in fair water with a little salt, and a faggot of tyme and rosemary bound up hard, some parsley and fennil-roots, being picked and finely cleansed, and two or three blades of large mace; being almost boil'd, put in two whole onions boil'd and strained with oyster liquor, a little verjuyce, grated bread, and some beaten pepper, give it a warm or two, and serve the capon or chicken on fine carved sippets. Garnish it with orange peel boil'd in strong broth, and some French beans boil'd, and put in thick butter, or some skirret, cardones, artichocks, slic't lemon, mace, or orange.

To boil a Capon or Chicken with sugar Pease.

When the cods be but young, string them and pick off the husks; then take two or three handfuls, and put them into a pipkin with half a pound of sweet butter, a quarter of a pint of fair water, gross pepper, salt, mace, and some sallet oyl: stew them till they be very tender, and strain to them three or four yolks of eggs, with six spoonfuls of sack.

To boil a Capon or Chicken with Colliflowers.

Cut off the buds of your flowers, and boil them in milk with a little mace till they be very tender; then take the yolks of two eggs, and strain them with a quarter of a pint of sack; then take as much thick butter being drawn with a little vinegar and slic't lemon, brew them together; then take the flowers out of the milk, put them to the butter and sack, dish up your capon being tender boil'd upon sippets finely carved, and pour on the sauce, serve it to the table with a little salt.

To boil a Capon or Chicken with Sparagus.

Boil your capon or chicken in fair water and some salt, then put in their bellies a little mace, chopped parsley, and sweet butter; being boild, serve them on sippets, and put a little of the broth on them: then have a bundle or two of sparagus boil'd, put in beaten butter, and serve it on your capon or chicken.

To boil a Capon or Chicken with Rice.

Boil the capon in fair water and salt, then take half a pound of rice, and boil it in milk; being half boil'd, put away the milk, and boil it in two quarts of cream, put to it a little rose-water and large mace, or nutmeg, with the foresaid materials. Being almost boil'd, strain the yolks of six or seven eggs with a little cream, and stir all together; give them a warm, and dish up the capon or chicken, then pour on the rice being seasoned with sugar and salt, and serve it on fine carved sippets. Garnish the dish with scraped sugar, orange, preserved barberries, slic't lemon, or pomegranate kernels, as also the Capon or chicken, and marrow on them.

Divers Meats boiled with Bacon hot or cold; as Calves-head, any Joynt of Veal, lean Venison, Rabits, Turkey, Peacock, Capons, Pullets, Pheasants, Pewets, Pigeons, Partridges, Ducks, Mallards, or any Sea Fowl.

Take a leg of veal and soak it in fair water, the blood being well soaked from it, and white, boil it, but first stuff it with parsley and other sweet herbs chopped small, as also some yolks of hard eggs minced, stuff it and boil it in water and salt, then boil the bacon by it self either stuffed or not, as you please; the veal and bacon being boil'd white, being dished serve them up, and lay the bacon by the veal with the rinde on in a whole piece, or take off the rinde and cut it in four, six, or eight thin slices; let your bacon be of the ribs, and serve it with parsley strowed on it, green sauce in saucers, or others, as you may see in the Book of Sauces.

Cold otherways.

Boil any of the meats, poultry, or birds abovesaid with the ribs of bacon, when it is boil'd take off the rind being finely kindled[2] from the rust and filth, slice it into thin slices, and season it with nutmeg, cinamon, cloves, pepper, and Fennil-seed all finely beaten, with fine sugar amongst them, sprinkle over all rose vinegar, and put some of the slices into your boild capon or other fowl, lay some slices on it, and lay your capon or other fowl on some blank manger in a clean dish, and serve it cold.

To boil Land Fowl, Sea Fowl, Lamb, Kid, or any Heads in the French *Fashion, with green Pease or Hasters.*

Take pease, shell them, and put them all into boiling mutton broth, with some thin slices of interlarded bacon; being almost boiled, put in chopped parsley, some anniseeds, and strain some of the pease, thicken them or not, as you please; then put some pepper, give it a warm, and serve Kids or Lambs head on sippets, and stick it otherways with eggs and grated cheese, or some of the pease or flower strained; sometimes for variety you may use saffron or mint.

To boil all other small Fowls, as Ruffes, Brewes, Godwits, Knots, Dotterels, Strenits, Pewits, Ollines, Gravelens, Oxeyes, Red-shanks, &c.

Half roast any of these fowls, and stick on one side a few cloves as they roast, save the gravy, and being half roasted, put them into a pipkin, with the gravy, some claret wine, as much strong broth as will cover them, some broild houshold-bread strained, also mace, cloves pepper, ginger, some fried onions and salt; stew all well together, and serve them on fine carved sippets; sometimes for change add capers and samphire.

To boil all manner of small Birds, or Land Fowl, as Plovers, Quails, Rails, Black-birds, Thrushes, Snites, Wheat-ears, Larks, Sparrows, Martins.

Take them and truss them, or cut off the legs & heads, and boil them in strong

---

[2]   ...when it is boil'd take off the rind being finely kindled...

broth or water, scum them, and put in large mace, white-wine, washed currans, dates, marrow, pepper, and salt; being well stewed, dish them on fine carved sippets, thicken the broth with strained almonds, rose-water, and sugar, and garnish them with lemon, barberries, sugar, or grated bread strewed about the dish. For Leir otherways, strained bread and hard eggs, with verjuyce and broth.

Sometimes for variety garnish them with potatoes, farsings, or little balls of farsed manchet.

To boil a Swan, Whopper, wilde or tame Goose, Crane, Shoveller, Hern, Ducks, Mallard, Bittorn, Widgeons, Gulls, or Curlews.

Take a Swan and bone it, leave on the legs and wings, then make a farsing of some beef-suet or minced lard, some minced mutton or venison being finely minced with some sweet herbs, beaten nutmeg, pepper, cloves, and mace; then have some oysters parboil'd in their own liquor, mingle them amongst the minced meat, with some raw eggs, and fill the body of the fowl, prick it up close on the back, and boil it in a stewing-pan or deep dish, then put to the fowl some strong broth, large mace, white-wine, a few cloves, oyster-liquor, and some boil'd marrow; stew them all well together: then have oysters stewed by themselves with an onion or two, mace, pepper, butter, and a little white-wine. Then have the bottoms of artichocks ready boild, and put in some beaten butter, and boil'd marrow; dish up the fowl on fine carved sippets, then broth them, garnish them with stewed oysters, marrow, artichocks, gooseberries, slic't lemon, barberries or grapes and large mace; garnish the dish with grated bread, oysters, mace, lemon and artichocks, and run the fowl over with beaten butter.

Otherways fill the body with a pudding made of grated bread, yolks of eggs, sweet herbs minced small, with an onion, and some beef-suet minced, some beaten cloves, mace, pepper, and salt, some of the blood of the fowl mixed with it, and a little cream; fill the fowl, and stew it or boil it as before.

To boil any large Water Fowl otherways, a Swan, Whopper, wild or tame Geese.

Take a goose and salt it two or three days, then truss it to boil, cut lard as big as your little finger, and lard the breast; season the lard with pepper, mace, and salt; then boil it in beef-broth, or water and salt, put to it pepper grosly beaten, a bundle of bay-leaves, tyme, and rosemary bound up very well, boil them with the fowl; then prepare some cabbidge boild tender in water and salt, squeeze out the water from it, and put it in a pipkin with strong broth, claret wine, and a good big onion or two; season it with pepper, mace, and salt, and three or four anchovies dissolved; stew these together with a ladleful of sweet butter, and a little vinegar: and when the goose is boil'd enough, and your cabbidge on sippets, lay on the goose with some cabbidge on the breast, and serve it up. Thus you may dress any large wild Fowl.

To boil all manner of small Sea or Land Fowl.

Boil the fowl in water and salt, then take some of the broth, and put to it some beefs-udder boild, and slic't into thin slices with some pistaches blanch'd, some slic't sausages stript out of the skin, white-wine, sweet, herbs, and large mace;

stew these together till you think it sufficiently boiled, then put to it beet-root cut into slices, beat it up with butter, and carve up the Fowl, pour the broth on it, and garnish it with sippets, or what you please.

Or thus.

Take and lard them, then half roast them, draw them, and put them in a pipkin with some strong broth or claret wine, some chesnuts, a pint of great oysters, taking the breads from them, two or three onions minced very small, some mace, a little beaten ginger, and a crust of *French* bread grated; thicken it, and dish them up on sops: If no oysters, chesnuts, or artichock bottoms, turnips, colliflowers, interlarded bacon in thin slices, and sweetbreads, &c.

Otherways.

Take them and roast them, save the gravy, and being roasted, put them in a pipkin, with the gravy, some slic't onions, ginger, cloves, pepper, salt, grated bread, claret wine, currans, capers, mace, barberries, and sugar, serve them on fine sippets, and run them over with beaten butter, slic't lemon, and lemon peel; sometimes for change use stewed oysters or cockles.

To boil or dress any Land Fowl, or Birds in the Italian fashion, in a Broth called Bro-do-Lardiero.

Take six Pigeons being finely cleansed, and trust, put them into a pipkin with a quart of strong broth, or water, and half wine, then put therein some fine slices of interlarded bacon, when it boils scum it, and put in nutmeg, mace, ginger, pepper, salt, currans, sugar, some sack, raisins of the sun, prunes, sage, dryed cherries, tyme, a little saffron, and dish them on fine carved sippets.

To stew Pigeons in the French *fashion.*

The Pigeons being drawn and trust, make a fearsing or stopping of some sweet herbs minced, then mince some beef-suet or lard, grated bread, currans, cloves, mace, pepper, ginger, sugar, & 3 or 4 raw eggs. The pigeons being larded & half roasted, stuff them with the foresaid fearsing, and put boil'd cabbidge stuck with a few cloves round about them; bind up every Pigeon several with pack-thread, then put them in a pipkin a boiling with strong mutton broth, three or four yolks of hard eggs minced small, some large mace, whole cloves, pepper, salt, and a little white-wine; being boil'd, serve them on fine carved sippets, and strow on cinamon, ginger, and sugar.

Otherways in the French *Fashion.*

Take Pigeons ready pull'd or scalded, take the flesh out of the skin, and leave the skin whole with the legs and wings hanging to it, mince the bodies with some lard or beef suet together very small, then put to them some sweet herbs finely minced, and season all with cloves, mace, ginger, pepper, some grated bread or parmisan grated, and yolks of eggs; fill again the skins, and prick them up in the back, then put them in a dish with some strong broth, and sweet herbs chopped, large mace, gooseberries, barberries, or grapes; then cabbidge-lettice boil'd in water and salt, put to them butter, and the Pigeons being boil'd, serve them on sippets.

To boil Pigeons otherways.

Being trussed, put them in a pipkin, with some strong broth or fair water, boil and scum them, then put in some mace, a faggot of sweet herbs, white endive, marigold flowers, and salt; and being finely boiled, serve them on sippets, and garnish the dish with mace and white endive flowers.

Otherways you may add Cucumbers in quarters either pickled or fresh, and some pickled capers; or boil the cucumbers by themselves, and put them in beaten butter, and sweet herbs chopped small.

Or boil them with capers, samphire, mace, nutmeg, spinage, endive, and a rack or chine of mutton boil'd with them.

Or else with capers, mace, salt, and sweet herbs in a faggot; then have some cabbidge or colliflowers boil'd very tender in fair water and salt, pour away the water, and put them in beaten butter, and when the fowls be boil'd, serve the cabbidge on them.

To boil Pigeons otherwaies.

Take Pigeons being finely cleansed and trust, put them in a pipkin or skillet clean scowred, with some mutton broth or fair water; set them a boiling and scum them clean, then put to them large mace, and well washed currans, some strained bread strained with vinegar and broth, put it to the Pigeons with some sweet butter and capers; boil them very white, and being boil'd, serve them on fine carved sippets in the broth with some sugar; garnish them with lemon, fine sugar, mace, grapes, gooseberries, or barberries, and run them over with beaten butter; garnish the dish with grated manchet.

Pottages.

Pottage in the Italian *Fashion.*

Boil green pease with some strong broth, and interlarded bacon cut into slices; the pease being boiled, put to them some chopped parsley, pepper, anniseed, and strain some of the pease to thicken the broth; give it a walm and serve it on sippets, with boil'd chickens, pigeons, kids, or lambs-heads, mutton, duck, mallard, or any poultry.

Sometimes for variety you may thicken the broth with eggs.

Pottage otherways in the Italian Fashion.

Boil a rack of mutton, a few whole cloves, mace, slic't ginger, all manner of sweet herbs chopped, and a little salt; being finely boiled, put in some strained almond-paste, with grape verjuyce, saffron, grapes, or gooseberries; give them a warm, and serve your meat on sippets.

Pottage of Mutton, Veal, or Beef, in the English *Fashion.*

Cut a rack of mutton in two pieces, and take a knuckle of veal, and boil it in a gallon pot or pipkin, with good store of herbs, and a pint of oatmeal chopped amongst the herbs, as tyme, sweet marjoram, parsley, chives, salet, succory, mari-gold-leaves and flowers, strawberry-leaves, violet-leaves, beets, borage, sorrel, bloodwort, sage, pennyroyal; and being finely boil'd, serve them on fine carved sippets with the mutton and veal, &c.

To stew a Shoulder of Mutton with Oysters.

Take a shoulder of mutton, and roast it, and being half roasted or more, take off the upper skin whole, & cut the meat into thin slices, then stew it with claret, mace, nutmeg, anchovies, oyster-liquor, salt, capers, olives, samphire, and slices of orange; leave the shoulder blade with some meat on it, and hack it, save also the marrow bone whole with some meat on it, and lay it in a clean dish; the meat being finely stewed, pour it on the bones, and on that some stewed oysters and large oysters over all, with slic't lemon and lemon peel.

The skin being first finely breaded, stew the oysters with large mace, a great onion or two, butter, vinegar, white wine, a bundle of sweet herbs, and lay on the skin again over all, &c.

To roast a Shoulder of Mutton with Onions and Parsley, and baste it with Oranges.

Stuff it with parsley and onions, or sweet herbs, nutmeg, and salt, and in the roasting of it, baste it with the juyce of oranges, save the gravy and clear away the fat; then stew it up with a slice or two of orange and an anchovie, without any fat on the gravy, &c.

Other Hashes of Scotch Collops.

Cut a leg of mutton into thin slices as thin as a shilling, cross the grain of the leg, sprinkle them lightly with salt, and fry them with sweet butter, serve them with gravy or juice of oranges, and nutmeg, and run them over with beaten butter, lemon, &c.

Otherways the foresaid Collops.

For variety, sometimes season them with coriander-seed, or stamped fen-nil-seed, pepper and salt; sprinkle them with white wine, then flower'd, fryed, and served with juice of orange, for sauce, with sirrup of rose-vinegar, or elder vinegar.

Other Hashes or Scotch Collop of any Joint of Veal, either in Loyn, Leg, Rack or Shoulder.

Cut a leg into thin slices, as you do Scotch collops of mutton, hack and fry them with small thin slices of interlarded bacon as big as the slices of veal, fry them with sweet butter; and being finely fried, dish them up in a fine dish, put from them the butter that you fried them with, and put to them beaten butter with lemon, gravy, and juyce of orange.

A Hash of a Leg of Mutton in the French fashion.

Parboil a leg of mutton, then take it up, pare off some thin slices on the upper and under side, or round it, prick the leg through to let out the gravy on the slices; then bruise some sweet herbs, as tyme, parsly, marjoram, savory, with the back of a ladle, and put to it a piece of sweet butter, pepper, verjuyce; and when your mutton is boild, pour all over the slices herbs and broth on the leg into a clean dish.

Another Hash of Mutton or Lamb, either hot or cold.

Roast a shoulder of mutton, and cut it into slices, put to it oysters, white wine, raisins of the sun, salt, nutmeg, and strong broth, (or no raisins) slic't lemon or orange; stew it all together, and serve it on sippets, and run it over with beaten butter and lemon, &c.

Another Hash of a Joynt of Mutton or Lamb hot or cold.

Cut it in very thin slices, then put them in a pipkin or dish, and put to it a pint of claret wine, salt, nutmeg, large mace, an anchovie or two, stew them well together with a little gravy; and being finely stewed serve them on carved sippets with some beaten butter & lemon, &c.

Otherways.

Cut it into thin slices raw, and fry it with a pint of white wine till it be brown, and put them into a pipkin with slic't lemon, salt, fried parsley, gravy, nutmeg, and garnish your dish with nutmeg and lemon.

Other Hashes of a Shoulder of Mutton.

Boil it and cut it in thin slices, hack the shoulder-blade, and put all into a pipkin or deep dish, with some salt, gravy, white-wine, some strong broth, and a faggot of sweet herbs, oyster-liquor, caper-liquor, and capers; being stewed down, bruse some parsley, and put to it some beaten cloves and mace, and serve it on sippets.

Divers made Dishes or Capilotado's.

First, a Dish of Chines of Mutton, Veal, Capon, Pigeons, or other Fowls.

Boil a pound of rice in mutton broth, put to it some blanched chesnuts, pine apple-seeds, almonds or pistaches; being boil'd thick, put to it some marrow or fresh butter, salt, cinamon, and sugar; then cut your veal into small bits or peices, and break up the fowl; then have a fair dish, and set it on the embers, and put some of your rice, and some of the meat, and more of the rice and sugar, and cinamon, and pepper over all, and some marrow.

Capilotado, in the Lumbardy *fashion of a Capon.*

Boil rice in mutton broth till it be very thick, and put to it some salt and sugar.

Then have also some Bolonia Sausages boil'd very tender, minced very small, or grated, and some grated cheese, sugar, and cinamon mingled together; then cut up the boil'd or roast capon, and lay it upon a clean dish with some of the rice, strow on cinamon and sausage, grated cheese and sugar, and lay on yolks of raw eggs; thus make two or three layings and more, eggs and some butter or marrow on the top of all, and set it on the embers, and cover it, or in a warm oven.

Capilotado of Pigeons or wild Ducks, or any Land or Sea Fowls roasted.

Take a pound of almond-paste, and put to it a Capon minc't and stamped with the almonds, & some crums of manchet, some sack or white-wine, three pints of strong broth cold, and eight or ten yolks of raw eggs; strain all the foresaid together, and boil it in a skillet with some sugar to a pretty thickness, put to it some cinamon, nutmeg, and a few whole cloves, then have roast Pigeons, or any small birds roasted, cut them up, and do as is aforesaid, and strow on sugar and cinamon.

Capilotado *for roast Meats, as Partridges, Pigeons, eight or twelve, or any other the like; or Sea Fowls, Ducks, or Widgeons.*

Take a pound of almonds, a pound of currans, a pound of sugar, half a pound of muskefied bisket-bread, a pottle of strong broth cold, half a pint of grape verjuyce, pepper half an ounce, nutmegs as much, an ounce of cinamon, and a few cloves; all these aforesaid stamped, strained, and boil'd with the aforesaid liquor, and in all points as the former, only toasts must be added.

Other Capilotado *common.*

Take two pound of parmisan grated, a minced kidney of veal, a pound of other fat cheese, ten cloves of garlick boil'd, broth or none, two capons minced and stamped, rost or boil'd, and put to it ten yolks of eggs raw, with a pound of sugar: temper the foresaid with strong broth, and boil all in a broad skillet or brass pan, in the boiling stir it continually till it be incorporated, and put to it an ounce of cinamon, a little pepper, half an ounce of cloves, and as much nutmeg beaten, some saffron; then break up your roast fowls, roast lamb, kid, or fried veal, make three bottoms, and set it into a warm oven, till you serve it in, &c.

Capilotado, *or Custard, in the Hungarian fashion, in the pot, or baked in an Oven.*

Take two quarts of goat or cows milk, or two quarts of cream, and the whites of five new laid eggs, yolks and all, or ten yolks, a pound of sugar, half an ounce of cinamon, a little salt, and some saffron; strain it and bake it in a deep dish; being baked, put on the juyce of four or five oranges, a little white wine, rose-water, and beaten ginger, &c.

Capilotado Francois.

Roast a leg of mutton, save the gravy, and mince it small, then strain a pound of almond paste with some mutton or capon broth cold, some three pints and a half of grape verjuyce, a pound of sugar, some cinamon, beaten pepper, and salt; the meat and almonds being stamp'd and strained, put it a boiling softly, and stir it continually, till it be well incorporate and thick; then serve it in a dish with some roast chickens, pigeons, or capons: put the gravy to it, and strow on sugar, some marrow, cinamon, &c.

Sometimes you may add some interlarded bacon instead of marrow, some sweet herbs, and a kidney of veal.

Sometimes eggs, currans, saffron, gooseberries, &c.

Other made Dishes, or little Pasties called in Italian Tortelleti.

Take a rost or boil'd capon, and a calves udder, or veal, mince it and stamp it with some marrow, mint, or sweet marjoram, put a pound of fat parmisan grated to it, half a pound of sugar, and a quarter of a pound of currans, some chopped sweet herbs, pepper, saffron, nutmeg, cinamon, four or five yolks of eggs, and two whites; mingle all together and make a piece of paste of warm or boiling liquor, and some rose-water, sugar, butter; make some great and some very little, rouls or stars, according to the judgment of the Cook; boil them in broth, milk, or cream. Thus also fish. Serve them with grated fat cheese or parmisan, sugar, and beaten cinamon on them in a dish, &c.

Tortelleti, or little Pasties.

Mince some interlarded bacon, some pork or any other meat, with some calves udder, and put to it a pound of fresh cheese, fat cheese, or parmisan, a pound of sugar, and some roasted turnips or parsnips, a quarter of a pound of currans, pepper, cloves, nutmegs, eight eggs, saffron; mingle all together, and make your pasties like little fishes, stars, rouls, or like beans or pease, boil them in flesh broth, and serve them with grated cheese and sugar, and serve them hot.

Tortelleti, *or little Pasties otherwayes, of Beets or Spinage chopped very small.*

Being washed and wrung dry, fry them in butter, put to them some sweet herbs chopped small, with some grated parmisan, some cinamon, cloves, saffron, pepper, currans, raw eggs, and grated bread: Make your pasties, and boil them in strong broth, cream, milk, or almond-milk: thus you may do any fish. Serve them with sugar, cinamon, and grated cheese.

Tortelleti, *of green Pease, French Beans, or any kind of Pulse green or dry.*

Take pease gren or dry, French beans, or garden beans green or dry, boil them tender, and stamp them; strain them through a strainer, and put to them some fried onions chopped small, sugar, cinamon, cloves, pepper, and nutmeg, some grated parmisan, or fat cheese, and some cheese-curds stamped.

Then make paste, and make little pasties, boil them in broth, or as beforesaid, and serve them with sugar, cinamon, and grated cheese in a fine clean dish.

To boil a Capon or chicken with Colliflowers in the French Fashion.

Cut off the buds of your flowers, and boil them in milk with a little mace till they be very tender; then take the yolks of 2 eggs, strain them with a quarter of a pint of sack; then take as much thick butter, being drawn with a little vinegar and a slic't lemon, brew them together; then take the flowers out of the milk, and put them into the butter and sack: then dish up your Capon, being tender boil'd, upon sippets finely carved, and pour on the sauce, and serve it to the Table with a little salt.

To boil Capons, Chickens, Pigeons, or any Land Fowls in the French Fashion.

Either the skin stuffed with minced meat, or boned, & fill the vents and body; or not boned and trust to boil, fill the bodies with any of the farsings following made of any minced meat, and seasoned with pepper, cloves, mace, and salt; then mince some sweet herbs with bacon and fowl, veal, mutton, or lamb, and mix with it three or four eggs, mingle all together with grapes, gooseberries, barberries, or red currans, and sugar, or none, some pine-apple-seed, or pistaches; fill the fowl, and stew it in a stewing-pan with some strong broth, as much as will cover them, and a little white wine; being stewed, serve them in a dish with sippets finely carved, and slic't oranges, lemons, barberries, gooseberries, sweet herbs chopped, and mace.

To boil Partridges, or any of the former Fowls stuffed with any the filling aforesaid.

Boil them in a pipkin with strong broth, white-wine, mace, sweet herbs chopped very fine, and put some salt, and stew them leisurely; being finely stewed, put some marrow, and strained almonds, with rosewater to thicken it, serve them on fine carved sippets, and broth them, garnish the dish with grated bread and pistaches, mace, and lemon, or grapes.

To boil Pigeons, Woodcocks, Snites, Black birds, Thrushes, Veldifers, Rails, Quails, Larks, Sparrows, Wheat ears, Martins, or any small Land Fowl.

Woodcocks or Snites.

Boil them either in strong broth or water and salt, and being boil'd, take out the guts, and chop them small with the liver, put to it some crumb of white-bread grated, a little of the broth of the cock, and some large mace, stew them together with some gravy; then dissolve the yolks of two eggs with some wine vinegar, and a little grated nutmeg, and when you are ready to dish it, put the eggs to it, and stir it amongst the sauce with a little butter, dish them on sippets, and run the sauce over them with some beaten butter and capers, lemon minced small, barberries or pickled grapes whole.

Sometimes with this sauce, boil some slic't onions and currans in a broth by it self: when you boil it not with onions, rub the bottom of the dish with a clove or two of garlick.

Boil Woodcocks or Larks otherways.

Take them with the guts in, and boil them in some strong broth or fair water, and three or four whole onions, larg mace, and salt; the cocks being boil'd, make sauce with the some thin slices of manchet, or grated, in another pipkin, and some of the broth where the fowl or cocks boil, and put to it some butter, the guts and liver minced, and then have some yolks of eggs dissolved with some vinegar & some grated nutmeg, put it to the other ingredients, and stir them together, and dish the fowl on fine sippets, and pour on the sauce and some slic't lemon, grapes, or barberries, and run it over with beaten buter.

To boil all manner of Sea Fowl, or any wild Fowl, as Swan, Whopper, Crane, Geese, Shoveler, Hern, Bittorn, Duck, Widgeons, Gulls, Curlew, Teels, Ruffs, &c.

Stuff either the skin with his own meat, being minced with lard or beef-suet, some sweet herbs, beaten nutmeg, cloves, mace, and parboil'd oysters; mix all together, fill the skin, and prick it fast on the back, boil it in a large stewing pan or deep dish, with some strong broth, claret or white-wine, salt, large mace, two or three cloves, a bundle of sweet herbs, or none, oyster-liquor and marrow, stew all well together. Then have stewed oysters by themselves ready stewed with an onion or two, mace, pepper, butter, and a little white-wine.

Then have the bottoms of artichocks put in beaten butter, and some boild marrow ready also; then again dish up the fowl on fine carved sippets, broth the fowl, & lay on the oysters, artichocks, marrow, barberries, slic't lemon, gooseberries, or grape; and garnish your dish with grated manchet strowed, and some oysters, mace, lemon, and artichocks, and run it over with beaten butter.

Otherways bone it and fill the body with a farsing or stuffing made of minced mutton with spices, and the same materials as aforesaid.

Otherways, Make a pudding and fill the body, being first boned, and make the pudding of grated bread, sweet herbs chopped; onions, minced suet or lard, cloves, mace, pepper, salt, blood, and cream; mingle all together, as beforesaid in all points.

Or a bread pudding without blood or onions, and put minced meat to it, fruit, and sugar.

Otherways, boil them in strong broth, claret-wine, mace, cloves, salt, pepper, saffron, marrow, minced, onions, and thickned with strained sweet-breads of veal; or hard eggs strained with broth, and garnished with barberries, lemon, grapes, red currans, or gooseberries.

To boil all manner of Sea Fowls, as Swan, Whopper, Geese, Ducks, Teels. &c.

Put your fowl being cleansed and trussed into a pipkin fit for it, and boil it with strong broth or fair spring water, scum it clean, and put in three or four slic't onions, some large mace, currans, raisins, some capers, a bundle of sweet herbs, grated or strained bread, white-wine, two or three cloves, and pepper; being finely boil'd, slash it on the breast, and dish it on fine carved sippets; broth it, and lay on slic't lemon and a lemon peel, barberries or grapes, run it over with beaten butter, sugar, or ginger, and trim the dish sides with grated bread in place of the beaten ginger.

To boil these Fowls otherways.

You may add some oyster liquor, barberries, grapes, gooseberries, or lemon.

And sometimes prunes, raisins, or currans.

Otherways, half roast any of your fowls, slash them down the breast, and put them in a pipkin with the breast downward, put to them two or three slic't onions and carrots cut like lard, some mace, pepper, and salt, butter, savory, tyme, some strong broth, and some white-wine; let the broth be half wasted, and stew it very softly; being finely stewed dish it up, serve it on sippets, and pour on the broth, &c.

Otherways boil the fowl and not roast them, boil them in strong mutton broth, and put the fowl into a pipkin, boil and scum them, put to it slic't onions, a bunch of sweet herbs, some cloves, mace, whole pepper, and salt; then slash the breast from end to end 3 or four slashes, and being boil'd, dish it up on fine carved sippets, put some sugar to it, and prick a few cloves on the breast of the fowl, broth it and strow on fine sugar, and grated bread.

Otherways.

Put them in a stewing pan with some wine and strong broth, and when they boil scum them, then put to them some slices of interlarded bacon, pepper, mace, ginger, cloves, cinamon, sugar, raisins of the sun, sage flowers, or seeds or leaves of sage; serve them on fine carved sippets and trim the dish sides with sugar or grated bread.

Or you may make a farsing of any of the foresaid fowls, make it of grated cheese, and some of their own fat, two or three eggs, nutmeg, pepper, and ginger, sowe up the vents, boil them with bacon, and serve them with a sauce made of almond paste, a clove of garlick, and roasted turnips or green sauce.

To boil any old Geese, or any Geese.

Take them being powdered, and fill their bellies with oatmeal, being steeped first in warm milk or other liquor; then mingle it with some beef-suet, minced onions, and apples, seasoned with cloves, mace, some sweet herbs minced, and pepper, fasten the neck and vent, boil it, and serve it on brewes with colliflowers, cabbidge, turnips, and barberries, run it over with beaten butter.

Thus the smaller Fowls, as is before specified, or any other.

To boil wild Fowl otherways.

Boil your Fowl in strong broth or water, scum it clean, and put some white-wine to it, currans, large mace, a clove or two, some Parsley and Onions minced together:[3] then have some stewed turnips cut like lard, and stewed in a pot or little pipkin with butter, mace, a clove, white-wine, and sugar; Being finely stewed serve your fowl on sippets finely carved, broth the fowls, and pour on your Turnips, run it over with beaten butter, a little cream, yolks of eggs, sack and sugar. Scraped sugar to trim the dish, or grated bread.

Otherways.

Half roast your fowls, save the gravy, and carve the breast jagged; then put it in a pipkin, and stick here and there a clove, and put some slic't onions, chopped parsley, slic't ginger, pepper, and gravy, strained bread, with claret wine, currans, or capers, broth, mace, barberries, and sugar; being finely boil'd or stewed, serve it on carved sippets, and run it over with beaten butter, and a lemon peel.

To boil these aforesaid Fowls otherways, with Muscles, Oysters, or Cockcles; or fried Wickles in Butter, and after stewed with Butter, white Wine, Nutmeg, a slic't Orange, and gravy.

Either boil the Fowl or roast them, boil them by themselves in water and salt, scum them clean, and put to them mace, sweet herbs, and onions chopped together, some white-wine, pepper, and sugar, if you please, and a few cloves stuck in the fowls, some grated or strained bread with some of the broth, and give it a warm; dish up the fowls on fine sippets, or French bread, and carve the breast, broth it, and pour on your shell-fish, run it over with beaten butter, and slic't lemon or orange.

Otherways in the French Fashion.

---

[3]   some Parsley and Onions minced together:

Half roast the fowls, and put them in a pipkin with the gravy, then have time, parsley, sage, marjoram, & savory; mince all together with a handful of raisins of the Sun, put them into the pipkin with some mutton broth, some sack or white-wine, large mace, cloves, salt, and sugar.

Then have the other half of the fruit and herbs being minced, beat them with the white of an egg, and fry it in suet or butter as big as little figs and they will look green.

Dish up the fowls on sippets, broth it, and serve the fried herbs with eggs on them and scraped sugar.

To boil Goose-Giblets, or the Giblets of any Fowl.

Boil them whole, being finely scalded; boil them in water and salt, two or three blades of mace, and serve them on sippets finely carved with beaten butter, lemon, scalded gooseberries, and mace, or scalded grapes, barberries or slic't lemon.

Or you may for variety use the yolks of two or three eggs, beatten butter, cream, a little sack, and sugar, for lear.

Otherways.

Boil them whole, or in pieces, and boil them in strong broth or fair water, mace, pepper, and salt, being first finely scummed, put two or three whole onions, butter, and gooseberries, run it over with beaten butter, being first dished on sippetts; make a pudding in the neck, as you may see in the Book of all manner of Puddings and Farsings, &c.

Otherways.

Boil them with some white-wine, strong broth, mace, slic't ginger, butter, and salt; then have some stewed turnips or carrots cut like lard, and the giblets being finely dished on sippets, put on the stewed turnips, being thickned with eggs, verjuyce, sugar, and lemon, &c.

To bake Goose Giblets, or of any Fowl, several ways for the Garnish.

Take Giblets being finely scalded and cleansed, season them lightly with pepper, salt, and nutmeg, and put them into a Pye, being well joynted, and put to them an onion or two cut in halves, and put some butter to them, and close them up, and bake them well, and soak them some three hours.

Sauce for green-Geese.

1. Take the juyce of sorrell mixed with scalded goose-berries, and served on sippets and sugar with beaten butter, &c.

Otherways.

2. Their bellies roasted full of gooseberies, and after mixed with sugar, butter, verjuyce, and cinamon, and served on sippets.

To make a grand Sallet of minced Capon, Veal, roast Mutton, Chicken or Neats tongue.

Minced capon or veal, &c. dried Tongues in thin slices, lettice shred small as the tongue, olives, capers, mushrooms, pickled samphire, broom-buds, lemon or oranges, raisins, almonds, blew figs, Virginia potato, caparones, or crucifix pease, currans, pickled oysters, taragon.

How to dish it up.

Any of these being thin sliced, as is shown above said, with a little minced taragon and onion amongst it; then have lettice minced as small as the meat by it self, olives by themselves, capers by themselves, samphire by it self, broom-buds by it self, pickled mushrooms by themselves, or any of the materials abovesaid.

Garnish the dish with oranges and lemons in quarters or slices, oyl and vinegar beaten together, and poured over all, &c.

To boil all manner of Land Fowl, as followeth.

Turkey, Bustard Peacock, Capon, Pheasant, Pullet, Heath-pouts, Partridge, Chickens, Woodcocks, Stock-Doves, Turtle-Doves, tame Pigeons, wild Pigeons, Rails, Quails, Black-Birds, Thrushes, Veldifers, Snites, Wheatears, Larks, Sparrows, and the like.

Sauce for the Land Fowl.

Take boil'd prunes and strain them with the blood of the fowl, cinamon, ginger, and sugar, boil it to an indifferent thickness and serve it in saucers, and serve in the dish with the fowl, gravy, sauce of the same fowl.

To boil Pigeons.

Take Pigeons, and when you have farsed and boned them, fry them in butter or minced lard, and put to them broth, pepper, nutmeg, slic't ginger, cinamon beaten, coriander seed, raisins of the sun, currans, vinegar, and serve them with this sauce, being first steep'd in it four or five hours, and well stewed down.

Or you may add some quince or dried cherries boil'd amongst.

In summer you may use damsins, swet herbs chopped, grapes, bacon in slices, white-wine.

Thus you may boil any small birds, Larks, Veldifers, Black-birds, &c.

Pottage in the French Fashion.

Cut a breast of mutton into square bits or pieces, fry them in butter, & put them in a pipkin with some strong broth, pepper, mace, beaten ginger, and salt; stew it with half a pound of strained almonds, some mutton broth, crumbs of manchet, and some verjuyce; give it a warm, and serve it on sippets.

If you would have it yellow, put in saffron; sometimes for change white-wine, sack, currans, raisins, and sometimes incorporated with eggs and grated cheese.

Otherways change the colour green, with juyce of spinage, and put to it almonds strained.

Pottage otherways in the French Fashion of Mutton, Kid, or Veal.

Take beaten oatmeal and strain it with cold water, then the pot being boiled and scummed, put in your strained oatmeal, and some whole spinage, lettice, endive, colliflowers, slic't onions, white cabbidge, and salt; your pottage being almost boil'd, put in some verjuyce, and give it a warm or two; then serve it on sippets, and put the herbs on the meat.

Pottage in the English Fashion.

Take the best old pease you can get, wash and boil them in fair water, when they boil scum them, and put in a piece of interlarded bacon about two pound, put in also a bundle of mint, or other sweet herbs; boil them not too thick, serve the bacon on sippets in thin slices, and pour on the broth.

Pottage without sight of Herbs.

Mince your herbs and stamp them with your oatmeal, then strain them through a strainer with some of the broth of the pot, boil them among your mutton, & some salt; for your herbs take violet leaves, strawberry leaves, succory, spinage, lang de beef, scallions, parsley, and marigold flowers, being well boil'd, serve it on sippets.

To make Sausages.

Take the lean of a leg of pork, and four pound of beef-suet, mince them very fine, and season them with an ounce of pepper, half an ounce of cloves and mace, a handful of sage minced small, and a handful of salt; mingle all together, then brake in ten eggs, and but two whites; mix these eggs with the other meat, and fill the hogs guts; being filled, tie the ends, and boil them when you use them.

Otherways.

You may make them of mutton, veal, or beef, keeping the order abovesaid.

To make most rare Sausages without skins.

Take a leg of young pork, cut off all the lean, and mince it very small, but leave none of the strings or skins amongst it; then take two pound of beef-suet shred small, two handfuls of red sage, a little pepper, salt, and nutmeg, with a small peice of an onion; mince them together with the flesh and suet, and being finely minced, put the yolks of two or three eggs, and mix all together, make it into a paste, and when you will use it, roul out as many peices as you please in the form of an ordinary sausage, and fry them. This paste will keep a fortnight upon occasion.

Otherways.

Stamp half the meat and suet, and mince the other half, and season them as the former.

To make Links.

Take the fillet or a leg of pork, and cut it into dice work, with some of the fleak of the pork cut in the same form, season the meat with cloves, mace and pepper, a handful of sage fine minced, with a handful of salt; mingle all together, fill the guts and hang them in the air, and boil them when you spend them. These Links will serve to stew with divers kinds of meats.

SECTION II.

An hundred and twelve excellent wayes for the dressing of Beef.

To boil Oxe-Cheeks.

T Ake them and bone them, soak them in fair water four or five hours, then wash out the blood very clean, pair off the ruff of the mouth, and take out the balls of the eyes; then stuff them with sweet herbs, hard eggs, and fat, or beef-suet, pepper, and salt; mingle all together, and stuff them on the inside, prick both the insides together; then boil them amongst the other beef, and being very tender boild, serve them on brewis with interlarded bacon and *Bolonia* sausages, or boiled links made of pork on the cheeks, cut the bacon in thin slices, serve them with saucers of mustard, or with green sauce.

To dress Oxe-Cheeks Otherways.

Take out the bones and the balls of the eyes, make the mouth very clean, soak it, and wash out the blood; then wipe it dry with a clean cloath, and season it with pepper, salt, and nutmeg; then put it in a pipkin or earthen pan, with two or three great onions, some cloves, and mace, cut the jaw bones in pieces, & cut out the teeth, lay the bones on the top of the meat, then put to it half a pint of claret wine, and half as much water; close up the pot or pan with a course piece of paste, and set it a baking in an oven over night for to serve next day at dinner, serve it on toasts of fine manchet fried, then have boil'd carrots and lay on it with toasts of manchet laid round the dish; as also fried greens to garnish it, and run it over with beaten butter. This way you may also dress a leg of beef.

Or thus.

Take them and cleanse them as before, then roast them, and season them with pepper, salt, and nutmeg, save the gravy, and being roasted put them in a pipkin with some claret wine, large mace, a clove or two, and some strong broth, stew them till they be very tender, then put to them some fryed onions, and some prunes, and serve them on toasts of fried bread, or slices of French bread, and slices of orange on them, garnish the dish with grated bread.

To dress Oxe Cheeks in Stofado, or the Spanish fashion.

Take the cheeks, bone them and cleanse them, then lay them in steep in claret or white-wine, and wine vinegar, whole cloves, mace, beaten pepper, salt, slic't nutmeg, slic't ginger, and six or seven cloves of garlick, steep them the space of five or six hours, and close them up in an earthen pot or pan, with a piece of paste, and the same liquor put to it, set it a baking over night for next day dinner, serve it on toasts of fine manchet fried: then have boil'd carrots and lay on it, with the toasts of manchet laid round the dish: garnish it with slic't lemons or oranges, and fried toasts, and garnish the dish with bay-leaves.

To marinate Oxe-Cheeks.

Being boned, roast or stew them very tender in a pipkin with some claret, slic't nutmegs, pepper, salt, and wine-vinegar; being tender stewed, take them up, and put to the liquor in a pipkin a quart of wine-vinegar, and a quart of white-wine, boil it with some bay leaves, whole pepper, a bundle of rosemary, tyme, sweet marjoram, savory, sage, and parsley, bind them very hard the streightest sprigs, boil also in the liquor large mace, cloves, slic't ginger, slic't nutmegs and salt; then put the cheeks into the barrel, and put the liquor to them, and some slic't lemons, close up the head and keep them. Thus you may do four or five heads together, and serve them hot or cold.

Oxe Cheeks in Sallet.

Take oxe cheeks being boned and cleansed, steep them in claret, white-wine, or wine vinegar all night, the next day season them with nutmegs, cloves, pepper, mace, and salt, roul them up, boil them tender in water, vinegar, and salt, then press them, and being cold, slice them in thin slices, and serve them in a clean dish with oyl and vinegar.

To bake Oxe cheeks in a Pasty or Pie.

Take them being boned and soaked, boil them tender in fair water, and cleanse them, take out the balls of the eyes, and season them with pepper, salt, and nut-meg, then have some beef-suet and some buttock beef minced and laid for a bed, then lay the cheeks on it, and a few whole cloves, make your Pastie in good crust; to a gallon of flower, two pound and a half of butter, five eggs whites and all, work the butter and eggs up dry into the flower, then put in a little fair water to make it up into a stiff paste, and work up all cold.

To dress Pallets, Noses, and Lips of any Beast, Steer, Oxe, or Calf.

Take the pallats, lips, or noses, and boil them very tender, then blanch them, and cut them in little square pieces as broad as a sixpence, or like lard, fry them in sweet butter, and being fryed, pour away the butter, and put to it some anchovies, grated nutmeg, mutton gravy, and salt; give it a warm on the fire, and then dish it in a clean dish with the bottom first rubbed with a clove of garlick, run it over with beaten butter, juyce of oranges, fried parsley, or fried marrow in yolks of two eggs, and sage leaves.

Sometimes add yolks of eggs strained, and then it is a fricase.

Otherways.

Take the pallets, lips, or noses, and boil them very tender, blanch them, and cut them two inches long, then take some interlarded bacon and cut it in the like proportion, season the pallets with salt, and broil them on paper; being tender broil'd put away the fat, and put them in a dish being rubbed with a clove of gar-lick, put some mutton gravy to them on a chaffing dish of coals, and some juyce of orange, &c.

To fricase Pallets.

Take beef pallets being tender boil'd and blanched, season them with beaten cloves, nutmeg, pepper, salt, and some grated bread; then the pan being ready over the fire, with some good butter fry them brown, then put them in a dish, put to them good mutton gravy, and dissolve two or three anchovies in the sauce, a lit-tle grated nutmeg, and some juyce of lemons, and serve them up hot.

To stew Pallets, Lips, and Noses.

Take them being tender boild and blanched, put them into a pipkin, and cut to the bigness of a shilling, put to them some small cucumbers pickled, raw calves udders, some artichocks, potatoes boil'd or musk-mellon in square pieces, large mace, two or three whole cloves, some small links or sausages, sweetbreads of veal, some larks, or other small birds, as sparrows, or ox-eyes, salt, butter, strong broth, marrow, white-wine, grapes, barberries, or gooseberries, yolks of hard eggs, and stew them all together, serve them on toasts of fine French bread, and slic't lemon; sometimes thicken the broth with yolks of strained eggs and verjuyce.

To marinate Pallets, Noses, and Lips.

Take them being tender boil'd and blancht, fry them in sweet sallet oyl, or clarified butter, and being fryed make a pickle for them with whole pepper, large mace, cloves, slic't ginger, slic't nutmeg, salt and a bundle of sweet herbs, as rose-mary, tyme, bay-leaves, sweet marjoram, savory, parsley, and sage; boil the spices and herbs in wine vinegar and white-wine, then put them in a barrel with the pallets, lips and noses, and lemons, close them up for your use, and serve them in a dish with oyl.

To dress Pallets, Lips, and Noses, with Collops of Mutton and Bacon.

Take them being boild tender & blanch'd, cut them as broad as a shilling, as also some thin collops of interlarded bacon, and of a leg of mutton, finely hack'd with the back of a knife, fry them all together with some butter, and being finely fried, put out the butter, and put unto it some gravy, or a little mutton broth, salt, grated nutmeg, and a dissolved anchove; give it a warm over the fire and dish it, but rub the dish with a clove of garlick, and then run it over with butter, juyce of orange; and salt about the dish.

To make a Pottage of Beef Pallets.

Take beef pallets that are tender boi'd and blanched, cut each pallet in two pieces, and set them a stewing between two dishes with a fine piece of interlarded bacon, a handful of champignions, and five or six sweet-breads of veal, a ladle full of strong broth, and as much mutton gravy, an onion or two, two or three cloves, a blade or two of large mace, and an orange; as the pallets stew make ready a dish with the bottoms and tops of French bread slic't and steeped in mutton gravy, and the broth the pallets were stewed in; then you must have the marrow of two or three beef bones stewed in a little strong broth by it self in good big gobbets: and when the pallets, marrow, sweet-breads and the rest are enough, take out the bacon, onions, and spices, and dish up the aforesaid materials on the dish of steeped bread, lay the marrow uppermost in pieces, then wring on the juyce of two or three oranges, and serve it to the table very hot.

To rost a dish of Oxe Pallets with great Oysters, Veal, Sweet-breads, Lamb stones, peeping Chickens, Pigeons, slices of interlarded Bacon, large Cockcombs, and Stones, Marrow, Pistaches, and Artichocks.

Take the oxe pallets and boil them tender, blanch them and cut them 2 inches long, lard one half with smal lard, then have your chickens & pigeon peepers scalded, drawn, and trust; set them, and lard half of them; then have the lambstones, parboil'd and blanched, as also the combs, and cock-stones, next have interlarded bacon, and sage; but first spit the birds on a small bird-spit, and between each chicken or pigeon put on first a slice of interlarded bacon, and a sage leaf, then another slice of bacon and a sage leaf, thus do till all the birds be spitted; thus also the sweet-breads, lamb-stones, and combs, then the oysters being parboild, lard them with lard very small, and also a small larding prick, then beat the yolks of two or 3 eggs, and mix them with a little fine grated manchet, salt, nutmeg, time, and rosemary minced very small, and when they are hot at the fire baste them often, as also the lambstones and sweet-breads with the same ingredients; then have the bottoms of artichocks ready boil'd, quartered, and fried, being first dipped in butter and kept warm, and marrow dipped in butter and fried, as also the fowls and other ingredients; then dish the fowl piled up in the middle upon another roast material round about them in the dish, but first rub the dish with a clove of garlick: the pallets by themselves, the sweet-breads by themselves, and the cocks stones, combs, and lamb-stones by themselves; then the artichocks, fryed marrow, and pistaches by themselves; then make a sauce with some claret wine, and gravy, nutmeg, oyster liquor, salt, a slic't or quartered onion, an anchove or two dissolved, and a little sweet butter, give it a warm or two, and put to it two or three slices of an orange, pour on the sauce very hot, and garnish it with slic't oranges and lemons.

The smallest birds are fittest for this dish of meat, as wheat-ears, martins, larks, ox-eyes, quails, snites, or rails.

Oxe Pallets in Jellies.

Take two pair of neats or calves feet, scald them, and boil them in a pot with two gallons of water, being first very well boned, and the bone and fat between the claws taken out, and being well soaked in divers waters, scum them clean; and boil them down from two gallons to three quarts; strain the broth, and being cold take off the top and bottom, and put it into a pipkin with whole cinamon, ginger, slic't and quartered nutmeg, two or three blades of large mace, salt, three pints of white-wine, and half a pint of grape-verjuyce or rose vinegar, two pound and a half of sugar, the whites of ten eggs well beaten to froth, stir them all together in a pipkin, being well warmed and the jelly melted, put in the eggs, and set it over a charcoal-fire kindled before, stew it on that fire half an hour before you boil it up, and when it is just a boiling take it off, before you run it let it cool a little, then run it through your jelly bag once or twice; then the pallets being tender boild and blanched, cut them into dice-work with some lamb-stones, veal, sweet-breads, cock-combs, and stones, potatoes, or artichocks all cut into dice-work, preserved barberries, or calves noses, and lips, preserved quinces, dryed or green neats tongues, in the same work, or neats feet, all of these together, or any one of them; boil them in white-wine or sack, with nutmeg, slic't ginger, coriander, caraway, or fennil-seed, make several beds, or layes of these things, and run the jelly over them many times after one is cold, according as you have sorts of colours of jellies, or else put all at once; garnish it with preserved oranges, or green citron cut like lard.

To bake Beef-Pallets.

Provide pallets, lips, and noses, boild tender and blanched, cock-stones, and combs, or lamb stones, and sweet-breads cut into pieces, scald the stones, combs, and pallets slic't or in pieces as big as the lamb stones, half a pint of great oysters parboil'd in their own liquor, quarter'd dates, pistaches a handful, or pine kernels, a few pickled broom buds, some fine interlarded bacon slic't in thin slices being also scalded, ten chestnuts roasted & blanched; season all these together with salt, nutmeg, and a good quantity of large mace, fill the pie, and put to it good butter, close it up and bake it, make liquor for it, then beat some butter, and three or four yolks of eggs with white or claret wine, cut up the lid, and pour it on the meat, shaking it well together, then lay on slic't lemon and pickled barberries, &c.

To dress a Neats-Tongue boil'd divers ways.

Take a Neats-tongue of three or four days powdering, being tender boil'd, serve it on cheat bread for brewis, dish on the tongue in halves or whole, and serve an udder with it being of the same powdering and salting, finely blanched, put to them the clear fat of the beef on the tongue, and white sippets round the dish, run them over with beaten butter, &c.

Otherways.

For greater service two udders and two tongues finely blanched and served whole.

Sometimes for variety you may make brewis with some fresh beef or good mutton broth, with some of the fat of the beef-pot; put it in a pipkin with some large mace, a handful of parsley and sorrel grosly chopped, and some pepper, boil them together, and scald the bread, then lay on the boil'd tongue, mace, and some of the herbs, run it over with beaten butter, slic't lemon, gooseberries, barberries, or grapes.

Or for change, put some pared turnips boiling in fair water, & being tender boil'd, drain the water from them, dish them in a clean dish, and run them over with beaten butter, dish your tongues and udders on them, and your colliflowers on the tongues and udders, run them over with beaten butter; or in place of colli-flowers, carrots in thin quarters, or sometimes on turnips and great boil'd onions, or butter'd cabbidge and carrots, or parsnips, and carrots buttered.

Neats Tongues and a fresh Udder in Stoffado.

Season them with pepper, salt, and nutmeg, then lard them with great lard, and steep them all night in claret-wine, wine vinegar, slic't nutmegs and ginger, whole cloves, beaten pepper, and salt; steep them in an earthen pot or pan, and cover or close them up, bake them, and serve them on sops of French bread, and the spices over them with some slic't lemon, and sausages or none.

Neats Tongues stewed whole or in halves.

Take them being tender boil'd, and fry them whole or in halves, put them in a pipkin with some gravy or mutton-broth, large mace, slic't nutmeg, pepper, claret, a little wine vinegar, butter, and salt; stew them well together, and being almost stewed, put to the meat two or three slices of orange, sparagus, skirrets, chesnuts, and serve them on fine sippets; run them over with beaten butter, slic't lemon, and boil'd marrow over all.

Sometimes for the broth put some yolks of eggs, beaten with grape-verjuyce.

To stew a Neats Tongue otherwayes.

Make a hole in the but-end of it, and mince it with some fat bacon or beef-suet, season it with nutmeg, salt, the yolk of a raw egg, some sweet herbs minced small, & grated parmisan, or none, some pepper, or ginger, and mingle all together, fill the tongue and wrap it in a caul of veal, boil it till it will blanch, and being blancht, wrap about it some of the searsing with a caul of veal; then put it in a pipkin with some claret and gravy, cloves, salt, pepper, some grated bread, sweet herbs chopped small, fried onions, marrow boild in strong broth, and laid over all, some grapes, gooseberries, slic't orange or lemon, and serve it on sippets, run it over with beaten butter, and stale grated manchet to garnish the dish.

Or sometimes in a broth called *Brodo Lardiero.*

To hash or stew a Neats tongue divers wayes.

Take a Neats-tongue being tender boil'd and blancht, slice it into thin slices, as big and as thick as a shilling, fry it in sweet butter; and being fried, put to it some strong broth, or good mutton-gravy, some beaten cloves, mace, nutmeg, salt, and saffron; stew them well together, then have some yolks of eggs dissolved with grape verjuyce, and put them into the pan, give them a toss or two, and the gravy and eggs being pretty thick, dish it on fine sippets.

Or make the same, and none of those spices, but only cinamon, sugar, and saffron.

Sometimes sliced as aforesaid, but in slices no bigger nor thicker than a three pence, and used in all points as before, but add some onions fried, with the tongue, some mushrooms, nutmegs, and mace; and being well stewed, serve it on fine sippets, but first rub the dish with a clove of garlick, and run all over with beaten butter, a shred lemon, and a spoonful of fair water.

Sometimes you may add some boil'd chesnuts, sweet herbs, capers, marrow, and grapes or barberries.

Or stew them with raisins put in a pipkin, with the sliced tongue, mace, slic't dates, blanched almonds, or pistaches, marrow, claret-wine, butter, salt, verjuyce, sugar, strong broth, or gravy; and being well stewed, dissolve the yolks of six eggs with vinegar or grape verjuyce, and dish it up on fine sippets, slic't lemon, and beaten butter over all.

To marinate a Neats-Tongue either whole or in halves.

Take seven or eight Neats-tongues, or Heifer, Calves, Sheeps, or any tongues, boil them till they will blanch; and being blanched, lard them or not lard them, as you please; then put them in a barrel, then make a pickle of whole pepper, slic't ginger, whole cloves, slic't nutmegs, and largemace: next have a bundle of sweet herbs, as tyme, rosemary; bay-leaves, sage-leaves, winter-savory, sweet marjoram, and parsley; take the streightest sprigs of these herbs that you can get, and bind them up hard in a bundle every sort by it self, and all into one; then boil these spices and herbs in as much wine vinegar and white wine as will fill the vessel where the tongues are, and put some salt and slic't lemons to them; close them up being cold, and keep them for your use upon any occasion; serve them with some of the spices, liquor, sweet herbs, sallet oyl, and slic't lemon or lemon-peel, Pack them close.

To fricase Neats-Tongues.

Being tender boil'd, slice them into thin slices, and fry them with sweet butter; being fried put away the butter, and put to them some strong gravy or broth, nutmeg, pepper, salt, some sweet herbs chopped small, as tyme, savory, sweet marjoram, and parsley; stew them well together, then dissolve some yolks of eggs with wine-vinegar or grape-verjuyce, some whole grapes or barberries. For the thickening use fine grated manchet, or almond-paste strained, and some times put saffron to it. Thus you may fricase any Udder being tender boil'd, as is before-said.

To dress Neats-Tongues in Brodo Lardiero, or the Italian way.

Boil a Neats-tongue in a pipkin whole, halves, or in gubbings till it may be blanched, cover it close, and put to it two or three blades of large mace, with some strong mutton or beef broth, some sack or white-wine, and some slices of interlarded bacon, scum it when it boils, and put to it large mace, nutmeg, ginger, pepper, raisins, two or three whole cloves, currans, prune, sage-leaves, saffron, and divers cherries; stew it well, and serve it in a fine clean scoured dish, on slices of French-Bread.

To dress Neats-Tongues, as Beefs Noses, Lips, and Pallets.

Take Neats-tongues, being tender boild and blancht, slice them thin, and fry them in sweet butter, being fried put away the butter, and put to them anchovies, grated nutmeg, mutton gravy, and salt; give them a warm over the fire, and serve them in a clean scoured dish: but first rub the dish with a clove of garlick, and run the meat over with some beaten butter, juyce of oranges, fried parsley, fried marrow, yolks of eggs, and sage leaves.

To hash a Neats-tongue whole or in slices.

Boil it tender and blanch it, then slice it into thin slices, or whole, put to it some boil'd or roast chesnuts, some strong broth, whole cloves, pepper, salt, claret wine, large mace and a bundle of sweet herbs; stew them all together very leisurely, and being stewed serve it on fine carved sippets, either with slic't lemon, grapes, gooseberries, or barberries, and run it over with beaten butter.

To dry Neats Tongues.

Take salt beaten very fine, and salt-peter of each alike, rub your tongues very well with the salts, and cover them all over with it, and as it wasts, put on more, when they are hard and stiff they are enough, then roul them in bran, and dry them before a soft fire, before you boil them, let them lie in pump water one night, and boil them in pump water.

Otherways powder them with bay-salt, and being well smoakt, hang them up in a garret or cellar, and let them come no more at the fire till they be boil'd.

To prepare a Neats-tongue or Udder to roast, a Stag, Hind, Buck, Doe, Sheep, Hog, Goat, Kid, or Calf.

Boil them tender and blanch them, being cold lard them, or roast them plain without lard, baste them with butter, and serve them on gallendine sauce.

To roast A Neats Tongue.

Take a Neats-tongue being tender boil'd, blanched, and cold, cut a hole in the but-end, and mince the meat that you take out, then put some sweet herbs finely minced to it, with a minced pippin or two, the yolks of eggs slic't, some minced beef-suet, or minced bacon, beaten ginger and salt, fill the tongue, and stop the end with a caul of veal, lard it and roast it; then make sauce with butter, nutmeg, gravy, and juyce of oranges; garnish the dish with slic't lemon, lemon peel and barberries.

To roast a Neats-Tongue or Udder otherways.

Boil it a little, blanch it, lard it with pretty big lard all the length of the tongue, as also udders; being first seasoned with nutmeg, pepper, cinamon, and ginger, then spit and roast them, and baste them with sweet butter; being rosted, dress them with grated bread and flower, and some of the spices abovesaid, some sugar, and serve it with juyce of oranges, sugar, gravy, and slic't lemon on it.

To make minced Pies of a Neats tongue.

Take a fresh Neats-tongue, boil, blanch, and mince it hot or cold, then mince four pound of beef-suet by it self, mingle them together, and season them with an ounce of cloves and mace beaten, some salt, half a preserved orange, and a little lemon-peel minced, with a quarter of a pound of sugar, four pound of currans, a little verjuyce, and rose-water, and a quarter of a pint of sack, stir all together, and fill your Pies.

To bake Neats tongues to eat cold, according to these figures.

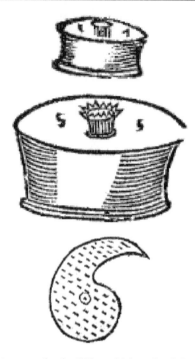

Take the tongues being tender boil'd and blanched, leave on the fat of the roots of the tongue, and season them well with nutmeg, pepper, and salt; but first lard them with pretty big lard, and put them in the Pie with some whole cloves and some butter, close them and bake them in fine or course paste, made only of boiling liquor and flour, and baste the crust with eggs, pack the crust very close in the filling with the raw beef or mutton.

To bake two Neats-tongues in a Pie to eat hot, according to these Figures.

Take one of the tongues, and mince it raw, then boil the other very tender, blanch it, and cut it into pieces as big as a walnut, lard them with small lard being cold & seasoned; then have another tongue being raw, take out the meat, and mince it with some beef-suet or lard: then lay some of the minced tongues in the bottom of the Pie, and the pieces on it; then make balls of the other meat as big as the pieces of tongue, with some grated bread, cream, yolks of eggs, bits of artichocks, nutmeg, salt, pepper, a few sweet herbs, and lay them in a Pie with some boild artichocks, marrow, grapes, chesnuts blanch't, slices of interlarded bacon, and butter; close it up & bake it, then liquor it with verjuyce, gravy, and yolks of eggs.

To bake a Neats tongue hot otherways.

Boil a fresh tongue very tender, and blanch it; being cold slice it into thin slices, and season it lightly with pepper, nutmeg, cinamon, and ginger finely beaten; then put into the pie half a pound of currans, lay the meat on, and dates in halves, the marrow of four bones, large mace, grapes, or barberries, and butter; close it up and bake it, and being baked, liquor it with white or claret wine, butter, sugar, and ice it.

Otherways.

Boil it very tender, and being blanched and cold, take out some of the meat at the but-end, mince it with some beef-suet, and season it with pepper, ginger beaten fine, salt, currans, grated bread, two or three yolks of eggs, raisins minced, or in place of currans, a little cream, a little orange minced, also sweet herbs chopped small: then fill the tongue and season it with the foresaid spices, wrap it in a caul of veal, and put some thin slices of veal under the tongue, as also thin slices of interlarded bacon, and on the top large mace, marrow, and barberries, and butter over all; close it up and bake it, being baked, liquor it, and ice it with butter, sugar, white-wine, or grape-verjuyce.

For the paste a pottle of flower, and make it up with boiling liquor, and half a pound of butter.

To roast a Chine, Rib, Loin, Brisket, or Fillet of Beef.

Draw them with parsley, rosemary, tyme, sweet marjoram, sage, winter savory, or lemon, or plain without any of them, fresh or salt, as you please; broach it, or spit it, roast it and baste it with butter; a good chine of beef will ask six hours roasting.

For the sauce take strait tops of rosemary, sage-leaves, picked parsley, tyme, and sweet marjoram; and strew them in wine vinegar, and the beef gravy; or otherways with gravy and juyce of oranges and lemons. Sometimes for change in saucers of vinegar and pepper.

To roast a Fillet of Beef.

Take a fillet which is the tenderest part of the beef, and lieth in the inner part of the surloyn, cut it as big as you can, broach it on a broach not too big, and be careful not to broach it through the best of the meat, roast it leisurely, & baste it with sweet butter, set a dish to save the gravy while it roasts, then prepare sauce for it of good store of parsley, with a few sweet herbs chopp'd smal, the yolks of three or four eggs, sometimes gross pepper minced amongst them with the peel of an orange, and a little onion; boil these together, and put in a little butter, vinegar, gravy, a spoonful of strong broth, and put it to the beef.

Otherways.

Sprinkle it with rose-vinegar, claret-wine, elder-vinegar, beaten cloves, nutmeg, pepper, cinamon, ginger, coriander-seed, fennil-seed, and salt; beat these things fine, and season the fillet with it, then roast it, and baste it with butter, save the gravy, and blow off the fat, serve it with juyce of orange or lemon, and a little elder-vinegar.

Or thus.

Powder it one night, then stuff it with parsley, tyme, sweet marjoram, beets, spinage, and winter-savory, all picked and minced small, with the yolks of hard eggs mixt amongst some pepper, stuff it and roast it, save the gravy and stew it with the herbs, gravy, as also a little onion, claret wine, and the juyce of an orange or two; serve it hot on this sauce, with slices of orange on it, lemons, or barberries.

To stew a fillet of Beef in the Italian Fashion.

Take a young tender fillet of beef, and take away all the skins and sinews clean from it, put to it some good white-wine (that is not too sweet) in a bowl, wash it, and crush it well in the wine, then strow upon it a little pepper, and a powder called *Tamara* in Italian, and as much salt as will season it, mingle them together very well, and put to it as much white-wine as will cover it, lay a trencher upon it to keep it down in a close pan with a weight on it, and let it steep two nights and a day; then take it out and put it into a pipkin with some good beef-broth, but put none of the pickle to it, but only beef-broth, and that sweet, not salt; cover it close, and set it on the embers, then put to it a few whole cloves and mace, let it stew till it be enough, it will be very tender, and of an excellent taste; serve it with the same broth as much as will cover it.

To make this *Tamara*, take two ounces of coriander-seed, an ounce of anniseed, an ounce of fennel-seed, two ounces of cloves, and an ounce of cinamon; beat them into a gross powder, with a little powder of winter-savory, and put them into a viol-glass to keep.

To make an excellent Pottage called Skinke.

Take a leg of beef, and chop it into three pieces, then boil it in a pot with three pottles of spring-water, a few cloves, mace, and whole pepper: after the pot is scum'd put in a bundle of sweet morjoram, rosemary, tyme, winter-savory, sage, and parsley bound up hard, some salt, and two or three great onions whole, then about an hour before dinner put in three marrow bones and thicken it with some strained oatmeal, or manchet slic't and steeped with some gravy, strong broth, or some of the pottage; then a little before you dish up the Skinke, put into it a little fine powder of saffron, and give it a warm or two: dish it on large slices of French Bread, and dish the marrow bones on them in a fine clean large dish; then have two or three manchets cut into toasts, and being finely toasted, lay on the knuckle of beef in the middle of the dish, the marrow bones round about it, and the toasts round about the dish brim, serve it hot.

To stew a Rump, or the fat end of a Brisket of Beef in the French Fashion.

Take a Rump of beef, boil it & scum it clean in a stewing pan or broad mouthed pipkin, cover it close, & let it stew an hour; then put to it some whole pepper, cloves, mace, and salt, scorch the meat with your knife to let out the gravy, then put in some claret-wine, and half a dozen of slic't onions; having boiled, an hour after put in some capers, or a handfull of broom-buds, and half a dozen of cab-

bidge-lettice being first parboil'd in fair water, and quartered, two or three spoonfuls of wine vinegar, and as much verjuyce, and let it stew till it be tender; then
serve it on sippets of French bread, and dish it on those sippets; blow the fat clean
off the broth, scum it, and stick it with fryed bread.

A Turkish Dish of Meat.

Take an interlarded piece of beef, cut it into thin slices, and put it into a pot
that hath a close cover, or stewing-pan; then put it into a good quantity of clean
picked rice, skin it very well, and put it into a quantity of whole pepper, two or
three whole onions, and let this boil very well, then take out the onions, and dish
it on sippets, the thicker it is the better.

To boil a Chine, Rump, Surloin, Brisket, Rib, Flank, Buttock, or Fillet of Beef poudered.

Take any of these, and give them in Summer a weeks powdering, in Winter
a fortnight, stuff them or plain; if you stuff them, do it with all manner of sweet
herbs, fat beef minced, and some nutmeg; serve them on brewis, with roots of cabbidge boil'd in milk, with beaten butter. &c.

To pickle roast Beef, Chine, Surloin, Rib, Brisket, Flank, or Neats-Tongues.

Take any of the foresaid beef, as chine or fore-rib, & stuff it with penniroyal, or
other sweet herbs, or parsley minced small, and some salt, prick in here & there a
few whole cloves, roast it; and then take claret wine, wine vinegar, whole pepper,
rosemary, and bayes, and tyme, bound up close in a bundle, and boil'd in some
claret-wine, and wine-vinegar, make the pickle, and put some salt to it; then pack
it up close in a barrel that will but just hold it, put the pickle to it, close it on the
head, and keep it for your use.

To stew Beef in gobbets, in the French Fashion.

Take a flank of beef, or any part but the leg, cut it into slices or gobbits as big
as a pullets egg, with some gobbits of fat, and boil it in a pot or pipkin with some
fair spring water, scum it clean, and put to it an hour after it hath boil'd carrots,
parsnips, turnips, great onions, salt, some cloves, mace, and whole pepper, cover
it close, and stew it till it be very tender; then half an hour before dinner, put into
it some picked tyme, parsley, winter-savory, sweet marjoram, sorrel and spinage,
(being a little bruised with the back of a ladle) and some claret-wine; then dish it
on fine sippets, and serve it to the table hot, garnish it with grapes, barberries, or
gooseberries, sometimes use spices, the bottoms of boil'd artichocks put into beat-
en butter, and grated nutmeg, garnished with barberries.

Stewed Collops of Beef.

Take some of the buttock of beef, and cut it into thin slices cross the grain of
the meat, then hack them and fry them in sweet butter, and being fryed fine and
brown put them in a pipkin with some strong broth, a little claret wine, and some
nutmeg, stew it very tender; and half an hour before you dish it, put to it some
good gravy, elder-vinegar, and a clove or two; when you serve it, put some juyce
of orange, and three or four slices on it, stew down the gravy somewhat thick, and
put into it when you dish it some beaten butter.

Olives of Beef stewed and roast.

Take a buttock of beef, and cut some of it into thin slices as broad as your hand, then hack them with the back of a knife, lard them with small lard, and season them with pepper, salt, and nutmeg, then make a farsing with some sweet herbs, tyme, onions, the yolks of hard eggs, beef-suet or lard all minced, some salt, barberries, grapes or gooseberris, season it with the former spices lightly, and work it up together, then lay it on the slices, and roul them up round with some caul of veal, beef, or mutton, bake them in a dish within the oven, or roast them, then put them in a pipkin with some butter, and saffron, or none; blow off the fat from the gravy, and put it to them, with some artichocks, potato's, or skirrets blanched, being first boil'd, a little claret-wine, and serve them on sippets with some slic't orange, lemon, barberries, grapes or gooseberries.

To Make a Hash of raw Beef.

Mince it very small with some beef-suet or lard, and some sweet herbs, some beaten cloves and mace, pepper, nutmeg and a whole onion or two, stew all together in a pipkin, with some blanched chesnuts, strong broth, and some claret; let it stew softly the space of three hours, that it may be very tender, then blow off the fat, dish it, and serve it on sippets, garnish it with barberries, grapes, or gooseberries.

To make a Hash of Beef otherways.

Take some of the buttock, cut it into thin slices, and hack them with the back of your knife, then fry them with sweet butter, and being fried put them into a pipkin with some claret, strong broth, or gravy, cloves, mace, pepper, salt, and sweet butter; being tender stewed serve them on fine sippets, with slic't lemon, grapes, barberries, or goosberries, and rub the dish with a clove of garlick.

Otherways.

Cut some buttock-beef into thin slices, and hack it with the back of a knife, then have some slices of interlarded bacon; stew them together in a pipkin, with some gravy, claret-wine, and strong broth, cloves, mace, pepper, and salt; being tender stewed, serve it on French bread sippets.

Otherways.

Being roasted and cold cut it into very fine thin slices, then put some gravy to it, nutmeg, salt, a little thin slic't onion, and claret-wine, stew it in a pipkin, and being well stewed dish it and serve it up, run it over with beaten butter and slic't lemon, garnish the dish with sippets, &c.

Carbonadoes of Beef, raw, roasted, or toasted.

Take a fat surloin, or the fore-rib, and cut it into steaks half an inch thick, sprinkle it with salt, and broil it on the embers on a very temperate fire, and in an hour it will be broild enough; then serve it with gravy, and onions minced and boil'd in vinegar, and pepper, or juyce of oranges, nutmeg, and gravy, or vinegar, and pepper only, or gravy alone.

Or steep the beef in claret wine, salt, pepper, nutmeg, and broil them as the former, boil up the gravy where it was steeped, and serve it for sauce with beaten butter.

As thus you may also broil or toast the sweet-breads when they are new, and serve them with gravy.

To Carbonado, broil or toast Beef in the Italian fashion.

Take the ribs, cut them into steaks & hack them, then season them with pepper, salt, and coriander-seed, being first sprinkled with rose-vinegar, or elder vinegar, then lay them one upon another in a dish the space of an hour, and broil or toast them before the fire, and serve them with the gravy that came from them, or juyce of orange and the gravy boild together. Thus also you may do hiefers' udders, oxe-cheeks, or neats-tongues, being first tender broild or roasted.

In this way also you may make Scotch Collops in thin slices, hack them with your knife, being salted, and fine and softly broil'd serve them with gravy.

Beef fried divers ways, raw or roasted.

1. Cut it in slices half an inch thick, and three fingers broad, salt it a little, and being hacked with the back of your knife, fry it in butter with a temperate fire.

2. Cut the other a quarter of an inch thick; and fry it as the former.

3. Cut the other collop to fry as thick as half a crown, and as long as a card: hack them and fry them as the former, but fry them not to hard.

Thus you may fry sweetbreads of the beef.

Beef fried otherways, being roasted and cold.

Slice it into good big slices, then fry them in butter, and serve them with butter and vinegar, garnish them with fried parsley.

Sauces for the raw fried Beef.

1. Beaten butter, with slic't lemon beaten together.

2. Gravy and butter.

3. Mustard, butter, and vinegar.

4. Butter, vinegar, minced capers, and nutmeg.

For the garnish of this fried meat, either parsley, sage, clary, onions, apples, carrots, parsnips, skirrets, spinage, artichocks, pears, quinces, slic't oranges, or lemons, or fry them in butter.

Thus you may fry sweet-breads, udders, and tongues in any of the foresaid ways, with the same sauces and garnish.

To bake Beef in Lumps several ways, or Tongues in lumps raw, or Heifer Udders raw or boil'd.

Take the buttock, brisket, fillet, or fore-rib, cut it into gobbets as big as a pullets egg, with some equal gobbets of fat, season them with pepper, salt, and nutmeg, and bake them with some butter or none.

Make the paste with a quarter of a pound of butter, and boiling liquor, boil the butter in the liquor, make up the paste quick and pretty stiff for a round Pie.

To bake Beef, red-Deer-fashion in Pies or Pasties either Surloin, Brisket, Buttock, or Fillet, larded or not.

Take the surloin, bone it, and take off the great sinew that lies on the back, lard the leanest parts of it with great lard, being season'd with nutmegs, pepper, and lard three pounds; then have for the seasoning four ounces of pepper, four ounces of nutmegs, two ounces of ginger, and a pound of salt, season it and put it into the Pie: but first lay a bed of good sweet butter, and a bay-leaf or two, half an ounce of whole cloves, lay on the venison, then put on all the rest of the seasoning, with a few more cloves, good store of butter, and a bay-leaf or two, close it up and bake it, it will ask eight hours soaking, being baked and cold, fill it up with clarified butter, serve it, and a very good judgment shall not know it from red Deer. Make the paste either fine or course to bake it hot or cold; if for hot half the seasoning, and bake it in fine paste.

To this quantity of flesh you may have three gallons of fine flower heapt measure, and three pound of butter; but the best way to bake red deer, is to bake it in course paste either in pie or pasty, make it in rye meal to keep long.

Otherways, you may make it of meal as it comes from the mill, and make it only of boiling water, and no stuff in it.

Otherways to be eaten cold.

Take two stone of buttock beef, lard it with great lard, and season it with nutmeg, pepper, and the lard, then steep it in a bowl, tray, or earthen pan, with some wine-vinegar, cloves, mace, pepper, and two or three bay-leaves: thus let it steep four or five days, and turn it twice or thrice a day: then take it and season it with cloves, mace, pepper, nutmeg, and salt; put it into a pot with the back-side downward, with butter under it, and season it with a good thick coat of seasoning, and some butter on it, then close it up and bake it, it will ask six or seven hours baking. Being baked draw it, and when it is cold pour out the gravy, and boil it again in a pipkin, and pour it on the venison, then fill up the pot with the clarified butter, &c.

To make minced Pies of Beef.

Take of the buttock of beef, cleanse it from the skins, and cut it into small pieces, then take half as much more beef-suet as the beef, mince them together very small, and season them with pepper, cloves, mace, nutmeg, and salt; then have half as much fruit as meat, three pound of raisins, four pound of currans, two pound of prunes, &c. or plain without fruit, but only seasoned with the same spices.

To make a Collar of Beef.

Take the thinnest end of a coast of beef, boil it a little and lay in pump water, & a little salt three days, shifting it once a day; the last day put a pint of claret wine to it, and when you take it out of the water let it lie two or three hours a draining; then cut it almost to the end in three slices, and bruise a little cochinel and a very little allum, and mingle it with a very little claret wine, colour the meat all over with it; then take a douzen of anchoves, wash and bone them, lay them on the beef, & season it with cloves, pepper, mace, two handfuls of salt, a little sweet marjoram, and tyme; & when you make it up, roull the innermost slice first, & the other two upon it, being very well seasoned every where and bind it up hard with tape, then put it into a stone pot a little bigger than the collar, and pour upon it a pint of claret wine, and half a pint of wine vinegar, a sprig of rosemary, and a few bay-leaves; bake it very well, and before it be quite cold, take it out of the pot, and you may keep it dry as long as you please.

To bake a Flank of Beef in a Collar.

Take flank of beef, and lay it in pump water four days and nights, shift it twice a day, then take it out & dry it very well with clean cloaths, cut it in three layers, and take out the bones and most of the fat; then take three handfuls of salt, and good store of sage chopped very small, mingle them, and strew it between the three layers, and lay them one upon another; then take an ounce of cloves and mace, and another of nutmegs, beat them very well, and stew it between the layers of beef, roul it up close together, then take some packthred and tie it up very hard, put it in a long earthen pot, which is made of purpose for that use, tie up the top of the pot with cap paper, and set it in an oven; let it stand eight hours, when you draw it, and being between hot and cold, bind it up round in a cloth, tie it fast at both ends with packthred, and hang it up for your use.

Sometimes for variety you may use slices of bacon btwixt the layers, and in place of sage sweet herbs, and sometimes cloves of garlick. Or powder it in saltpeter four or five days, then wash it off, roul it and use the same spices as abovesaid, and serve it with mustard and sugar, or Gallendine.

To stuff Beef with Parsley to serve cold.

Pick the parsley very fine and short, then mince some suet not to small, mingle it with the parsley, and make little holes in ranks, fill them hard and full, and being boiled and cold, slice it into thin slices, and serve it with vinegar and green parsley.

To make Udders either in Pie or Pasty, according to these Figures.

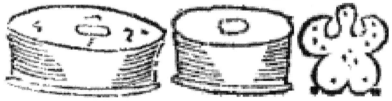

Take a young Udder and lard it with great lard, being seasoned with nutmeg, pepper, cloves, and mace, boil it tender, and being cold wrap it in a caul of veal, but first season it with the former spices and salt; put it in the Pie with some slices of veal under it, season them, and some also on the top, with some slices of lard and butter; close it up, and being baked, liquor it with clarified butter. Thus for to eat cold; if hot, liquor it with white-wine, gravy and butter.

To bake a Heifers Udder in the Italian fashion.

The Udder being boil'd tender, and cold, cut it into dice-work like small dice, and season them with some cloves, mace, cinamon, ginger, salt, pistaches, or pine-kernels, some dates, and bits of marrow; season the aforesaid materials lightly and fit, make your Pie not above an inch high, like a custard, and of custard-paste, prick it, and dry it in the oven, and put in the abovesaid materials; put to it also some custard-stuff made of good cream, ten eggs, and but three whites, sugar, salt, rose-water, and some dissolved musk; bake it and stick it with slic't dates, canded pistaches, and scrape fine sugar on it.

Otherways, boil the udder very tender, & being cold slice it into thin slices, as also some thin slices of parmisan & interlarded bacon, some sweet herbs chopt small, some currans, cinamon, nutmeg, sugar, rose-water, and some butter, make three bottoms of the aforesaid things in a dish, patty-pan, or pie, with a cut cover, and being baked, scrape sugar on it, or rice it.

Otherways to eat hot.

Take an Udder boil'd and cold, slice it into thin slices, and season it with pepper, cinamon, nutmeg, ginger, and salt, mingle some currans among the slices and fill the pie; put some dates on the top, large mace, barberries, or grapes, butter, and the marrow of 2 marrow-bones, close it up and bake it, being baked ice it; but before you ice it, liquor it with butter, verjuyce and sugar.

To stew Calves or Neats Feet.

Boil and blanch them, then part them in halves, and put them into a pipkin with some strong broth, a little powder of saffron, sweet butter, pepper, sugar, and some sweet herbs finely minced, let them stew an hour and serve them with a little grape verjuyce, stewed among them.

Neats feet being soust serve them cold with mustard.

To make a fricase of Neats-Feet.

Take them being boild and blancht, fricase them with some butter, and being finely fried make a sauce with six yolks of eggs, dissolved with some wine-vinegar, grated nutmeg, and salt.

Otherways.

First bone and prick them clean, then being boiled, blanched, or cold, cut them into gubbings, and put them in a frying-pan with a ladle-full of strong broth, a piece of butter, and a little salt; after they have fried awhile, put to them a little chopt parsley, green chibbolds, young spear-mint, and tyme, all shred very small, with a little beaten pepper: being almost fried, make a lear for them with the yolks of four or five eggs, some mutton gravy, a little nutmeg, and the juyce of a lemon wrung therein; put this lear to the neats feet as they fry in the pan, then toss them once or twice, and so serve them.

Neats Feet larded, and roasted on a spit.

Take neats feet being boil'd, cold, and blanched, lard them whole, and then roast them, being roasted, serve them with venison sauce made of claret wine, wine-vinegar, and toasts of houshold bread strained with the wine through a strainer, with some beaten cinamon and ginger, put it in a dish or pipkin, and boil it on the fire, with a few whole cloves, stir it with a sprig of rosemary, and make it not too thick.

To make Black Puddings of Beefers Blood.

Take the blood of a beefer when it is warm, put in some salt, and then strain it, and when it is through cold put in the groats of oatmeal well pic't, and let it stand soaking all night, then put in some sweet herbs, pennyroyal, rosemary, tyme, savoury, fennil, or fennil-seed, pepper, cloves, mace, nutmegs, and some cream or good new milk; then have four or five eggs well beaten, and put in the blood with good beef-suet not cut too small; mix all well together and fill the beefers guts, being first well cleansed, steeped, and scalded.

To dress a Dish of Tripes hot out of the pot or pan.

Being tender boil'd, make a sauce with some beaten butter, gravy, pepper, mustard, and wine-vinegar, rub a dish with a clove of garlick, and dish them therein; then run the sauce over them with a little bruised garlick amongst it, and a little wine vinegar sprinkled over the meat.

To make Bolonia-Sausages.

Take a good leg of pork, and take away all the fat, skins, and sinews, then mince and stamp it very fine in a wooden or brass mortar, weigh the meat, and to every five pound thereof take a pound of good lard cut as small as your little finger about an inch long, mingle it amongst the meat, and put to it half an ounce of whole cloves, as much beaten pepper, with the same quantity of nutmegs and mace finely beaten also, an ounce of whole carraway-seed, salt eight ounces, cocherel bruised with a little allom beaten and dissolved in sack, and stamped amongst the meat: then take beefers guts, cut of the biggest of the small guts, a yard long, and being clean scoured put them in brine a week or eight days, it strengthens and makes them tuff to hold filling. The greatest skill is in the filling of them, for if they be not well filled they will grow rusty; then being filled put them a smoaking three or four days, and hang them in the air, in some *Garret* or in a *Cellar*, for they must not come any more at the fire; and in a quarter of a year they will be eatable.

SECTION III.

The A-la-mode ways of dressing the Heads of any Beasts.

To boil a Bullocks Cheek in the Italian way.

BReak the bones and steep the head in fair water, shift it, and scrape off the slime, let it lie thus in steep about twelve hours, then boil in fair water with some *Bolonia* sausage and a piece of interlarded bacon; the cheeks and the other materials being very tender boiled, dish it up and serve it with some flowers and greens on it, and mustard in saucers.

To stew Bullocks Cheeks.

Take the Cheeks being well soaked or steeped, spit and half roast them, save the gravy, and put them into a pipkin with some claret-wine, gravy, and some strong broth, slic't nutmeg, ginger, pepper, salt and some minced onions fried; stew it the space of two hours on a soft fire, and being finely stewed, serve it on carved sippets.

Otherways.

Take out the bones, balls of the eyes, and the ruff of the mouth, steep it well in fair water and shift it often: being well cleans'd from the blood and slime, take it out of the water, wipe it dry, and season it with nutmeg, pepper, and salt, put them in an earthen pot one upon another, and put to them a pint of claret wine, a few whole cloves, a little fair water, and two three whole onions; close up the pot and bake it, it will ask six hours bakeing; being tender baked, serve it on toasts of fine manchet.

Or thus.

Being baked or stewed, you may take out the bones and lay them close together, pour the liquor to them, and being cold slice them into slices, and serve them cold with mustard and sugar.

To boil a Calves Head.

Take the head, skin, and all unflayed, scald it, and soak it in fair water a whole night or twelve hours, then take out the brains and boil them with some sage, parsley, or mint; being boil'd chop them small together, butter them and serve them in a dish with fine sippets about them, the head being finely cleansed, boil it in a clean cloth and close it up together again in the cloth; being boil'd, lay it one side by another with some fine slices of boil'd bacon, and lay some fine picked parsley upon it, with some borage or other flowers.

To hash a Calves Head.

Take a calves head well steeped and cleansed from the blood and slime, boil it tender, then take it up and let it be through cold, cut it into dice-work, as also the brains in the same form, and some think slices interlarded bacon being first boil'd put some gooseberries to them, as also some gravy or juyce of lemon or orange, and some beaten butter; stew all together, and being finely stewed, dish it on carved sippets, and run it over with beaten butter.

Otherways.

The head being boil'd and cold, slice it in to thin slices, with some onions and the brains in the same manner, then stew them in a pipkin with some gravy or strong mutton, broth, with nutmeg, some mushrooms, a little white wine and beaten butter; being well stewed together dish them on fine sippets, and garnish the meat with slic't lemon or barberries.

To souce a Calves Head.

First scald it and bone it, then steep it in fair water the space of six hour, dry it with a clean cloth, and season it with some salt and bruised garlick (or none) then roul it up in a collar, bind it close, and boil it in white wine, water, and salt; being boil'd keep it in that souce drink, and serve it in the collar, or slice it, and serve it with oyl, vinegar, and pepper. This dish is very rare, and to a good judgment scarce discernable.

To roast a Calves head.

Take a calves head, cleave it and take out the brains, skins, and blood about it, then steep them and the head in fair warm water the space of four or five hours, shift them three or four times and cleanse the head; then boil the brains, & make a pudding with some grated bread, brains, some beef-suet minced small, with some minced veal & sage; season the pudding with some cloves, mace, salt, ginger, sugar, five yolks of eggs, & saffron; fill the head with this pudding, then close it up and bind it fast with some packthread, spit it, and bind on the caul round the head with some of the pudding round about it, rost it & save the gravy, blow off the fat, and put to the gravy; for the sauce a little white-wine, a slic't nutmeg & a piece of sweet butter, the juyce of an orange, salt, and sugar. Then bread up the head with some grated bread; beaten cinamon, minced lemon peel, and a little salt.

To roast a Calves Head with Oysters.

Split the head as to boil, and take out the brains washing them very well with the head, cut out the tongue, boil it a little, and blanch it, let the brains be parbol'd as well as tongue, then mince the brains and tongue, a little sage, oysters, beef-suet, very small; being finely minced, mix them together with three or four yolks of eggs, beaten ginger, pepper, nutmegs, grated bread, salt, and a little sack, if the brains and eggs make it not moist enough. This being done parboil the calves head a little in fair water, then take it up and dry it well in a cloth filling the holes where the brains and tongue lay with this farsing or pudding; bind it up close together, and spit it, then stuff it with oysters being first parboil'd in their own liquor, put them into a dish with minced tyme, parsley, mace, nutmeg, and pepper beaten very small; mix all these with a little vinegar, and the white of an egg, roul the oysters in it, and make little holes in the head, stuff it as full as you can, put the oysters but half way in, and scuer in them with sprigs of tyme, roast it and set the dish under it to save the gravy, wherein let there be oysters, sweet herbs minced, a little white-wine and slic't nutmeg. When the head is roasted set the dish where-in the sauce is on the coals to stew a little, then put in a piece of butter, the juyce of an orange, and salt, beating it up together: dish the head, and put the sauce to it, and serve it up hot to the table.

To bake a Calves Head in Pye or Pasty to eat hot or cold.

Take a calves head and cleave it, then cleanse it & boil it, and being almost boil'd, take it up, & take it from the bones as whole as you can, when it is cold stuff it with sweet herbs, yolks of raw eggs, both finely minced with some lard or beef-suet, and raw veal; season it with nutmeg, pepper, and salt, brake two or three raw eggs into it; and work it together, and stuff the cheeks: the Pie being made, season the head with the spices abovesaid, and first lay in the bottom of the Pie some thin slices of veal, then lay on the head, and put on it some more season-ing, and coat it well with the spices, close it up with some butter, and bake it, being baked liquor it with clarified butter, and fill it up.

If you bake the aforesaid Pie to eat hot, give it but half the seasoning, and put some butter to it, with grapes, or gooseberries or barberries; then close it up and bake it, being baked liquor it with gravy and butter beat up thick together; with the juyce of two oranges.

To make a Calves-foot Pye, or Neats-foot Pye, or Florentine in a dish of Puff-Paste; but the other Pye in short paste, and the Dish of Puff.

Take two pair of calves feet, and boil them tender & blanch them, being cold bone them & mince them very small, and season them with pepper, nutmeg, ci-namon, and ginger lightly, and a little salt, and a pound of currans, a quarter of a pound of dates, slic't, aquarter of a pound of fine sugar, with a little rose-water verjuyce, & stir all together in a dish or tray, and lay a little butter in the bottom of the Pie, & lay on half the meat in the Pie; then have the marrow of three mar-row-bones, and lay that on the meat in the Pie, and the other half of the meat on the marrow, & stick some dates on the top of the meat & close up the Pie, & bake it, & being half bak't liquor it with butter, white-wine, or verjuyce, and ice it, and set in the oven again till it be iced, and ice it with butter, rose-water, and sugar.

Or you may bake them in halves with the bones in, and use for change some grapes, gooseberries, or barberries, with currans or without, and dates in halves, and large mace.

To Stew a Calves-Head.

First boil it in fair water half an hour, then take it up and pluck it pieces, then put it into a pipkin with great oysters and some of the broth, which boil'd it, (if you have no stronger) a pint of white-wine or claret, a quarter of a pound of interlarded bacon, some blanched chesnuts, the yolks of three or four hard eggs cut into halves, sweet herbs minced, and a little horseradish-root scraped, stew all these an hour, then slice the brains (being parboil'd) and strew a little ginger, salt, and flower, you may put in some juyce of spinage, and fry them green with butter; then dish the meat, and lay the fried brains, oysters, chesnuts, half yolks of eggs, and sippet it, serve it up hot to the table.

To hash a Calves Head.

Take a calves-head, boil it tender, and let it be through cold, then take one half and broil or roast it, do it very white and fair, then take the other half and slice it into thin slices, fry it with clarified butter fine and white, then put it in a dish a stewing with some sweet herbs, as rosemary, tyme, savory, salt, some white-wine or claret, some good roast mutton gravy, a little pepper and nutmeg; then take the tongue being ready boil'd, and a boil'd piece of interlarded bacon, slice it into thin slices, and fry it in a batter made of flower, eggs, nutmeg, cream, salt, and sweet herbs chopped small, dip the tongue & bacon into the batter, then fry them & keep them warm till dinner time, season the brains with nutmegs, sweet herbs minced small, salt, and the yolks of three or four raw eggs, mince all together, and fry them in spoonfuls, keep them warm, then the stewed meat being ready dish it, and lay the broild side of the head on the stewed side, then garnish the dish with the fried meats, some slices of oranges, and run it over with beaten butter and juyce of oranges.

To broil A Calves Head.

Take a calves head being cleft and cleansed, and also the brains, boil the head very white and fine, then boil the brains with some sage and other sweet herbs, as tyme and sweet marjoram, chop and boil them in a bag, being boil'd put them out and butter them with butter, salt, and vinegar, serve them in a little dish by themselves with fine thin sippits about them.

Then broil the head, or toast it against the fire, being first salted and scotched with your knife, baste it with butter, being finely broil'd, bread it with fine manchet and fine flour, brown it a little and dish it on a sauce of gravy, minced capers; grated nutmeg, and a little beaten butter.

To bake Lamb.

Season Lamb (as you may see in page 209) with nutmegs, pepper, and salt, as you do veal, (in page 225) or as you do chickens, in pag. 197, & 198. for hot or cold pies.

To boil a Lambs Head in white broth.

Take a lambs head, cleave it, and take out the brains, then open the pipes of the appurtenances, and wash and soak the meat very clean, set it a boiling in fair water & when it boils scum it, & put in some large mace, whole cinamon, slic't dates, some marrow, & salt, & when the heads is boil'd, dish it up on fine carved sippets, & trim the dish with scraping sugar: then strain six or seven yolks of eggs with sack or white-wine, and a ladleful of cream, put it into the broth, and give it a warm on the fire, stir it, and broth the head, then lay on the head some slic't lemon, gooseberries, grapes, dates, and large mace.

To stew a Lambs Head.

Take a lambs head, cleave it, and take out the brains, wash and pick the head from the slime and filth, and steep it in fair water, shift it twice in an hour, as also the appurtenances, then set it a boiling on the fire with some strong broth, and when it boils scum it, and put in a large mace or two, some capers, quarters of pears, a little white wine, some gravy, marrow, and some marigold flowers; being finely stewed, serve it on carved sippets, and broth it, lay on it slic't lemon, and scalded gooseberries or barberries.

To boil a Lambs Head otherways.

Make a forcing or pudding of the brains, being boil'd and cold cut them into bits, then mince a little veal or lamb with some beef-suet, and put to it some grated bread, nutmeg, pepper, salt, some sweet herbs minced, small, and three or four raw eggs, work all together, and fill the head with this pudding, being cleft, steeped, and after dried in a clean cloth, stew it in a stewing-pan or between two dishes with some strong broth; then take the remainder of this forcing or pudding, and make it into balls, put them a boiling with the head, and add some white-wine, a whole onion, and some slic't, pipins or pears, or square bits like dice, some bits of artichocks, sage-leaves, large mace, and lettice boil'd and quartered, and put in beaten butter; being finely stewed, dish it up on sippets, and put the balls and the other materials on it, broth it and run it over with beaten butter and lemon.

SECTION IV.

The rarest Ways of dressing of all manner of Roast Meats, either of Flesh or Fowl, by Sea or land, with their Sauces that properly belong to them.

Divers ways of breading or dredging of Meats and Fowl.

1. Grated bread and flower.

2. Grated bread, and sweet herbs minced, and dried, or beat to powder, mixed with the bread.

3. Lemon in powder, or orange peel mixt with bread and flower, minced small or in powder.

4. Cinamon, bread, flour, sugar made fine or in powder.

5. Grated bread, Fennil seed, coriander-seed, cinamon, and sugar.

6. For pigs, grated bread, flour, nutmeg, ginger, pepper, sugar; but first baste it with the jucye of lemons, or oranges, and the yolks of eggs.

7. Bread, sugar, and salt mixed together.

Divers Bastings for roast Meats.

1. Fresh butter.

2. Clarified suet.

3. Claret wine, with a bundle of sage, rosemary, tyme, and parsley, baste the mutton with these herbs and wine.

4. Water and salt.

5. Cream and melted butter, thus flay'd pigs commonly.

6. Yolks of eggs, juyce of oranges and biskets, the meat being almost rosted, comfits for some fine large fowls, as a peacock, bustard, or turkey.

To roast a shoulder of Mutton in a most excellent new way with Oysters and other materials.

Take three pints of great oysters and parboil them in their own liquor, then put away the liquor and wash them with some white-wine, then dry them with a clean cloth and season them with nutmeg and salt, then stuff the shoulder, and lard it with some anchoves; being clean washed spit it, and lay it to the fire, and baste it with white or claret wine, then take the bottoms of six artichocks, pared from the leaves and boil'd tender, then take them out of the liquor and put them into beaten butter, with the marrow of six marrow-bones, and keep them warm by a fire or in an oven, then put to them some slic'd nutmeg, salt, the gravy of a leg of roast mutton, the juyce of two oranges, and some great oysters a pint, being first parboil'd, and mingle with them a little musk or ambergreese; then dish up the shoulder of mutton, and have a sauce made for it of gravy which came from the roast shoulder of mutton stuffed with oysters, and anchovies, blow off the fat, then put to the gravy a little white-wine, some oyster liquor, a whole onion, and some stript tyme, and boil up the sauce, then put it in a fair dish, and lay the shoulder of mutton on it, and the bottoms of the artichocks round the dish brims, and put the marrow and the oysters on the artichoke bottoms, with some slic't lemon on the shoulder of mutton, and serve it up hot.

To roast a Shoulder of Mutton with Oysters otherways.

Take great oysters, and being opened, parboil them in their own liquor, beard them and wash them in some vinegar, then wipe them dry, and put to them grated nutmeg, pepper, some broom-buds, and two or three anchoves; being finely cleansed, washed, and cut into little bits, the yolk of a raw egg or two dissolved, some salt, a little samphire cut small, and mingle all together, then stuff the shoulder, roast it, and baste it with sweet butter, and being roasted make sauce with the gravy, white wine, oyster liquor, and some oysters, then boil the sauce up and blow off the fat, beat it up thick with the yolk of an egg or two and serve the shoulder up hot with the sauce, and some slic't lemon on it.

Otherways.

The oysters being opened parboil them in their liquor, beard them and wipe them dry, being first washed out of their own liquor with some vinegar, put them in a dish with some time, sweet marjoram, nutmeg, and lemon-peel all minced very small, but only the oysters whole, and a little salt, and mingle all together, then make little holes in the upper side of the mutton, and fill them with this composition. Roast the shoulder of mutton, and baste it with butter, set a dish under it to save the gravy that drippeth from it; then for the sauce take some of the oysters, and a whole onion, stew them together with some of the oyster-liquor they were parboil'd in, and the gravy that dripped from the shoulder, (but first blow off the fat) and boil up all together pretty thick, with the yolk of an egg, some verjuyce, the slice of an orange; and serve the mutton on it hot.

Or make sauce with some oysters being first parboil'd in their liquor, put to them some mutton gravy, oyster-liquor, a whole onion, a little white-wine, and large mace, boil it up and garnish the dish with barberries, slic't lemon, large mace and oysters.

Othertimes for change make sauce with capers, great oysters, gravy, a whole onion, claret-wine, nutmeg, and the juyce of two or three oranges beaten up thick with some butter and salt.

To roast a Shoulder of Mutton with Oysters.

Take a shoulder of mutton and rost it, then make sauce with some gravy, claret-wine, pepper, grated nutmeg, slic't lemon, and broom-buds, give it a warm or two, then dish the mutton, and put the sauce to it, and garnish it with barberries, and slic't lemon.

To roast a Chine of Mutton either plain or with divers stuffings, lardings and sauces.

First lard it with lard, or lemon peel cut like lard, or with orange-peel, stick here and there a clove, or in place of cloves, tops of rosemary, tyme, sage, winter-savory or sweet marjoram, baste it with butter, and make sauce with mutton-gravy, and nutmeg, boil it up with a little claret and the juyce of an orange, and rub the dish you put it in with a clove of garlick.

Or make a sauce with pickled or green cucumbers slic't and boil'd in strong broth or gravy; with some slic't onions, an anchove or two, and some grated nutmeg, stew them well together, and serve the mutton with it hot.

Divers Sauces for roast Mutton.

1. Gravy, capers, samphire, and salt, and stew them well together.

2. Watter, onion, claret-wine, slic't nutmeg and gravy boiled up.

3. Whole onions stewed in strong broth or gravy, white-wine, pepper, pickled capers, mace, and three or four slices of a lemon.

4. Mince a little roast mutton hot from the spit, and add to it some chopped parsley and onions, verjuyce or vinegar, ginger, and pepper; stew it very tender in a pipkin, and serve it under any joynt with some gravy of mutton.

5. Onions, oyster-liquor, claret, capers, or broom-buds, gravy, nutmeg, and salt boiled together.

6. Chop't parsley, verjuyce, butter, sugar, and gravy.

7. Take vinegar, butter, and currans, put them in a pipkin with sweet herbs finely minced, the yolks of two hard eggs, and two or three slices of the brownest of the leg, mince it also, some cinamon, ginger, sugar, and salt.

8. Pickled capers, and gravy, or gravy, and samphire, cut an inch long.

9. Chopped parsley and vinegar.

10. Salt, pepper, and juyce of oranges.

11. Strained prunes, wine, and sugar.

12. White-wine, gravy, large mace, and butter thickned with two or three yolks of eggs.

Oyster Sauce.

13. Oyster-liquor and gravy boil'd together, with eggs and verjuyce to thicken it, then juyce of orange, and slices of lemon over all.

14. Onions chipped with sweet herbs, vinegar, gravy and salt boil'd together.

To roast Veal divers ways with many excellent farsings, Puddings and Sauces, both in the French, Italian, and English fashion.

To make a Pudding in a Breast of Veal.

Open the lower end with a sharp knife close between the skin and the ribs, leave hold enough of the flesh on both sides, that you may put in your hand between the ribs, and the skin; then make a pudding of grated white bread, two or three yolks of eggs, a little cream, clean washt currans pick't and dried, rose-water, cloves, and mace fine beaten, a little saffron, salt, beef-suet minced fine, some slic't dates and sugar; mingle all together, and stuff the breast with it, make the pudding pretty stiff, and prick on the sweetbread wrapped in the caul, spit it and roast it; then make sauce with some claret-wine, grated nutmeg, vinegar, butter, and two or three slices of orange, and boil it up, &c.

To roast a Breast of Veal otherways.

Parboil it, and lard it with small lard all over, or the one half with lard; and the other with lemon-peel, sage-leaves, or any kind of sweet herbs; spit it and roast it, and baste it with sweet butter, and being roasted, bread it with grated bread, flower, and salt; make sauce with gravy, juyce of oranges, and slic't lemons laid on it.

Or thus.

Make stuffing or farsing with a little minced veal, and some tyme minced, lard, or fat bacon, a few cloves and mace beaten, salt, and two or three yolks of eggs; mingle them all together, and fill the breast, scuer it up with a prick or scuer, then make little puddings of the same stuff you stuffed the breast, and having spitted the breast, prick upon it those little puddings, as also the sweetbreads, roast all together, and baste them with good sweet butter, being finely roasted, make sauce with juyce of oranges and lemons.

To roast a Loyn of Veal.

Spit it and lay it to the fire, baste it with sweet butter, then set a dish under it with some vinegar, two or three sage-leaves, and two or three tops of rosemary and tyme; let the gravy drop on them, and when the veal is finely roasted, give the herbs and gravy a warm or two on the fire, and serve it under the veal.

Another Sauce for a Loin of Veal.

All manner of sweet herbs minced very small, the yolks of two or three hard eggs minced very small, and boil them together with a few currans, a little grated bread, beaten cinamon, sugar, and a whole clove or two, dish the veal on this sauce, with two or three slices of an orange.

To roast Olives on a Leg of Veal.

Cut a leg of veal into thin slices, and hack them with the back of a knife; then strew on them a little salt, grated nutmeg, sweet herbs finely minced, and the yolks of some herd eggs minced also, grated bread, a little beef-suet minced, currans, and sugar, mingle all together, and strew it on the olives, then roul it up in little rouls, spit them and roul the caul of veal about them, roast them and baste them in sweet butter; being roasted, make sauce with some of the stuffing, verjuyce, the gravy that drops from them, and some sugar, and serve the olives on it.

To roast a Leg or Fillet of Veal.

Take it and stuff it with beef-suet, seasoned with nutmeg, salt, and the yolks of two or three raw eggs, mix them with suet, stuff it and roast it; then make sauce with the gravy that dripped from it, blow off the fat, and give it two or three warms on the fire, and put to it the juyce of two or three oranges.

To roast Veal in pieces.

Take a leg of veal, and cut it into square pieces as big as a hens egg, season them with pepper, salt, some beaten cloves, and fennil-seed; then spit them with slices of bacon between every piece; being spitted, put the caul of the veal about them and roast them, then make the sauce of the gravy and the juyce of oranges. Thus you may do of veal sweet-breads, and lamb-stones.

To roast Calves Feet.

First boil them tender and blanch them, and being cold lard them thick with small lard, then spit them on a small spit and roast them, serve them with a sauce made of vinegar, cinamon, sugar, and butter.

To roast a Calves Head with Oysters.

Take a Calves head and cleave it, take out the brains and wash them very well with the head, cut out the tongue, and boil, blanch, and parboil the brains, as also the head and tongue; then mince the brain and tongue with a little sage, oysters, marrow, or beef-suet very small, mix with it three or four yolks of eggs, beaten ginger, pepper, nutmeg, grated bread, salt, and a little sack, this being done, then take the calves head, and fill it with this composition where the brains and tongue lay: bind it up close together, spit it, and stuff it with oysters, compounded with nutmeg, mace, tyme, graded bread, salt, and pepper: Mix all these with a little vinegar, and the white of an egg, and roul the oysters in it; stuff the head with it as full as you can, and roast it thorowly, setting a dish under it to catch the gravy, wherein let there be oysters, sweet herbs minced, a little white wine and slic't nutmeg; when the head is roasted, set the dish wherein the sauce is on the coals to stew a little, then put in a peice of butter, the juyce of an orange, and salt, beating it up thick together, dish the head, and put the sauce to it, and serve it hot to the table.

Several Sauces for roast Veal.

1. Gravy, claret, nutmeg, vinegar, butter, sugar, and oranges.

2. Juyce of orange, gravy, nutmeg, and slic't lemon on it.

3. Vinegar and butter.

4. All manner of sweet herbs chopped small with the yolks of two or three eggs, and boil them in vinegar, butter, a few bread crumbs, currans, beaten cinamon, sugar, and a whole clove or two, put it under the veal, with slices of orange and lemon about the dish.

5. Claret sauce, of boil'd carrots, and boil'd quinces stamped and strained, with lemon, nutmeg, pepper, rose-vinegar, sugar, and verjuyce, boil'd to an indifferent height or thickness, with a few whole cloves.

To roast red Deer.

Take a side, or half hanch, and either lard them with small lard, or stick them with cloves; but parboil them before you lard them, then spit and roast them.

Sauces for red Deer.

1. The gravy and sweet herbs chopped small and boil'd together, or the gravy only.

2. The juyce of oranges or lemons, and gravy.

3. A Gallendine sauce made with strained bread, vinegar, claret wine, cinamon, ginger, and sugar; strain it, and being finely beaten with the spices boil it up with a few whole cloves and a sprig of rosemary.

4. White bread boil'd in water pretty thick without spices, and put to it some butter, vinegar, and sugar.

If you will stuff or farse any venison, stick them with rosemary, tyme, savory, or cloves, or else with all manner of sweet herbs, minced with beef-suet, lay the caul over the side or half hanch, and so roast it.

To roast pork with the Sauces belonging to it.

Take a chine of Pork, draw it with sage on both sides being first spitted, then roast it; thus you may do of any other Joynt, whether Chine, Loyn, Rack, Breast, or spare-rib, or Harslet of a bacon hog, being salted a night of two.

Sauces.

1. Gravy, chopped sage, and onions boil'd together with some pepper.

2. Mustard, vinegar, and pepper.

3. Apples pared, quartered, and boil'd in fair water, with some sugar and butter.

4. Gravy, onions, vinegar, and pepper.

To roast Pigs divers ways with their different sauces.

To roast a Pig with the hair on.

Take a pig and draw out his intrails or guts, liver and lights, draw him very clean at vent, and wipe him, cut off his feet, truss him, and prick up the belly close, spit it, and lay it to the fire, but scorch it not, being a quarter roasted, the skin will rise up in blisters from the flesh; then with your knife or hands pull off the skin and hair, and being clean flayed, cut slashes down to the bones, baste it with butter and cream, being but warm, then bread it with grated white bread, currans, sugar, and salt mixed together, and thus apply basting upon dregging, till the body be covered an inch thick; then the meat being throughly roasted, draw it and serve it up whole, with sauce made of wine-vinegar, whole cloves, cinamon, and sugar boiled to a syrrup.

Otherways.

You may make a pudding in his belly, with grated bread, and some sweet herbs minced small, little beef-suet also minced, two or three yolks of raw eggs, grated nutmeg, sugar, currans, cream, salt, pepper, &c. Dredge it or bread it with flower, bread, sugar, cinamon slic't nutmeg.

To dress a Pig the French way.

Take and spit it, the Pig being scalded and drawn, and lay it down to the fire, and when the Pig is through warm, take off the skin, and cut it off the spit, and divide it into twenty pieces, more or less, (as you please) then take some white-wine, and some strong broth, and stew it therein with an onion or two minc't very small, and some stripped tyme, some pepper, grated nutmeg, and two or three anchoves, some elder vinegar, a little butter, and some gravy if you have it; dish it up with the same liquor it was stewed in, with some French bread in slices under it, with oranges, and lemons upon it.

To roast a Pig the plain way.

Scald and draw it, wash it clean, and put some sage in the belly, prick it up, and spit it, roast it and baste with butter, and salt it; being roasted fine and crisp, make sauce with chopped sage and currans well boil'd in vinegar and fair water, then put to them the gravy of the Pig, a little grated bread, the brains, some barberries, and sugar, give these a warm or two, and serve the Pig on this sauce with a little beaten butter.

To roast a Pig otherways.

Take a Pig, scald and draw it, then mince some sweet herbs, either sage or penny-royal, and roul it up in a ball with some butter, prick it up in the pigs belly and roast him; being roasted, make sauce with butter, vinegar, the brains, and some barberries.

Otherways.

Draw out his bowels, and flay it but only the head-truss the head looking over his back; and fill his belly with a pudding made of grated bread, nutmeg, a little minced beef-suet, two or three yolks of raw eggs, salt, and three or four spoonfuls of good cream, fill his belly and prick it up, roast it and baste it with yolks of eggs; being roasted, wring on the juyce of a lemon, and bread it with grated bread, pepper, nutmeg, salt, and ginger, bread it quick with the bread and spices.

Then make sauce with vinegar, butter, and the yolks of hard eggs minced, boil them together with the gravy of the Pig, and serve it on this sauce.

To roast Hares with their several stuffings and sauces.

Take a hare, flay it, set it, and lard it with small lard, stick it with cloves, and make a pudding in his belly with grated bread, grated nutmeg, beaten cinamon, salt, currans, eggs, cream, and sugar; make it good, and stiff, fill the hare and roast it: if you would have the pudding green, put juyce of spinage, if yellow, saffron.

Sauce.

Beaten cinamon, nutmeg, ginger, pepper, boil'd prunes, and currans strained, muskefied bisket-bread, beaten into powder, sugar, and cloves, all boiled up as thick as water-grewel.

To roast a Hare with the skin on.

Draw a hare (that is, the bowels out of the body) wipe it clean, and make a farsing or stuffing of all manner of sweet herbs, as tyme, winter-savory, sweet Marjo-ram, and parsley, mince them very small, and roul them in some butter, make a ball thereof, and put it in the belly of the hare, prick it up close, and roast it with the skin and hair on it, baste it with butter, and being almost roasted flay off the skin, and stick a few cloves on the hare; bread it with fine grated manchet, flower, and cinamon, bread it good and thick, froth it up, and dish it on sauce made of grated bread, claret-wine, wine-vinegar, cinamon, ginger, sugar, and barberries, boil it up to an indifferency.

Several Sauces belonging to Rabits.

1. Beaten butter, and rub the dish with a clove of garlick.

2. Sage and parsley minced, roul it in a ball with some butter, and fill the belly with this stuffing.

3. Beaten butter with lemon and pepper.

4. In the French fashion, onions minced small and fried, and mingled with mustard and pepper.

5. The rabits being roasted, wash the belly with the gravy of mutton, and add to it a slice or two of lemon.

To roast Woodcocks in the English Fashion.

First pull and draw them, then being washt and trust, roast them, baste them with butter, and save the gravy, then broil toasts and butter them; being roasted, bread them with bread and flower, and serve them in a clean dish on the toast and gravy.

Otherways in the French Fashion.

Being new and fresh kil'd that day you use them, pull, truss, & lard them with a broad piece of lard or bacon pricked over the breast: being roasted, serve them on broil'd toast, put in verjuyce, or the juyce of orange with the gravy, and warmed on the fire.

Or being stale, draw them, and put a clove or two in the bellies, with a piece of bacon.

To roast a Hen or Pullet.

Take a Pullet or Hen full of eggs, draw it and roast it; being roasted break it up, and mince the brauns in thin slices, save the wings whole, or not mince the brauns, and leave the rump with the legs whole; stew all in the gravy and a little salt.

Then have a minced lemon, and put it into the gravy, dish the minced meat in the midst of the dish, and the thighs, wings, and rumps about it. Garnish the dish, with oranges and lemons quartered, and serve them up covered.

Sauce with Oysters and Bacon.

Take Oysters being parboil'd and clenged from the grunds, mingle them with pepper, salt, beaten nutmeg, time, and sweet marjoram, fill the Pullets belly, and roast it, as also two or three ribs of interlarded bacon, serve it in two pieces into the dish with the pullet; then make sauce of the gravy, some of the oysters liquor, oysters and juice of oranges boil'd together, take some of the oysters out of the pullets belly, and lay on the breast of it, then put the sauce to it with slices of lemon.

Sauce for Hens or Pullets to prepare them to roast.

Take a pullet, or hen, if lean, lard it, if fat, not; or lard either fat or lean with a piece or slice of bacon over it, and a peice of interlarded bacon in the belly, seasoned with nutmeg, and pepper, and stuck with cloves.

Then for the sauce take the yolks of six hard eggs minced small, put to them white-wine, or wine vinegar, butter, and the gravy of the hen, juyce of orange, pepper, salt, and if you please add thereto mustard.

Several other Sauces for roast Hens.

1. Take beer, salt, the yolks of three hard eggs, minced small, grated bread, three or four spoonfuls of gravy; and being almost boil'd, put in the juyce of two or three oranges, slices of a lemon and orange, with lemon-peel shred small.

2. Beaten butter with juice of lemon or orange, white or claret wine.

3. Gravy and claret wine boil'd with a piece of an onion, nutmeg, and salt, serve it with the slices of orange or lemons, or the juyce in the sauce.

4. Or with oyster-liquor, an anchove or two, nutmeg, and gravy, and rub the dish with a clove of garlick.

5. Take the yolks of hard eggs and lemon peel, mince them very small, and stew them in white-wine, salt, and the gravy of the fowl.

Several Sauces for roast Chickens.

1. Gravy, and the juyce or slices of orange.

2. Butter, verjuyce, and gravy of the chicken, or mutton gravy.

3. Butter and vinegar boil'd together, put to it a little sugar, then make thin sops of bread, lay the roast chicken on them, and serve them up hot.

4. Take sorrel, wash and stamp it, then have thin slices of manchet, put them in a dish with some vinegar, strained sorrel, sugar, some gravy, beaten cinamon, beaten butter, and some slices of orange or lemon, and strew thereon some cinamon and sugar.

5. Take slic't oranges, and put to them a little white wine, rose-water, beaten mace, ginger, some sugar, and butter; set them on a chafing dish of coals and stew them; then have some slices of manchet round the dish finely carved, and lay the chickens being roasted on the sauce.

6. Slic't onions, claret wine, gravy, and salt boil'd up.

Sauces for roast Pigeons or Doves.

1. Gravy and juyce of orange.

2. Boil'd parsley minced, and put amongst some butter and vinegar beaten up thick.

3. Gravy, claret wine, and an onion stewed together, with a little salt.

4. Vine-leaves roasted with the Pigeons minced and put in claret-wine and salt, boil'd together, some butter and gravy.

5. Sweet butter and juyce of orange beat together, and made thick.

6. Minced onions boil'd in claret wine almost dry, then put to it nutmeg, sugar, gravy of the fowl, and a little pepper.

7. Or gravy of the Pigeons only.

Sauces for all manner of roast Land-Fowl, as Turkey, Bustard, Peacock, Pheasant, Partridge, &c.

1. Slic't onions being boil'd, stew them in some water, salt, pepper, some grated bread, and the gravy of the fowl.

2. Take slices of white-bread and boil them in fair water with two whole onions, some gravy, half a grated nutmeg, and a little salt; strain them together through a strainer, and boil it up as thick as water grewel; then add to it the yolks of two eggs dissolved with the juyce of two oranges, *&c.*

3. Take thin slices of manchet, a little of the fowl, some sweet butter, grated nutmeg, pepper, and salt; stew all together, and being stewed, put in a lemon minced with the peel.

4. Onions slic't and boil'd in fair water, and a little salt, a few bread crumbs beaten, pepper, nutmeg, three spoonful of white wine, and some lemon-peel finely minced, and boil'd all together: being almost boil'd put in the juyce of an orange, beaten butter, and the gravy of the fowl.

5. Stamp small nuts to a paste, with bread, nutmeg, pepper, saffron, cloves, juyce of orange, and strong broth, strain and boil them together pretty thick.

6. Quince, prunes, currans, and raisins, boil'd, muskefied bisket stamped and strained with white wine, rose vinegar, nutmeg, cinamon, cloves, juyce of oranges and sugar, and boil it not too thick.

7. Boil carrots and quinces, strain them with rose vinegar, and verjuyce, sugar, cinamon, pepper, and nutmeg, boil'd with a few whole cloves, and a little musk.

8. Take a manchet, pare off the crust and slice it, then boil it in fair water, and being boil'd some what thick put in some white wine, wine vinegar, rose, or elder vinegar, some sugar and butter, *&c.*

9. Almond-paste and crumbs of manchet, stamp them together with some sugar, ginger, and salt, strain them with grape-verjuyce, and juyce of oranges; boil it pretty thick.

Sauce for a stubble or fat Goose.

1. The Goose being scalded, drawn, and trust, put a handful of salt in the belly of it, roast it, and make sauce with sowr apples slic't, and boil'd in beer all to mash, then put to it sugar and beaten butter. Sometime for veriety add barberries and the gravy of the fowl.

2. Roast sowr apples or pippins, strain them, and put to them vinegar, sugar, gravy, barberries, grated bread, beaten cinamon, mustard, and boil'd onions strained and put to it.

Sauces for a young stubble Goose.

Take the liver and gizzard, mince it very small with some beets, spinage, sweet herbs, sage, salt, and some minced lard; fill the belly of the goose, and sow up the rump or vent, as also the neck; roast it, and being roasted, take out the farsing and put it in a dish, then add to it the gravy of the goose, verjuyce, and pepper, give it a warm on the fire, and serve it with this sauce in a clean dish.

The French sauce for a goose is butter, mustard, sugar, vinegar, and barberries.

Sauce for a Duck.

Onions slic't and carrots cut square like dice, boil'd in white-wine, strong broth, some gravy, minced parsley, savory chopped, mace, and butter; being well stewed together, it will serve for divers wild fowls, but most proper for water fowl.

Sauces for Duck and Mallard in the French fashion.

1. Vinegar and sugar boil'd to a syrrup, with two or three cloves, and cinamon, or cloves only.

2. Oyster liquor, gravy of the fowl, whole onions boil'd in it, nutmeg, and anchove. If lean, farse and lard them.

Sauces for any kind of roast Sea Fowl, as Swan, Whopper, Crane, Shoveler, Hern, Bittern, or Geese.

Make a gallendine with some grated bread, beaten cinamon, and ginger, a quartern of sugar, a quart of claret wine, a pint of wine vinegar, strain the aforesaid materials and boil them in a skillet with a few whole cloves; in the boiling stir it with a spring of rosemary, add a little red sanders, and boil it as thick as water grewel.

Green Sauce for Pork, Goslings, Chickens, Lamb, or Kid.

Stamp sorrel with white-bread and pared pipkins in a stone or wooden mortar, put sugar to it, and wine vinegar, then strain it thorow a fine cloth, pretty thick, dish it in saucers, and scrape sugar on it.

Otherways.

Mince sorrel and sage, and stamp them with bread, the yolks of hard eggs, pepper, salt, and vinegar, but no sugar at all.

Or thus.

Juyce of green white, lemon, bread, and sugar.

To make divers sorts of Vinegar.

Take good white-wine, and fill a firkin half full, or a lesser vessel, leave it unstopped, and set it in some hot place in the sun, or on the leads of a house, or gutter.

If you would desire to make vinegar in haste, put some salt, pepper, sowr leven mingled together, and a hot steel, stop it up and let the Sun come hot to it.

If more speedy, put good wine into an earthen pot or pitcher, stop the mouth with a piece of paste, and put it in a brass pan or pot, boil it half an hour, and it will grow sowr.

Or not boil it, and put into it a beet root, medlars, services, mulberries, unripe flowers, a slice of barley bread hot out of the oven, or the blossoms of services in their season, dry them in the sun in a glass vessel in the manner, of rose vinegar, fill up the glass with clear wine vinegar, white or claret wine, and set it in the sun, or in a chimney by the fire.

To make Vinegar of corrupt Wine.

Boil it, and scum it very clean, boil away one third part, then put it in a vessel, put to it some charnel, stop the vessel close, and in a short time it will prove good vinegar.

To make Vinegar otherways.

Take six gallons of strong ale of the first running, set it abroad to cool, and being cold put barm to it, and head it very thorowly; then run it up in a firkin, and lay it in the sun, then take four or five handfuls of beans, and parch them on a fire-shovel, or pan, being cut like chesnuts to roast, put them into the vinegar as hot as you can, and stop the bung-hole with clay; but first put in a handful of rye leven, then strain a good handful of salt, and put in also; let it stand in the sun from *May* to *August*, and then take it away.

Rose Vinegar.

Keep Roses dried, or dried Elder flowers, put them into several double glasses or stone bottles, write upon them, and set them in the sun, by the fire, or in a warm oven; when the vinegar is out, put in more flowers, put out the old, and fill them up with the vinegar again.

Pepper Vinegar.

Put whole pepper in a fine clothe, bind it up and put it in the vessel or bottle of vinegar the space of eight Days.

Vinegar for Digestion and Health.

Take eight drams of Sea-onions, a quart of vinegar, and as much pepper as onions, mint, and Juniper-berries.

To Make strong Wine Vinegar into Balls.

Take bramble berries when they are half ripe, dry them and make them into powder, with a little strong vinegar, make little balls, and dry them in the sun, and when you will use them, take wine and heat it, put in some of the ball or a whole one, and it will be turned very speedily into strong vinegar.

To make Verjuyce.

Take crabs as soon as the kernels turn black, and lay them in a heap to sweat, then pick them from stalks and rottenness; and then in a long trough with stamping beetles stamp them to mash, and make a bag of course hair-cloth as square as the press; fill it with stamped crabs, and being well pressed, put it up in a clean barrel or hogs-head.

To make Mustard divers ways.

Have good seed, pick it, and wash it in cold water, drain it, and rub it dry in a cloth very clean; then beat it in a mortar with strong wine-vinegar; and being fine beaten, strain it and keep it close covered. Or grind it in a mustard quern, or a bowl with a cannon bullet.

Otherways.

Make it with grape-verjuyce, common-verjuyce, stale beer, ale, butter, milk, white-wine, claret, or juyce of cherries.

Mustard of Dijon, or French Mustard.

The seed being cleansed, stamp it in a mortar, with vinegar and honey, then take eight ounces of seed, two ounces of cinamon, two of honey, and vinegar as much as will serve, good mustard not too thick, and keep it close covered in little oyster-barrels.

To make dry Mustard very pleasant in little Loaves or Cakes to carry in ones Pocket, or to keep dry for use at any time.

Take two ounces of seamy, half an ounce of cinamon, and beat them in a mortar very fine with a little vinegar, and honey, make a perfect paste of it, and make it into little cakes or loaves, dry them in the sun or in an oven, and when you would use them, dissolve half a loaf or cake with some vinegar, wine, or verjuyce.

SECTION V.

The best way of making all manner of Sallets

To make a grand Sallet of divers Compounds.

T Ake a cold roast capon and cut it into thin slices square and small, (or any other roast meat as chicken, mutton, veal, or neats tongue) mingle with it a little minced taragon and an onion, then mince lettice as small as the capon, mingle all together, and lay it in the middle of a clean scoured dish. Then lay capers by themselves, olives by themselves, samphire by it self, broom buds, pickled mushrooms, pickled oysters, lemon, orange, raisins, almonds, blue-figs, Virginia Potato, caperons, crucifix pease, and the like, more or less, as occasion serves, lay them by themselves in the dish round the meat in partitions. Then garnish the dish sides with quarters of oranges, or lemons, or in slices, oyl and vinegar beaten together, and poured on it over all.

On fish days, a roast, broil'd, or boil'd pike boned, and being cold, slice it as abovesaid.

Another way for a grand Sallet.

Take the buds of all good sallet herbs, capers, dates, raisins, almonds, currans, figs, orangado. Then first of all lay it in a large dish, the herbs being finely picked and washed, swing them in a clean napkin; then lay the other materials round the dish, and amongst the herbs some of all the aforesaid fruits, some fine sugar, and on the top slic't lemon, and eggs scarse hard cut in halves, and laid round the side of the dish, and scrape sugar over all; or you may lay every fruit in partitions several.

Otherways.

Dish first round the centre slic't figs, then currans, capers, almonds, and raisins together; next beyond that, olives, beets, cabbidge-lettice, cucumbers, or slic't lemon carved; then oyl and vinegar beaten together, the beast oyl you can get, and sugar or none, as you please; garnish the brims of the dish with orangado, slic't lemon jagged, olives stuck with slic't almonds, sugar or none.

Another grand Sallet.

Take all manner of knots of buds of sallet herbs, buds of pot-herbs, or any green herbs, as sage, mint, balm, burnet, violet-leaves, red coleworts streaked of divers fine colours, lettice, any flowers, blanched almonds, blue figs, raisins of the sun, currans, capers, olives; then dish the sallet in a heap or pile, being mixed with some of the fruits, and all finely washed and swung in a napkin, then about the centre lay first slic't figs, next capers and currans, then almonds and raisins, next olives, and lastly either jagged beats, jagged lemons, jagged cucumbers, or cabbidge lettice in quarters, good oyl and wine vinegar, sugar or none.

Otherways.

The youngest and smallest leaves of spinage, the smallest also of sorrel, well washed currans, and red beets round the centre being finely carved, oyl and vinegar, and the dish garnished with lemon and beets.

Other Grand Sallets.

Take green purslain and pick it leaf by leaf, wash it and swing it in a napkin, then being disht in a fair clean dish, and finely piled up in a heap in the midst of it lay round about the centre of the sallet pickled capers, currans, and raisins of the sun, washed, pickled, mingled, and laid round it: about them some carved cucumbers in slices or halves, and laid round also. Then garnish the dish brims with borage, or clove jelly-flowers. Or otherways with jagged cucumber-peels, olives, capers, and raisins of the sun, then the best sallet-oyl and wine-vinegar.

Other Grand Sallets.

All sorts of good herbs, the little leaves of red sage, the smallest leaves of sorrel, and the leaves of parsley pickt very small, the youngest and smallest leaves of spinage, some leaves of burnet, the smallest leaves of lettice, white endive and charvel all finely pick't and washed, and swung in a strainer or clean napkin, and well drained from the water; then dish it in a clean scowred dish, and about the centre capers, currans, olives, lemons carved and slic't, boil'd beet-roots carved and slic't, and dished round also with good oyl and vinegar.

A good Sallet otherways.

Take corn-sallet, rampons, Alexander-buds, pickled mushrooms, and make a sallet of them, then lay the corn sallet through the middle of the dish from side to side, and on the other side rampons, then Alexander-buds, and in the other four quarter of mushrooms, salt, over all, and put good oyl and vinegar to it.

Other grand Sallet.

Take the tenderest, smallest, and youngest ellicksander-buds, and small sallet, or young lettice mingled together, being washed and pickled, with some capers. Pile it or lay it flat in a dish, first lay about the centre, olives, capers, currans, and about those carved'd oranges and lemons, or in a cross partition-ways, and salt, run oyl and vinegar over all.

Otherways.

Boil'd parsnips in quarters laid round the dish, and in the midst some small sallet, or water cresses finely washed and picked, on the water-cresses some little small lettice finely picked and washed also, and some elicksander-buds in halves, and some in quarters, and between the quarters of the parsnips, some small lettice, some water-cresses and elicksander-buds, oyl and vinegar, and round the dish some slices of parsnips.

Another grand Sallet.

Take small sallet of all good sallet herbs, then mince some white cabbidge leaves, or striked cole-worts, mingle them among the small sallet, or some lilly-flowers slit with a pin; then first lay some minced cabbidge in a clean scowred dish, and the minced sallet round about it; then some well washed and picked capers, currans, olives, or none; then about the rest, a round of boild red beets, oranges, or lemons carved. For the garnish of the brim of the dish, boild colliflowers, carved lemons, beets, and capers.

Sallet of Scurvy grass.

Being finely pick't short, well soak't in clean water, and swung dry, dish it round in a fine clean dish, with capers and currans about it, carved lemon and orange round that, and eggs upon the centre not boil'd too hard, and parted in halves, then oyl and vinegar; over all scraping sugar, and trim the brim of the dish.

A grand Sallet of Alexander-buds.

Take large Alexander-buds, and boil them in fair water after they be cleansed and washed, but first let the water boil, then put them in, and being boil'd, drain them on a dish bottom or in a cullender; then have boil'd capers and currans, and lay them in the midst of a clean scowred dish, the buds parted in two with a sharp knife, and laid round about upright, or one half on one side, and the other against it on the other side, so also carved lemon, scrape on sugar, and serve it with good oyl and wine vinegar.

Other grand Sallet of Watercresses.

Being finely picked, washed and laid in the middle of a clean dish with slic't oranges and lemons finely carved one against the other, in partitions or round the dish, with some Alexander-buds boil'd or raw, currans, pers, oyl, and vinegar, sugar, or none.

A grand Sallet of pickled capers.

Pickled capers and currans basted and boil'd together, disht in the middle of a clean dish, with red beets boil'd and jagged, and dish't round the capers and currans, as also jagg'd lemon, and serve it with oyl and vinegar.

To pickle Samphire, Broom-buds, Kitkeys, Crucifix Pease, Purslane, or the like.

Take Samphire, and pick the branches from the dead leaves or straws, then lay it in a pot or barrel, & make a strong brine of white or bay-salt, in the boiling scum it clean; being boil'd and cold put it to the samphire, cover it and keep it for all the year, and when you have any occasion to use it, take and boil it in fair water, but first let the water boil before you put it in, being boiled and become green, let it cool, then take it out of the water, and put it in a little bain or double viol with a broad mouth, put strong wine vinegar to it, close it up close and keep it.

Otherways.

Put samphire in a brass pot that will contain it, and put to it as much wine-vinegar as water, but no salt; set it over a charcoal-fire, cover it close, and boil it till it become green, then put it up in a barrell with wine-vinegar close on the head, and keep it for use.

To pickle Cucumbers.

Pickle them with salt, vinegar, whole pepper, dill-seed, some of the stalks cut, charnell, fair water, and some sicamore-leaves, and barrel them up close in a barrel.

Pickled Quinces the best way.

1. Take quinces not cored nor pared, boil them in fair water not too tender, and put them in a barrel, fill it up with their liquor, and close on the head.

2. Pare them and boil them with white-wine, whole cloves, cinamon, and slic't ginger, barrel them up and keep them.

3. In the juyce of sweet apples, not cored, but wiped, and put up raw.

4. In white-wine barrel'd up raw.

5. Being pared and cored, boil them up in sweet-wort and sugar, keep them in a glazed pipkin close covered.

6. Core them and save the cores, cut some of the crab-quinces, and boil them after the quinces be parboil'd & taken up; then boil the cores, and some of the crab-quinces in quarters, the liquor being boild strain it thorow a strainer, put it in a barrel with the quinces, and close up the barrel.

To pickle Lemon.

Boil them in water and salt, and put them up with white-wine.

To pickle any kind of Flowers.

Put them into a gally-pot or double glass, with as much sugar as they weigh, fill them up with wine vinegar; to a pint of vinegar a pound of sugar, and a pound of flowers; so keep them for sallets or boild meats in a double glass covered over with a blade and leather.

To pickle Capers, Gooseberries, Barberries, red and white Currans.

Pick them and put them in the juyce of crab-cherries, grape-verjuyce, or other verjuyce, and then barel them up.

To Candy Flowers for Sallets, as Violets, Cowslips, Clove-gilliflowers, Roses, Primroses, Borrage, Bugloss, &c.

Take weight for weight of sugar candy, or double refined sugar, being beaten fine, searsed, and put in a silver dish with rose-water, set them over a charecoal fire, and stir them with a silver spoon till they be candied, or boil them in a Candy sirrup height in a dish or skillet, keep them in a dry place for your use, and when you use them for sallets, put a little wine-vinegar to them, and dish them.

For the compounding and candying the foresaid pickled and candied Sallets,

Though they may be served simply of themselves, and are both good and dainty, yet for better curiosity and the finer ordering of a table, you may thus use them.

First, if you would set forth a red flower that you know or have seen, you shall take the pot of preserv'd gilliflowers, and suiting the colours answerable to the flower, you shall proportion it forth, and lay the shape of a flower with a purslane stalk, make the stalk of the flower, and the dimensions of the leaves and branches with thin slices of cucumbers, make the leaves in true proportion jagged or otherways, and thus you may set forth some blown some in the bud, and some half blown, which will be very pretty and curious; if yellow, set it forth with cowslip or primroses; if blue take violets or borrage; and thus of any flowers.

SECTION VI.

To make all manner of Carbonadoes, either of Flesh or Fowl; as also all manner of fried Meats of Flesh, Collops and Eggs, with the most exquisite way of making Pancakes, Fritters, and Tansies.

To carbonado a Chine of Mutton.

T Ake a Chine of Mutton, salt it, and broil it on the embers, or toast it against the fire; being finely broil'd, baste it, and bread it with fine grated manchet, and serve it with gravy only.

To carbonado a Shoulder of Mutton.

Take a Shoulder of Mutton, half boil it, scotch it and salt it, save the gravy, and broil it on a soft fire being finely coloured and fitted, make sauce with butter, vinegar, pepper, and mustard.

To carbonado a Rack of Mutton.

Cut it into steaks, salt and broil them on the embers, and being finely soaked, dish them and make sauce of good mutton-gravy, beat up thick with a little juyce of orange, and a piece of butter.

To carbonado a Leg of Mutton.

Cut it round cross the bone about half an inch thick, then hack it with the back of a knife, salt it, and broil it on the embers on a soft fire the space of an hour; being finely broil'd, serve it with gravy sauce, and juyce of orange.

Thus you may broil any hanch of venison, and serve it with gravy only.

To broil a chine of Veal.

Cut it in three or four pieces, lard them (or not) with small lard, season them with salt and broil them on a soft fire with some branches of sage and rosemary between the gridiron and the chine; being broil'd, serve it with gravy, beaten butter, and juyce of lemon or orange.

To broil a Leg of Veal.

Cut it into rowls, or round the leg in slices as thick as ones finger, lard them or not, then broil them softly on embers, and make sauce with beaten butter, gravy, and juyce of orange.

To carbonado a Rack of Pork.

Take a Rack of Pork, take off the skin, and cut it into steaks, then salt it, and strow on some fennil seeds whole and broil it on a soft fire, being finely broil'd, serve it on wine-vinegar and pepper.

To broil a Flank of Pork.

Flay it and cut it into thin slices, salt it, and broil it on the embers in a dripping-pan of white paper, and serve it on the paper with vinegar and pepper.

To broil Chines of Pork.

Broil them as you do the rack, but bread them and serve them with vinegar and pepper, or mustard and vinegar.

Or sometimes apples in slices, boil'd in beer and beaten butter to a mash.

Or green sauce, cinamon, and sugar.

Otherways, sage and onions minced, with vinegar and pepper boil'd in strong broth till they be tender.

Or minced onions boil'd in vinegar and pepper.

To broil fat Venison.

Take half a hanch, and cut the fattest part into thick slices half an inch thick; salt and broil them on the warm embers, and being finely soaked, bread them, and serve them with gravy only.

Thus you may broil a side of venison, or boil a side, fresh in water and salt, then broil it and dredge it, and serve it with vinegar and pepper.

Broil the chine raw as you do the half hanch, bread it and serve it with gravy.

To fry Lambs or Kids Stones.

Take the stones, parboil them, then mince them small and fry them in sweet butter, strain them with some cream, some beaten cinamon, pepper, and grated cheese being put to it when it is strained, then fry them, and being fried, serve them with sugar and rose-water.

Thus may you dress calves or lambs brains.

To carbonado Land or Water Fowl.

Being roasted, cut them up and sprinkle them with salt, then scoch and broil them and make sauce with vinegar and butter, or juyce of orange.

To dress a dish of Collops and Egg the best way for service.

Take fine young and well coloured bacon of the ribs, the quantity of two pound, cut it into thine slices and lay them in a clean dish, toste them before the fire fine and crisp; then poche the eggs in a fair scrowred skillet white and fine, dish them on a dish and plate, and lay on the colops, some upon them, and some round the dish.

To broil Bacon on Paper.

Make the fashion of two dripping-pans of two sheets of white paper, then take two pound of fine interlarded bacon, pare off the top, and cut the bacon into slices as thin as a card, lay them on the papers, then put them on a gridiron, and broil them on the embers.

To broil Brawn.

Cut a Collar into six or seven slices round the Collar, and lay it on a plate in the oven, being broil'd serve it with juyce of orange, pepper, gravy, and beaten butter.

To fry Eggs.

Take fifteen eggs and beat them in a dish, then have interlarded bacon cut into square bits like dice, and fry them with chopped onions, and put to them cream, nutmeg, cloves, cinamon, pepper, and sweet herbs chopped small, (or no herbs nor spice) being fried, serve them on a clean dish, with sugar and juyce of orange.

To fry an Egg as round as a Ball.

Take a broad frying posnet, or deep frying pan, and three pints of clarified butter or sweet suet, heat it as hot as you do for fritters; then take a stick and stir it till it run round like to a whirle-pit; then break an egg into the middle of the whirle, and turn it round with your stick till it be as hard as a soft poached egg, and the whirling round of the butter or suet will make round as a ball; then take it up with a slice, and put it in a warm pipkin or dish, set it a leaning against the fire, so you may do as many as you please, they will keep half an hour yet be soft; you may serve them with fried or toasted collops.

To make the best Fritters.

Take good mutton-broth being cold, and no fat, mix it with flour and eggs, some salt, beaten nutmeg and ginger, beat them well together, then have apples or pippins, pare and core them, and cut them into dice-work, or square bits, and when you will fry them, put them in the batter, and fry them in clear clarified suet, or clarified butter, fry them white and fine, and sugar them.

Otherways.

Take a pint of sack, a pint of ale, some ale-yeast or barm, nine eggs yolks and whites beaten very well, the eggs first, then all together, then put in some ginger, salt, and fine flour, let it stand an hour or two, then put in apples, and fry them in beef-suet clarified, or clarified butter.

Other Fritters.

Take a quart of flour, three pints of cold mutton broth, a nutmeg, a quartern of cinamon, a race of ginger, five eggs, and salt, and strain the foresaid materials; put to them twenty slic't pippins, and fry them in six pound of suet.

Sometimes make the batter of cream, eggs, cloves, mace, nutmeg, saffron, barm, ale, and salt.

Other times flour, grated bread, mace, ginger, pepper, salt, barm, saffron, milk, sack, or white wine.

Sometimes you may use marrow steeped in musk and rose-water, and pleasant pears or quinces.

Or use raisins, currans, and apples cut like square dice, and as small, in quarters or in halves.

Fritters in the Italian Fashion.

Take a pound of the best Holland cheese or parmisan grated, a pint of fine flower, and as much fine bisket bread muskefied beaten to powder, the yolks of four or five eggs, some saffron and rosewater, sugar, cloves, mace, and cream, make it into stiff paste, then make it into balls, and fry them in clarified butter. Or stamp this paste in a mortar, and make the balls as big as a nutmeg or musket bullet.

Otherways in the Italian Fashion.

Take a pound of rice and boil it in a pint of cream, being boil'd something thick, lay it abroad in a clean dish to cool, then stamp it in a stone mortar, with a pound of good fat cheese grated, some musk, and yolks of four or five hard eggs, sugar, and grated manchet or bisket bread; then make it into balls, the paste being stiff, and you may colour them with marigold flowers stamped, violets, blue bottles, carnations or pinks, and make them balls of two or three colours. If the paste be too tender, work more bread to them and flour, fry them, and serve them with scraping sugar and juyce of orange. Garnish these balls with stock fritters.

Fritters of Spinage.

Take spinage, pick it and wash it, then set on a skillet of fair water, and when it boileth put in the spinage, being tender boil'd put it in a cullender to drain away the liquor; then mince it small on a fair board, put it in a dish and season it with cinamon, ginger, grated manchet, fix eggs with the whites and yolks, a little cream or none, make the stuff pretty thick, and put in some boil'd currans. Fry it by spoonfuls, and serve it on a dish and plate with sugar.

Thus also you may make fritters of beets, clary, borrage, bugloss, or lattice.

To make Stock-Fritters or Fritters of Arms.

Strain half a pint of fine flower, with as much water, and make the batter no thicker, than thin cream; then heat the brass moulds in clarified butter; being hot wipe them, dip the moulds half way in the batter and fry them, to garnish any boil'd fish meats or stewed oysters. View their forms.

Other fried Dishes of divers forms, or Stock-Fritters in the Italian Fashion.

Take a quart of fine flower, and strain it with some almond milk, leven, white wine, sugar and saffron; fry it on the foresaid moulds, or dip clary on it, sage leaves, or branches of rosemary, then fry them in clarified butter.

Little Pasties, Balls, or Toasts fried.

Take a boil'd or raw Pike, mince it and stamp it with some good fat old cheese grated, season them with cinamon, sugar, boil'd currans, and yolks of hard eggs, make this stuff into balls, toasts or pasties, and fry them.

Otherways.

Make your paste into little pasties, stars, half moons, scollops, balls, or suns.

Or thus.

Take grated bread, cake, or bisket bread, and fat cheese grated, almond paste, eggs, cinamon, saffron, and fry them as abovesaid.

Otherways Pasties to fry.

Take twenty apples or pippins par'd, coard, and cut into bits like square dice, stew them in butter, and put to them three ounces of bisket bread, stamp all together in a stone mortar, with six ounces of fat cheese grated, six yolks of eggs, cinamon, six ounces of sugar, make it in little Pasties, or half moons, and fry them.

Otherways.

Take a quart of fine flower, wet it with almond milk, sack, white-wine, rose-water, saffron, and sugar, make thereof a paste into balls, cakes, or any cut or carved branches, and fry them in clarified butter, and serve them with fine scraped sugar.

To fry Paste out of a Syringe or Butter-squirt.

Take a quart of fine flower, & a litle leven, dissolve it in warm water, & put to it the flour, with some white wine, salt, saffron, a quarter of butter, and two ounces of sugar; boil the aforesaid things in a skillet as thick as a hasty pudding, and in the boiling stir it continually, being cold beat it in a mortar, fry it in clarified butter, and run it into the butter through a butter-squirt.

To make Pancakes.

Take three pints of cream, a quart of flour, eight eggs, three nutmegs, a spoonful of salt, and two pound of clarified butter; the nutmegs being beaten, strain them with the cream, flour and salt, fry them into pancakes, and serve them with fine sugar.

Otherways.

Take three pints of spring-water, a quart of flour, mace, and nutmeg beaten, six cloves, a spoonful of salt, and six eggs, strain them and fry them into Pancakes.

Or thus.

Make stiff paste of fine flour, rose-water, cream, saffron, yolks of eggs, salt, and nutmeg, and fry them in clarified butter.

Otherways.

Take three pints of cream, a quart of flour, five eggs, salt, three spoonfuls of ale, a race of ginger, cinamon as much, strain these materials, then fry and serve them with fine sugar.

To make a Tansie the best way.

Take twenty eggs, and take away five whites, strain them with a quart of good thick sweet cream, and put to it grated nutmeg, a race of ginger grated, as much cinamon beaten fine, and a penny white loaf grated also, mix them all together with a little salt, then stamp some green wheat with some tansie herbs, strain it into the cream and eggs, and stir all together; then take a clean frying-pan, and a quarter of a pound of butter, melt it, and put in the tansie, and stir it continually over the fire with a slice, ladle, or saucer, chop it, and break it as it thickens, and being well incorporated put it out of the pan into a dish, and chop it very fine; then make the frying pan very clean, and put in some more butter, melt it, and fry it whole or in spoonfuls; being finely fried on both sides, dish it up, and sprinkle it with rose-vinegar, grape-verjuyce, elder-vinegar, couslip-vinegar, or the juyce of three or four oranges, and strew on good store of fine sugar.

Otherways.

Take a little tansie, featherfew, parsley, and violets stamp and strain them with eight or ten eggs and salt, fry them in sweet butter, and serve them on a plate and dish with some sugar.

A Tansie for Lent.

Take tansie and all manner of herbs as before, and beaten almond, stamp them with the spawn of pike or carp and strain them with the crumb of a fine manchet, sugar, and rose-water, and fry it in sweet butter.

Toasts of Divers sorts.

First, in Butter or Oyl.

Take a cast of fine rouls or round manchet, chip them, and cut them into toasts, fry them in clarified butter, frying oyl, or sallet oyl, but before you fry them dip them in fair water, and being fried, serve them in a clean dish piled one upon another, and sugar between.

Otherways.

Toste them before the fire, and run them over with butter, sugar, or oyl.

Cinamon Toasts.

Cut fine thin toasts, then toast them on a gridiron, and lay them in ranks in a dish, put to them fine beaten cinamon mixed with sugar and some claret, warm them over the fire, and serve them hot.

French Toasts.

Cut French bread, and toast it in pretty thick toasts on a clean gridiron, and serve them steeped in claret, sack, or any wine, with sugar and juyce of orange.

SECTION VII.

The most Excellent Ways of making All sorts of Puddings.

A boil'd Pudding.

BEat the yolks of three eggs, with rose-water, and half a pint of cream, warm it with a piece of butter as big as a walnut, and when it is melted mix the eggs and that together, and season it with nutmeg, sugar, and salt; then put in as much bread as will make it as thick as batter, and lay on as much flour as will lie on a shilling, then take a double cloth, wet it, and flour it, tie it fast, and put it in the pot; when it is boil'd, serve it up in a dish with butter, verjuice, and sugar.

Otherways.

Take flour, sugar, nutmeg, salt, and water, mix them together with a spoonful of gum-dragon, being steeped all night in rose-water, strain it, then put in suet, and boil it in a cloth.

To boil a Pudding otherways.

Take a pint of cream or milk, and boil it with a stick of cinamon, being boil'd let it cool, then put in six eggs, take out three whites, and beat the eggs before you put them in the milk, then slice a penny-roul very thin and being slic't beat all together, then put in some sugar, and flour the cloth; being boil'd for sauce, put butter, sack, and sugar, beat them up together, and scrape sugar on it.

Other Pudding.

Sift grated bread through a cullender, and mix it with flour, minc't dates, currans, nutmeg, cinamon, minc't suet, new milk warm, sugar and eggs, take away some of the whites and work all together, then take half the pudding for one side, and half for the other side, and make it round like a loaf, then take butter and put it into the midst, and the other side aloft on the top, when the liquor boils, tie it in a fair cloth and boil it, being boil'd, cut it in two, and so serve it in.

To make a Cream Pudding to be boil'd.

Take a quart of cream and boil it with mace, nutmeg and ginger quartered, put to it eight eggs, and but four whites beaten, a pound of almonds blanched, beaten, and strained in with the cream, a little rose-water, sugar, and a spoonful of fine flower; then take a thick napkin, wet it and rub it with flour, and tie the pudding up in it: being boil'd make sauce for it with sack, sugar, and butter beat up thick together with the yolk of an egg, then blanch some almonds, slice them, and stick the pudding with them very thick, and scrape sugar on it.

To make a green boil'd Pudding of sweet Herbs.

Take and steep a penny white loaf in a quart of cream and only eight yolks of eggs, some currans, sugar, cloves, beaten mace, dates, juyce of spinage, saffron, cinamon, nutmeg, sweet marjoram, tyme, savory, peniroyal minced very small, and some salt, boil it in beef-suet, marrow, (or none.) These puddings are excellent for stuffings of roast or boil'd Poultrey, Kid, Lamb, or Turkey, Veal, or Breasts of Mutton.

To make a Pudding in haste.

Take a pint of good Milk or Cream, put thereto a handful of raisins of the Sun, with as many currans, and a piece of butter, then grate a manchet and a nutmeg, and put thereto a handful of flour; when the milk boils, put in the bread, let it boil a quarter of an hour, then dish it up on beaten butter.

To make a Quaking Pudding.

Slice the crumbs of a penny manchet, and infuse it three or four hours in a pint of scalding hot cream, covering it close, then break the bread with a spoon very small, and put to it eight eggs, and put only four whites, beat them together very well, and season it with sugar, rose-water, and grated nutmeg: if you think it too stiff, put in some cold cream and beat them well together; then wet the bag or napkin and flour it, put in the pudding, tie it hard, and boil it half an hour, then dish it and put to it butter, rose-water, and sugar, and serve it up to the table.

Otherways baked.

Scald the bread with a pint of cream as abovesaid, then put to it a pound of almonds blanched and beaten small with rose-water in a stone mortar, or walnuts, and season it with sugar, nutmeg, salt, the yolks of six eggs, a quarter of a pound of dates slic't and cut small a handful of currans boil'd and some marrow minced, beat them all together and bake it.

To make a Quaking Pudding either boil'd or baked.

Take a pint of good thick cream, boil it with some large mace, whole cinamon, and slic't nutmeg, then take six eggs, and but three whites, beat them well, and grate some stale manchet, the quantity of a half penny loaf, put it to the eggs with a spoonful of flour, then season the cream according to your own taste with sugar and salt; beat all well together, then wet a cloth or butter it, and put in the pudding when the water boils; an hour will bake it or boil it.

Otherways.

Take a penny white loaf, pare off the crust, and slice the crumb, steep it in a quart of good thick cream warmed, some beaten nutmeg, six eggs, whereof but two whites, and some salt. Sometimes you may use boil'd currans, or boil'd raisins.

If to bake, make it a little stiffer, sometimes add saffron; on flesh-days use beef-suet, or marrow; (or neither) for a boil'd pudding butter the napkin being first wetted in water, and bind it up like a ball, an hour will boil it.

To make a Shaking Pudding.

Take a pint of cream and boil it with large mace, slic't nutmeg, and ginger, put in a few almonds blanched and beaten with rose-water, strain them all together, then put to it slic't ginger, grated bread, salt and sugar, flour the napkin or cloth, and put in the pudding, tie it hard, and put it in boiling water; (as you must do all puddings) then serve it up verjuyce, butter, and sugar.

To make a Hasty-Pudding in a Bag.

Boil a pint of thick cream with a spoonful of flour, season it with nutmeg, sugar, and salt, wet the cloth and flour it, then pour in the cream being hot into the cloth, and when it is boil'd butter it as a hasty pudding. If it be well made, it will be as good as a Custard.

To make a Hasty-Pudding otherways.

Grate a two penny manchet, and mingle it with a quarter of a pint of flour nut-meg, and salt, a quarter of sugar, and half a pound of butter; then set it a boiling on the fire in a clean scowred skillet, a quart, or three pints of good thick cream, and when it boils put in the foresaid materials, stir them continual, and being half boil'd, put in six yolks of eggs, stir them together, and when it is boil'd, serve it in a clean scowred dish, and stick it with some preserved orange-peel thin sliced, run it over with beaten butter, and scraping sugar.

To make an Almond Pudding.

Blanch and beat a pound of almonds, strain them with a quart of cream, a grat-ed, penny manchet searsed, four eggs, some sugar, nutmeg grated, some dates, & salt; boil it, and serve it in a dish with beaten butter, stick it with some muskedines, or wafers, and scraping sugar.

Otherways.

Take a pound of almond-paste, some grated bisket-bread, cream, rose-water, yolks of eggs, beaten cinamon, ginger, nutmeg, some boil'd currans, pistaches, and musk, boil it in a napkin, and serve it as the former.

To make an Almond Pudding in Guts.

Take a pound of blanched almonds, beat them very small, with rosewater, and a little good new milk or cream with two or three blades of mace, and some sliced nutmegs; when it is boil'd take the spice clean from it, then grate a penny loaf and searse it through a cullender, put it into the cream, and let it stand till it be pretty cool, then put in the almonds, five or six yolks of eggs, salt, sugar and good store of marrow or beef-suet finely minced, and fill the guts.

To make a Rice Pudding to bake.

Boil the rice tender in milk, then season it with nutmeg, mace, rose-water, sugar, yolks of eggs, with half the whites, some grated bread, and marrow minced with amber-greese, and bake it in a buttered dish.

To make Rice Puddings in guts.

Boil half a pound of rice with three pints of milk, and a little beaten mace, boil it until the rice be dry, but never stir it, if you do, you must stir it continually, or else it will burn, pour your rice into a cullender or strainer, that the moisture may run clean from it, then put to it six eggs, (put away the whites of three) half a pound of sugar, a quarter of a pint of rose-water, a pound of currans, and a pound of beef-suet shred small, season it with nutmeg, cinamon, and salt, then dry the small guts of a hog, sheep, or beefer, and being, finely cleansed for the purpose, steep and fill them, cut the guts a foot long, and fill them three quarters full, tie both ends together, and put them in boiling water, a quarter of an hour will boil them.

Otherways.

Boil the rice first in water, then in milk, after with salt, in cream; then take six eggs, grated bread, good store of marrow minced small, some nutmeg, sugar, and salt; fill the guts and put them into a pipkin, and boil them in milk and rose-water.

Otherways.

Steep it in fair water all night, then boil it in new milk, and drain out the milk through a cullender, then mince a good quantity of beef-suet not too small, and put it into the rice in some bowl or tray, with currans being first boil'd, yolks of eggs, nutmeg, cinamon, sugar, and barberries, mingle all together; then wash the second guts, fill them, and boil them.

To make a Cinamon Pudding.

Take and steep a penny white loaf in a quart of cream, six yolks of eggs, and but two whites, dates, half an ounce of beaten cinamon, and some almond paste. Sometimes add rose-water, salt, and boil'd currans, either bake or boil it for stuffings.

To make a Haggas Pudding.

Take a calves chaldron being well scowred or boiled, mince it being cold, very fine and small, then take four or five eggs, and leave out half the whites, thick cream, grated bread, sugar, salt, currans, rose-water, some beef-suet or marrow, (and if you will) sweet marjoram, time, parsley, and mix all together; then having a sheeps maw ready dressed, put it in and boil it a little.

Otherways.

Take good store of parsley, tyme, savory, four or five onions, and sweet marjoram, chop them with some whole oatmeal, then add to them pepper, and salt, and boil them in a napkin, being boil'd tender, butter it, and serve it on sippets.

To make a Chiveridge Pudding.

Lay the fattest of a hog in fair water and salt to scowr them, then take the longest and fattest gut, and stuff it with nutmeg, sugar, ginger, pepper, and slic't dates, cut them and serve them to the table.

To make Leveridge Puddings.

Boil a hogs liver, and let it be thorowly cold, then grate and sift it through a cullender, put new milk to it and the fleck of a hog minced small put into the liver, and some grated bread, divide the meat in two parts, then take store of herbs, mince them fine, and put the herbs into one part with nutmeg, mace, pepper, anniseed, rosewater, cream, and eggs, fill them up and boil them. To the other part or sort put barberries, slic't dates, currans, cream, and eggs.

Other Leveridge Puddings.

Boil a hogs liver very dry, and when it is cold grate it and take as much grated manchet as liver, sift them through a cullender; and season them with cloves, mace, and cinamon, as much of all the other spices, half a pound of sugar, a pound and a half of currans, half a pint of rose-water, three pound of beef suet minced small, eight eggs and but four whites.

A Swan or Goose Pudding.

Strain the swan or goose blood, and steep with it oatmeal or grated bread in milk or cream, with nutmeg, pepper, sweet herbs minced, suet, rose-water, minced lemon peels very small and a small quantity of coriander-seed.

This for a Pudding in a swan or gooses neck.

To make a Farsed Pudding.

Mince a leg of mutton with sweet herbs, grated bread, minced dates, currans, raisins of the sun, a little orangado or preserved lemon sliced thin, a few coriander-seeds, nutmeg, pepper, and ginger, mingle all together with some cream, and raw eggs, and work it together like a pasty, then wrap the meat in a caul of mutton or veal, and so you may either boil or bake them. If you bake them, indorse them with yolks of eggs, rose-water, and sugar, and stick them with little sprigs of rosemary and cinamon.

To make a Pudding of Veal.

Mince raw veal very fine, and mingle it with lard cut into the form of dice, then mince some sweet marjoram, penniroyal, camomile, winter-savory, nutmeg, ginger, pepper, salt, work all together with good store of beaten cinamon, sugar, barberries, sliced figs, blanched almonds, half a pound of beef-suet finely minced, put these into the guts of a fat mutton or hog well cleansed, and cut an inch and a half long, set them a boiling in a pipkin of claret wine with large mace; being almost boil'd, have some boil'd grapes in small bunches, and barberries in knots, then dish them on French bread being scalded with the broth of some good mutton gravy, and lay them on garnish of slic't lemons.

To make a Pudding of Wine in guts.

Slice the crumbs, of two manchets, and take half a pint of wine, and some sugar, the wine must be scalded; then take eight eggs, and beat them with rose-water, put to them sliced dates, marrow, and nutmeg, mix all together, and fill the guts to boil.

Bread Puddings in guts.

Take cream and boil it with mace, and mix beaten almonds with rose-water, then take cream, eggs, nutmeg, currans, salt, and marrow, mix them with as much bread as you think fit, and fill the guts.

To make an Italian Pudding.

Take a fine manchet and cut it in square pieces like dice, then put to it half a pound of beef-suet minced small, raisins of the sun, cloves, mace, minced dates, sugar, marrow, rose-water, eggs, and cream, mingle all these together, put them into a buttered dish, in less than an hour it will be baked, and when you serve it, scrapesugar on it.

Other Pudding in the Italian Fashion with blood of Beast or Fish.

Take half a pound of grated cheese, a penny manchet grated, sweet herbs chopped very small, cinamon, pepper, salt, nutmeg, cloves, mace, four eggs, sugar, and currans, bake it in a dish or pie, or boil it in a napkin, and bind it up in a ball, being boil'd serve it with beaten butter, sugar, and beaten cinamon.

To make a French Pudding.

Take half a pound of raisins of the sun, a penny white loaf pared and cut into dice-work, half a pound of beef-suet finely minced, three ounces of sugar, eight slic't dates, a grain of musk, twelve or sixteen lumps of marrow, salt, half a pint of cream, three eggs beaten with it, and poured on the pudding, cloves, mace, nutmeg, salt, and a pome-water, or a pippin or two pared, slic't, and put in the bottom of the dish before you bake the pudding.

To make a French Barley Pudding.

Boil the barley, & put to one quart of barley, a manchet grated, then beat a pound of almonds, & strain them with cream, then take eight eggs, & but four whites, & beat them with rose-water, season it with nutmeg, mace, salt, and marrow, or beef-suet cut small, mingle all together, then fill the guts and boil them.

To make an excellent Pudding.

Take crumbs of white-bread, as much fine flour, the yolks of four eggs, but one white, and as much good cream as will temper it as thick as you would make pancake batter, then butter the dish, bake it, and scrape sugar on it being baked.

Puddings of Swines Lights.

Parboil the lights, mince them very small with suet, and mix them with grated bread, cream, curans, eggs, nutmeg, salt, and rose-water, and fill the guts.

To make an Oatmeal Pudding.

Pick a quart of whole oatmeal, being finly picked and cleansed, steep it in warm milk all night, next morning drain it, and boil it in three pints of cream; being boil'd and cold put to it six yolks of eggs and but three whites, cloves, mace, saffron, salt, dates slic't, and sugar, boil it in a napkin, and boil it as the bread-pudding, serve it with beaten butter, and stick it with slic't dates, and scrape sugar; or you may bake these foresaid materials in dish, pye, &c.

Sometimes add to this pudding raisins of the sun, and all manner of sweet herbs, chopped small, being seasoned as before.

Other Oatmeal Pudding.

Take great oatmeal, pick it and scale it in cream being first put in a dish or bason, season it with nutmeg, cinamon, ginger, pepper, and currans, bake it in a dish, or boil it in a napkin, being baked or boiled, serve it with beaten butter, and scraping sugar.

Otherways.

Season it with cloves, mace, saffron, salt, and yolks of eggs, and but five that have whites, and some cream to steep the groats in, boil it in a napkin, or bake it in a dish or pye.

To make Oatmeal Pudding-pies.

Steep oatmeal in warm milk three or four hours, then strain some blood into it of flesh or fish, mix it with cream, and add to it suet minced small, sweet herbs chopped fine, as tyme, parsley, spinage, succory, endive, strawberry leaves, violet leaves, pepper, cloves mace, fat beef-suet, and four eggs; mingle all together, and so bake them.

To make an Oatmeal Pudding boil'd.

Take the biggest oatmeal, mince what herbs you like best and mix with it, season it with pepper and salt, tye it strait in a bag, and when it is boild, butter it and serve it up.

Oatmeal Pudding otherwise of fish or flesh blood.

Take a quart of whole oatmeal, steep it in warm milk over night, & then drain the groats from it, boil them in a quart or three pints of good cream; then the oatmeal being boil'd and cold, have tyme, penniroyal, parsley, spinage, savory, endive, marjoram, sorrel, succory, and strawberry leaves, of each a little quantity, chop them fine, and put them to the oatmeal, with some fennil-seed, pepper, cloves, mace, and salt, boil it in a napkin, or bake it in a dish, pie, or guts.

Sometimes of the former pudding you may leave out some of the herbs, and add these, penniroyal, savory, leeks, a good big onion, sage, ginger, nutmeg, pepper, salt, either for fish or flesh days, with butter or beef-suet, boil'd or baked in a dish, napkin, or pie.

To make a baked Pudding.

Take a pint of cream, warm it, and put to it eight dates minced, four eggs, marrow, rose-water, nutmegs raced and beaten, mace and salt, butter the dish, and put it in; and if you please, lay puff paste on it, and scrape sugar on it and in it.

To make a baked Pudding otherways.

Take a pint and a half of cream, and a pound of butter; set the same on fire till the butter be melted, then take three or four eggs, season it with nutmeg, rose-water, sugar, and salt, make it as thin as pankake batter, butter the dish, and baste it with a garnish of paste about it.

Otherways.

Take a penny loaf, pare it, slice it, and put it into a quart of cream with a little rose-water, break it very small, then take four ounces of almon-paste, and put in eight eggs beaten, the marrow of three or four marrow bones, three or four pippins slic't thin, or what way you please; mingle these together with a little ambergreese, and butter, then dish and bake it.

Otherways.

Take a quart of cream, put thereto a pound of beef-suet minced small, put it into the cream, and season it with nutmeg, cinamon, and rose-water, put to it eight eggs, and but four whites, and two grated manchets; mingle them well together, and put them in a butter'd dish, bake it, and being baked, scrape on sugar, and serve it.

To make black Puddings.

Take half the oatmeal, pick it, and take the blood while it is warm from the hog, strain it and put it in the oatmeal as soon us you can, let it stand all night; then take the other part of the oatmeal, pick it also, and boil it in milk till it be tender, and all the milk consumed, then put it to the blood and stir it well together, put in good store of beef or hog suet, and season it with good pudding herbs, salt, pepper, and fennil-seed, fill not the guts too full, and boil them.

To make black Puddings otherways.

Take the blood of the hog while it is warm, put in some salt, and when it is thorough cold put in the groats or oatmeal well picked; let it stand soaking all night, then put in the herbs, which must be rosemary, tyme, penniroyal, savory, and fennel, make the blood soft with putting in some good cream until the blood look pale; then beat four or five eggs, whites and all, and season it with cloves, mace, pepper, fennil-seed, and put good store of hogs fat or beef-suet to the stuff, cut not the fat too small.

To make black Puddings an excellent way.

After the hogs Umbles are tender boil'd, take some of the lights with the heart, and all the flesh about them, picking from them all the sinewy skins, then chop the meat as small as you can, and put to it a little of the liver very finely searsed, some grated nutmeg, four or five yolks of eggs, a pint of very good cream, two or three spoonfuls of sack, sugar, cloves, mace, nutmeg, cinamon, caraway-seed, a little rose-water, good store of hogs fat, and some salt: roul it in rouls two hours before you go to fill them in the guts, and lay the guts in steep in rose-water till you fill them.

SECTION VIII.

The rarest Ways of making all manner of Souces and Jellies.

To souce a Brawn.

Ake a fat brawn of two or three years growth, and bone the sides, cut off the head close to the ears, and cut five collars of a side, bone the hinder leg, or else five collars will not be deep enough, cut the collars an inch deeper in the belly, then on the back; for when the collars come to boiling, they will shrink more in the belly than in the back, make the collars very even when you bind them up, not big at one end, & little at the other, but fill them equally, and lay them again in a soaking in fair water; before you bind them up, let them be well watered the space of two days, and twice a day soak & scrape them in warm water, then cast them in cold fair water, before you roul them up in collors, put them into white clouts, or sow them up with white tape.

Or bone him whole, & cut him cross the flitches, make but four or five collars in all, & boil them in cloths, or bind them up with white tape, then have your boiler ready, make it boil, and put in your collars of the biggest bulk first, a quarter of an hour before the other lessor; boil them at the first putting in the space of an hour with a quick fire, & keep the boiler continually fil'd up with warm clean liquor, scum off the fat clean still as it riseth; after an hour let it boil leisurely, and keep it still filled up to the brim; being fine and tender boil'd, that you may put a straw thorow it, draw your fire, and let your brawn rest till the next morning. Then being between hot and cold, take it into molds of deep hoops, bind them about with packthred, and being cold, take them out and put them into souce drink made of boil'd oatmeal ground or beaten, and bran boil'd in fair water; being cold, strain it thorow a cullender into the tub or earthen pot, put salt into it, and close up the vessel close from the air.

Or you may make other souse-drink of whey and salt beaten together, it will make your brawn look more white and better.

To make Pig Brawn

Take a white or red Pig, for a spotted one is not so handsome, take a good large fat one, and being scalded and drawn bone it whole, but first cut off the head and the hinder quarters, (and leave the bone in the hinder quarters) the rest being boned cut it into 2 collars overwart both the sides, or bone the wole Pig but only the head: then wash them in divers-waters, and let it soak in clean water two hours, the bloud being well soaked out, take them and dry the collars in a clean cloth, and season them in the inside with minced lemon-peel and salt, roul them up, & put them into fine clean clouts, but first make your collars very equal at both ends, round and even, bind them up at the ends and middle hard & close with packthred; then let your Pan boil, and put in the collars, boil them with water and salt, and keep it filled up with warm water as you do the brawn, scum off the fat very clean, and being tender boil'd put them in a hoop as deep as the collar, bind it and frame it even, being cold put it into your souce drink made of whey and salt, or oatmeal boil'd and strained, then put them in a pipkin or little barrel, and stop them close from the air.

When you serve it, dish it on a dish and plate, the two collars, two quarters and head, or make but two collars of the whole Pig.

To garnish Brawn or Pig Brawn.

Leach your brawn, and dish it on a plate in a fair clean dish, then put a rosemary branch on the top being first dipped in the white of an egg well beaten to froth, or wet in water and sprinkled with flour, or a sprig of rosemary gilt with gold; the brawn spotted also with gold and silver leaves, or let your sprig be of a streight sprig of yew tree, or a streight furz bush, and put about the brawn stuck round with bay-leaves three ranks round, and spotted with red and yellow jelly about the dish sides, also the same jelly and some of the brawn leached, jagged, or cut with tin moulds, and carved lemons, oranges and barberries, bay-leaves gilt, red beets, pickled barberries, pickled gooseberries, or pickled grapes.

To souce a Pig.

Take a pig being scalded, cut off the head, and part it down the back, draw it and bone it, then the sides being well cleansed from the blood, and soaked in several clean waters, take the pig and dry the sides, season them with nutmeg, ginger, and salt, roul them and bind them up in clean clouts as the pig brawn aforesaid, then have as much water as will cover it in a boiling pan two inches over and two bottles of white-wine over and above; first let the water boil, then put in the collars with salt, mace, slic't ginger, parsley-roots and fennil-roots scraped and picked; being half boiled put in two quarts of white-wine, and when it is boil'd quite, put in slices of lemon to it, and the whole peel of a lemon.

Otherways in Collars.

Season the sides with beaten nutmeg, salt, and ginger, or boil the sides whole or not bone them; boil also a piece or breast of veal with them, being well joynted and soaked two hours in fair water, boil it in half wine and half water, mace, slic't ginger, parsley, and fennil-roots, being boil'd leave it in this souce, and put some slic't lemon to it, with the whole pieces: when it is cold serve it with yellow, red, and white jelly, barberries, slic't lemon, and lemon-peel.

Or you may make but one collar of both the sides to the hinder quarters, or bone the two sides, and make but two collars of all, and save the head only whole, or souce a pig in quarters or halves, or make of a good large fat pig but one collar only, and the head whole.

Or souce it with two quarts of white wine to a gallon of water, put in your wine when your pig is almost boil'd, and put to it four maces, a few cloves, two races of slic't ginger, salt, a few bay-leaves, whole pepper, some slices of lemon, and lemon-peel; before you boil your pig, season the sides or collars with nutmeg, salt, cloves, and mace.

To souce a Pig otherways.

Scald it and cut it in four quarters, bone it, and let it ly in water a day and a night, then roul it up (like brawn) with sage leaves, lard in thin slices, & some grated bread mix't with the juyce of orange, beaten nutmeg, mace, and salt: roul it up in the quarters of the pig very hard and binde it up with tape, then boil it with fair water, white-wine, large mace, slic't ginger, a little lemon-peel, a faggot of sweet herbs, and salt; being boil'd put it in an earthen pot to cool in the liquor, and souce there two days, then dish it out on plates, or serve it in collars with mustard and sugar.

Otherways.

Season the sides with cloves, mace, and salt, then roul it in collars or sides with the bones in it; then take two or 3 gallons of water, a pottle of white-wine, and when the liquor boils put in the pig, with mace, cloves, slic't ginger, salt, bay-leaves, and whole pepper; being half boil'd, put in the wine, &c.

Otherways.

Season the collars with chopped sage, beaten nutmeg, pepper, and salt.

To souce or jelly a Pig in the Spanish fashion.

Take a pig being scalded, boned, and chined down the back, then soak the collars clean from the blood the space of two hours, dry them in a clean cloth, and season the sides with pepper, salt, and minced sage; then have two dryed neats-tongues that are boil'd tender and cold, that they look fine and red, pare them and slice them from end to end the thickness of a half crown piece, lay them on the inside of the seasoned pig, one half of the tongue for one side, and the other for the other side; then make two collars and bind them up in fine white clouts, boil them as you do the soust pigs with wine, water, salt, slic't ginger and mace, keep it dry, or in souce drink of the pig brawn.

If dry serve it in slices as thick as a trencher cut round the collar or slices in jelly, and make jelly of the liquor wherein it was boil'd, adding to it juyce of lemon, ising-glass, spices, sugar clarified with eggs, and run it through the bag.

How to divide a Pig into Collars divers ways, either for Pig Brawn, or soust Pig.

1. Cut a large fat Bore-pig into one collar only, bone it whole, and not chine it, the head only cut off.

2. Take out the hinder-quarters and buttocks with the bones in them, bone all the rest whole, only the head cut off.

3. Take off the hinder quarters and make two collars, bone all the rest, only cut off the head & leave it whole.

4. Cut off the head, and chine it through the back, and collar both sides at length from end to end.

5. Chine it as before with the bones in, and souce it in quarters.

To souce a Capon.

Take a good bodied Capon, young, fat, and finely pulled, drawn and trussed, lay it in soak two or three hours with a knuckle of veal well joynted, and after set them a boiling in a fine deep brass-pan, kettle, or large pipkin, in a gallon of fair water; when it boils, scum it, and put in four or five blades of mace, two or three races of ginger slic't, four fennil-roots, and four parsley-roots, scraped and picked, and salt. The Capon being fine and tender boild take it up, and put it in other warm liquor or broth, then put to your souced broth a quart of white-wine, and boil it to a jelly; then take it off, and put it into an earthen pan or large pipkin, put your capon to it, with two or three slic't lemons, and cover it close, serve it at your pleasure, and garnish it with slices and pieces of lemon, barberries, roots, mace, nutmeg, and some of the jelly.

Some put to this souc't capon, whole pepper, & a faggot of sweet herbs, but that maketh the broth very black.

In that manner you may souce any Land Fowl.

To souce a Breast of Veal, Side of Lamb, or any Joynt of Mutton, Kid, Fawn, or Venison.

Bone a breast of veal & soak it well from the blood, then wipe it dry, and season the side of the breast with beaten nutmeg, ginger, some sweet herbs minced small, whole coriander-seed, minced lemon-peel, and salt, and lay some broad slices of sweet lard over the seasoning, then roul it into a collar, and bind it up in a white clean cloth, put it into boiling liquor, scum it well, and then put in slic't ginger, slic't nutmeg, salt, fennil, and parsley-roots, being almost boild, put in a quart of white-wine, and when it is quite boild take it off, and put in slices of lemon, the peel of two lemons whole, and a douzen bay leaves, boil it close covered to make the veal look white.

Thus you may do a breast of mutton, either roul'd, or with the bones in, and season them with nutmeg, pepper & salt, roul them, & bake them in a pot with wine and water, any Sea or Land fowl, being stuffed or farsed; and filled up with butter afterwards, and served dry, or lard the Fowls, bone and roul them.

To souce a Leg of Veal.

Take a leg of veal, bone it and lard it, but first season the lard with pepper, cloves, & mace, lard it with great lard as big as your little finger, season the veal also with the same seasoning & some salt with it; lard it very thick then have all manner of sweet herbs minc't and strew'd on it, roul it like a collar of brawn, and boil it or stew it in the oven in a pipkin, with water, salt, and white-wine, serve it in a collar cold, whole or in slices, or put away the liquor, and fill it up with butter, or bake it with butter in a roul, jelly it, and mix some of the broth with almond milk, and jellies in slices of two collars, when you serve it.

Otherways.

Stuff or farse a leg of veal; with sweet herbs minc't, beef-suet, pepper, nutmeg, and salt, collar it, and boil or bake it; being cold, either serve it dry in a collar, or in slices, or in a whole collar with gallendines of divers sorts, or in thin slices with oyl and vinegar.

Thus you may dress any meat, venison, or Fowls.

To souce Bullocks Cheeks, a Flank, Brisket, or Rand of Beef, &c.

Take a bullocks cheek or flank of beef and lay it in peter salt four days, then roul it as even as you can, that the collar be not bigger in one place than in another boil it in water and salt, or amongst other beef, boil it very tender in a cloth as you do brawn, and being tender boil'd take it up, and put it into a hoop to fashion it upright and round, then keep it dry, and take it out of the clout, and serve it whole with mustard and sugar, or some gallendines. If lean, lard it with groat Lard.

To collar a Surloin, Flank, Brisket, Rand, or Fore-Rib of Beef.

Take the flank of beef, take out the sinewy & most of the fat, put it in pickle with as much water as will cover it, and put a handful of peter-salt to it, let it steep three days and not sift it, then take it out and hang it a draining the air, wipe it dry, then have a good handful of red sage, some tops of rosemary, savory, marjoram, tyme, but twice as much sage, mince them very small, then take quarter of an ounce of mace, and half as many cloves, with a little ginger, and half an ounce of pepper, and likewise half an ounce of peter-salt; mingle them together, then take your beef, splat it, and lay it even that it may roul up handsomely in a collar; then take your seasoning of herbs and spices, and strow it all over, roul it up close, and bind it fast with packthred, put it into an earthen pipkin or pot, and put a pint of claret wine to it, an onion and two or three cloves of garlick, close it up with a piece of course paste, and bake it in a bakers oven, it will ask six hours soaking.

To souce a Collar of Veal in the same manner, or Venison, Pork, or Mutton.

Take out the bones, and put them in steep in the picle with peter-salt, as was aforesaid, steep them three days, and hang them in the air one day, lard them (or not lard them) with good big lard, and season the lard with nutmeg, pepper, and herbs, as is aforesaid in the collar of beef, strow it over with the herbs, and spices, being mingled together, and roul up the collar, bind it fast, and bake it tender in a pot, being stopped close, and keep it for your use to serve either in slices or in the whole collar, garnish it with bays and rosemary.

To make a Jelly for any kind of souc't Meats, Dishes, or other Works of that nature.

Take six pair of calves feet, scald them and take away the fat betwixt the claws, & also the long shank-bones, lay them in soak in fair water 3 or 4 hours, and boil them in two gallons of fair spring-water, to three quarts of stock; being boild strain it through a strainer, & when the broth is cold, take it from the grounds, & divide it into three pipkins for three several colours, to every pipkin a quart of white-wine, and put saffron in one, cutchenele in another, and put a race of ginger, two blades of mace, and a nutmeg to each pipkin, and cinamon to two of the pipkins, the spices being first slic't, then set your pipkins on the fire, and melt the jelly; then have a pound and a half of sugar for each pipkin: but first take your fine sugar being beaten, and put in a long dish or tray, and put to it whites of eighteen eggs, and beat them well together with your rouling pin, and divide it into three parts, put each part equally into the several pipkins, and stir it well together; the broth being almost cold, then set them on a charcoal fire and let them stew leisurely, when they begin to boil over, take them off, let it cool a little, run them through the bags once or twice and keep it for your use.

For variety sometimes in place of wine, you may use grapes stamped and strained, wood-sorrel, juyce of lemons, or juyce of oranges.

To jelly Hogs or Porkers Feet, Ears, or Snouts.

Take twelve feet, six ears, & six snouts or noses, being finely scalded, & lay them in soak twenty four hours, shift & scrape them very white, then boil them in a fair clean scoured brass pot or pipkin in three gallons of liquor, five quarts of water, three of wine-vinegar, or verjuyce, and four of white-wine, boil them from three gallons to four quarts waste, being scum'd, put in an ounce of pepper whole, an ounce of nutmegs in quarters, an ounce of ginger slic't, and an ounce of cinamon, boil them together, as is abovesaid, to four quarts.

Then take up the meat, and let them cool, divide them into dishes, & run it over with the broth or jelly being a little first setled, take the clearest, & being cold put juice or orange over all, serve it with bay-leaves about the dish.

To make a Crystal Jelly.

Take three pair of calves feet, and scald off the hair very clean, knock off the claws, and take out the great bones & fat, & cast them into fair water, shift them three or four times in a day and a night, then boil them next morning in a glazed pipkin or clean pot, with six quarts of fair spring water, boil it and scum it clean, boil away three quarts or more; then strain it into a clean earthen pan or bason, & let it be cold: then prepare the dross from the bottom, and take the fat of the top clean, put it in a large pipkin of six quarts, and put into it two quarts of old clear white-wine, the juyce of four lemons, three blades of mace, and two races of ginger slic't; then melt or dissolve it again into broth, and let it cool. Then have four pound of hard sugar fine beaten, and mix it with twelve whites of eggs in a great dish with your rouling pin, and put it into your pipkin to your jelly, stir it together with a grain of musk and ambergriese, put it in a fine linnen clout bound up, and a quarter of a pint of damask rose-water, set it a stewing on a soft charcoal fire, before it boils put in a little ising glass, and being boil'd up, take it, and let it cool a little, and run it.

Other Jelly for service of several colours.

Take four pair of calves feet, a knuckle of veal, a good fleshie capon, and prepare these things as is said in the crystal jelly: boil them in three gallons of fair water, till six quarts be wasted, then strain it in an earthen pan, let it cool, and being cold pare the bottom, and take off the fat on the top also; then dissolve it again into broth, and divide it into 4 equal parts, put it into four several pipkins, as will contain five pints a piece each pipkin, put a little saffron into one of them, into another cutchenele beaten with allum, into another turnsole, and the other his own natural white; also to every pipkin a quart of white-wine, and the juyce of two lemons. Then also to the white jelly one race of ginger pare'd and slic't & three blades of large mace, to the red jelly 2 nutmegs, as much in quantity of cinamon as nutmegs, also as much ginger; to the turnsole put also the same quantity, with a few whole cloves; then to the amber or yellow color, the same spices and quantity. Then have eighteen whites of eggs, & beat them with six pound of double refined sugar, beaten small and stirred together in a great tray or bason with a rouling pin divide it into four parts in the four pipkins & stir it to your jelly broth, spice, & wine, being well mixed together with a little musk & ambergriese. Then have new bags, wash them first in warm water, and then in cold, wring them dry, and being ready strung with packthread on sticks, hang them on a spit by the fire from any dust, and set new earthen pans under them being well seasoned with boiling liquor.

Then again set on your jelly on a fine charcoal fire, and let it stew softly the space of almost an hour, then make it boil up a little, and take it off, being somewhat cold run it through the bag twice or thrice, or but once if it be very clear; and into the bags of colors put in a sprig of rosemary, keep it for your use in those pans, dish it as you see good, or cast it into what mould you please; as for example these.

Scollop shells, Cockle shells, Egg shells, half Lemon, or Lemon-peel, Wilks, or Winkle shells, Muscle shells, or moulded out of a butter-squirt.

Or serve it on a great dish and plate, one quarter of white, another of red, another of yellow, the fourth of another colour, & about the sides of the dish oranges in quarters of jelly, in the middle whole lemon full of jelly finely carved, or cast out of a wooden or tin mould, or run into little round glasses four or five in a dish, on silver trencher plates, or glass trencher plates.

The quantities for a quart of Jelly Broth for the true making of it.

A quart of white-wine, a pound and a half of sugar, eggs, two nutmegs, or mace, two races of ginger, as much cinamon, two grains of musk and ambergriese, calves feet, or a knuckle of veal.

Sometimes for variety, in place of wine, use grape-verjuyce; if juyce of grapes a quart, juyce of lemons a pint, juyce of oranges a quart, juyce of wood-sorrel a quart, and juyce of quinces a quart.

How to prepare to make a good Stock for Jellies of all sorts, and the meats most proper for them, both for service and sick-folks; also the quantities belonging to a quart of Jellie.

For the stock for service.

Two pair of calves feet finely cleansed, the fat and great bones taken out and parted in halves; being well soaked in fair water twenty four hours, and often shifted, boil them in a brass pot or pipkin close covered, in the quantity of a gallon of water, boil them to three pints, then strain the broth through a clean strong canvas into an earthen pan or bason; when it is cold take off the top, and pare off the dregs from the bottom. Put it in a clean well glazed pipkin of two quarts, with a quart of white-wine, a quarter of a pint of cinamon-water, as much of ginger-water, & as much of nutmeg-water, or these spices sliced. Then have two pound of double refined sugar beaten with eggs, in a deep dish or bason, your jelly being new melted, put in the eggs with sugar, stir all the foresaid materials together, and set it astewing on a soft charcoal fire the space of half an hour or more, being well digested and clear run.

Take out the bone and fat of any meat for jellies, for it doth but stain the stock, and is the cause that it will never be white nor very clear.

Meats proper for Jelly for service or sick folks.

1. Three pair of calves feet.

2. Three pair of calves feet, a knuckle of veal, and a fine well fleshed capon.

3. One pair of calves feet, a well fleshed capon, and half a pound of harts-horn of ising-glass.

4. An old cock and a knuckle of veal.

5. Harts horn jelly only, or with a poultrey.

6. Good bodied capons.

7. Ising-glass only, or with a cock or capon.

8. Jelly of hogs feet, ears, and snouts.

9. Sheeps feet, lambs feet, and calves feet.

Neats feet for a Jelly for a Neats-Tongue.

Being fresh and tender boil'd and cold, lard it with candied cittern candied orange, lemon, or quinces, run it over with jelly, and some preserved barberries or cherries.

To make a Jelly as white as snow of Jorden-Almonds.

Take a pound of almonds, steep them in cold water till they will blanch, which will be in six hours; being blanched into cold water, beat them with a quart of rose water: then have a decoction of half a pound of ising-glass, boil'd with a gallon of fair spring-water, or else half wine, boil it till half be wasted, then let it cool, strain it, and mingle it with your almonds, and strain with them a pound of double refined sugar, the juyce of two lemons, and cast it into egg shells; put saffron to some of it, and make some of it blue, some of it green, and some yellow; cast some into oranges, and some into lemon rindes candied: mix part of it with some almond paste colored; and some with cheese-curds; serve of divers of these colours on a great dish and plate.

To make other white Jelly.

Boil two capons being cleansed, the fat and lungs taken out, truss them and soak them well in clean water three of four hours; then boil them in a pipkin, or pot of two gallons or less, put to them a gallon or five quarts of white wine, scum them, and boil them to a jelly, next strain the broth from the grounds and blow off the fat clean; then take a quart of sweet cream, a quart of the jelly broth, a pound and half of refined sugar, and a quarter of a pint of rose water, mingle them all together, and give them a warm on the fire with half an ounce of fine searsed ginger;

then set it a cooling, dish it, or cast it in lemon or orange-peels, or in any fashion of the other jellies, in moulds or glasses, or turn it into colours; for sick folks in place of cream use stamped almonds.

To make Jellies for sauces, made dishes, and other works.

Take six pair of calves feet, scald them and take away the fat between the claws, as also the great long shank bones, and lay them in water four or five hours; then boil them in two gallons of fair spring water, scum them clean and boil them from two gallons to three quarts, then strain it through a strong canvas, and let the broth cool; being cold cleanse it from the grounds, pare off the top and melt it, then put to it in a good large pipkin, three quarts of white-wine, three races of ginger slic't, some six blades of mace, a quarter of an ounce of cinamon, a grain of musk, and eighteen whites of eggs beaten with four pound of sugar, mingle them with the rest in the pipkin, and the juyce of three lemons, set all on the fire, and let it stew leisurely; then have your bag ready washed, and when your pipkin boils up, run it, &c.

Harts horn Jelly.

Take half a pound of harts-horn, boil it in fair spring water leisurely, close covered, and in a well glazed pipkin that will contain a gallon, boil it till a spoonful will stand stiff being cold, then strain it through a fine thick canvas or fine boultering, and put it again into another lesser pipkin, with the juyce of eight or nine good large lemons, a pound and half of double refined sugar, and boil it again a little while, then put it in a gally pot, or small glasses, or cast it into moulds, or any fashions of the other jellies. It is held by the Physicians for a special Cordial.

Or take half a pound of harts-horn grated, and a good capon being finely cleansed and soaked from the blood, and the fat taken off, truss it, and boil it in a pot or pipkin with the harts-horn, in fair spring water, the same things as the former, &c.

To make another excellent Jelly of Harts horn and Ising-glass for a Consumption.

Take half a pound of ising-glass, half a pound of harts-horn, half a pound of slic't dates, a pound of beaten sugar, half a pound of slic't figs, a pound of slic't prunes half an ounce of cinamon, half an ounce of ginger, a quarter of an ounce of mace, a quarter of an ounce of cloves, half an ounce of nutmegs, and a little red sanders, slice your spices, and also a little stick of liquorish and put in your cinamon whole.

To make a Jelly for weakness in the back.

Take two ounces of harts-horn, and a wine quart of spring-water, put it into a pipkin, and boil it over a soft fire till it be one half consumed, then take it off the fire, and let it stand a quarter of an hour, and strain it through a fine holland cloth, crushing the harts-horn gently with a spoon: then put to it the juyce of a lemon, two spoonfulls of red rose-water, half a spoonful of cinamon-water, four or five ounces of fine sugar, or make it sweet according to the parties taste; then put it out into little glasses or pipkins, and let it stand twenty four hours, then you may take of it in the morning, or at four of the clock in the afternoon, what quantity you please. To put two or three spoonfuls of it into broth is very good.

To make another dish of meat called a Press, for service.

Do in this as you may see in the jelly of the porker, before spoken of; take the feet, ears, snouts, and cheeks, being finely and tender boil'd to a jelly with spices, and the same liquor as is said in the Porker; then take out the bones and make a lay of it like a square brick, season it with coriander or fennil-seed, and bind it up like a square brick in a strong canvas with packthred, press it till it be cold, and serve it in slices with bay-leaves, or run it over with jellies.

To make a Sausage for Jelly.

Boil or roast a capon, mince and stamp it with some almond paste, then have a fine dried neats-tongue, one that looks fine and red ready boil'd, cut it into little pieces, square like dice, half an inch long, and as much of interlarded bacon cut into the same form ready boil'd and cold, some preserved quinces and barberries, sugar, and cinamon, mingle all together with some scraped ising-glass amongst it warm; roul it up in a sausage, knit it up at the ends, and sow the sides; then let it cool, slice it, and serve it in a jelly in a dish in thin slices, and run jelly over it, let it cool and lay on more, that cool, run more, and thus do till the dish be full; when you serve it, garnish the dish with jelly and preserved barberries, and run over all with juyce of lemon.

To make Leach a most excellent way in the French Fashion.

Take a quart of sweet cream, twelve spoonfuls of rose-water, four grains of musk dissolved in rose-water, and four or five blades of large mace boil'd with half a pound of ising-glass, being steeped and washed clean, and put to it half a pound of sugar, and being boil'd to a jelly, run it through your jelly bag into a dish, and being cold slice it into chequer-work, and serve it on a plate or glasses, and sometimes without sugar in it, &c.

To make the best Almond Leach.

Take an ounce of ising-glass, and lay it two hours in water, shift it, and boil it in fair water, let it cool; then take two pound of almonds, lay them in the water till they will blanch, then stamp them and put to them a pint of milk, strain them, and put in large mace and slic't ginger, boil them till it taste well of the spice, then put in your digested ising-glass, sugar, and a little rose-water, run it through a strainer, and put it into dishes.

Some you may colour with saffron, turnsole, or green wheat, and blew-bottles for blew.

To keep Sparagus all the year.

Parboil them very little, and put them into clarified butter, cover them with it, the butter being cold, cover them with a leather, and about a month after refresh the butter, melt it, and put it on them again, then set them under ground being

covered with a leather.

SECTION IX.

The best way of making all manner of baked Meats.

To make a Bisk or Batalia Pie.

Take six peeping Pigeons, and as many peeping small chickens, truss them to bake; then have six oxe pallets well boil'd and blancht, and cut in little pieces; then take six lamb-stones, and as many good veal sweet-breads cut in halves and parboil'd, twenty cocks-combs boil'd and blanch'd, the bottoms of four artichocks boiled and blanched, a quart of great oysters parboil'd and bearded, also the marrow of four bones seasoned with pepper, nutmeg, mace, and salt; fill the pye with the meat, and mingle some pistaches amongst it, cock-stones, knots, or yolks of hard eggs, and some butter, close it up and bake it (an hour and half will bake it) but before you set it in the oven, put into it a little fair water: Being baked pour out the butter, and liquor it with gravy, butter beaten up thick, slic't lemon, and serve it up.

Or you may bake this bisk in a patty-pan or dish.

Sometimes use sparagus and interlarded bacon.

For the paste of this dish, take three quarts of flour, and three quarters of a pound of butter, boil the butter in fair water, and make up the paste hot and quick.

Otherways in the summer time, make the paste of cold butter; to three quarts of flour take a pound and a half of butter, and work it dry into the flour, with the yolks of four eggs and one white, then put a little water to it, and make it up into a stiff paste.

To bake Chickens or Pigeons.

Take either six pigeon peepers or six chicken peepers, if big cut them in quarters, then take three sweet-breads of veal slic't very thin, three sheeps tongues boil'd tender, blanched and slic't, with as much veal, as much mutton, six larks, twelve cocks combs, a pint of great oysters parboild and bearded, calves udder cut in pieces, and three marrow bones, season these foresaid materials with pepper, salt, and nutmeg, then fill them in pies of the form as you see, and put on the top some chesnuts, marrow, large mace, grapes, or gooseberries; then have a little piece of veal and mince it with as much marrow, some grated bread, yolks of eggs, minced dates, salt, nutmeg, and some sweet marjoram, work up all with a little cream, make it up in little balls or rouls, put them in the pie, and put in a little mutton-gravy, some artichock bottoms, or the tops of boild sparagus, and a little butter; close up the pie and bake it, being baked liquor it with juyce of oranges, one lemon, and some claret wine, shake it well together, and so serve it.

To Make a Chicken Pie otherways.

Take and truss them to bake, then season them lightly with pepper, salt, and nutmeg; lay them in the pie, and lay on them some dates in halves, with the marrow of three marrow-bones, some large mace, a quarter of a pound of eringo roots, some grapes or barberries, and some butter, close it up, and put it in the oven; being half baked, liquor it with a pound of good butter; a quarter of a pint of grape-verjuyce, and a quartern of refined sugar, ice it and serve it up.

Otherways you may use the giblets, and put in some pistaches, but keep the former order as aforesaid for change.

Liquor it with caudle made of a pint of white-wine or verjuyce, the yolks of five or six eggs, suger, and a quarter of a pound of good sweet butter; fill the pye, and shake this liquor well in it, with the slices of a lemon. Or you may make the caudle green with the juyce of spinage; ice these pies, or scrape sugar on them.

Otherways for the liquoring or garnishing of these Pies, for variety you may put in them boil'd skirrets, bottom of artichocks boil'd, or boil'd cabbidge lettice.

Sometimes sweet herbs, whole yolks of hard eggs, interlarded bacon in very thin slices, and a whole onion; being baked, liquor it with white-wine, butter, and the juyce of two oranges.

Or garnish them with barberries, grapes, or gooseberries, red or white currans, and some sweet herbs chopped small, boil'd in gravy; and beat up thick with butter.

Otherways liquor it with white-wine, butter, sugar, some sweet marjoram, and yolks of eggs strained.

Or bake them with candied lettice stalks, potatoes, boil'd and blanch'd, marrow, dates, and large mace; being baked cut up the pye, and lay on the chickens, slic't lemon, then liquor the pye with white-wine, butter, and sugar, and serve it up hot.

You may bake any of the foresaid in a patty-pan or dish, or bake them in cold butter paste.

To bake Turkey, Chicken, Pea-Chicken, Pheasant-Pouts, Heath Pouts, Caponets, or Partridge for to be eaten cold.

Take a turkey-chicken, bone it, and lard it with pretty big lard, a pound and half will serve, then season it with an ounce of pepper, an ounce of nutmegs, and two ounces of salt, lay some butter in the bottom of the pye, then lay on the fowl, and put in it six or eight whole cloves, then put on all the seasoning with good store of butter, close it up, and baste it over with eggs, bake it, and being baked fill it up with clarified butter.

Thus you may bake them for to be eaten hot, giving them but half the seasoning, and liquor it with gravy and juyce of orange.

Bake this pye in fine paste; for more variety you may make a stuffing for it as followeth; mince some beef-suet and a little veal very fine, some sweet herbs, grated nutmeg, pepper, salt, two or three raw yolks of eggs, some boil'd skirrets or pieces of artichocks, grapes, or gooseberries, &c.

To bake Pigeons wild or tame, Stock-Doves, Turtle-Doves, Quails, Rails, &c. to be eaten cold.

Take six pigeons, pull, truss, and draw them, wash and wipe them dry, and season them with nutmeg, pepper, and salt, the quantity of two ounces of the foresaid spices, and as much of the one as the other, then lay some butter in the bottom of the pye, lay on the pigeons, and put all the seasoning on them in the pye, put butter to it, close it up and bake it, being baked and cold, fill it up with clarified butter.

Make the paste of a pottle of fine flour, and a quarter of a pound of butter boil'd in fair water made up quick and stiff.

If you will bake them to be eaten hot, leave out half the seasoning: Bake them in dish, pie, or patty-pan, and make cold paste of a pottle of flour, six yolks of raw eggs, and a pound of butter, work into the flour dry, and being well wrought into it, make it up stiff with a little fair water.

Being baked to be eaten hot, put it into yolks of hard eggs, sweet-breads, lamb-stones, sparagus, or bottoms of artichocks, chesnuts, grapes, or gooseberries.

Sometimes for variety make a lear of butter, verjuyce, sugar, some sweet marjoram chopped and boil'd up in the liquor, put them in the pye when you serve it up, and dissolve the yolk of an egg into it; then cut up the pye or dish, and put on it some slic't lemon, shake it well together, and serve it up hot.

In this mode or fashion you bake larks, black-birds, thrushes, veldifers, sparrows, or wheat-ears.

To bake all manner of Land Fowl, as Turkey, Bustard, Peacock, Crane, &c. to be eaten cold.

Take a turkey and bone it, parboil and lard it thick with great lard as big as your little finger, then season it with 2 ounces of beaten pepper, two ounces of beaten nutmeg, and three ounces of salt, season the fowl, and lay it in a pie fit for it, put first butter in the bottom, with some ten whole cloves, then lay on the turkey, and the rest of the seasoning on it, lay on good store of butter, then close it up and baste it either with saffron water, or three or four eggs beaten together with their yolks; bake it, and being baked and cold, liquor it with clarified butter, &c.

To bake all manner of Sea-Fowl, as Swan, Whopper, to be eaten cold.

Take a swan, bone, parboil and lard it with great lard, season the lard with nutmeg and pepper only, then take two ounces of pepper, three of nutmeg, and four of salt, season the fowl, and lay it in the pie, with good store of butter, strew a few whole cloves on the rest of the seasoning, lay on large sheets of lard over it, and good store of butter; then close it up in rye-paste or meal course boulted, and made up with boiling liquor, and make it up stiff: or you may bake them to eat hot, only giving them half the seasoning.

In place of baking any of these fowls in pyes, you may bake them in earthen pans or pots, for to be preserved cold, they will keep longer.

In the same manner you may bake all sorts of wild geese, tame geese, bran geese, muscovia ducks, gulls, shovellers, herns, bitterns, curlews, heath-cocks, teels, olines, ruffs, brewes, pewits, mewes, sea-pies, dap chickens, strents, dotter-ils, knots, gravelins, oxe-eyes, red shanks, &c.

In baking of these fowls to be eaten hot, for the garnish put in a big onion, gooseberries, or grapes in the pye, and sometimes capers or oysters, and liquor it with gravy, claret, and butter.

To dress a Turkey in the French mode, to eat cold, called a la doode.

Take a turkey and bone it, or not bone it, but boning is the best way, and lard it with good big lard as big as your little finger and season it with pepper, cloves, and mace, nutmegs, and put a piece of interlarded bacon in the belly with some rosemary and bayes, whole pepper, cloves and mace, and sew it up in a clean cloth, and lay it in steep all night in white-wine, next morning close it up with a sheet of course paste in a pan or pipkin, and bake it with the same liquor it was steept in; it will ask four hours baking, or you may boil the liquor; then being baked and cold, serve it on a pie-plate, and stick it with rosemary and bays, and serve it up with mustard and sugar in saucers, and lay the fowl on a napkin folded square, and the turkey laid corner-ways.

Thus any large fowl or other meat, as a leg of mutton, and the like.

Meats proper for a stofado may be any large fowl, as,

Turkey, Swan, Goose, Bustard, Crane, Whopper, wild Geese, Brand Geese, Hearn, Shoveler, or Bittern, and many more; as also Venison, Red Deer, Fallow Deer, Legs of Mutton, Breasts of Veal boned and larded, Kid or Fawn, Pig, Pork, Neats-tongues, and Udders, or any Meat, a Turkey, Lard one pound, Pepper one ounce, Nutmegs, Ginger, Mace, Cloves, Wine a quart, Vinegar half a pint, a quart of great Oysters, Puddings, Sausages, two Lemons, two Cloves of Garlick.

A Stofado.

Take two turkeys, & bone them and lard them with great lard as big as your finger, being first seasoned with pepper, & nutmegs, & being larded, lay it in steep in an earthen pan or pipkin in a quart of white-wine, & half as much wine-vine-gar, some twenty whole cloves, half an ounce of mace, an ounce of beaten pepper, three races of slic't ginger, half a handful of salt, half an ounce of slic't nutmegs, and a ladleful of good mutton broth, & close up the pot with a sheet of coarse paste, and bake it; it will ask four hours baking; then have a fine clean large dish, with a six penny French bread slic't in large slices, and then lay them in the bottom of a dish, and steep them with some good strong mutton broth, and the same broth that it was baked in, and some roast mutton gravy, and dish the fowl, garnish it with the spices and some sausages, and some kind of good puddings, and marrow and carved lemons slic't, and lemon-peels.

To bake any kind of Heads, and first of the Oxe or Bullocks Cheeks to be eaten hot or cold.

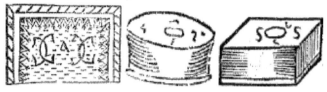

Being first cleansed from the slime and filth, cut them in pieces, take out the bones, and season them with pepper, salt, and nutmeg, then put them in a pye with a few whole cloves, a little seasoning, slices of bacon, and butter over all; bake them very tender, and liquor them with butter and claret wine.

Or boil your chickens, take out the bones and make a pasty with some minced meat, and a caul of mutton under it, on the top spices and butter, close it up in good crust, and make your pies according to these forms.

Otherways.

Bone and lard them with lard as big as your little finger seasoned with pepper, salt, and nutmeg, and laid into the pye or pasty, with slices of interlarded bacon, and a clove or two, close it up, and bake it with some butter; make your pye or pasty of good fine crust according to these forms. Being baked fill it up with good sweet butter.

Otherways.

You may make a pudding of some grated bread, minced veal, beef-suet, some minced sweet herbs, a minced onion, eggs, cream, nutmeg, pepper, and salt, and lay it on the top of your meat in the pye, and some butter, close it up and bake it.

Otherways.

Take a calves head, soak it well and take out the brains, boil the head and take out the bones, being cold stuff it with sweet herbs and hard eggs chopped small, minced bacon, and a raw egg or two, nutmeg, pepper, and salt; and lay in the bottom of the pye minced veal raw, and bacon; then lay the cheeks on it in the pye, and slices of bacon on that, then spices, butter, and grapes or lemon, close it up, bake it, and liquor it with butter only.

Otherways.

Boil it and take out the bones, cleanse it, and season it with pepper, salt, and nutmeg, put some minced veal or suet in the bottom of the pye, then lay on the cheeks, and on them a pudding made of minced veal raw and suet, currans, grated bread or parmisan, eggs, saffron, nutmeg, pepper, and salt, put it on the head in the pye, with some thin slices of interlarded bacon, thin slices also of veal and butter, close it up, and make it according to these forms, being baked, liquor it with butter only.

To bake a Calves Chaldron.

Boil it tender, and being cold mince it, and season it with nutmeg, pepper, cinamon, ginger, salt, caraway seeds, verjuyce, or grapes, some currans, sugar, rose-water and dates stir them all together and fill your pye, bake it, and being baked ice it.

Minced Pies of Calves Chaldrons, or Muggets.

Boil it tender, and being cold mince it small, then put to it bits of lard cut like dice, or interlarded bacon, some yolks of hard eggs cut like dice also, some bits of veal and mutton cut also in the same bigness, as also lamb, some gooseberries, grapes or barberries, and season it with nutmeg, pepper, and salt, fill your pye, and lay on it some thin slices of interlarded bacon, and butter; close it up, and bake it, liquor it with white-wine beaten with butter.

To bake a Calves Chaldron or Muggets in a Pye or little Pasties, or make a Pudding of it, adding two or three Eggs.

Being half boil'd, mince it small, with half a pound of beef-suet, and season it with beaten cloves and mace, nutmegs, a little onion and minced lemon peel, and put to it the juyce of an orange, and mix all together. Then make a piece of puff-paste and bake it in a dish as other Florentines, and close it up with the other half of the paste, and being baked put into it the juyce of two or three oranges, and stir the meat with the orange juyce well together and serve it, &c.

To bake a Pig to be eaten cold called a Maremaid Pye.

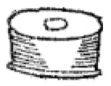

Take a Pig, flay it and quarter it, then bone it, take also a good Eel flayed, speated, boned, and seasoned with pepper, salt, and nutmeg, then lay a quarter of your pig in a round pie; and part of the Eel on that quarter, then lay another quarter on the other and then more eel, and thus keep the order till your pie be full, then lay a few whole cloves, slices of bacon, and butter, and close it up, bake it in good fine paste, being baked and cold, fill it up with good sweet butter.

Otherways.

Scald it, and bone it being first cleansed, dry the sides in a clean cloth, and season them with beaten nutmeg, pepper, salt, and chopped sage; then have two neats-tongues dryed, well boild, and cold, slice them out all the length, as thick as a half crown, and lay a quarter of your pig in a square or round pie, and slices of the tongue on it, then another quarter of a pig and more tongue, thus do four times double; and lay over all slices of bacon, a few cloves, butter, and a bay-leafe or two; then bake it, and being baked, fill it up with good sweet butter. Make your paste white of butter and flower.

Otherways.

Take a pig being scalded, flayed, and quartered, season it with beaten nutmeg, pepper, salt, cloves, and mace, lay it in your pie with some chopped sweet herbs, hard eggs, currans, (or none) put your herbs between every lay, with some gooseberries, grapes, or barberries, and lay on the top slices of interlarded bacon and butter, close it up, and bake it in good fine crust, being baked, liquor it with butter, verjuyce, and sugar. If to be eaten cold, with butter only.

Otherways to be eaten hot.

Cut it in pieces, and make a pudding of grated bread, cream, suet, nutmeg, eggs, and dates, make it into balls, and stick them with slic't almonds; then lay the pig in the pye, and balls on it, with dates, potato, large mace, lemon, and butter; being baked liquor it.

To bake four Hares in a Pie.

Bone them and lard them with great lard, being first seasoned with nutmeg, and pepper, then take four ounces of pepper, four ounces of nutmegs, and eight ounces of salt, mix them together, season them, and make a round or square pye of course boulted rye and meal; then the pie being made put some butter in the bottom of it, and lay on the hares one upon another; then put upon it a few whole cloves, a sheet of lard over it, and good store of butter, close it up and bake it, being first basted over with eggs beaten together, or saffron; when it is baked liquor them with clarified butter.

Or bake them in white paste or pasty, if to be eaten hot, leave out half the seasoning.

To bake three Hares in a Pie to be eaten cold.

Bone three hares, mince them small, and stamp them with the seasoning of pepper, salt, and nutmeg, then have lard cut as big as ones little finger, and as long as will reach from side to side of the pye; then lay butter in the bottom of it, and a lay of meat, then a lay of lard, and a lay of meat, and thus do five or six times, lay your lard all one way, but last of all a lay of meat, a few whole cloves, and slices of bacon over all, and some butter, close it up and bake it, being baked fill it up with sweet butter, and stop the vent.

Thus you may bake any venison, beef, mutton, veal, or rabits; if you bake them in earthen pans they will keep the longest.

To bake a Hare with a Pudding in his belly.

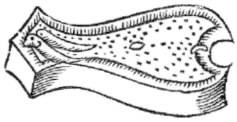

For to make this pie you must take as followeth, a gallon of flour, half an ounce of nutmegs, half an ounce of pepper, salt, capers, raisins, pears in quarters, prunes, with grapes, lemon, or gooseberries, and for the liquor a pound of sugar, a pint of claret or verjuyce, and some large mace.

Thus also you may bake a fawn, kid, lamb, or rabit: Make your Hare-Pie according to the foregoing form.

To make minced Pies of a Hare.

Take a Hare, flay it, and cleanse it, then take the flesh from the bones, and mince it with the fat bacon, or beef-suet raw, season it with pepper, mace, nutmeg, cloves, and salt; then mingle all together with some grapes, gooseberries, or barberries; fill the pie, close it up and bake it.

Otherways.

Mince it with beef-suet, a pound and half of raisins minced, some currans, cloves, mace, salt, and cinamon, mingle all together, and fill the pie, bake it and liquor it with claret.

To make a Pumpion Pie.

Take a pound of pumpion and slice it, a handful of time, a little rosemary, and sweet marjoram stripped off the stalks, chop them small, then take cinamon, nutmeg, pepper, and a few cloves all beaten, also ten eggs, and beat them, then mix and beat them all together, with as much sugar as you think fit, then fry them like a froise, after it is fried, let it stand till it is cold, then fill your pie after this manner. Take sliced apples sliced thin round ways, and lay a layer of the froise, and a layer of apples, with currans betwixt the layers. While your pie is fitted, put in a good deal of sweet butter before you close it. When the pie is baked, take six yolks of eggs, some white-wine or verjuyce, and make a caudle of this, but not too thick, cut up the lid, put it in, and stir them well together whilst the eggs and pumpion be not perceived, and so serve it up.

To make a Lumber-Pie.

Take some grated bread, and beef-suet cut into bits like great dice, and some cloves and mace, then some veal or capon minced small with beef-suet, sweet herbs, salt, sugar, the yolks of six eggs boil'd hard and cut in quarters, put them to the other ingredients, with some barberries, some yolks of raw eggs, and a little cream, work up all together and put it in the cauls of veal like little sausages; then bake them in a dish, and being half baked, have a pie made and dried in the oven; put these puddings into it with some butter, verjuyce, sugar, some dates on them, large mace, grapes, or barberries, and marrow; being baked, serve it with a cut cover on it, and scrape sugar on it.

Otherways.

Take some minc't meat of chewits of veal, and put to it some three or four raw eggs, make it into balls, then put them in a pye fitted for them according to this form, first lay in the balls, then lay on them some slic't dates, large mace, marrow, and butter; close it up and bake it, being baked, liquor it with verjuyce, sugar, and butter, then ice it, and serve it up.

To make an Olive Pye.

Take tyme, sweet marjorarm, savory, spinage, parsley, sage, endive, sorrel, violet leaves, and strawberry leaves, mince them very small with some yolks of hard eggs, then put to them half a pound of currans, nutmeg, pepper, cinamon, sugar, and salt, minced raisins, gooseberries, or barberries, and dates minc'd small, mingle alltogether, then have slices of a leg of veal, or a leg or mutton, cut thin and hacked with the back of a knife, lay them on a clean board and strow on the foresaid materials, roul them up and put them in a pye; then lay on them some dates, marrow, large mace, and some butter, close it up and bake it, being baked cut it up, liquor it with butter, verjuyce, and sugar, put a slic't lemon into it, and serve it up with scraped sugar.

To bake a Loin, Breast, or Rack of Veal or Mutton.

If you bake it with the bones, joynt a loin very well and season it with nutmeg, pepper, and salt, put it in your pye, and put butter to it, close it up, and bake it in good crust, and liquor it with sweet butter.

Thus also you may bake the brest, either in pye or pasty, as also the rack or shoulder, being stuffed with sweet herbs, and fat of beef minced together and baked either in pye or pasty.

In the summer time you may add to it spinage, gooseberries, grapes, barberries, or slic't lemon, and in winter, prunes, and currans, or raisins, and liquor it with butter, sugar, and verjuyce.

To make a Steak Pye the best way.

Cut a neck, loyn, or breast into steaks, and season them with pepper, nutmeg, and salt; then have some few sweet herbs minced small with an onion, and the yolks of three or four hard eggs minced also; the pye being made, put in the meat and a few capers, and strow these ingredients on it, then put in butter, close it up and bake it three hours moderately, &c. Make the pye round and pretty deep.

Otherways.

The meat being prepared as before, season it with nutmeg, ginger, pepper, a whole onion, and salt; fill the pye, then put in some large mace, half a pound of currans, and butter, close it up and put it in the oven; being half baked put in a pint of warmed clearet, and when you draw it to send it up, cut the lid in pieces, and stick it in the meat round the pye; or you may leave out onions, and put in sugar and verjuyce.

Otherways.

Take a loyn of mutton, cut it in steaks, and season it with nutmeg, pepper, and salt, then lay a layer of raisins and prunes in the bottom of the pye, steaks on them, and then whole cinamon, then more fruit and steaks, thus do it three times, and on the top put more fruit, and grapes, or slic't orange, dates, large mace, and butter, close it up and bake it, being baked, liquor it with butter, white wine and sugar, ice it, and serve it hot.

To bake Steak Pies the French way.

Season the steaks with pepper, nutmeg, and salt lightly, and set them by; then take a piece of the leanest of a leg of mutton, and mince it small with some beef suet and a few sweet herbs, as tops of tyme, penniroyal, young red sage, grated bread, yolks of eggs, sweet cream, raisins of the sun, &c. work all together, and make it into little balls, and rouls, put them into a deep round pye on the steaks, then put to them some butter, and sprinkle it with verjuyce, close it up and bake it, being baked cut it up, then roul sage leaves in butter, fry them, and stick them in the balls, serve the pye without a cover, and liquor it with the juyce of two or three oranges or lemons.

Otherways.

Bake these steaks in any of the foresaid-ways in patty-pan or dish, and make other paste called cold butter paste; take to a gallon of flower a pound and a half of butter, four or five eggs and but two whites, work up the butter and eggs into the flour, and being well wrought, put to it a little fair cold water, and make it up a stiff paste.

To bake a Gammon of Bacon.

Steep it all night in water, scrape it clean, and stuff it with all manner of sweet herbs, as sage, tyme, parsley, sweet marjoram, savory, violet-leaves, strawberry leaves, fennil, rose-mary, penniroyal, &c. being cleans'd and chopped small with some yolks of hard eggs, beaten nutmeg, and pepper, stuff it and boil it, and being fine and tender boil'd and cold, pare the under side, take off the skin, and season it with nutmeg and pepper, then lay it in your pie or pasty with a few whole cloves, and slices of raw bacon over it, and butter; close it up in pye or pasty of short paste, and bake it.

To bake wild Bore.

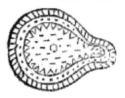

Take the leg, season it, and lard it very well with good big lard seasoned with nutmeg, pepper, and beaten ginger, lay it in a pye of the form as you see, being seasoned all over with the same spices and salt, then put a few whole cloves on it, a few bay-leaves, large slices of lard, and good store of butter, bake it in fine or course crust, being baked, liquor it with good sweet butter, and stop up the vent.

If to keep long, bake it in an earthen pan in the abovesaid seasoning, and being baked fill it up with butter, and you may keep it a whole year.

To bake your wild Bore that comes out of France.

Lay it in soak two days, then parboil it, and season it with pepper, nutmeg, cloves, and ginger; and when it is baked fill it up with butter.

To bake Red Deer.

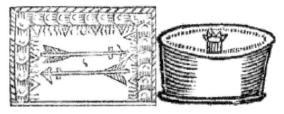

Take a side of red deer, bone it and season it, then take out the back sinew and the skin, and lard the fillets or back with great lard as big as your middle finger; being first seasoned with nutmeg, and pepper; then take four ounces of pepper, four ounces of nutmeg, and six ounces of salt, mix them well together, and season the side of venison; being well slashed with a knife in the inside for to make the seasoning enter; being seasoned, and a pie made according to these forms, put in some butter in the bottom of the pye, a quarter of an ounce of cloves, and a bay-leaf or two, lay on the flesh, season it, and coat it deep, then put on a few cloves, and good store of butter, close it up and bake it the space of eight or nine hours, but first baste the pie with six or seven eggs, beaten well together; being baked and cold fill it up with good sweet clarified butter.

Take for a side or half hanch of red deer, half a bushel of rye meal, being coursly searsed, and make it up very stiff with boiling water only.

If you bake it to eat hot, give it but half the seasoning, and liquor it with claret-wine, and good butter.

To bake Fallow-Dear to be eaten hot or cold.

Take a side of venison, bone and lard it with great lard as big as your little finger, and season it with two ounces of pepper, two ounces of nutmeg, and four ounces of salt; then have a pie made, and lay some butter in the bottom of it, then lay in the flesh, the inside downward, coat it thick with seasoning, and put to it on the top of the meat, with a few cloves, and good store of butter, close it up and bake it, the pye being first basted with eggs, being baked and cold, fill it up with clarified butter, and keep it to eat cold. Make the paste as you do for red deer, course drest through a boulter, a peck and a pottle of this meal will serve for a side or half hanch of a buck.

To bake a side or half Hanch to be eaten hot.

Take a side of a buck being boned, and the skins taken away, season it only with two ounces of pepper, and as much salt, or half an ounce more, lay it on a sheet of fine paste with two pound of beef-suet, finely minced and beat with a little fair water, and laid under it, close it up and bake it, and being fine and tender baked, put to it a good ladle-full of gravy, or good strong mutton broth.

To make a Paste for it.

Take a peck of flour by weight, and lay it on the pastery board, make a hole in the midst of the flour, and put to it five pound of good fresh butter, the yolks of six eggs and but four whites, work up the butter and eggs into the flour, and being well wrought together, put some fair water to it, and make it into a stiff paste.

In this fashion of fallow deer you may bake goat, doe, or a pasty of venison.

To make meer sauce, or a Pickle to keep Venison in that is tainted.

Take strong ale and as much vinegar as will make it sharp, boil it with some bay salt, and make a strong brine, scum it, and let it stand till it be cold, then put in your vinison twelve hours, press it, parboil it, and season it, then bake it as before is shown.

Other Sauce for tainted Venison.

Take your venison, and boil water, beer, and wine-vinegar together, and some bay-leaves, tyme, savory, rosemary, and fennil, of each a handful, when it boils put in your venison, parboil it well and press it, and season it as aforesaid, bake it for to be eaten cold or hot, and put some raw minced mutton under it.

Otherways to preserve tainted Venison.

Bury it in the ground in a clean cloth a whole night, and it will take away the corruption, savour, or stink.

Other meer Sauces to counterfeit Beef, or Muton to give it a Venison colour.

Take small beer and vinegar, and parboil your beef in it, let it steep all night, then put in some turnsole to it, and being baked, a good judgment shall not discern it from red or fallow deer.

Otherways to counterfeit Ram, Wether, or any Mutton for Venison.

Bloody it in sheeps, Lambs, or Pigs blood, or any good and new blood, season it as before, and bake it either for hot or cold. In this fashion you may bake mutton, lamb, or kid.

To make Umble-Pies.

Lay minced beef-suet in the bottom of the pie, or slices of interlarded bacon, and the umbles cut as big as small dice, with some bacon cut in the same form, and seasoned with nutmeg, pepper, and salt, fill your pyes with it, and slices of bacon and butter, close it up and bake it, and liquor it with claret, butter, and stripped tyme.

To make Pies of Sweet-breads or Lamb stones.

Parboil them and blanch them, or raw sweetbreads or stones, part them in halves, & season them with pepper, nutmeg, and salt, season them lightly; then put in the bottom of the pie some slices of interlarded bacon, & some pieces of artichocks or mushrooms, then sweet-breads or stones, marrow, gooseberries, barberries, grapes, or slic't lemon, close it up and bake it, being baked liquor it with butter only. Or otherwise with butter, white-wine, and sugar, and sometimes add some yolks of eggs.

To make minced Pies or Chewits of a Leg of Veal, Neats-Tongue, Turkey, or Capon.

Take to a good leg of veal six pound of beef-suet, then take the leg of veal, bone it, parboil it, and mince it very fine when it is hot; mince the suet by it self very fine also, then when they are cold mingle them together, then season the meat with a pound of sliced dates, a pound of sugar, an ounce of nutmegs, an ounce of pepper, an ounce of cinamon, half an ounce of ginger, half a pint of ver-juyce, a pint of rose-water, a preserved orange, or any peel fine minced, an ounce of caraway-comfits, and six pound of currans; put all these into a large tray with half a handful of salt, stir them up all together, and fill your pies, close them up, bake them, and being baked, ice them with double refined sugar, rose-water, and butter.

Make the paste with a peck of flour, and two pound of butter boil'd in fair water or liquor, make it up boiling hot.

To make minced Pies of Mutton.

Take to a leg of mutton four pound of beef-suet, bone the leg and cut it raw into small pieces, as also the suet, mince them together very fine, and being minc't season it with two pound of currans, two pound of raisins, two pound of prunes, an ounce of caraway seed, an ounce of nutmegs, an ounce of pepper, an ounce of cloves, and mace, and six ounces of salt; stir up all together, fill the pies, and bake them as the former.

To make minced Pies of Beef.

Take a stone or eight pound of beef, also eight pound of suet, mince them very small, and put to them eight ounces of salt, two ounces of nutmegs, an ounce of pepper, an ounce of cloves and mace, four pound of currans, and four pound of raisins, stir up all these together, and fill your pies.

Minced in the French fashion, called Pelipate, or in English Petits, made of Veal, Pork, or Lamb, or any kind of Venison, Beef, Poultrey, or Fowl.

Mince them with lard, and being minced, season them with salt, and a little nutmeg, mix the meat with some pine-apple-seed, and a few grapes or gooseber-ries; fill the pies and bake them, being baked liquor them with a little gravy.

Sometimes for variety in the Winter time, you may use currans instead of grapes or gooseberries, and yolks of hard eggs minced among the meat.

Minced Pies in the Italian Fashion.

Parboil a leg of veal, and being cold mince it with beef-suet, and season it with pepper, salt, and gooseberries; mix with it a little verjuyce, currans, sugar, and a little saffron in powder.

Forms of minced Pyes.

To make an extraordinary Pie, or a Bride Pye of several Compounds, being several distinct Pies on one bottom.

Provide cock-stones and combs, or lamb-stones, and sweet-breads of veal, a little set in hot water and cut to pieces; also two or three ox-pallats blanch't and slic't, a pint of oysters, slic't dates, a handful of pine kernels, a little quantity of broom buds, pickled, some fine interlarded bacon slic't; nine or ten chesnuts rosted and blancht season them with salt, nutmeg, and some large mace, and close it up with some butter. For the caudle, beat up some butter, with three yolks of eggs, some white or claret wine, the juyce of a lemon or two; cut up the lid, and pour on the lear, shaking it well together; then lay on the meat, slic't lemon, and pickled barberries, and cover it again, let these ingredients be put in the moddle or scollops of the Pye.

Several other Pies belong to the first form, but you must be sure to make the three fashions proportionably answering one the other; you may set them on one bottom of paste, which will be more convenient; or if you set them several you may bake the middle one full of flour, it being bak't and cold, take out the flour in the bottom, & put in live birds, or a snake, which will seem strange to the beholders, which cut up the pie at the Table. This is only for a Wedding to pass away the time.

Now for the other pies you may fill them with several ingredients, as in one you may put oysters, being parboild and bearded, season them with large mace, pepper, some beaten ginger, and salt, season them lightly and fill the Pie, then lay on marrow & some good butter, close it up and bake it. Then make a lear for it with white wine, the oyster liquor, three or four oysters bruised in pieces to make it stronger, but take out the pieces, and an onion, or rub the bottom of the dish with a clove of garlick; it being boil'd, put in a piece of butter, with a lemon, sweet herbs will be good boil'd in it, bound up fast together, cut up the lid, or make a hole to let the lear in, &c.

Another you may make of prawns and cockles, being seasoned as the first, but no marrow: a few pickled mushrooms, (if you have them) it being baked, beat up a piece of butter, a little vinegar, a slic't nutmeg, and the juyce of two or three oranges thick, and pour it into the Pye.

A third you may make a Bird pie; take young Birds, as larks pull'd and drawn, and a forced meat to put in the bellies made of grated bread, sweet herbs minced very small, beef-suet, or marrow minced, almonds beat with a little cream to keep them from oyling, a little parmisan (or none) or old cheese; season this meat with nutmeg, ginger, and salt, then mix them together, with cream and eggs like a pudding, stuff the larks with it, then season the larks with nutmeg, pepper, and salt, and lay them in the pie, put in some butter, and scatter between them pine-kernels, yolks of eggs and sweet herbs, the herbs and eggs being minced very small; being baked make a lear with the juyce of oranges and butter beat up thick, and shaken well together.

For another of the Pies, you may boil artichocks, and take only the bottoms for the Pie, cut them into quarters or less, and season them with nutmeg. Thus with several ingredients you may fill your other Pies.

For the outmost Pies they must be Egg-Pies.

Boil twenty eggs and mince them very small, being blanched, with twice the weight of them of beef-suet fine minced also; then have half a pound of dates slic't with a pound of raisins, and a pound of currans well washed and dryed, and half an ounce of cinamon fine beaten, and a little cloves and mace fine beaten, sugar a quarter of a pound, a little salt, a quarter of a pint of rose-water, and as much verjuyce, and stir and mingle all well together, and fill the pies, and close them, and bake them, they will not be above two hours a baking, and serve them all seventeen upon one dish, or plate, and ice them, or scrape sugar on them; every one of these Pies should have a tuft of paste jagged on the top.

To make Custards divers ways.

Take to a quart cream, ten eggs, half a pound of sugar, half a quarter of an ounce of mace, half as much ginger beaten very fine, and a spoonful of salt, strain them through a strainer; and the forms being finely dried in the oven, fill them full on an even hearth, and bake them fair and white, draw them and dish them on a dish and plate; then strow on them biskets red and white, stick muskedines red and white, and scrape thereon double refined sugar.

Make the paste for these custards of a pottle of fine flour, make it up with boiling liquor, and make it up stiff.

To make an Almond Custard.

Take two pound of almonds, blanch and beat them very fine with rosewater, then strain them with some two quarts of cream, twenty whites of eggs, and a pound of double refined sugar; make the paste as beforesaid, and bake it in a mild oven fine and white, garnish it as before and scrape fine sugar over all.

To make a Custard without Eggs.

Take a pound of almonds, blanch and beat them with rose-water into a fine paste, then put the spawn or row of a Carp or Pike to it, and beat them well together, with some cloves, mace, and salt, the spices being first beaten, and some ginger, strain them with some fair spring water, and put into the strained stuff half a pound of double refined sugar and a little saffron; when the paste is dried and ready to fill, put into the bottom of the coffin some slic't dates, raisins of the sun stoned, and some boiled currans, fill them and bake them; being baked, scrape sugar on them. Be sure always to prick your custards or forms before you set them in the oven.

If you have no row or spawn, put rice flour instead hereof.

To make an extraordinary good Cake.

Take half a bushel of the best flour you can get very finely searsed, and lay it upon a large Pastry board, make a hole in the midst thereof, and put to it three pound of the best butter you can get; with fourteen pound of currans finely picked and rubbed, three quarts of good new thick cream warm'd, two pound of fine sugar beaten, three pints of good new ale, barm or yeast, four ounces of cinamon fine beaten and searsed, also an ounce of beaten ginger, two ounces of nutmegs fine beaten and searsed; put in all these materials together, and work them up into an indifferent stiff paste, keep it warm till the oven be hot, then make it up and bake it, being baked an hour and a half ice it, then take four pound of double refined sugar, beat it, and searse it, and put it in a deep clean scowred skillet the quantity of a gallon, boil it to a candy height with a little rose-water, then draw the cake, run it all over, and set it into the oven, till it be candied.

To make a Cake otherways.

Take a gallon of very fine flour and lay it on the pastry board, then strain three or four eggs with a pint of barm, and put it into a hole made in the middle of the flour with two nutmegs finely beaten, an ounce of cinamon, and an ounce of cloves and mace beaten fine also, half a pound of sugar, and a pint of cream; put these into the flour with two spoonfuls of salt, and work it up good and stiff, then take half the paste, and work three pound of currans well picked & rubbed into it, then take the other part and divide it into two equal pieces, drive them out as broad as you wold have the cake, then lay one of the sheets of paste on a sheet of paper, and upon that the half that hath the currans, and the other part on the top, close it up round, prick it, and bake it; being baked, ice it with butter, sugar, and rose water, and set it again into the oven.

To make French Bread the best way.

Take a gallon of fine flour, and a pint of good new ale barm or yeast, and put it to the flour, with the whites of six new laid eggs well beaten in a dish, and mixt with the barm in the middle of the flour, also three spoonfuls of fine salt; then warm some milk and fair water, and put to it, and make it up pretty stiff, being well wrought and worked up, cover it in a boul or tray with a warm cloth till your oven be hot; then make it up either in rouls, or fashion it in little wooden dishes and bake it, being baked in a quick oven, chip it hot.

SECTION X.

To bake all manner of Curneld Fruits in Pyes, Tarts, or made Dishes, raw or preserved, as Quinces, Warden, Pears, Pippins, &c.

To bake a Quince Pye.

Take fair Quinces, core and pare them very thin, and put them in a Pye, then put it in two races of ginger slic't, as much cinamon broken into bits, and some eight or ten whole cloves, lay them in the bottom of the Pye, and lay on the Quinces close packed, with as much fine refined sugar as the Quinces weigh, close it up and bake it, and being well soaked the space of four or five hours, ice it.

Otherways.

Take a gallon of flour, a pound and a half of butter, six eggs, thirty quinces, three pound of sugar, half an ounce of cinamon, half an ounce of ginger, half an ounce of cloves, and some rose-water, make them in a Pye or Tart, and being baked stew on double refined sugar.

Otherways.

Bake these Quinces raw, slic't very thin, with beaten cinamon, and the same quantity of sugar, as before, either in tart, patty-pan, dish, or in cold butter-paste, sometimes mix them with wardens, pears or pipins, and some minced citron.

To make a Quince Pye otherways.

Take Quinces and preserve them, being first coared and pared, then make a sirrup of fine sugar and spring water, take as much as the quinces weigh, and to every pound of sugar a pint of fair water, make your sirrup in a preserving pan; being scumm'd and boil'd to sirrup, put in the quinces, boil them up till they be well coloured, & being cold, bake them in pyes whole or in halves, in a round tart, dish, or patty-pan with a cut cover, or in quarters; being baked put in the same sirrup, but before you bake them, put in more fine sugar, and leave the sirrups to put in afterwards, then ice it.

Thus you may do of any curnel'd fruits, as wardens, pippins pears, pearmains, green quodlings, or any good apples, in laid tarts, or cuts.

To make a slic't Tart of Quinces, Wardens, Pears, Pippins, in slices raw of divers Com-

pounds.

The foresaid fruits being finely pared, and slic't in very thine slices; season them with beaten cinamon, and candied citron minced, candied orange, or both, or raw orange peel, raw lemon peel, fennil-seed, or caraway-seed or without any of these compounds or spices, but the fruits alone one amongst the other; put to ten pippins six quinces, six wardens, eight pears, and two pound of sugar; close it up, bake it; and ice it as the former tarts.

Thus you may also bake it in patty-pan, or dish, with cold butter paste.

To bake Quinces, Wardens, Pears, Pippins, or any Fruits preserved to be baked in pies, Tarts, Patty-pan or Dish.

Preserve any of the foresaid in white-wine & sugar till the sirrup grow thick, then take the quinces out of it, and lay them to cool in a dish, then set them into the pye, and prick cloves on the tops with some cinamon, and good store of refined sugar, close them up with a cut cover, and being baked, ice it, and fill it up with the syrrup they were first boiled in.

Otherways.

You may bake them in an earthen pot with some claret-wine and sugar, and keep them for your use.

To make a Trotter Pye of Quinces, Wardens, Pears, &c.

Take them either severally or all together in quarters, or slic't raw, if in quarters put some whole ones amongst them, if slic't beaten spices, and a little butter and sugar; take to twelve quinces a pound of sugar, and a quarter of a pound of butter, close it up and bake it, and being bak't cut it up and mash the fruit to pieces, then put in some cream, and yolks of eggs beaten together, and put it into the Pye, stir all together, and cut the cover into five or six pieces like Lozenges, or three square, and scrape on sugar.

To make a Pippin Pye.

Take thirty good large pippins, pare them very thin, and make the Pye, then put in the pippins, thirty cloves, a quarter of an ounce of whole cinamon, and as much pared and slic't, a quarter of a pound of orangado, as much of lemon in sucket, and a pound & half of refined sugar, close it up and bake it, it will ask four hours baking, then ice it with butter, sugar, and rose-water.

To make a Pippin Tart according to this form.

Take fair pippins and pare them, then cut them in quarters, core them and stew them, in claret-wine, whole cinamon, and slic't ginger; stew them half an hour, then put them into a dish, and break them not, when they are cold, lay them one by one into the tart, then lay on some green cittern minced small, candied orange or coriander, put on sugar and close it up, bake it, and ice it, then scrape on sugar and serve it.

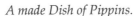

To make a Pippin Tart, either in Tart, Patty-Pan, or Dish.

Take ten fair pippins, preserve them in white wine, sugar, whole cinamon, slic't ginger, and eight or ten cloves, being finely preserved and well coloured, lay them on a cut tart of short paste; or in place of preserving you may bake them between two dishes in the oven for the foresaid use.

A made Dish of Pippins.

Take pippins, pare and slice them, then boil them in claret-wine in a pipkin, or between two dishes with some sugar, and beaten cinamon, when 'tis boiled good and thick, mash it like marmalade, and put in a dish of puff paste or short paste; acording to this form with a cut cover, and being baked ice it.

To preserve Pippins in slices.

Make pippins and slice them round with the coars or kernels in, as thick as a half crown piece, and some lemon-peel amongst them in slices, or else cut like small lard, or orange peel first boil'd and cut in the same manner; then make the syrup weight for weight, and being clarified and scummed clean, put in the pipins and boil them up quick; to a pound of sugar put a pint of fair water, or a pint of white-wine or claret, and make them of two colours.

To make a Warden or a Pear Tart quartered.

Take twenty good wardens, pare them, and cut them in a tart, and put to them two pound of refined sugar, twenty whole cloves, a quarter of an ounce of cinamon broke into little bits, and three races of ginger pared and slic't thin; then close up the tart and bake it, it will ask five hours baking, then ice it with a quarter of a pound of double refined sugar, rose-water, and butter.

Other Tart of Warden, Quinces, or Pears.

First bake them in a pot, then cut them in quarters, and coar them, put them in a tart made according to this form, close it up, and when it is baked, scrape on sugar.

To make a Tart of Green Pease.

Take green pease and boil them tender, then pour them out into a cullender, season them with saffron, salt, and put sugar to them and some sweet butter, then close it up and bake it almost an hour, then draw it forth of the oven and ice it, put in a little verjuyce, and shake them well together, then scrape on sugar, and serve it in.

To make a Tart of Hips.

Take hips, cut them, and take out the seeds very clean, then wash them and season them with sugar, cinamon, and ginger, close the tart, bake it, ice it, scrape on sugar, and serve it in.

To make a Tart of Rice.

Boil the rice in milk or cream, being tender boil'd pour it into a dish, & season it with nutmeg, ginger, cinamon, pepper, salt, sugar, and the yolks of six eggs, put it in the tart with some juyce of orange; close it up and bake it, being baked scrape on sugar, and so serve it up.

To make a tart of Medlers.

Take medlers that are rotten, strain them, and set them on a chaffing dish of coals, season them with sugar, cinamon, and ginger, put some yolks of eggs to them, let it boil a little, and lay it in a cut tart; being baked scrape on sugar.

To make a Cherry-Tart.

Take out the stones, and lay the cherries into the tart, with beaten cinamon, ginger, and sugar, then close it up, bake it, and ice it; then make a sirrup of muskedine, and damask water, and pour it into the tart, scrape on sugar, and so serve it.

To make a Strawberry-Tart.

Wash the strawberries, and put them into the Tart, season them with cinamon, ginger, and a little red wine, then put on sugar, bake it half an hour, ice it, scrape on sugar, and serve it.

To make a Taffety-Tart.

First wet the paste with butter and cold water, roul it very thin, then lay apples in the lays, and between every lay of apples, strew some fine sugar, and some lem-on-peel cut very small, you may also put some fennel-seed to them; let them bake an hour or more, then ice them with rose-water, sugar, and butter beaten together, and wash them over with the same, strew more fine sugar on them, and put them into the oven again, being enough serve them hot or cold.

To make an Almond Tart.

Strain beaten almonds with cream, yolks of eggs, sugar, cinamon, and ginger, boil it thick, and fill your tart, being baked ice it.

To make a Damson Tart.

Boil them in wine, and strain them with cream, sugar, cinamon, and ginger, boil it thick, and fill your tart.

To make a Spinage Tart of three colours, green, yellow, and white.

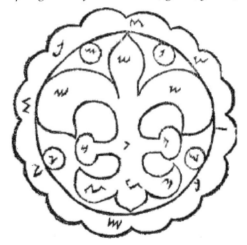

Take two handfuls of young tender spinage, wash it and put it into a skillet of boiling liquor; being tender boil'd have a quart of cream boil'd with some whole cinamon, quarterd nutmeg, and a grain of musk; then strain the cream, twelve yolks of eggs, and the boil'd spinage into a dish, with some rose-water, a little sack, and some fine sugar, boil it over a chaffing dish of coals, and stir it that it curd not, keep it till the tart be dried in the oven, and dish it in the form of three colours, green, white, and yellow.

To make Cream Tarts.

Thicken cream with muskefied bisket bread, and serve it in a dish, stick wa-fers round about it, and slices of preserved citron, and in the middle a preserved orange with biskets, the garnish of the dish being of puff paste.

Or you may boil quinces, wardens, pares, and pippins in slices or quarters, and strain them into cream, as also these fruits, melacattons, necturnes, apricocks, peaches, plumbs, or cherries, and make your tart of these forms.

To make a French Tart.

Take a pound of almonds, blanch and beat them into fine paste in a stone mortar, with rose-water, then beat the white breast of a cold roast turkey, being minced, and beat with it a pound of lard minc't, with the marrow of four bones, and a pound of butter, the juyce of three lemons, two pounds of hard sugar, being fine beaten, slice a whole green piece of citron in small slices, a quarter of a pound of pistaches, and the yolks of eight or ten eggs, mingle all together, then make a paste for it with cold butter, two or three eggs, and cold water.

To make a Quodling Pie.

Take green quodlings and quodle them, peel them and put them again into the same water, cover them close, and let them simmer on embers till they be very green, then take them up and let them drain, pick out the noses, and leave them on the stalks, then put them in a pie, and put to them fine sugar, whole cinamon, slic't ginger, a little musk, and rose-water, close them up with a cut cover, and as soon as it boils up in the oven, draw it, and ice it with rose-water, butter, and sugar.

Or you may preserve them and bake them in a dish with paste, tart, or pat-ty-pan.

To make a Dish in the Italian Fashion.

Take pleasant pears, slice them into thin slices, and put to them half as much sugar as they weigh, then mince some candied citron and candied orange small, mix it with the pears, and lay them on a bottom of cold butter paste in a patty-pan with some fine beaten cinamon, lay on the sugar and close it up, bake it, being baked, ice it with rose-water, fine sugar, and butter.

For the several Colours of Tarts.

If to have them yellow, preserved quinces, apricocks, necturnes, and melacat-tons, boil them up in white-wine with sugar, and strain them.

Otherways, strained yolks of eggs and cream.

For green tarts take green quodlings, green preserved apricocks, green pre-served plums, green grapes, and green gooseberries.

For red tarts, quinces, pippins, cherries, rasberries, barberries, red currans, red gooseberries, damsins.

For black tarts, prunes, and many other berries preserved.

For white tarts, whites of eggs and cream.

Of all manner of tart-stuff strained, that carries his colour black, as prunes, damsons, &c. For lard of set Tarts dishes, or patty-pans.

Tart stuff of damsons.

Take a postle of damsons and good ripe apples, being pared and cut into quarters, put them into an earthen pot with a little whole cinamon, slic't ginger, and sugar, bake them and being cold strain them with some rose-water, and boil the stuff thick, &c.

Other Tart stuff that carries its colour black.

Take three pound of prunes, and eight fair pippins par'd and cor'd, stew them together with some claret wine, some whole cinamon, slic't ginger, a sprig of rosemary, sugar, and a clove or two, being well stew'd and cold, strain them with rose-water, and sugar.

To make other black Tart Stuff.

Take twelve pound of prunes, and sixteen pound of raisins, wash them clean, and stew them in a pot with water, boil them till they be very tender, and then strain them through a course strainer; season it with beaten ginger and sugar, and give it a warm on the fire.

Yellow Tart Stuff.

Take twelve yolks of eggs, beat them with a quart of cream, and bake them in a soft oven; being baked strain them with some fine sugar, rose-water, musk, ambergriese, and a little sack, or in place of baking, boil the cream and eggs.

White Tart-Stuff.

Make the white tart stuff with cream, in all points as the yellow, and the same seasoning.

Green Tart-Stuff.

Take spinage boil'd, green peese, green apricocks, green plums quodled, peaches quodled, green necturnes quodled, gooseberries quodled, green sorrel, and the juyce of green wheat.

To bake Apricocks green.

Take young green apricocks, so tender that you may thrust a pin through the stone, scald them and scrape the out side, of putting them in water as you peel them till your tart be ready, then dry them and fill the tart with them, and lay on good store of fine sugar, close it up and bake it, ice it, scrape on sugar, and serve it up.

To bake Mellacattons.

Take and wipe them clean, and put them in a pie made scollop ways, or in some other pretty work, fill the pie, and put them in whole with weight for weight in refined sugar, close it up and bake it, being baked ice it.

Sometimes for change you may add to them some chips or bits of whole cinamon, a few whole cloves, and slic't ginger.

To preserve Apricocks, or any Plums green.

Take apricocks when they are so young and green, that you may put a needle through stone and all, but all other plums may be taken green, and at the highest growth, then put them in indifferent hot water to break them, & let them stand close cover'd in that hot water till a thin skin will come off with scraping, all this while they will look yellow; then put them into another skillet of hot water, and let them stand covered until they turn to a perfect green, then take them out, weigh them, take their weight in sugar and something more, and so preserve them. Clarifie the sugar with the white of an egg, and some water.

To preserve Apricocks being ripe.

Stone them, then weigh them with sugar, and take weight for weight, pare them and strow on the sugar, let them stand till the moisture of the apricocks hath wet the sugar, and stand in a sirrup: then set them on a soft fire, not suffering them to boil, till your sugar be all melted; then boil them a pretty space for half an hour, still stirring them in the sirrup, then set them by two hours, and boil them again till your sirrup be thick, and your apricocks look clear, boil up the sirrup higher, then take it off, and being cold put in the apricocks into a gally-pot or glass, close them up with a clean paper, and leather over all.

To preserve Peaches after the Venetian way.

Take twenty young peaches, part them in two, and take out the stones, then take as much sugar as they weigh, and some rose-water, put in the peaches, and make a sirrup that it may stand and stick to your fingers, let them boil softly a while, then lay them in a dish, and let them stand in the same two or three days, then set your sirrup on the fire, let it boil up, and then put in the peaches, and so preserve them.

To preserve Mellacattons.

Stone them and parboil them in water, then peel off the outward skin of them, they will boil as long as a piece of beef, and therefore you need not fear the breaking of them; when they are boil'd tender make sirrup of them as you do of any other fruit, and keep them all the year.

To preserve Cherries.

Take a pound of the smallest cherries, but let them be well coloured, boil them tender in a pint of fair water, then strain the liquor from the cherries and take two pound of other fair cherries, stone them, and put them in your preserving-pan, with a laying of cherries and a laying of sugar, then pour the sirrup of the other strained cherries over them, and let them boil as fast as maybe with a blazing fire, that the sirrup may boil over them; when you see that the sirrup is of a good colour, something thick, and begins to jelly, set them a cooling, and being cold pot them; and so keep them all the year.

To preserve Damsins.

Take damsins that are large and well coloured, (but not throw ripe, for then they will break) pick them clean and wipe them one by one; then weigh them, and to every pound of damsins you must take a pound of Barbary sugar, white & good, dissolved in half a pint or more of fair water; boil it almost to the height of a sirrup, and then put in the damsins, keeping them with a continual scuming and stirring, so let them boil on a gentle fire till they be enough, then take them off and keep them all the year.

To preserve Grapes as green as Grass.

Take grapes very green, stone them and cut them into little bunches, then take the like quantity of refin'd sugar finely beaten, & strew a row of sugar in your preserving pan, and a lay of grapes upon it, then strow on some more sugar upon them, put to them four or five spoonfuls of fair water, and boil them up as fast as you can.

To preserve Barberries.

Take barberries very fair and well coloured, pick out the stones, weigh them, and to every ounce of barberries take three ounce of hard sugar, half an ounce of pulp of barberries, and an ounce of red rose-water to dissolve the sugar; boil it to a sirrup, then put in the barberries and let them boil a quarter of an our, then take them up, and being cool pot them, and they will keep their colour all the year. Thus you may preserve red currans, &c.

To preserve Gooseberries green.

Take some of the largest gooseberries that are called Gascoyn gooseberries, set a pan of water on the fire, and when it is lukewarm put in the berries, and cover them close, keep them warm half an hour; then have another posnet of warm water, put them into that, in like sort quoddle them three times over in hot water till they look green; then pour them into a sieve, let all the water run from them, and put them to as much clarified sugar as will cover them, let them simmer leisurely close covered, then your gooseberries will look as green as leek blades, let them stand simmering in that sirrup for an hour, then take them off the fire, and let the sirrup stand till it be cold, then warm them once or twice, take them up, and let the sirrup boil by it self, pot them, and keep them.

To preserve Rasberries.

Take fair ripe rasberries, (but not over ripe) pick them from the stalk, then take weight for weight of double refined sugar, and the juyce of rasberries; to a pound of rasberries take a quarter of a pint of raspass juyce, and as much of fair water, boil up the sugar and liquor, and make the sirrup, scum it, and put in the raspass, stir them into the sirrup, and boil them not too much; being preserved take them up, and boil the sirrup by it self, not too long, it will keep the colour; being cold, pot them and keep them. Thus you may also preserve strawberries.

The time to preserve Green Fruits.

Gooseberries must be taken about *Whitsuntide*, as you see them in bigness, the long gooseberry will be sooner than the red; the white wheat plum, which is ever ripe in Wheat harvest, must be taken in the midst of *July*, the pear plum in the midst of *August*, the peach and pippin about *Bartholomew-tide*, or a little before; the grape in the first week of *September*. Note that to all your green fruits in general that you will preserve in sirup, you must take to every pound of fruit, a pound and two ounces of sugar, and a grain of musk; your plum, pippin and peach will have three quarters of an hour boiling, or rather more, and that very softly, keep the fruit as whole as you can; your grapes and gooseberries must boil half an hour something fast and they will be the fuller. Note also, that to all your Conserves you take the full weight of sugar, then take two skillets of water, and when they are scalding hot put the fruits first into one of them and when that grows cold put them in the other, changing them till they be about to peel, then peel them, and afterwards settle them in the same water till they look green, then take them and put them into sugar sirrup, and so let them gently boil till they come to a jelly; let them stand therein a quarter of an hour, then put them into a pot and keep them.

SECTION XI.

To make all manner of made Dishes, with or without Paste.

To make a Paste for a Pie.

T Ake to a gallon of flour a pound of butter, boil it in fair water, and make the paste up quick.

To make cool Butter Paste for Patty-Pans or Pasties.

Take to every peck of flour five pound of butter, the whites of six eggs, and work it well together with cold spring water; you must bestow a great deal of pains, and but little water, or you put out the millers eyes. This paste is good only for patty-pan and pasty.

Sometimes for this paste put in but eight yolks of eggs, and but two whites, and six pound of butter.

To make Paste for thin bak'd Meats.

The paste for your thin and standing bak'd meats must be made with boiling water, then put to every peck of flour two pound of butter, but let your butter boil first in your liquor.

To make Custard Paste.

Let it be only boiling water and flour without butter, or put sugar to it, which will add to the stiffness of it, & thus likewise all pastes for Cuts and Orangado Tarts, or such like.

Paste for made-Dishes in the Summer.

Take to a gallon of flour three pound of butter, eight yolks of eggs, and a pint of cream or almond milk, work up the butter and eggs dry into the flour, then put cream to it, and make it pretty stiff.

Paste Royal for made Dishes.

Take to a gallon of flour a pound of sugar, a quart of almond milk, a pound and half of butter, and a little saffron, work up all cold together, with some beaten cinamon, two or three eggs, rose-water, and a grain of ambergriese and musk.

Otherways.

Take a pottle of flour, half a pound of butter, six yolks of eggs, a pint of cream, a quarter of a pound of sugar, and some fine beaten cinamon, and work up all cold.

Otherways.

Take to a pottle of flour four eggs, a pound and a half of butter, and work them up dry in the flour, then make up the paste with a pint of white-wine, rose-water, and sugar.

To make Paste for Lent for made Dishes.

Take a quart of flour, make it up with almond-milk, half a pound of butter, and some saffron.

To make Puff-Paste divers ways.

The First Way.

Take a pottle of flour, mix it with cold water, half a pound of butter, and the whites of five eggs; mix them together very well and stiff, then roul it out very thin, and put flour under it and over it, then take near a pound of butter, and lay it in bits all over, double it in five or six doubles, this being done roul it out the second time, and serve it as at the first, then roul it out and cut it into what form, or for what use you please; you need not fear the curle, for it will divide it as often as you double it, which ten or twelve times is enough for any use.

The second way.

Take a quart of flour, and a pound and a half of butter, work the half pound of butter dry into the flour, then put three or four eggs to it, and as much cold water as will make it leith paste, work it in a piece of a foot long, then strew a little flour on the table, take it by the end, and beat it till it stretch to be long, then put the ends together, and beat it again, and so do five or six times, then work it up round, and roul it up broad; then beat your pound of butter with a rouling pin that it may be little, take little bits thereof, and stick it all over the paste, fold up your paste close, and coast it down with your rouling pin, roul it out again, and so do five or six times, then use it as you will.

The third way.

Break two eggs into three pints of flour, make it with cold water and roul it out pretty thick and square, then take so much butter as paste, lay it in ranks, and divide your butter in five pieces, that you may lay it on at five several times, roul your paste very broad, and stick one part of the butter in little pieces all over your paste, then throw a handful of flour slightly on, fold up your paste and beat it with a rowling-pin, so roul it out again, thus do five times, and make it up.

The fourth way.

Take to a quart of flour four whites and but two yolks of eggs, and make it up with as much cream as will make it up pretty stiff paste, then roul it out, and beat three quarters of a pound of butter of equal hardness of the paste, lay it on the paste in little bits at ten several times; drive out your paste always one way; and being made, use it as you will.

The fifth way.

Work up a quart of flour with half a pound of butter, three whites of eggs, and some fair spring water, make it a pretty stiff paste, and drive it out, then beat half a pound of more butter of equal hardness of the paste, and lay it on the paste in little bits at three several times, roul it out, and use it for what use you please.

Drive the paste out every time very thin.

A made Dish or Florentine of any kind of Tongue in Dish, Pye, or Patty-pan.

Take a fresh neats tongue, boil it tender and blanch it, being cold, cut it into little square bits as big as a nutmeg, and lard it with very small lard, then have another tongue raw, take off the skin, and mince it with beef-suet, then lay on one half of it in the dish or patty pan upon a sheet of paste; then lay on the tongue being larded and finely seasoned with nutmeg, pepper, and salt; and with the other minced tongue put grated bread to it, some yolks of raw eggs, some sweet herbs minced small, and made up into balls as big as a walnut, lay them on the other tongue, with some chesnuts, marrow, large mace, some grapes, gooseberries or barberries, some slices of interlarded bacon and butter, close it up and bake it, being baked liquor it with grape-verjuyce, beaten butter, and the yolks of three or four eggs strained with the verjuyce.

A made Dish of Tongues otherways.

Take neats-tongues or smaller tongues, boil them tender, and slice them thin, then season them with nutmeg, pepper, beaten cinamon; salt, and some ginger, season them lightly, and lay them in a dish on a bottom or sheet of paste mingled with some currans, marrow, large mace, dates, slic't lemon, grapes, barberries, or gooseberries and butter, close up the dish, and being almost baked, liquor it with white wine, butter, and sugar, and ice it.

Made Dish in Paste of two Rabits, with sweet liquor.

Take the rabits, flay them, draw them and cut them into small pieces as big as a walnut, then wash and dry them with a clean cloth, and season them with pepper, nutmeg, and salt; lay them on a bottom of paste, also lay on them dates, preserved lettice stalks, marrow, large mace, grapes, and slic't orange or lemon, put butter to it, close it up and bake it, being baked, liquor it with sugar, white-wine and butter; or in place of wine, grape-verjuyce, and strained yolks of raw eggs.

In winter bake them with currans, prunes, skirrets, raisins of the sun, *&c.*

A made Dish of Florentine, or a Partridge or Capon.

Being roasted and minced very small with as much beef-marrow, put to it two ounces of orangado minced small with as much green citron minced also, season the meat with a little beaten cloves, mace, nutmeg, salt, and sugar, mix all together, and bake it in puff paste; when it is baked, open it, and put in half a grain of musk or ambergriese, dissolved with a little rose-water, and the juyce of oranges, stir all together amongst the meat, cover it again, and serve it to the table.

To make a Florentine, or Dish, without Paste, or on Paste.

Take a leg of mutton or veal, shave it into thin slices, and mingle it with some sweet herbs, as sweet marjoram, tyme, savory, parsley, and rosemary, being

minced very small, a clove of garlick, some beaten nutmeg, pepper, a minced onion, some grated manchet, and three or four yolks of raw eggs, mix all together
with a little salt, some thin slices of interlarded bacon, and some oster-liquor, lay
the meat round the dish on a sheet of paste, or in the dish without paste, bake it,
and being baked, stick bay leaves round the dish.

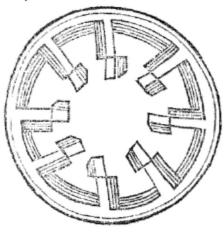

To bake Potatoes, Artichocks in a Dish, Pye, or Patty-pan either in Paste, or little Pasties.

Take any of these roots, and boil them in fair water, but put them not in till the
water boils, being tender boil'd, blanch them, and season them with nutmeg, pepper, cinamon, and salt, season them lightly, then lay on a sheet of paste in a dish,
and lay on some bits of butter, then lay on the potatoes round the dish, also some
eringo roots, and dates in halves, beef marrow, large mace, slic't lemon, and some
butter, close it up with another sheet of paste, bake it, and being baked, liquor it
with grape-verjuyce, butter and sugar, and ice it with rose-water and sugar.

To make a made Dish of Spinage in Paste baked.

Take some young spinage, and put it in boiling hot fair water, having boil'd
two or three walms, drain it from the water, chop it very small, and put it in a dish
with some beaten cinamon, salt, sugar, a few slic't dates, a grain of musk dissolved
in rose-water, some yolks of hard eggs chopped small, some currans and butter;
stew these foresaid materials on a chaffing dish of coals, then have a dish of short
paste on it, and put this composition upon it, either with a cut, a close cover, or
none; bake it, and being baked, ice it with some fine sugar, water, and butter.

Other made Dish of Spinage in Paste baked.

Boil spinage as beforesaid, being tender boil'd, drain it in a cullender, chop it
small, and strain it with half a pound of almond-paste, three or four yolks of eggs,
half a grain of musk, three or four spoonfuls of cream, a quartern of fine sugar,
and a little salt; then bake it on a sheet of paste on a dish without a cover, in a very
soft oven, being fine and green baked, stick it with preserved barberries, or strow
on red and white biskets, or red and white muskedines, and scrape on fine sugar.

A made Dish of Spinage otherways.

Take a pound of fat and well relished cheese, and a pound of cheese curds, stamp them in a mortar with some sugar, then put in a pint of juyce of spinage, a pint of cream, ten eggs, cinamon, pepper, nutmeg, and cloves, make your dish without a cover, according to this form, being baked ice it.

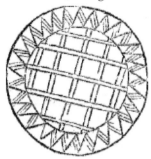

To make a made Dish of Barberries.

Take a good quantity of them and boil them with claret-wine, rose-water and sugar, being boil'd very thick, strain them, and put them on a bottom of puff paste in a dish, or short fine paste made of sugar, fine flour, cold butter, and cold water, and a cut cover of the same paste, bake it and ice it, and cast bisket on it, but before you lay on the iced cover, stick it with raw barberries in the pulp or stuff.

To make a Peasecod Dish, in a Puff Paste.

Take a pound of almonds, and a quarter of a pound of sugar, beat the almonds finely to a paste with some rose-water, then beat the sugar amongst them, mingle some sweet butter with it, and make this stuff up in puff paste like peasecods, bake them upon papers, and being baked, ice it with rose-water, butter, and fine sugar.

In this fashion you may make peasecod stuff of preserved quinces, pippins, pears, or preserved plums in puff paste.

Make Dishes of Frogs in the Italian Fashion.

Take the thighs and fry them in clarified butter, then have slices of salt Eels watered, flay'd, bon'd, boil'd, and cold, slice them in thin slices, and season both with pepper, nutmeg, and ginger, lay butter on your paste, and lay a rank of frog, and a rank of Eel, some currans, gooseberries or grapes, raisins, pine-apple seeds, juyce of orange, sugar, and butter; thus do three times, close up your dish, and being baked ice it.

Make your paste of almond milk, flour, butter, yolks of eggs, and sugar.

In the foresaid dish you may add fryed onions, yolks of hard eggs, cheese-curds, almond-paste, or grated cheese.

To make a made Dish of Marrow.

Take the marrow of two or three marrow-bones, cut it into pieces like great square dice, and put to it a penny manchet grated fine, some slic't dates, half a quartern of currans, a little cream, rosted wardens, pippins or quinces slic't, and two or three yolks of raw eggs, season them with cinamon, ginger, and sugar, and mingle all together.

A made Dish of Rice in Puff Paste.

Boil your rice in fair water very tender, scum it, and being boil'd put it in a dish, then put to it butter, sugar, nutmeg, salt, rose-water, and the yolks of six or eight eggs, put it in a dish, of puff paste, close it up and bake it, being baked, ice it, and caste on red and white biskets, and scraping sugar.

Sometimes for change you may add boil'd currans and beaten cinamon, and leave out nutmeg.

Otherways of Almond-Paste, and boiled Rice.

Mix all together with some cream, rose-water, sugar, cinamon, yolks of eggs, salt, some boil'd currans, and butter; close it up and bake it in puff-paste, ice it, and cast on red and white biskets and scrape on sugar.

Otherways a Made Dish of Rice and Paste.

Wash the rice clean, and boil it in cream till it be somewhat thick, then put it out into a dish, and put to it some sugar, butter, six or eight yolks of eggs, beaten cinamon, slic't dates, currans, rose-water, and salt, mix all together, and bake it in puff paste or short paste, being baked ice it, and cast biskets on it.

To make a made Dish of Rice, Flour, and Cream.

Take half a pound of rice, dust and pick it clean, then wash it, dry it, lay it abroad in a dish as thin as you can or dry it in a temperate oven, being well dried, rub it, and beat it in a mortar till it be as fine as flour; then take a pint of good thick cream, the whites of three new laid eggs, well beaten together, and a little rose-water, set it on a soft fire, and boil it till it be very thick, then put it in a platter and let it stand till it be cold, then slice it out like leach, cast some bisket upon it, and so serve it.

To make a made Dish of Rice, Prunes, and Raisins.

Take a pound of prunes, and as many raisins of the sun, pick and wash them, then boil them with water and wine, of each a like quantity; when you first set them on the fire, put rice flour to them, being tender boil'd strain them with half a pound of sugar, and some rose-water, then stir the stuff till it be thick like leach, put it in a little earthen pan, being cold slice it, dish it, and cast red and white bisket on it.

To make a made Dish of Blanchmanger.

Take a pint of cream, the whites of six new laid eggs, and some sugar; set them over a soft fire in a skillet and stir it continually till it be good and thick, then strain it, and being cold, dish it on a puff-paste bottom with a cut cover, and cast biskets on it.

A made Dish of Custard stuff, called an Artichock Dish.

Boil custard stuff in a clean scowred skillet, stir it continually, till it be something thick, then put it in a clean strainer, and let it drain in a dish, strain it with a little musk or ambergriese, then bake a star of puff paste on a paper, being baked take it off the paper, and put it in a dish for your stuff, then have lozenges also ready baked of puff paste, stick it round with them, and scrape on fine sugar.

A made Dish of Butter and eggs.

Take the yolks of twenty four eggs, and strain them with cinamon, sugar, and salt; then put melted butter to them, some fine minced pippins, and minced citron, put it on your dish of paste, and put slices of citron round about it, bar it with puff paste, and the bottom also, or short paste in the bottom.

To make a made dish of Curds.

Take some tender curds, wring the wehy from them very well, then put to them two raw eggs, currans, sweet butter, rose-water, cinamon, sugar, and mingle all together, then make a fine paste with flour, yolks of egs, rose-water, & other water, sugar, saffron, and butter, wrought up cold, bake it either in this paste or in puff-paste, being baked ice it with rose-water, sugar, and butter.

To make a Paste of Violets, Cowslips, Burrage, Bugloss, Rosemary Flowers, &c.

Take any of these flowers, pick the best of them, and stamp them in a stone mortar, then take double refined sugar, and boil it to a candy height with as much rosewater as will melt it, stir it continually in the boiling, and being boiled thick, cast it into lumps upon a pye plate, when it is cold, box them, and keep them all the year in a stove.

To make the Portugal Tarts for banquetting.

Take a pound of marchpane paste being finely beaten, and put into it a grain of musk, six spoonfuls of rose-water, and the weight of a groat of Orris Powder, boil all on a chaffing dish of coals till it be something stiff; then take the whites of two eggs, beaten to froth, put them into it, and boil it again a little, let it stand till it be cold, mould it, and roul it out thin; then take a pound more of almond-paste unboil'd, and put to it four ounces of caraway-seed, a grain of musk, and three drops of oyl of lemons, roul the paste into small rouls as big as walnuts, and lay these balls into the first made paste, flat them down like puffs with your thumbs a little like figs and bake them upon marchpane wafers.

To make Marchpane.

Take two pounds of almonds blanch't and beaten in a stone mortar, till they begin to come to a fine paste, then take a pound of sifted sugar, put it in the mortar with the almonds, and make it into a perfect paste, putting to it now and then in the beating of it a spoonful of rose-water, to keep it from oyling; when you have beat it to a puff paste, drive it out as big as a charger, and set an edge about it as you do upon a quodling tart, and a bottom of wafers under it, thus bake it in an oven or baking pan; when you see it is white, hard, and dry, take it out, and ice it with rose-water and sugar being made as thick as butter for fritters, to spread it on with a wing feather, and put it into the oven again; when you see it rise high, then take it out and garnish it with some pretty conceits made of the same stuff, slick long comfets upright on it, and so serve it.

To make Collops like Bacon of Marchpane.

Take some of your Marchpane paste and work it with red sanders till it be red, then roul a broad sheet of white marchpane paste, and a sheet of red paste, three of white, and four of red, lay them one upon another, dry it, cut it overthwart, and it will look like collops of bacon.

To make Almond Bread.

Take almonds, and lay them in water all night, blanch them and slice them, take to every pound of almonds a pound of fine sugar finely beat, & mingle them together, then beat the whites of 3 eggs to a high froth, & mix it well with the almonds & sugar; then have some plates and strew some flour on them, lay wafers on them and almonds with edges upwards, lay them as round as you can, and scrape a little sugar on them when they are ready to set in the oven, which must not be so hot as to colour white paper;[4] being a little baked take them out, set them on a plate, then put them in again, and keep them in a stove.

To make Almond Bisket.

Take the whites of four new laid eggs and two yolks, beat them together very well for an hour, then have in readiness a quarter of a pound of the best almonds blanched in cold water, beat them very small with rosewater to keep them from oiling, then have a pound of the best loaf sugar finely beaten, beat it in the eggs a while, then put in the almonds, and five or six spoonfuls of fine flour, so bake them on paper, plates, or wafers; then have a little fine sugar in a piece of tiffany, dust them over as they go into the oven, and bake them as you do bisket.

To make Almond-Cakes.

Take a pound of almonds, blanch them and beat them very small in a little rose-water where some musk hath been steeped, put a pound of sugar to them fine beaten, and four yolks of eggs, but first beat the sugar and the eggs well together,

---

[4] which must not be so hot as to colour white paper; Text as printed at page break:

then put them to the almonds and rose-water, and lay the cakes on wafers by half spoonfuls, set them into an oven after manchet is baked.

To make Almond-Cakes otherways.

Take a pound of the best Jordan almonds, blanch them in cold water as you do marchpane, being blanched wipe them dry in a clean cloth, & cut away all the rotten from them, then pound them in a stone-motar, & sometimes in the beating put in a spoonful of rose-water wherein you must steep some musk; when they are beaten small mix the almonds with a pound of refined sugar beaten and searsed; then put the stuff on a chafing-dish of coals in a made dish, keep it stirring, and beat the whites of seven eggs all to froth, put it into the stuff and mix it very well together, drop it on a white paper, put it on plates, and bake them in an oven; but they must not be coloured.

To make white Ambergriese Cakes.

Take the purest refined sugar that can be got, beat it and searse it; then have six new laid eggs, and beat them into a froth, take the froth as it riseth, and drop it into the sugar by little and little, grinding it still round in a marble mortar and pestle, till it be throughly moistened, and wrought thin enough to drop on plates; then put in some ambergriese, a little civet, and some anniseeds well picked, then take your pie plates, wipe them, butter them, and drop the stuff on them with a spoon in form of round cakes, put them into a very mild oven and when you see them be hard and rise a little, take them out and keep them for use.

To make Sugar-Cakes or Jambals.

Take two pound of flour, dry it, and season it very fine, then take a pound of loaf sugar, beat it very fine, and searse it, mingle your flour and sugar very well; then take a pound and a half of sweet butter, wash out the salt and break it into bits into the flour and sugar, then take the yolks of four new laid eggs, four or five spoonfuls of sack, and four spoonfuls of cream, beat all these together, put them into the flour, and work it up into paste, make them into what fashion you please, lay them upon papers or plates, and put them into the oven; be careful of them, for a very little thing bakes them.

To make Jemelloes.

Take a pound of fine sugar, being finely beat, and the yolks of four new laid eggs, and a grain of musk, a thimble full of caraway seed searsed, a little gum dragon steeped in rose-water, and six spoonfuls of fine flour beat all these in a thin paste a little stiffer then butter, then run it through a butter-squirt of two or three ells long bigger then a wheat straw, and let them dry upon sheets of paper a quarter of an hour, then tie them in knots or what pretty fashion you please, and when they be dry, boil them in rose-water and sugar; it is an excellent sort of banqueting.

To make Jambals.

Take a pint of fine wheat flour, the yolks of three or four new laid eggs, three or four spoonfuls of sweet cream, a few anniseeds, and some cold butter, make it into paste, and roul it into long rouls, as big as a little arrow, make them into divers knots, then boil them in fair water like simnels; bake them, and being baked, box them and keep them in a stove. Thus you may use them, and keep them all the year.

To make Sugar Plate.

Take double refined sugar, sift it very small through a fine searse, then take the white of an egg, gum dragon, and rose-water, wet it, and beat it in a mortar till you are able to mould it, but wet it not to much at the first. If you will colour it, and the colour be of a watry substance, put it in with the rose-water, if a powder, mix it with your sugar before you wet it; when you have beat it in the mortar, and that it is all wet, and your colour well mixt in every place, then mould it and make it into what form you please.

To make Muskedines called Rising Comfits or Vissing Comfits.

Take half a pound of refined sugar, being beaten and searsed, put into it two grains of musk, a grain of civet, two grains of ambergriese, and a thimble full of white orris powder, beat all these with gum-dragon steeped in rose-water; then roul it as thin as you can, and cut it into little lozenges with your iging-iron, and stow them in some warm oven or stove, then box them and keep them all the year.

To make Craknels.

Take half a pound of fine flour dryed and searsed, and as much fine sugar searsed, mingled with a spoonfull of coriander-seed bruised, and two ounces of butter rubbed amongst the flour and sugar, wet it with the yolks of two eggs, half a spoonful of white rose-water, and two spoonfuls of cream, or as much as will wet it, work the paste till it be soft and limber to roul and work, then roul it very thin, and cut them round by little plats, lay them upon buttered papers, and when they go into the oven, prick them, and wash the tops with the yolk of an egg, beaten and made thin with rose-water or fair water; they will give with keeping, therfore before they are eaten they must be dried in a warm oven to make them crisp.

To make Mackeroons.

Take a pound of the finest sugar, and a pound of the best Jordan-almonds, steep them in cold water, blanch them and pick out the spots: then beat them to a perfect paste in a stone mortar, in the beating of them put rose-water to them to keep them from oyling, being finely beat, put them in a dish with the sugar, and set them over a chafing-dish of coals, stir it till it will come clean from the bottom of the dish, then put in two grains of musk, and three of ambergriese.

To make the Italian Chips.

Take some paste of flowers, beat them to fine powder, and searse or sift them; then take some gum-dragon steeped in rose-water, beat it to a perfect paste in a marble mortar, then roul it thin, and lay one colour upon another in a long roul, roul them very thin, then cut them overthwart, and they will look of divers pretty colours like marble.

To make Bisket Bread.

Take a pound of sugar searsed very fine, a pound of flour well dryed, twelve eggs and but six whites, a handful of caraway-seed, and a little salt; beat all these together the space of an hour, then your oven being hot, put them into plates or tin things, butter them and wipe them, a spoonful into a plate is enough, so set them into the oven, and make it as hot as to bake them for manchet.

To make Bisquite du Roy.

Take a pound of fine searsed sugar, a pound of fine flour, and six eggs, beat them very well, then put them all into a stone mortar, and pound them for the space of an hour and a half, let it not stand still, for then it will be heavy, and when you have beaten it so long a time, put in halfe an ounce of anniseed; then butter over some pie plates, and drop the stuff on the plate as fast as two or three can with spoons, shape them round as near as you can, and set them into an oven as hot as for manchet, but the less they are coloured the better.

Bisquite du Roy otherways.

Take to a pound of flour a pound of sugar, and twelve new laid eggs, beat them in a deep dish, then put to them two grains of musk dissolved, rose-water, anniseed, and coriander-seed, beat them the space of an hour with a wooden spatter; then the oven being ready, have white tin molds butter'd, and fill them with this Bisquite, strow double refined sugar in them, and bake them when they rise out of the moulds, draw them and put them on a great pasty-plate or pye-plate, and dry them in a stove, and put them in a square lattin box, and lay white papers betwixt every range or rank, have a padlock to it, and set it over a warm oven, so keep them, and thus for any kind of bisket, mackeroons, marchpane, sugar plates, or pasties, set them in a temperate place where they may not give with every change of weather, and thus you may keep them very long.

To make Shell Bread.

Take a quarter of a pound of rice flour, a quarter of a pound of fine flour, the yolks of four new laid eggs, and a little rose-water, and a grain of musk; make these into a perfect paste, then roul it very thin and bake it in great muscle-shells, but first roast the shells in butter melted where they be baked, boil them in melted sugar as you boil a simmel, then lay them on the bottom of a wooden sieve, and they will eat as crisp as a wafer.

To make Bean Bread.

Take two pound of blanched almonds and slice them, take to them two pound of double refined sugar finely beaten and searsed, five whites of eggs beaten to froth, a little musk steeped to rose-water and some anniseeds, mingle them all together in a dish, and bake them on pewter-plates buttered, then afterwards dry them and them.

To make Ginger-Bread.

Take a pound of Jordan Almonds, and a penny manchet grated and sifted and mingled among the almond paste very fine beaten, an ounce of slic't ginger, two thimble fuls of liquoras and anniseed in powder finely searsed, beat all in a mortar together, with two or three spoonfuls of rose-water, beat them to a perfect paste with half a pound of sugar, mould it, and roul it thin, then print it and dry it in a stove, and guild it if you please.

Thus you may make gingerbread of sugar plate, putting sugar to it as above-said.

To make Ipocras.

Take to a gallon of wine, three ounces of cinamon, two ounces of slic't ginger, a quarter of an ounce of cloves, an ounce of mace, twenty corns of pepper, an ounce of nutmegs, three pound of sugar, and two quarts of cream.

Otherways.

Take to a pottle of wine, an ounce of cinamon, an ounce of ginger, an ounce of nutmegs, a quarter of an ounce of cloves, seven corns of pepper, a handful of rosemary-flowers, and two pound of sugar.

To make excellent Mead much commended.

Take to every quart of honey a gallon of fair spring water, boil it well with nutmeg and ginger bruised a little, in the boiling scum it well, and being boil'd set it a cooling in severall vessels that it may stand thin, then the next day put it in the vessel, and let it stand a week or two, then draw it in bottles.

If it be to drink in a short time you may work it as beer, but it will not keep long.

Or take to every gallon of water, a quart of honey, a quarter of an ounce of mace, as much ginger and cinnamon, and half as much cloves, bruise them, and use them as abovesaid.

Otherways.

Take five quarts and a pint of water, warm it, and put to it a quart of honey, and to every gallon of liquor one lemon, and a quarter of an ounce of nutmegs; it must boil till the scum rise black, and if you will have it quickly ready to drink, squeeze into it a lemon when you tun it, and tun it cold.

To make Metheglin.

Take all sorts of herbs that are good and wholesome as balm, mint, rosemary, fennil, angelica, wild time, hysop, burnet, agrimony, and such other field herbs, half a handful of each, boil and strain them, and let the liquor stand till the next day, being setled take two gallons and a half of honey, let it boil an hour, and in the boiling scum it very clean, set it a cooling as you do beer, and when it is cold, take very good barm and put it into the bottom of the tub, by a little & a little as to beer, keeping back the thick setling that lieth in the bottom of the vessel that it is cooled in; when it is all put together cover it with a cloth and let it work very near three days, then when you mean to put it up, skim off all the barm clean, and put it up into a vessel, but you must not stop the vessel very close in three or four days, but let it have some vent to work; when it is close stopped you must look often to it, and have a peg on the top to give it vent, when you heare it make a noise as it will do, or else it will break the vessel.

Sometimes make a bag and put in good store of slic't ginger, some cloves and cinamon, boil'd or not.

SECTION XII.

To make all manner of Creams, Sack-Possets, Sillabubs, Bla-mangers, White-Pots, Fools, Wassels, &c.

To make Apple Cream.

T Ake twelve pippins, pare and slice, or quarter them, put them into a skillet with some claret wine, and a race of ginger sliced thin, a little lemon-peel cut small, and some sugar; let all these stew together till they be soft, then take them off the fire and put them in a dish, and when they be cold take a quart of cream boil'd with a little nutmeg, and put in of the apple stuff to make it of what thickness you please, and so serve it up.

To make Codling Cream.

Take twenty fair codlings being peeld and codled tender and green, put them in a clean silver-dish, filled half full of rose-water, and half a pound of sugar, boil all this liquor together till half be consumed, and keep it stirring till it be ready, then fill up the dish with good thick and sweet cream, stir it till it be well mingled, and when it hath boil'd round about the dish, take it off, sweeten it with fine sugar, and serve it cold.

Otherways.

Codle forty fair codlings green and tender, then peel and core them, and beat them in a mortar, strain them with a quart of cream, and mix them well together in a dish with fine sugar, sack, musk, and rose-water. Thus you may do with any fruit you please.

To boil Cream with Codlings.

Boil a quart of cream with mace, sugar, two yolks of eggs, two spoonfulls of rose water, and a grain of ambergriese, put it into the cream, and set them over the fire till they be ready to boil, then set them to cool, stirring it till it be cold; then take a quart of green codling stuff strained, put it into a silver dish, and mingle it with cream.

To make Quince-Cream.

Take and boil them in fair water, but first let the water boil, then put them in and being tender boil'd take them up and peel them, strain them and mingle it with fine sugar, then take some very good and sweet cream, mix all together and make it of a fit thickness, or boil the cream with a stick of cinamon, and let it stand till it be cold before you put it to the quinces. Thus you may do wardens or pears.

To make Plum Cream.

Take any kind of Plums, Apricocks, or the like, and put them in a dish with some sugar, white-wine, sack, claret, or rose-water, close them up with a piece of paste between two dishes; being baked and cold, put to them cream boil'd with eggs, or without, or raw, and scrape on sugar, &c.

To make Gooseberry Cream.

Codle them green, and boil them up with sugar, being preserved put them into the cream strain'd as whole, scrape sugar on them, and so serve them cold in boil'd or raw cream. Thus you may do strawberries, raspas, or red currans, put in raw cream whole, or serve them with wine and sugar in a dish without cream.

To make Snow Cream.

Take a quart of cream, six whites of eggs, a quartern of rose-water, a quarter of a pound of double refined sugar, beat them together in a deep bason or a boul dish, then have a fine silver dish with a penny manchet, the bottom and upper crust being taken away, & made fast with paste to the bottom of the dish, and a streight sprig of rosemary set in the middle of it; then beat the cream and eggs together, and as it froatheth take it off with a spoon and lay it on the bread and rosemary till you have fill'd the dish. You may beat amongst it some musk and ambergriese dissolv'd, and gild it if you please.

To make Snow Cream otherways.

Boil a quart of cream with a stick of cinamon, and thicken it with rice flour, the yolks of two or three eggs, a little rose-water, sugar, and salt, give it a walm, and put it in a dish, lay clouted cream on it, and fill it up with whip cream or cream that cometh out of the top of a churn when the butter is come, disht out of a squirt or some other fine way, scrape on sugar, sprinkle it with rosewater, and stick some pine-apple-seeds on it.

Otherways.

Take three pints of cream, and the whites of seven eggs, strain them together, with a little rosewater and as much sugar as will sweeten it; then take a stick of a foot long, and split it in four quarters, beat the cream with it, or else with a whisk, and when the snow riseth, put it in a cullender with a spoon, that the thin may run from it, when you have snow enough, boil the rest with cinamon, ginger, and cloves, seeth it till it be thick, then strain it and when it is cold, put it in a clean dish, and lay your snow upon it.

To make Snow Cream otherways with Almonds.

Take a quart of good sweet cream, and a quarter of a pound of almond paste fine beaten with rose-water, and strained with half a pint of white-wine, put some orange-peel to it, a slic't nutmeg, and three sprigs of rosemary, let it stand two or three hours in steep; then put some double refined sugar to it, and strain it into a bason, beat it till it froth and bubble, and as the froth riseth, take it off with a spoon, and lay it in the dish you serve it up in.

To make a Jelly of Almonds as white as Snow.

Take a pound of almonds, steep them in cold water six hours, and blanch them into cold water, then make a decoction of half a pound of ising-glass, with two quarts of white wine and the juyce of two lemons, boil it till half be wasted, then let it cool and strain it, mingle it with the almonds, and strain them with a pound of double refined sugar, & the juyce of two lemons, turn it into colours, red, white, or yellow, and put it into egg shells, or orange peels, and serve them on a pye plate upon a dish.

To Make Almond Cream.

Take half a pound of almond paste beaten with ros-water, and strain it with a quart of cream, put it in a skillet with a stick of cinamon and boil it, stir it continually, and when it is boiled thick, put sugar to it, and serve it up cold.

To make Almond Cream otherways.

Take thick almond milk made with fair spring-water, and boil it a little then take it from the fire, and put to a little salt and vinegar, cast it into a clean strainer and hang it upon a pin over a dish, then being finely drained, take it down and put it in a dish, put to it some fine beaten sugar, and a little sack, muskedine, or white wine, dish it on a silver dish, and strow on red Biskets.

Otherways.

Take a quart of cream, boil it over night, then in the morning have half a pound of almonds blanched and fine beaten, strain them with the cream, and put to it a quarter of a pound of double refined sugar, a little rose-water, a little fine ginger and cinamon finely searsed, and mixed all together, dish it in a clean silver dish with fine carved sippets round about it.

To make Almond Cheese.

Take almonds being beaten as fine as marchpane paste, then have a sack-posset with cream and sack, mingle the curd of the posset with almond paste, and set it on a chafing-dish of coals, put some double refined sugar to it and some rose-water; then fashion it on a pye-plate like a fresh cheese, put it in a dish, put a little cream to it, scrape sugar, on it, and being cold serve it up.

To make an excellent Cream.

Take a quart of cream, and set it a boiling, with a large mace or two, whilst it is boiling cut some thin sippets, and lay them in a very fine clean dish, then have seven or eight yolks of eggs strained with rose-water, put some sugar to them, then take the cream from the fire, put in the eggs, and stir all together, then pour it on the slices of fine manchet, and being cold scrape on sugar, and so serve it.

To make Cream otherways.

Take a quart of cream, and boil it with four or five large maces, and a stick of whole cinamon; when it hath boiled a little while, have seven or eight yolks of eggs dissolved with a little cream, take the cream from the fire and put in the eggs, stir them well into the boiled cream, and put it in a clean dish, take out the spices, and when it is cold stick it with those maces and cinamon. Thus you may do with the whites of the eggs with cream.

To make cast Cream.

Take a quart of cream, a pint of new milk, and the whites of six eggs, strain them together and boil it, in the boiling stir it continnally till it be thick, then put to it some verjuyce, and put it into a strainer, hang it on a nail or pin to drain the whey from it, then strain it, put some sugar to it and rose-water; drain it in a fair dish, and strow on some preserved pine-kernels, or candied pistaches. In this fashion you may do it of the yolks of eggs.

To make Clouted Cream.

Take three galons of new milk, and set it on the fire in a clean scowred brass pan or kettle till it boils, then make a hole in the middle of the milk, & take three pints of good cream and put into the hole as it boileth, boil it together half an hour, then divide it into four milk pans, and let it cool two days, if the weather be not too hot, then take it up with a slice or scummer, put it in a dish, and sprinkle it with rose-water, lay one clod upon another, and scrape on sugar.

To make clouted Cream otherways extraordinary.

Take four gallons of new milk from the cow, set it over the fire in clean scowred pan or kettle to scald ready to boil, strain it through a clean strainer and put it into several pans to cool, then take the cream some six hours after, and put it in the dish you mean to serve it in, season it with rose-water, sugar, and musk, put some raw cream to it, and some snow cream on that.

To make clouted Cream otherways.

Take a gallon of new milk from the cow, two quarts of cream and twelve spoonfuls of rose-water, put these together in a large milk-pan, and set it upon a fire of charcoal well kindled, (you must be sure the fire be not too hot) and let it stand a day and a night, then take it off and dish it with a slice or scummer, let no milk be in it, and being disht and cut in fine little pieces, scrape sugar on it.

To make a very good Cream.

When you churn butter, take out half a pint of cream just as it begins to turn to butter, (that is, when it is a little frothy) then boil a quart of good thick and new cream, season it with sugar and a little rose-water, when it is quite cold, mingle it very well with that you take out of the churn, and so dish it.

To make a Sack Cream.

Take a quart of cream, and set it on the fire, when it is boiled, drop in six or eight drops of sack, and stir it well to keep it from curdling, then season it with sugar and strong water.

To make Cabbidge Cream.

Set six quarts of new milk on the fire, and when it boils empty it into ten or twelve earthen pans or bowls as fast as you can without frothing, set them where they may come, and when they are a little cold, gather the cream that is on the top with your hand, rumpling it together, and lay it on a plate, when you have laid three or four layers on one another, wet a feather in rose-water and musk and stroke over it, then searse a little grated nutmeg, and fine sugar, (and if you please, beat some musk and ambergriese in it) and lay three or four lays more on as before; thus do till you have off all the cream in the bowls, then put all the milk to boil again, and when it boils set it as you did before in bowls, and so use it in like manner; it will yield four or five times seething, which you must use as before, that it may lye round and high like a cabbige; or let one of the first bowls stand because the cream may be thick and most crumpled, take that up last to lay on uppermost, and when you serve it up searse or scrape sugar on it; this must be made over night for dinner, or in the morning for supper.

To make Stone Cream.

Take a quart of cream, two or three blades of large mace, two or three little sticks of cinamon, and six spoonfulls of rosewater, season it sweet with sugar, and boil it till it taste well of the spice, then dish it, and stir it till it be as cold as milk from the cow, then put in a little runnet and stir it together, let it stand and cool, and serve it to the table.

To make Whipt Cream.

Take a whisk or a rod and beat it up thick in a bowl or large bason, till it be as thick as the cream that comes off the top of a churn, then lay fine linning clouts on saucers being wet, lay on the cream, and let it rest two or three hours, then turn them into a fine silver dish, put raw cream to them, and scrape on sugar.

To make Rice Cream.

Take a quart of cream, two handfuls of rice flour, and a quarter of a pound of sugar, mingle the flour and sugar very well together, and put it in the cream; then beat the yolk of an egg with a little rose-water, put it to the cream and stir them all together, set it over a quick fire, keeping it continually stirring till it be as thick as pap.

To make another rare Cream.

Take a pound of almond paste fine beaten with rose-water, mingle it with a quart of cream, six eggs, a little sack, half a pound of sugar, and some beaten nutmeg; strain them and put them in a clean scowred skillet, and set it on a soft fire, stir it continually, and being well incorporated, dish it, and serve it with juyce of orange, sugar, and stick it full of canded pistaches.

To make a white Leach of Cream.

Take a quart of cream, twelve spoonfuls of rose-water, two grains of musk, two drops of oyl of mace, or two large maces, boil them with half a pound of sugar, and half a pound of the whitest ising-glass; being first steeped and washed clean, then run it through your jelly-bag, into a dish; when it is cold slice it into chequerwork, and serve it on a plate. This is the best way to make leach.

To make other Leach with Almonds.

Take two ounces of ising-glass, lay it two hours in fair water; then boil it in clear spring water, and being well digested set it to cool; then have a pound of almonds beaten very fine with rose-water, strain them with a pint of new milk, and put in some mace and slic't ginger, boil them till it taste well of the spices, then put into it the digested ising-glass, some sugar, and a little rose-water, give it a warm over the fire, and run it through a strainer into dishes, and slice it into dishes.

To make a Cream Tart in the Italian fashion to eat cold.

Take twenty yolks of eggs, and two quarts of cream, strain it with a little salt, saffron, rose-water, juyce of orange, a little white-wine, and a pound of fine sugar, then bake it in a deep dish with some fine cinamon, and some canded pistaches stuck on it, and when it is baked, white muskedines.

Thus you may do with the whites of the eggs, and put in no spices.

To make Piramedis Cream.

Take a quart of water, and six ounces of harts-horn, put it into a bottle with gum-dragon, and gum-araback, of each as much as a walnut; put them all into the bottle, which must be so big as will hold a pint more, for if it be full it will break, stop it very close with a cork, and tye a cloth over it, put the bottle in the beef-pot, or boil it in a pot with water, let it boil three hours, then take as much cream as there is jelly, and half a pound of almonds well beaten with rose-water, mingle the cream and the almonds together, strain it, then put the jelly when it is cold into a silver bason, and the cream to it, sweeten it as you please, and put in two or three grains of musk and ambergriese, set it over the fire, and stir it continually till be seathing hot, but let it not boil; then put it in an old fashioned drinking glass, and let it stand till it be cold, when you will use it, put the glass in some warm water, and whelm it in a dish, then take pistaches boil'd in white-wine and sugar, stick it all over, and serve it in with cream.

French Barley Cream.

Take a porringer full of French perle barley, boil it in eight or nine several waters very tender, then put it in a quart of cream, with some large mace, and whole cinamon, boil it about a quarter of an hour; then have two pound of almonds blanched and beaten fine with rose-water, put to them some sugar, and strain the almonds with some cold cream, then put all over the fire, and stir it till it be half cold, then put to it two spoonfuls of sack or white-wine, and a little salt, and serve it in a dish cold.

To make Cheesecakes.

Let your paste be very good, either puff-paste or cold butter-paste, with sugar mixed with it, then the whey being dried very well from the cheese-curds which must be made of new milk or butter, beat them in a mortar or tray, with a quarter of a pound of butter to every pottle of curds, a good quantity of rose-water, three grains of ambergriese or musk prepared, the crums of a small manchet rubbed through a cullender, the yolks of ten eggs, a grated nutmeg, a little salt, and good store of sugar, mix all these well together with a little cream, but do not make them too soft; instead of bread you may take almonds which are much better; bake them in a quick oven, and let them not stand too long in, least they should be to dry.

To make Cheesecakes otherways.

Make the crust of milk & butter boil'd together, put it into the flour & make it up pretty stiff, to a pottle of fine flour, take half a pound of butter; then take a fresh cheese made of morning milk, and a pint of cream, put it to the new milk, and set the cheese with some runnet, when it is come, put it in a cheese-cloth and press it from the whey, stamp in the curds a grated fine small manchet, some cloves and mace, a pound and a half of well washed and pick't currans, the yolks of eight eggs, some rose-water, salt, half a pound of refined white sugar, and a nutmeg or two; work all these materials well together with a quarter of a pound of good sweet butter, and some cream, but make it not too soft, and make your cheesecakes according to these formes.

To make Cheesecakes otherways.

Make the paste of a pottle of flour, half a pound of butter, as much ale barm as two egg shells will hold, and a little saffron made into fine powder, and put into the flour, melt the butter in milk, and make up the paste; then take the curds of a gallon of new milk cheese, and a pint of cream, drain the whey very well from it, pound it in a mortar, then mix it with half a pound of sugar, and a pound of well washed and picked currans, a grated nutmeg, some fine beaten cinamon, salt, rose-water, a little saffron made into fine powder, and some eight yolks of eggs, work it up very stiff with some butter and a little cream.

Otherways.

Take six quarts of new milk, run it pretty cold, and when it is tender come, drain from it the whey, and hang it up in a strainer, press the whey from it, and beat it in a mortar till it be like butter, then strain it through a strainer, and mingle it with a pound of butter with your hand; then beat a pound of almonds with rose-water till they be as fine as the curds; put to them the yolks of twenty eggs, a quart of cream, two grated nutmegs, and a pound and a half of sugar, when the coffins are ready to be set into the oven, then mingle them together, and let them bake half an hour; the paste must be made of milk and butter warmed together, dry the coffins as you do for a custard, make the paste very stiff, and make them into works.

To make Cheesecakes without Milk.

Take twelve eggs, take away six whites, and beat them very well, then take a quart of cream, and boil it with mace, take it off the fire, put in the eggs, and stir them well together, then set it on the fire again, and let it boil till it curds; then set it off, and put to it a good quantity of sugar, some grated nutmeg, and beaten mace; then dissolve musk & ambergriese in rose-water, three or four spoonfuls of grated bread, with half a pound of almonds beat small, a little cream, and some currans; then make the paste for them of flour, sugar, cream, and butter, bake them in a mild oven; a quarter of an hour will bake them.

Cheesecakes otherways.

For the paste take a pottle of flour, half a pound of butter and the white of an egg, work it well into the flour with the butter, then put a little cold water to it, and work it up stiff; then take a pottle of cream, half a pound of sugar, and a pound of currans boil'd before you put them in, a whole nutmeg grated, and a little pepper fine beaten, boil these gently, and stir it continually with twenty eggs well beaten amongst the cream, being boil'd and cold, fill the cheesecakes.

To make Cheesecakes otherways.

Take eighteen eggs, and beat them very well, beat some flour amongst them to make them pretty thick; then have a pottle of cream and boil it, being boiled put in your eggs, flour, and half a pound of butter, some cinamon, salt, boil'd currans, and sugar, set them over the fire, and boil it pretty thick, being cold fill them and bake them, make the crust as beforesaid.

To make Cheesecakes in the Italian Fashion.

Take four pound of good fat Holland cheese, and six pound of good fresh cheese curd of a morning milk cheese or better, beat them in a stone or Wooden mortar, then put sugar to them, & two pound of well washed currans, twelve eggs, whites & all, being first well beaten, a pound of sugar, some cream, half an ounce of cinamon, a quarter of an ounce of mace, and a little saffron, mix them well together, & fill your talmouse or cheesecakes pasty-ways in good cold butter-paste; sometimes use beaten almonds amongst it, and some pistaches whole; being baked, ice them with yolks of eggs, rose-water, and sugar, cast on red and white biskets, and serve them up hot.

Cheesecakes in the Italian fashion otherways.

Take a pound of pistaches stamped with two pound of morning-milk cheese-curd fresh made, three ounces of elder flowers, ten eggs, a pound of sugar, a pound of butter, and a pottle of flour, strain these in a course strainer, and put them in short or puff past.

To make Cheesecakes otherways.

Take a good morning milk cheese, or better, of some eight pound weight, stamp it in a mortar, and beat a pound of butter amongst it, and a pound of sugar, then mix with it beaten mace, two pound of currans well picked and washed, a penny manchet grated, or a pound of almonds blanched and beaten with fine rose-water, and some salt; then boil some cream, and thicken it with six or eight yolks of eggs, mixed with the other things, work them well together, and fill the cheesecakes, make the curd not too soft, and make the paste of cold butter and water according to these forms.

To make a Triffel.

Take a quart of the best and thickest cream, set it on the fire in a clean skillet, and put to it whole mace, cinamon, and sugar, boil it well in the cream before you put in the sugar; then your cream being well boiled, pour it into a fine silver piece or dish, and take out the spices, let it cool till it be no more than blood-warm, then put in a spoonful of good runnet, and set it well together being cold scrape sugar on it, and trim the dish sides finely.

To make fresh Cheese and Cream.

Take a pottle of milk as it comes from the cow, and a pint of cream, put to it a spoonful of runnet, and let it stand two hours, then stir it up and put it in a fine cloth, let the whey drain from it, and put the curd into a bowl-dish, or bason; then put to it the yolk of an egg, a spoonful of rose-water, some salt, sugar, and a little nutmeg finely beaten, put it to the cheese in the cheese-fat on a fine cloth, then scrape on sugar, and serve it on a plate in a dish.

Thus you may make fresh cheese and cream in the *French* fashion called *Jonches*, or rush cheese, being put in a mould of rushes tyed at both ends, and being dished put cream to it.

To make a Posset.

Take the yolks of twenty eggs, then have a pottle of good thick sweet cream, boil it with good store of whole cinamon, and stir it continually on a good fire, then strain the eggs with a little raw cream; when the cream is well boiled and tasteth of the spice, take it off the fire, put in the eggs, and stir them well in the cream, being pretty thick, have some sack in a posset pot or deep silver bason, half a pound of double refined sugar, and some fine grated nutmeg, warm it in the bason and pour in the cream and eggs, the cinamon being taken out, pour it as high as you can hold the skillet, let it spatter in the bason to make it froth, it will make a most excellent posset, then have loaf-sugar fine beaten, and strow on it good store.

To the curd you may add some fine grated manchet, some claret or white-wine, or ale only.

To make a Posset otherways.

Take two quarts of new cream, a quarter of an ounce of whole cinamon, and two nutmegs quartered, boil it till it taste well of the spice, and keep it always stirring, or it will burn to, then take the yolks of fourteen or fifteen eggs beaten well together with a little cold cream, put them to the cream on the fire, and stir it till it begin to boil, then take it off and sweeten it with sugar, and stir it on till it be pretty cool; then take a pint and a quarter of sack, sweeten that also and set it on the fire till it be ready to boil, then put it in a fine clean scowred bason, or posset pot, and pour the cream into it, elevating your hand to make it froth, which is the grace of your posset; if you put it through a tunnel or cullender, it is held the more exquisite way.

To make Sack Posset otherways.

Take two quarts of good cream, and a quarter of a pound of the best almonds stamp't with some rose-water or cream, strain them with the cream, and boil with it amber and musk; then take a pint of sack in a bason, and set it on a chaffing dish till it be bloud warm; then take the yolks of twelve eggs with 4 whites, beat them very well together, and so put the eggs into the sack, make it good and hot, then stir all together in the bason, set the cream cool a little before you put it into the sack, and stir all together on the coals, till it be as thick as you would have it, then take some amber and musk, grind it small with sugar, and strew it on the top of the posset, it will give it a most delicate and pleasant taste.

Sack Posset otherways.

Take eight eggs, whites and yolks, beat them well together, and strain them into a quart of cream, season them with nutmeg and sugar, and put to them a pint of sack, stir them all together, and put it into your bason, set it in the oven no hotter then for a custard, and let it stand two hours.

To make a Sack Posset without Milk or Cream.

Take eighteen eggs, whites and all, take out the cock-treads, and beat them very well, then take a pint of sack, and a quart of ale boil'd scum it, and put into it three quarters of a pound of sugar, and half a nutmeg, let it boil a little together, then take it off the fire stirring the eggs still, put into them two or three ladlefuls of drink, then mingle all together, set it on the fire, and keep it stirring till you find it thick, and serve it up.

Other Posset.

Take a quart of cream, and a quarter of nutmeg in it, set it on the fire, and let it boil a little, as it is boling take a pot or bason that you may make the posset in, and put in three spoonfuls of sack, and some eight spoonfuls of ale, sweeten it with sugar, then set it on the coals to warm a little while; being warmed, take it off and let it stand till it be almost cold, then put it into the pot or bason, stir it a little, and let it stand to simmer over the fire an hour or more, the longer the better.

An excellent Syllabub.

Fill your Sillabub pot half full with sider, and good store of sugar, and a little nutmeg, stir it well together, and put in as much cream by two or three spoonfuls at a time, as hard as you can, as though you milkt it in; then stir it together very softly once about, and let it stand two hours before you eat it, for the standing makes it curd.

To make White Pots according to these Forms.

Take a quart of good thick cream, boil it with three or four blades of large mace, and some whole cinamon, then take the whites of four eggs, and beat them very well, when the cream boils up, put them in, and take them off the fire keeping them stirring a little while, & put in some sugar; then take five or six pippins, pare, and slice them, then put in a pint of claret wine, some raisins of the sun, some sugar, beaten cinamon, and beaten ginger; boil the pippins to pap, then cut some sippets very thin and dry them before the fire; when the apples and cream are boil'd & cold, take half the sippets & lay them in a dish, lay half the apples on them, then lay on the rest of the sippets and apples as you did before, then pour on the rest of the cream and bake it in the oven as a custard, and serve it with scraping sugar.

Bake these in paste, in dish or pan, or make the paste as you will do for a custard, make it three inches high in the foregoing forms.

Otherways to make a White Pot.

Take a quart of sweet cream and boil it, then put to it two ounces of picked rice, some beaten mace, ginger, cinamon, and sugar, let these steep in it till it be cold, and strain into it eight yolks of eggs and but two whites, then put in two ounces of clean washed and picked currans, and some salt, stir all well together, and bake it in paste, earthen pan, dish, or deep bason; being baked, trim it with some sugar, and comfits of orange, cinamon, or white biskets.

To make a Wassel.

Take muskedine or ale, and set it on the fire to warm, then boil a quart of cream and two or three whole cloves, then have the yolks of three or four eggs dissolved with a little cream; the cream being well boiled with the spices, put in the eggs and stir them well together, then have sops or sippets of fine manchet or french bread, put them in a bason, and pour in the warm wine, with some sugar and thick cream on that; stick it with blanched almonds and cast on cinamon, ginger, and sugar, or wafers, sugar plate, or comfits.

To make a Norfolk Fool.

Take a quart of good thick sweet cream, and set it a boiling in a clean scoured skillet, with some large mace and whole cinamon; then having boil'd a warm or two take the yolks of five or six eggs dissolved and put to it, being taken from the fire, then take out the cinamon and mace; the cream being pretty thick, slice a fine manchet into thin slices, as much as will cover the bottom of the dish, pour on the cream on them, and more bread, some two or three times till the dish be full, then trim the dish side with fine carved sippets, and stick it with slic't dates, scrape on sugar, and cast on red and white biskets.

To make Pap.

Take milk and flour, strain them, and set it over the fire till it boil, being boil'd, take it off and let it cool; then take the yolks of eggs, strain them, and put it in the milk with some salt, set it again on the embers, and stir it till it be thick, and stew leisurely, then put it in a clean scowred dish, and serve it for pottage, or in paste, add to it sugar and rose-water.

To make Blamanger according to these Forms.

Take a capon being boil'd or rosted & mince it small then have a pound of blanched almonds beaten to a paste, and beat the minced capon amongst it, with some rose-water, mingle it with some cream, ten whites of eggs, and grated manchet, strain all the foresaid things with some salt, sugar, and a little musk, boil them in a pan or broad skillet clean scowred as thick as pap, in the boiling stir it continually, being boil'd strain it again, and serve it in paste in the foregoing forms, or made dishes with paste royal.

To make your paste for the forms, take to a quart of flour a quarter of a pound of butter, and the yolks of four eggs, boil your butter in fair water, and put the yolks of the eight eggs on one side of your dish, make up your paste quick, not too dry, and make it stiff.

Otherways.

Take to a quart of fine flour a quarter of a pound of butter, a quarter of a pound of sugar, a little saffron, rose-water, a little beaten cinamon, and the yolk of an egg or two, work up all cold together with a little almond milk.

Blamanger otherways.

Take a boil'd or rost capon, and being cold take off the skin, mince it and beat it in a mortar, with some almond paste, then mix it with some capon broth, and crumbs of manchet, strained together with some rose-water, salt, and sugar; boil it to a good thickness, then put it into the paste of the former forms, of an inch high, or in dishes with paste royal, the paste being first baked.

In this manner you may make Blamanger of a Pike.

Otherways.

Boil or rost a capon, mince it, and stamp it with almond paste, & strain it either with capon broth, cream, goats-milk, or other milk, strain them with some rice flour, sugar, and rosewater, boil it in a pan like pap, with a little musk, and stir it continually in the boiling, then put in the forms of paste as aforesaid.

Sometimes use for change pine-apple-seeds and currans, other times put in dates, cinamon, saffron, figs, and raisins being minced together, put them in as it boils with a little sack.

To make Blamanger otherways.

Take half a pound of fine searsed rice flour, and put to it a quart of morning milk, strain them through a strainer into a broad skillet; and set it on a soft fire, stir it with a broad stick, and when it is a little thick take it from the fire, then put in a quartern of rose-water, set it to the fire again, and stir it well, in the stirring beat it with the stick from the one side of the pan to the other, and when it is as thick as pap, take it from the fire, and put it in a fair platter, when it is cold lay three slices in a dish, and scrape on sugar.

Blamanger otherways.

Take a capon or a pike and boil it in fair water very tender, then take the pulp of either of them and chop it small, then take a pound of blanched almonds beat to a paste, beat the pulp and the almonds together, and put to them a quart of cream, the whites of ten eggs, and the crumbs of a fine manchet, mingle all together, and strain them with some sugar and salt, put them in a clean broad stew pan and set them over the fire, stir it and boil it thick; being boiled put it into a platter till it be cold, strain it again with a little rose-water, and serve it with sugar.

Otherways.

Blanch some almonds & beat them very fine to a paste with the boil'd pulp of a pike or capon, & crums of fine manchet, strain all together with sugar, and boil it to the thickness of an apple moise, then let it cool, strain it again with a little rose-water, and so serve it.

To make Blamanger in the Italian fashion.

Boil a Capon in water and salt very tender, or all to mash, then beat Almonds, and strain them with your Capon-Broth, rice flour, sugar, and rose-water; boil it like pap, and serve it in this form; sometimes in place of Broth use Cream.

SECTION XIII.

OR,

THE FIRST SECTION FOR DRESSING OF F I S H .

Shewing divers ways, and the most excellent, for Dressing of Carps, either Boiled, Stewed, Broiled, Roasted, or Baked, &c.

To Boil a Carp in Corbolion.

T Ake as much wine as water, and a good handful of salt, when it boils, draw the carp and put it in the liquor, boil it with a continual quick fire, and being boiled, dish it up in a very clean dish with sippets round about it, and slic't lemon, make the sauce of sweet butter, beaten up with slic't lemon and grated nutmeg, garnish the dish with beaten ginger.

To boil a Carp the best way to be eaten hot.

Take a special male carp of eighteen inches, draw it, wash out the blood, and lay it in a tray, then put to it some wine-vinegar and salt, put the milt to it, the gall being taken from it; then have three quarts of white wine or claret, a quart of white wine vinegar, & five pints of fair water, or as much as will cover it; put the wine, water and vinegar, in a fair scowred pan or kettle, with a handful of salt, a quarter of an ounce of large mace, half a quartern of whole cloves, three slic'd nutmegs, six races of ginger pared and sliced, a quarter of an ounce of pepper, four or five great onions whole or sliced; then make a faggot of sweet herbs, of the tops of streight sprigs, of rosemary, seven or eight bay-leaves, 6 tops of sweet marjoram, as much of the streight tops of time, winter-savory, and parsley; being well bound up, put them into the kettle with the spices, and some orange and lemon-peels; make them boil apace before you put in the carp, and boil it up quick with a strong fire; being finely boil'd and crisp, dish it in a large clean scowred dish, lay on the herbs and spice on the carp, with slic't lemons and lemon-peels, put some of the broth to it, and run it over with beaten butter, put fine carved sippets round about it, and garnish the dish with fine searsed manchet.

Or you may make sauce for it only with butter beat up thick, with slices of lemon, some of the carp liquor, and an anchove or two, and garnish the dish with beatten ginger.

Or take three or four anchoves and dissolve them in some white-wine, put them in a pipkin with some slic't horse-raddish, gross pepper, some of the carp liquor, and some stewed oyster liquor, or stewed oysters, large mace, and a whole onion or two; the sauce being well stewed, dissolve the yolks of three or four eggs with some of the sauce, and give it a warm or two, pour it on the carp with some beaten butter, the stewed oysters and slic't lemon, barberries, or grapes.

Otherways.

Dissolve three or four anchoves, with a little grated bread and nutmeg, and give it a warm in some of the broth the carp was boiled in, beat it up thick with some butter, and a clove of garlick, or pour it on the carp.

Or make sauce with beaten butter, grape-verjuyce, white wine, slic't lemon, juyce of oranges, juyce of sorrel, or white-wine vinegar.

Or thus.

Take white or claret wine, put it in a pipkin with some pared or sliced ginger, large mace, dates quartered, a pint of great oysters with the liquor, a little vinegar and salt, boil these a quarter of an hour, then mince a handful of parsley, and some sweet herbs, boil it as much longer till half be consumed, then beat up the sauce with half a pound of butter and a slic't lemon, and pour it on the carp.

Sometimes for the foresaid carp use grapes, barberries, gooseberries, and horse-raddish, &c.

To make a Bisque of Carps.

Take twelve handsome male carps, and one larger than the rest, take out all the milts, and flea the twelve small carps, cut off their heads, take out their tongues, and take the fish from the bones, then take twelve large oysters and three or four yolks of hard eggs minc'd together, season it with cloves, mace, and salt, make thereof a stiff searse, add thereto the yolks of four or five eggs to bind, and fashion it into balls or rolls as you please, lay them into a deep dish or earthen pan, and put thereto twenty or thirty great oysters, two or three anchoves, the milts & tongues of the twelve carps, half a pound of fresh butter, the liquor of the oysters, the juyce of a lemon or two, a little white wine, some of the corbolion wherein the great carp is boil'd, & a whole onion, so set them a stewing on a soft fire, and make a soop therewith. For the great carp you must scald, draw him, and lay him for half an hour with other carps heads in a deep pan, with as much white wine vinegar as will cover and serve to boil him & the other heads in, then put therein pepper, whole mace, a race of ginger, slic't nutmeg, salt, sweet herbs, an onion or two slic't, & a lemon; when you have boiled the carps pour the liquor with the spices into the kettle where you boil him, when it boils put in the carp, and let it not boil too fast for breaking, after the carp hath boil'd a while put in the heads, and being boil'd, take off the liquor and let the carps and the heads keep warm in the kettle till you go to dish them. When you dress the bisk take a large silver dish, set it on the fire, lay therein slices of French bread, and steep it with a ladle full of the corbolion, then take up the great carp and lay him in the midst of the dish, range the twelve heads about the carp, then lay the fearse of the carp, lay that into the oysters, milts, and tongues, and pour on the liquor wherein the fearse was boil'd, wring in the juyce of a lemon and two oranges, and serve it very hot to the table.

To make a Bisk with Carps and other several Fishes.

Make the corbolion for the Bisk of some Jacks or small Carps boil'd in half white-wine and fair spring-water; some cloves, salt, and mace, boil it down to jelly, strain it, and keep it warm for to scald the bisk; then take four carps, four tenches, four perches, two pikes, two eels flayed and drawn; the carps being scalded, drawn, and cut into quarters, the tenches scalded and left whole, also the pearches and the pikes all finely scalded, cleansed, and cut into twelve pieces, three of each side, then put them into a large stewing-pan with three quarts of claret-wine, an ounce of large mace, a quarter of an ounce of cloves, half an ounce of pepper, a quarter of an ounce of ginger pared & slic't, sweet herbs chopped small, as stripped time, savory, sweet marjoram, parsley, rosemary, three or four bay-leaves, salt, chesnuts, pistaches, five or six great onions, and stew all together on a quick fire.

Then stew a pottle of oysters the greatest you can get, parboil them in their own liquor, cleanse them from the dregs, and wash them in warm water from the grounds and shells, put them into a pipkin with three or four great onions peeled, then take large mace, and a little of their own liquor, or a little wine vinegar, or white wine.

Next take twelve flounders being drawn and cleansed from the guts, fry them in clarified butter with a hundred of large smelts, being fryed stew them in a stew-pan with claret-wine, grated nutmeg, slic't orange, butter, and salt.

Then have a hundred of prawns, boiled, picked, and buttered, or fryed.

Next, bottoms of artichocks, boiled, blanched, and put in beaten butter, grated nutmeg, salt, white-wine, skirrets, and sparagus in the foresaid sauce.

Then mince a pike and an eel, cleanse them, and season them with cloves, mace, pepper, salt, some sweet herbs minct, some pistaches, barberries, grapes, or gooseberries, some grated manchet, and yolks of raw eggs, mingle all the foresaid things together, and make it into balls, or farse some cabbidge lettice, and bake the balls in an oven, being baked stick the balls with pine-apple seeds, and pistaches, as also the lettice.

Then all the foresaid things being made ready, have a large clean scowred dish, with large sops of French bread lay the carps upon them, and between them some tench, pearch, pike, and eels, & the stewed oysteres all over the other fish, then the fried flounders & smelts over the oysters, then the balls & lettice stuck with pistaches, the artichocks, skirrets, sparagus, butter prawns, yolks of hard eggs, large mace, fryed smelts, grapes, slic't lemon, oranges, red beets or pomegranats, broth it with the leer that was made for it, and run it over with beaten butter.

The best way to stew a Carp.

Dress the carp and take out the milt, put it in a dish with then carp, and take out the gall, then save the blood, and scotch the carp on the back with your knife; if the carp be eighteen inches, take a quart of claret or white wine, four or five blades of large mace, 10 cloves, two good races of ginger slic't, two slic't nutmegs, and a few sweet herbs, as the tops of sweet marjoram, time, savory, and parsley chopped very small, four great onions whole, three or four bay-leaves, and some salt; stew them all together in a stew-pan or clean scowred kettle with the wine, when the pan boils put in the carp with a quarter of a pound of good sweet butter, boil it on a quick fire of charcoal, and being well stew'd down, dish it in a clean large dish, pour the sauce on it with the spices, lay on slic't lemon and lemon-peel, or barber-ries, grapes, or gooseberries, and run it over with beaten butter, garnish the dish with dryed manchet grated and searsed, and carved sippets laid round the dish.

In feasts the carps being scal'd, garnish the body with stewed oysters, some fryed in white batter, some in green made with the juyce of spinage: sometimes in place of sippets use fritters of arms, somtimes horse-raddish, and rub the dish with a clove or two of garlick.

For more variety, in the order abovesaid, sometimes dissolve an anchove or two, with some of the broth it was stewed in, and the yolks of two eggs dissolved with some verjuyce, wine, or juyce of orange; sometimes add some capers, and hard eggs chopped, as also sweet herbs, &c.

To stew a Carp in the French fashion.

Take a Carp, split it down the back alive, & put it in boiling liquor, then take a good large dish or stew-pan that will contain the carp; put in as much claret wine as will cover it, and wash off the blood, take out the carp, and put into the wine in the dish three or four slic't onions, three or four blades of large mace, gross pep-per, and salt; when the stew-pan boils put in the carp and cover it close, being well stewed down, dish it up in a clean scowred dish with fine carved sippets round about it, pour the liquor it was boiled in on it, with the spices, onions, slic't lemon, and lemon-peel, run it over with beaten butter, and garnish the dish with dryed grated bread.

Another most excellent way to stew a Carp.

Take a carp and scale it, being well cleansed and dried with a clean cloth, then split it and fry it in clarified butter, being finely fryed put it in a deep dish with two or three spoonfuls of claret wine, grated nutmeg, a blade or two of large mace, salt, three or four slices of an orange, and some sweet butter, set it on a chafing dish of coals, cover it close, and stew it up quick, then turn it, and being very well stew'd, dish it on fine carv'd sippets, run it over with the sauce it was stewed in, the spices, beaten butter, and the slices of a fresh orange, and garnish the dish with dry manchet grated and searsed.

In this way you may stew any good fish, as soles, lobsters, prawns, oysters, or cockles.

Otherways.

Take a carp and scale it, scrape off the slime with a knife and wipe it clean with a dry cloth; then draw it, and wash the blood out with some claret wine into the pipkin where you stew it, cut it into quarters, halves, or whole, and put it into a broad mouthed pipkin or earthen-pan, put to it as much wine as water, a bundle of sweet herbs, some raisins of the sun, currans, large mace, cloves, whole cinamon, slic't ginger, salt, and some prunes boiled and strained, put in also some strained bread or flour, and stew them all together; being stewed, dish the carp in a clean scowred dish on fine carved sippets, pour the broth on the carp, and garnish it with the fruit, spices, some slic't lemon, barberries, or grapes, some orangado or preserved barberries, and scrape on sugar.

Otherways.

Do it as before, save only no currans, put prunes strained, beaten pepper, and some saffron.

To stew a Carp seven several ways.

1. Take a carp, scale it, and scrape off the slime, wipe it with a dry cloth, and give it a cut or two cross the back, then put it a boiling whole, parted down the back in halves, or quarters, put it in a broad mouthed pipkin with some claret or white-wine, some wine-vinegar, and good fresh fish broth or some fair water, three or four blades of large mace, some slic't onions fryed, currans, and some good butter; cover up the pipkin, and being finely stewed, put in some almond-milk, and some sweet herbs finely minced, or some grated manchet, and being well stewed, serve it up on fine carved sippets, broth it, and garnish the dish with some barberries or grapes, and the dish with some stale manchet grated and sears'd, being first dryed.

2. For the foresaid broth, yolks of hard eggs strained with some steeped manchet, some of the broth it is stewed in, and a little saffron.

3. For variety of garnish, carrots in dice-work, some raisins, large mace, a few prunes, and marigold flowers, boil'd in the foresaid broth.

4. Or leave out carrots and fruit, and put samphire and capers, and thicken it with French barley tender boil'd.

5. Or no fruit, but keep the order aforesaid, only adding sweet marjoram, stripped tyme, parsley, and savory, bruise them with the back of a ladle, and put them into the broth.

6. Otherways, stewed oysters to garnish the carp, and some boil'd bottoms of artichocks, put them to the stewed oysters or skirrets being boil'd, grapes, barberries, and the broth thickned with yolks of eggs strained with some sack, white wine, or caper liquor.

7. Boil it as before, without fruit, and add to it capers, carrots in dice-work, mace, faggot of sweet herbs, slic't onions chopp'd with parsley, and boil'd in the broth then have boil'd colliffowers, turnips, parsnips, sparagus, or chesnuts in place of carrots, and the leire strained with yolks of eggs and white wine.

To make French Herb Pottage for Fasting Days.

Take half a handful of lettice, as much of spinage, half as much of Bugloss and Borrage, two handfuls of sorrel, a little parsley, sage, a good handful of purslain, half a pound of butter, some pepper and salt, and sometimes, some cucumbers.

Other Broth or Pottage of a Carp.

Take a carp, scale it, and scrape off the slime, wash it, and wipe it with a clean cloth, then draw it, and put it in a broad mouthed pipkin that will contain it, put to it a pint of good white or claret wine, and as much good fresh fish broth as will cover it, or as much fair water, with the blood of the carp, four or five blades of large mace, a little beaten pepper, some slic't onions, a clove or two, some sweet herbs chopped, a handful of capers, and some salt, stew all together, the carp being well stewed, put in some almond paste, with some white-wine, give it a warm or two with some stewed oyster-liquor, & serve it on French bread in a fair scowr'd dish, pour on the liquor, and garnish it with dryed grated manchet.

To dress a Carp in Stoffado.

Take a carp alive, scale it, and lard it with a good salt eel, steep it in claret or white-wine, in an earthen pan, and put to it some wine-vinegar, whole cloves, large mace, gross pepper, slic't ginger, and four or five cloves of garlick, then have an earthen pan that will contain it, or a large pipkin, put to it some sweet herbs, three or four sprigs of rosemary, as many of time and sweet marjoram, two or three bay-leaves and parsley, put the liquor to it into the pan or pipkin wherein you will stew it, and paste on the cover, stew it in the oven, in an hour it will be baked, then serve it hot for dinner or supper, serve it on fine carved sippets of French bread, and the spices on it, with herbs, slic't lemon and lemon peel; and run it over with beaten butter.

To hash a Carp.

Take a carp, scale, and scrape off the slime with your knife, wipe it with a dry cloth, bone it, and mince it with a fresh water eel being flayed and boned; season it with beaten cloves, mace, salt, pepper, and some sweet herbs, as tyme, parsley, and some sweet marjoram minced very small, stew it in a broad mouthed pipkin, with some claret wine, gooseberries, or grapes, and some blanched chesnuts; being finely stewed, serve it on carved sippets about it, and run it over with beaten butter, garnish the dish with fine grated manchet searsed, and some fryed oysters in butter, cockles, or prawns.

Sometimes for variety, use pistaches, pine-apple-seeds, or some blanch't almonds stew'd amongst the hash, or asparagus, or artichock boil'd & cut as big as chesnuts, & garnish the dish with scraped horse-radish, and rub the bottom of the dish in which you serve the meat, with a clove or two of garlick. Sometimes mingle it with some stewed oysters, or put to it some oyster-liquor.

To marinate a Carp to be eaten hot or cold.

Take a carp, scale it, and scrape off the slime, wipe it clean with a dry cloth, and split it down the back, flour it, and fry it in sweet sallet oyl, or good clarified butter; being fine and crisp fryed, lay it in a deep dish or earthen pan, then have some white or claret wine, or wine-vinegar, put it in a broad mouthed pipkin with all manner of sweet herbs bound up in a bundle, as rosemary, tyme, sweet marjoram, parsley, winter-savory, bay-leaves, sorrel, and sage, as much of one as the other, put it into the pipkin with the wine, with some large mace, slic't ginger, gross pepper, slic't nutmeg, whole cloves, and salt, with as much wine and vinegar as will cover the dish, then boil the spices and wine with some salt a little while, pour it on the fish hot, and presently cover it close to keep in the spirits of the liquor, herbs, and spices for an hours space; then have slic't lemons, lemon-peels, orange and orange peels, lay them over the fish in the pan, and cover it up close; when you serve them hot lay on the spices and herbs all about it, with the slic't lemons, oranges, and their peels, and run it over with sweet sallet oyl, (or none) but some of the liquor it is soust in.

Or marinate the carp or carps without sweet herbs for hot or cold, only bay-leaves, in all points else as is abovesaid; thus you may marinate soles, or any other fish, whether sea or fresh-water fish.

Or barrel it, pack it close, and it will keep as long as sturgeon, and as good.

To broil or toast a Carp divers ways, either in sweet Butter or Sallet Oyl.

Take a carp alive, draw it, and wash out the blood in the body with claret wine into a dish, put to it some wine vinegar and oyl, then scrape off the slime, & wipe it dry both outside & inside, lay it in the dish with vinegar, wine, oyl, salt, and the streight sprigs of rosemary and parsley, let it steep there the space of an hour or two, then broil it on a clean scowred gridiron, (or toast it before the fire) broil it on a soft fire, and turn it often; being finely broil'd, serve it on a clean scowred dish, with the oyl, wine, and vinegar, being stew'd on the coals, put it to the fish, the rosemary and parsley round the dish, and some about the fish, or with beaten butter and vinegar, or butter and verjuyce, or juyce of oranges beaten with the butter, or juyce of lemons, garnish the fish with slices of orange, lemon, and branches of rosemary; boil the milt or spawn by it self and lay it in the dish with the Carp.

Or make sauce otherways with beaten butter, oyster liquor, the blood of the carp, grated nutmeg, juyce of orange, white-wine, or wine vinegar boil'd together, crumbs of bread, and the yolk of an egg boiled up pretty thick, and run it over the fish.

To broil a Carp in Staffado.

Take a live carp, scale it, and scrape off the slime, wipe it clean with a dry cloth, and draw it, wash out the blood, and steep it in claret, white-wine, wine-vinegar, large mace, whole cloves, two or three cloves of garlick, some slic't ginger, gross pepper, and salt; steep it in this composition in a dish or tray the space of two hours, then broil it on a clean scoured gridiron on a soft fire, & baste it with some sweet sallet oyl, sprigs of rosemary, time, parsley, sweet marjoram, and two or three bay-leaves, being finely broil'd; serve it with the sauce it was steeped in, boil'd up on the fire with a little oyster-liquor, the spices on it, and herbs round about it on the dish, run it over with sauce, either with sweet sallet oyl, or good beaten butter, and broil the milt or spawn by it self.

To roast a Carp.

Take a live carp, draw and wash it, and take away the gall, and milt, or spawn; then make a pudding with some grated manchet, some almond-paste, cream, currans, grated nutmeg, raw yolks of eggs, sugar, caraway-seed candied, or any peel, some lemon and salt, make a stiff pudding and put it through the gills into the belly of the carp, neither scale it, nor fill it too full; then spit it, and roust it in the oven upon two or three sticks cross a brass dish, turn it and let the gravy drop into the dish; being finely roasted, make sauce with the gravy, butter, juyce of orange or lemon, some sugar, and cinamon, beat up the sauce thick with the butter, and dish the carp, put the sauce over it with slices of lemon.

Otherways.

Scale it, and lard it with salt eel, pepper, and nutmeg, then make a pudding of some minced eel, roach, or dace, some sweet herbs, grated bread, cloves, mace, nutmeg, pepper, salt, yolks of eggs, pistaches, chesnuts, and the milt of the carp parboil'd and cut into dice-work, as also some fresh eel, and mingle it amongst the pudding or farse.

Sauces for Roast Carp.

1. Gravy and oyster liquor, beat it up thick with sweet butter, claret wine, nutmeg, slices of orange, and some capers, and give it a warm or two.

2. Beaten butter with slices of orange, and lemon, or the juyce of them only.

3. Butter, claret-wine, grated nutmeg, selt, slices of orange, a little wine-vinegar and the gravy.

4. A little white-wine, gravy of the carp, an anchove or two dissolved in it, some grated nutmeg, and a little grated manchet, beat them up thick with some sweet butter, and the yolk of an egg or two, dish the carp, and pour the sauce on it.

To make a Carp Pye a most excellent way.

Take carp, scale it and scrape off the slime, wipe it with a dry clean cloth, and split it down the back, then cut it in quarters or six pieces, three of each, and take out the milt or spawn, as also the gall; season it with nutmeg, pepper, salt, and beaten ginger, lay some butter in the pye bottom, then the carp upon it, and upon the carp two or three bay-leaves, four or five blades of large mace, four or five whole cloves, some blanched chesnuts, slices of orange, and some sweet butter, close it up and bake it, being baked liquor it with beaten butter, the blood of the carp, and a little claret wine.

For variety, in place of chesnuts, use pine apple-seeds, or bottoms of artichocks, gooseberries, grapes, or barberries. Sometimes bake great oysters with the carp, and a great onion or two; sometimes sweet herbs chopped, or sparagus boiled.

Or bake it in a dish as you do the pye.

To make paste for the pie, take two quarts and a pint of fine flour, four or five yolks of raw eggs, and half a pound of sweet butter,[5] boil the butter till it be melted, and make the paste with it.

Paste for a Florentine of Carps made in a dish or patty-pan.

Take a pottle of fine flour, three quarters of a pound of butter, and six yolks of

---

[5]   To make paste for the pie, take two quarts and a pint of fine flour, four or five yolks of raw eggs, and half a pound of sweet butter

eggs, and work up the butter, eggs, and flour, dry them, then put to it as much fair spring water cold as will make it up into paste.

To bake a Carp otherways to be eaten hot.

Take a carp, scale it alive, and scrape off the slime, draw it, and take away the gall and guts, scotch it, and season it with nutmeg, pepper, and salt lightly, lay it into the pye, and put the milt into the belly, then lay on slic't dates in halves, large mace, orange, or slic't lemon, gooseberries, grapes, or barberries, raisins of the sun, and butter; close it up and bake it, being almost baked liquor it with verjuyce, butter, sugar, claret or white-wine, and ice it.

Sometimes make a pudding in the carps belly, make it of grated bread, pepper, nutmegs, yolks of eggs, sweet herbs, currans, sugar, gooseberries, grapes, or barberries, orangado, dates, capers, pistaches, raisins, and some minced fresh eel.

Or bake it in a dish or patty pan in cold butter paste.

To bake a Carp with Oysters.

Scale a carp, scrape off the slime, and bone it; then cut it into large dice-work, as also the milt being parboil'd; then have some great oysters, parboil'd, mingle them with the bits of carp, and season them together with beaten pepper, salt, nutmeg, cloves, mace, grapes, gooseberries, or barberries, blanched chesnuts, and pistaches, season them lightly, then put in the bottom of the pie a good big onion or two whole, fill the pye, and lay upon it some large mace and butter, close it up and bake it, being baked liquor it with white wine, and sweet butter, or beaten butter only.

To make minced Pies of Carps and Eels.

Take a carp being cleansed, bone it, and also a good fat fresh water eel, mince them together, and season them with pepper, nutmeg, cinamon, ginger, and salt, put to them some currans, caraway-seed, minced orange-peel, and the yolks of six or seven hard eggs minced also, slic't dates, and sugar; then lay some butter in the bottom of the pyes, and fill them, close them up, bake them, and ice them.

To bake a Carp minced with an Eel in the French Fashion, called Peti Petes.

Take a carp, scale it, and scrape off the slime, then roast it with a flayed eel, and being rosted draw them from the fire, and let them cool, then cut them into little pieces like great dice, one half of them, & the other half minced small and seasoned with nutmeg, pepper, salt, gooseberries, barberries, or grapes, and some bottoms of artichocks boil'd and cut as the carp: season all the foresaid materials and mingle all together, then put some butter in the bottom of the pye, lay on the meat and butter on the top, close it up, and bake it, being baked liquor it with gravy, and the juyce of oranges, butter, and grated nutmeg.

Sometimes liquor it with verjuyce and the yolks of eggs strained, sugar, and butter.

Or with currans, white wine, and butter boil'd together, some sweet herbs chopped small, and saffron.

To bake a Carp according to these Forms to be eaten hot.

Take a carp, scale it, and scrape off the slime, bone it and cut it into dice-work, the milt being parboil'd, cut it into the same form, then have some great oysters parboild and cut into the same form also; put to it some grapes, goosberries, or barberries, the bottoms of artichocks boil the yolks of hard egs in quarters, boild, sparagus cut an inch long, and some pistaches, season all the foresaid things together with pepper, nutmegs, and salt, fill the pyes, close them up, and bake them, being baked, liquor them with butter, white-wine, and some blood of the carp, boil them together, or beaten butter, with juyce of oranges.

To bake a Carp with Eels to be eaten cold.

Take four large carps, scale them & wipe off the slime clean, bone them, and cut each side into two pieces of every carp, then have four large fresh water eels, fat ones, boned, flayed, and cut in as many pieces as the carps, season them with nutmeg, pepper, and salt; then have a pye ready, either round or square, put butter in the bottom of it, then lay a lay of eel, and a lay of carp upon that, and thus do till you have ended; then lay on some large mace and whole cloves on the top, some sliced nutmeg, sliced ginger, and butter, close it up and bake it, being baked and cold, fill it up with clarified butter.

Otherways.

Take eight carps, scale and bone them, scrape and wash off the slime, wipe them dry, and mince them very fine, then have four good fresh water eels, flay and bone them, and cut them into lard as big as your finger, then have pepper, cloves, mace, and ginger severally beaten and mingled with some salt, season the fish and also the eels, cut into lard; then make a pye according to this form, lay some butter in the bottom of the pye, then a lay of carp upon the butter, so fill it, close it up and bake it.

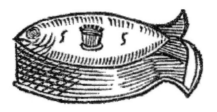

SECTION XIV.

OR,

THE SECOND SECTION OF F I S H.

Shewing the most Excellent Ways of Dressing of Pikes.

To boil a Pike.

Wash him very clean, then truss him either round whole, with his tail in his mouth, and his back scotched, or splatted and trust round like a hart, with his tail in his mouth, or in three pieces, & divide the middle piece into two pieces; then boil it in water, salt, and vinegar, put it not in till the liquor boils, & let it boil very fast at first to make it crisp, but afterwards softly; for the sauce put in a pipkin a pint of white wine, slic't ginger, mace, dates quartered, a pint of great oysters with the liquor, a little vinegar and salt, boil them a quarter of an hour; then mince a few sweet herbs & parsley, stew them till half the liquor be consumed; then the pike being boiled dish it, and garnish the dish with grated dry manchet fine searsed, or ginger fine beaten, then beat up the sauce, with half a pound of butter, minced lemon, or orange, put it on the pike, and sippet it with cuts of puff-paste or lozenges, some fried greens, and some yellow butter. Dish it according to these forms.

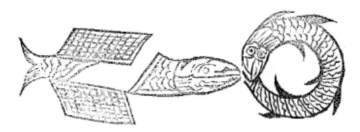

To boil a Pike otherways.

Take a male pike alive, splat him in halves, take out his milt and civet, and take away the gall, cut the sides into three pieces of a side, lay them in a large dish or tray, and put upon them half a pint of white wine vinegar, and half a handful of bay-salt beaten fine; then have a clean scowred pan set over the fire with as much rhenish or white-wine as will cover the pike, so set it on the fire with some salt, two slic't nutmegs, two races of ginger slic't, two good big onions slic't, five or six cloves of garlik, two or three tops of sweet marjoram, three or four streight sprigs of rosemary bound up in a bundle close, and the peel of half a lemon; let these boil with a quick fire, then put in the pike with the vinegar, and boil it up quick; whilest the pike is boiling, take a quarter of a pound of anchoves, wash and bone them, then mince them and put them in a pipkin with a quarter of a pound of butter, and 3 or four spoonfuls of the liquor the pike was boiled in; the pike being boiled dish it, & lay the ginger, nutmegs, and herbs upon it, run it over with the sauce, and cast dried searsed manchet on it.

This foresaid liquor is far better to boil another pike, by renewing the liquor with a little wine.

To boil a Pike and Eel together.

Take a quart of white-wine, a pint and a half of white wine vinegar, two quarts of water, almost a pint of salt, a handful of rosemary and tyme, let your liquor boil before you put in your fish, the herbs, a little large mace, and some twenty corns of whole pepper.

To boil a Pike otherways.

Boil it in water, salt, and wine vinegar, two parts water, and one vinegar, being drawn, set on the liquor to boil, cleanse the civet, and truss him round, scotch his back, and when the liquor boils, put in the fish and boil it up quick; then make sauce with some white-wine vinegar, mace, whole pepper, a good handful of cockles broiled or boiled out of the shells and washed with vinegar, a faggot of sweet herbs, the liver stamped and put to it, and horse raddish scraped or slic't, boil all the foresaid together, dish the pike on sippets, and beat up the sauce with some good sweet butter and minced lemon, make the sauce pretty thick, and garnish it as you please.

Otherways.

Take as much white-wine and water as will cover it, of each a like quantity, and a pint of vinegar, put to this liquor half an ounce of large mace, two lemon-peels, a quarter of an ounce of whole cloves, three slic't nutmegs, four races of ginger slic't, some six great onions slic't, a bundle of six or seven sprigs or tops of rosemary, as much of time, winter-savory, and sweet marjoram bound up hard in a faggot, put into the liquor also a good handful of salt, and when it boils, put in the fish being cleansed and trussed, and boil it up quick.

Being boiled, make the sauce with some of the broth where the pike was boiled, and put it in a dish with two or three anchoves being cleansed and minced, a little white wine, some grated nutmeg, and some fine grated manchet, stew it on a chafing dish, and beat it up thick with some sweet butter, and the yolk of an egg or two dissolved with some vinegar, give it a warm, and put to it three or four slices of lemon.

Then dish the pike, drain the liquor from it upon a chafing-dish of coals, pour on the sauce, and garnish the fish with slic't lemons, and the spices, herbs, and boil'd onions, run it over with beaten butter, and lay on some barberries or grapes.

Sometimes for change you may put some horse-raddish scraped, or the juyce of it.

To boil a Pike in White Broth.

Cut your pike in three pieces, then boil it in water, salt, and sweet herbs, put in the fish when the liquor boils; then take the yolks of six eggs, beat them with a little sack, sugar, melted butter, and some of the pike broth then put it on some embers to keep warm, stir it sometimes lest it curdle; then take up your pike, put the head and tail together in a clean dish, cleave the other piece in two, and take out the back-bone, put the one piece on one side, and the other piece on the other side, but blanch all, pour the broth on it, and garnish the fish with sippets, strow on fine ginger or sugar, wipe the edge of the dish round, and serve it.

To Boil a Pike in the French Fashion, a-la-Sauces d'Almaigne, or in the German Fashion.

Take a pike, draw him, dress the rivet, and cut him in three pieces, boil him in as much wine as water, & some lemon-peel, with the liquor boils put in the fish with a good handful of salt, and boil him up quick.

Then have a sauce made of beaten butter, water, the slices of two or three lemons, the yolks of two or three eggs, and some grated nutmeg; the pike being boiled dish it on fine sippets, and stick it with some fried bread run it over with the sauce, some barberries or lemon, and garnish the dish with some pared and slic't ginger, barberries, and lemon peel.

To boil a Pike in the City Fashion.

Take a live male pike, draw him and slit the rivet, wash him clean from the blood, and lay him in a dish or tray, then put some salt and vinegar to it, (or no vinegar; but only salt); then set on a kettle with some water & salt, & when it boils put in the pike, boil it softly, and being boiled, take it off the fire, and put a little butter into the kettle to it, then make a sauce with beaten butter, the juyce of a lemon or two, grape verjuyce or wine-vinegar, dish up the pike on fine carved sippets, and pour on the sauce, garnish the fish with scalded parsley, large mace barberries, slic't lemon, and lemon-peel, and garnish the dish with the same.

To stew a Pike in the French Fashion.

Take a pike, splat it down the back alive, and let the liquor boil before you put it in, then take a large deep dish or stewing pan that will contain the pike, put as much claret-wine as will cover it, & wash off the blood take out the pike, and put to the wine in the dish three or four slic't onions, four blades of large mace, gross pepper, & salt; when it boils put in the pike, cover it close, & being stewed down, dish it up in a clean scowred dish with carved sippets round abound it, pour on the broth it was stewed in all over it, with the spices and onions, and put some slic't lemon over all, with some lemon-peel; run it over with beaten butter, and garnish the dish with dry grated manchet. Thus you may also stew it with the scales on or off.

Sometimes for change use horse-raddish.

To stew a Pike otherways in the City Fashion.

Take a pike, splat it, and lay it in a dish, when the blood is clean washed out, put to it as much white-wine as will cover it, and set it a stewing; when it boils put in the fish, scum it, and put to it some large mace, whole cinamon, and some salt, being finely stewed dish it on sippets finely carved.

Then thicken the broth with two or three egg yolks, some thick cream, sugar, and beaten butter, give it a warm and pour it on the pike, with some boil'd currans, and boil'd prunes laid all over it, as also mace, cinamon, some knots of barberries, and slic't lemon, garnish the dish with the same garnish, and scrape on fine sugar.

In this way you may do Carp, Bream, Barbel, Chevin, Rochet, Gurnet, Conger, Tench, Pearch, Bace, or Mullet.

To hash a Pike.

Scale and bone it, then mince it with a good fresh eel, being also boned and flayed, put to it some sweet herbs fine stripped and minced small, beaten nutmeg, mace, ginger, pepper, and salt; stew it in a dish with a little white wine and sweet butter, being well stewed, serve it on fine carved sippets, and lay on some great stewed oysters, some fried in batter, some green with juyce of spinage, other yellow with saffron, garnish the dish with them, and run it over with beaten butter.

To souce a Pike.

Draw and wash it clean from the blood and slime, then boil it in water and salt, when the liquor boils put it to it, and boil it leisurely simmering, season it pretty savory of the salt, boil it not too much, nor in more water then will but just cover it.

If you intend to keep it long, put as much white-wine as water, of both as much as will cover the fish, some wine vinegar, slic't ginger, large mace, cloves, and some salt; when it boils put in the fish, spices, and some lemon-peel, boil it up quick but not too much; then take it up into a tray, and boil down the liquor to a jelly, lay some slic't lemon on it, pour on the liquor, and cover it up close; when you serve it in jelly, dish and melt some of the jelly, and run it all over, garnish it with bunches of barberries and slic't lemon.

Or being soust and not jellied, serve it with fennil and parsley.

When you serve it, you may lay round the dish divers Small Fishes, as Tench, Pearch, Gurnet, Chevin, Roach, Smelts, and run them over with jelly.

To souce and jelly Pike, Eeel, Tench, Salmon, Conger, &c.

Scale the foresaid fishes, being scal'd, cleansed and boned, season them with nutmeg and salt, or no spices at all, roul them up and bind them like brawn, being first rouled in a clean white cloth close bound up round it, boil them in water, white-wine, and salt, but first let the pan or vessel boil, put it in and scum it, then put in some large mace and slic't ginger. If you will only souce them boil them not down so much; if to jelly them, put to them some ising-glass, and serve them in collars whole standing in the jelly.

Otherways to souce and jelly the foresaid Fishes.

Make jelly of three tenches, three perches, and two carps, scale them, wash out the blood, and soak them in fair water three or four hours, leave no fat on them, then put them in a large pipkin with as much fair spring water as will cover them, or as many pints as pound of fish, put to it some ising-glass, and boil it close covered till two parts and a half be wasted; then take it off and strain it, let it cool, and being cold take off the fat on the top, pare the bottom, and put the jelly into three pipkins, put three quarts of white-wine to them, and a pound and a half of double refined sugar into each pipkin; then to make one red put a quarter of an ounce of whole cinamon, two races of ginger, two nutmegs, two or three cloves, and a little piece of turnsole dry'd, the dust rubbed out and steep'd in some claret-wine, put some of the wine into the jelly.

To make another yellow, put a little saffron-water, nutmeg, as much cinamon as to the red jelly, and a race of ginger sliced.

To the white put three blades of large mace, a race of ginger slic't, then set the jelly on the fire till it be melted, then have fifteen whites of eggs beaten, and four pound and a half of refined sugar, beat amongst the eggs, being first beaten to fine powder; then divide the sugar and eggs equally into the three foresaid pipkins, stir it amongst the sugar very well, set them on the fire to stew, but not to boil up till you are ready to run it; let each pipkin cool a little before you run it, put a rosemary branch in each bag, and wet the top of your bags, wring them before you run them, and being run, put some into orange rinds, some into scollop shells, or lemon rindes in halves, some into egg shells or muscle shells, or in moulds for Jellies. Or you may make four colours, and mix some of the jelly with almonds-milk.

You may dish the foresaid jellies on a pie-plate on a great dish in four quarters, and in the middle a lemon finely carved or cut into branches, hung with jellies, and orange peels, and almond jellies round about; then lay on a quarter of the white jelly on one quarter of the plate, another of red, and another of amber-jelly, the other whiter on another quarter, and about the outside of the plate of all the colours one by another in the rindes of oranges and lemons, and for the quarters, four scollop shells of four several colours, and dish it as the former.

Pike Jelly otherways.

Take a good large pike, draw it, wash out the blood, and cut it in pieces, then boil it in a gallon or 6 quarts of fair spring water, with half a pound of ising-glass close covered, being first clean scum'd, boil it on a soft fire till half be wasted; then strain the stock or broth into a clean bason or earthen pan, and being cold pare the bottom and top from the fat and dregs, put it in a pipkin and set it over the fire, melt it, and put it to the juyce of eight or nine lemons, a quart of white-wine, a race of ginger pared and slic't, three or four blades of large mace, as much whole cinamon, and a grain of musk and ambergriese tied up in a fine clean clout, then beat fifteen whites of eggs, and put to them in a bason four pound of double refined sugar first beaten to fine powder, stir it with the eggs with a rouling pin, and then put it among the jelly in the pipkin, stir them well together, and set it a stewing on a soft charcoal fire, let it stew there, but not boil up but one warm at least, let it stew an hour, then take it off and let it cool a little, run it through your jelly-bag, put a sprig of rosemary in the bottom of the bag, and being run, cast it into moulds. Amongst some of it put some almond milk or make it in other colours as aforesaid.

To make White Jelly of two Pikes.

Take two good handsome pikes, scale and draw them, and wash them clean from the blood, then put to them six quarts of good white-wine, and an ounce of ising-glass, boil them in a good large pipkin to a jelly, being clean scummed, then strain it and blow off the fat.

Then take a quart of sweet cream, a quart of the jelly, a pound and a half of double refined sugar fine beaten, and a quarter of a pint of rose-water, put all together in a clean bason, and give them a warm on the fire, with half an ounce of fine searsed ginger, then set it a cooling, dish it into dice-work, or cast it into moulds and some other coloured Jellies. Or in place of cream put in almond-milk.

To roast a Pike.

Take a pike, scour off the slime, and take out the entrails, lard the back with pickled herrings, (you must have a sharp bodkin to make the holes to lard it) then take some great oysters and claret-wine, season the oysters with pepper and nutmeg, stuff the belly with oysters, and intermix the stuffing with rosemary, tyme, winter savory, sweet marjoram, a little onion, and garlick, sow these in the belly of the pike; then prepare two sticks about the breadth of a lath, (these two sticks and the spit must be as broad as the pike being tied on the spit) tie the pike on winding packthred about it, tye also along the side of the pike which is not defended by the spit and the laths, rosemary, and bays, baste the pike with butter and claret wine with some anchoves dissolved in it; when the pike is wasted or roasted, take it off, rip up the belly, and take out the whole herbs quite away, boil up the gravy, dish the pike, put the wine to it, and some beaten butter.

To fry Pikes.

Draw them, wash off the slime and the blood clean, wipe them dry with a clean cloth, flour them, and fry them in clarifi'd butter, being fried crisp and stiff, make sauce with beaten butter, slic't lemon, nutmeg, and salt, beaten up thick with a little fried parsley.

Or with beaten butter, nutmeg, a little claret, salt, and slic't orange.

Otherways, oyster-liquor, a little claret, beaten butter, slic't orange, and nutmeg, rub the dish with a clove of garlick, give the sauce a warm, and garnish the fish with slic't lemon or orange and barberries. Small pikes are best to fry.

To fry a Pike otherways.

The pike being scalded and splatted, hack the white or inside with a knife, and it will be ribbed, then fry it brown and crisp in clarified butter, being fried, take it up, drain all the butter from it, and wipe the pan clean, then put it again into the pan with claret, slic't ginger, nutmeg, an anchove, salt, and saffron beat, fry it till it half be consumed, then put in a piece of butter, shake it well together with a minced lemon or slic't orange, and dish it, garnish it with lemon, and rub the dish with a clove of garlick.

To broil a Pike.

Take a pike, draw it & scale it, broil it whole, splat it or scotch it with your knife, wash out the blood clean, and lay it on a clean cloth, salt it, and heat the gridiron very hot, broil it on a soft fire, baste it with butter, and turn it often; being finely broil'd, serve it in a dish with beaten butter, and wine-vinegar, or juyce of lemons or oranges, and garnish the fish with slices of oranges or lemons, and bunches of rosemary.

Otherways.

Take a pike, as abovesaid, being drawn, wash it clean, dry it, and put it in a dish with some good sallet oyl, wine vinegar, and salt, there let it steep the space of half an hour, then broil it on a soft fire, turn it and baste it often with some fine streight sprigs of rosemary, parsley, and tyme, baste it out of the dish where the oyl and vinegar is; then the pike being finely broil'd, dish it in a clean dish, put the same basting to it being warmed on the coals, lay the herbs round the dish, with some orange or lemon slices.

To broil Mackarel or Horn kegg.

Draw the Mackarel at the gills, and wash them, then dry them, and salt and broil them with mints, and green fennil on a soft fire, and baste them with butter, or oyl and vinegar, and being finely broil'd, serve them with beaten butter and vinegar, or oyl and vinegar, with rosemary, time, and parsley; or other sauce, beaten butter, and slices of lemon or orange.

To broil Herrings, Pilchards, or Sprats.

Gill them, wash and dry them, salt and baste them with butter, broil them on a soft fire, and being broi'ld serve them with beaten butter, mustard, and pepper, or beaten butter and lemon; other sauce, take the heads and bruise them in a dish with beer and salt, put the clearest to the herrings.

To bake Pikes.

Bake your pikes as you do carp, as you may see in the foregoing Section, only remember that small pikes are best to bake.

SECTION XV.

OR,

THE THIRD SECTION FOR DRESSING OF FISH.

The most excellent ways of Dressing Salmon, Bace, or Mullet.

To Calver Salmon to be eaten hot or cold.

CHine it, and cut each side into two or three peices according to the bigness, wipe it clean from the blood and not wash it; then have as much wine and water as you imagine will cover it, make the liquor boil, and put in a good handful of salt; when the liquor boils put in the salmon, and boil it up quick with a quart of white-wine vinegar, keep up the fire stiff to the last, and being througly boil'd, which will be in the space of half an hour or less, then take it off the fire and let it cool, take it up into broad bottomed earthen pans, and being quite cold, which will be in a day, a night, or twelve hours, then put in the liquor to it, and so keep it.

Some will boil in the liquor some rosemary bound up in a bundle hard, two or three cloves, two races of slic't ginger, three or four blades of large mace, and a lemon peel. Others will boil it in beer only.

Or you may serve it being hot, and dish it on sippets in a clean scowred dish; dish it round the dish or in pieces and garnish it with slic't ginger, large mace, a clove or two, gooseberries, grapes, barberries, slic't lemon, fryed parsley, ellicksaders, sage, or spinage fried.

To make sauce for the foresaid salmon, beat some butter up thick with a little fair water, put 2 or three yolks of eggs dissolved into it, with a little of the liquor, grated nutmeg, and some slic't lemon, pour it on the salmon, and garnish the dish with fine searsed manchet, barberries, slic't lemon, and some spices, and fryed greens as aforesaid.

To stew a small Salmon, Salmon Peal, or Trout.

Take a salmon, draw it, scotch the back, and boil it whole in a stew-pan with white-wine, (or in pieces) put to it also some whole cloves, large mace, slic't ginger, a bay-leaf or two, a bundle of sweet herbs well and hard bound up, some whole pepper, salt, some butter, and vinegar, and an orange in halves; stew all together, and being well stewed, dish them in a clean scowred dish with carved sippets, lay on the spices and slic't lemon, and run it over with beaten butter, and some of the gravy it was stewed in; garnish the dish with some fine searsed manchet or searsed ginger.

Otherways a most excellent way to stew Salmon.

Take a rand or jole of salmon, fry it whole raw, and being fryed, stew it in a dish on a chaffing dish of coals, with some claret-wine, large mace, slic't nutmeg, salt, wine-vinegar, slic't orange, and some sweet butter; being stewed and the sauce thick, dish it on sippets, lay the spices on it, and some slices of oranges, garnish the dish with some stale manchet finely searsed and strewed over all.

To pickle Salmon to keep all the year.

Take a Salmon, cut it in six round pieces, then broil it in white-wine, vinegar, and a little water, three parts wine and vinegar, and one of water; let the liquor boil before you put in the salmon, and boil it a quarter of an hour; then take it out of the liquor, drain it very well, and take rosemary sprigs, bay-leaves, cloves, mace, and gross pepper, a good quantity of each, boil them in two quarts of white-wine, and two quarts of white-wine vinegar, boil it well, then take the salmon being quite cold, and rub it with pepper, and salt, pack it in a vessel that will but just contain it, lay a layer of salmon and a layer of spice that is boil'd in the liquor; but let the liquor and spice be very cold before you put it to it; the salmon being close packed put in the liquor, and once in half a year, or as it grows dry, put some white-wine or sack to it, it will keep above a year; put some lemon-peel into the pickle, let the salmon be new taken if possible.

An excellent way to dress Salmon, or other Fish.

Take a piece of fresh salmon, wash it clean in a little wine-vinegar, and let it lye a little in it in a broad pipkin with a cover, put to it six spoonfuls of water, four of vinegar, as much of white-wine, some salt, a bundle of sweet herbs, a few whole cloves, a little large mace, and a little stick of cinamon, close up the pipkin with paste, and set it in a kettle of seething water, there let it stew three hours; thus you may do carps, trouts, or eels, and alter the taste at your pleasure.

To hash Salmon.

Take salmon and set it in warm water, take off the skin, and mince a jole, rand, or tail with some fresh eel; being finely minced season it with beaten cloves, mace, salt, pepper, and some sweet herbs; stew it in a broad mouthed pipkin with some claret wine, gooseberries, barberries, or grapes, and some blanched chesnuts; being finely stewed serve it on sippets about it, and run it over with beaten butter, garnish the dish with stale grated manchet searsed, some fryed oysters in batter, cockles, or prawns; sometimes for variety use pistaches, asparagus boil'd and cut an inch long, or boil'd artichocks, and cut as big as a chesnut, some stewed oysters, or oyster-liquor, and some horse-raddish scraped, or some of the juyce; and rub the bottom of the dish wherein you serve it with a clove of garlick.

To dress Salmon in Stoffado.

Take a whole rand or jole, scale it, and put it in an earthen stew-pan, put to it some claret, or white-wine, some wine-vinegar, a few whole cloves, large mace, gross pepper, a little slic't ginger, salt, and four or five cloves of garlick, then have three or four streight sprigs of rosemary as much of time, and sweet marjoram, two or 3 bay leaves and parsley bound up into a bundle hard, and a quarter of a pound of good sweet butter, close up the earthen pot with course paste, bake it in an oven, & serve it on sippets of French bread, with some of the liquor and spices on it, run it over with beaten butter and barberries, lay some of the herbs on it, slic't lemon and lemon-peel.

To marinate Salmon to be eaten hot or cold.

Take a Salmon, cut it into joles and rands, & fry them in good sweet sallet oyl or clarified butter, then set them by in a charger, and have some white or claret-wine, & wine vinegar as much as will cover it, put the wine & vinegar into a pipkin with all maner of sweet herbs bound up in a bundle as rosemary, time, sweet marjoram, parsly winter-savory, bay-leaves, sorrel, and sage, as much of one as the other, large mace, slic't ginger, gross pepper, slic't nutmeg, whole cloves, and salt; being well boil'd together, pour it on the fish, spices and all, being cold, then lay on slic't lemons, and lemon-peel, and cover it up close; so keep it for present spending, and serve it hot or cold with the same liquor it is soust in, with the spices, herbs, and lemons on it.

If to keep long, pack it up in a vessel that will but just hold it, put to it no lemons nor herbs, only bay-leaves; if it be well packed, it will keep as long as sturgeon, but then it must not be splatted, but cut round ways through chine and all.

To boil Salmon in stewed Broth.

Take a jole, chine, or rand, put it in a stew-pan or large pipkin with as much claret wine and water as will cover it, some raisins of the sun, prunes, currans, large mace, cloves, whole cinamon, slic't ginger, and salt, set it a stewing over a soft fire, and when it boils put in some thickning of strain'd bread, or flour, strain'd with some prunes being finely stewed, dish it up on sippets in a clean scowred dish, put a little sugar in the broth, the fruit on and some slic't lemon.

To fry Salmon.

Take a jole, rand, or chine, or cut it round through chine and all half an inch thick, or in square pieces fry it in clarified butter; being stiff & crisp fryed, make sauce with two or three spoonfuls of claret-wine, some sweet butter, grated nutmeg, some slices of orange, wine-vinegar, and some oyster-liquor; stew them all together, and dish the salmon, pour on the sauce, and lay on some fresh slices of oranges and fryed parsley, ellicksander, sage-leaves fryed in batter, pippins sliced and fryed, or clary fryed in butter, or yolks of eggs, and quarters of oranges and lemons round the dish sides, with some fryed greens in halves or quarters.

To roast a Salmon according to this Form.

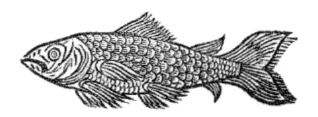

Take a salmon, draw it at the gills, and put in some sweet herbs in his belly whole; the salmon being scalded and the slime wip't off, lard it with pickled herrings, or a fat salt eel, fill his belly with some great oysters stewed, and some nutmeg; let the herbs be tyme, rosemary, winter savory, sweet marjoram, a little onion and garlick, put them in the belly of the salmon, baste it with butter, and set it in an oven in a latten dripping-pan, lay it on sticks and baste it with butter, draw it, turn it, and put some claret wine in the pan under it, let the gravy drip into it, baste it out of the pan with rosemary and bayes, and put some anchoves into the wine also, with some pepper and nutmeg; then take the gravy and clear off the fat, boil it up, and beat it thick with butter; then put the fish in a large dish, pour the sauce on it, and rip up his belly, take out some of the oysters, and put them in the sauce, and take away the herbs.

Otherways.

Take a rand or jole, cut it into four pieces, and season it with a little nutmeg and salt, stick a few cloves, and put it on a small spit, put between it some bay-leaves, and stick it with little sprigs of rosemary, roast it and baste it with butter, save the gravy, with some wine-vinegar, sweet butter, and some slices of orange; the meat being rosted, dish it, and pour on the sauce.

To broil or toast Salmon.

Take a whole salmon, a jole, rand, chine, or slices cut round it the thickness of an inch, steep these in wine-vinegar, good sweet sallet oyl and salt, broil them on a soft fire, and baste them with the same sauce they were steeped in, with some streight sprigs of rosemary, sweet marjoram, tyme, and parsley: the fish being broil'd, boil up the gravy and oyster-liquor, dish up the fish, pour on the sauce, and lay the herbs about it.

To broil or roast a Salmon in Stoffado.

Take a jole, rand, or chine, and steep it in claret-wine, wine-vinegar, white-wine, large mace, whole cloves, two or three cloves of garlick, slic't ginger, gross pepper and salt; being steeped about two hours, broil it on a soft fire, and baste it with butter, or very good sallet oyl, sprigs of rosemary, tyme, parsley, sweet marjoram, and some two or three bay-leaves, being broiled, serve it with the sauce it was steeped in, with a little oyster-liquor put to it, dish the fish, warm the sauce it was stewed in, and pour it on the fish either in butter or oyl, lay the spices and herbs about it; and in this way you may roast it, cut the jole, or rand in six pieces if it be large, and spit it with bayes and rosemary between, and save the gravy for sauce.

Sauces for roast or boil'd Salmon.

Take the gravy of the salmon, or oyster liquor, beat it up thick with beaten butter, claret wine, nutmeg, and some slices of orange.

Otherways, with gravy of the salmon, butter, juyce of orange or lemon, sugar, and cinamon, beat up the sauce with the butter pretty thick, dish up the salmon, pour on the sauce, and lay it on slices of lemon.

Or beaten butter, with slices of orange or lemon, or the juyce of them, or grape verjuyce and nutmeg.

Otherways, the gravy of the salmon, two or three anchoves dissolved in it, grated nutmeg, and grated bread beat up thick with butter, the yolk of an egg and slices of oranges, or the juyce of it.

To bake Salmon.

Take a salmon being new, scale it, draw it, and wipe it dry, scrape out the blood from the back-bone, scotch it on the back and side, then season it with pepper, nutmeg, and salt; the pie being made, put butter in the bottom of it, a few whole cloves, and some of the seasoning, lay on the salmon, and put some whole cloves on it, some slic't nutmeg, and butter, close it up and baste it over with eggs, or saffron water, being baked fill it up with clarified butter.

Or you may flay the salmon, and season as aforesaid with the same spices, and not scotch it but lay on the skin again, and lard it with Eels.

For the past only boiling liquor, with three gallons of fine or course flour made up very stiff.

To make minced Pies of Salmon.

Mince a rand of fresh salmon very small, with a good fresh water eel being flayed and boned; then mince, some violet leaves, sorrel, strawberry-leaves, parsley, sage, savory, marjoram, and time, mingle all together with the meat currans, cinamon, nutmeg, pepper, salt, sugar, caraways; rose-water, white-wine, and some minced orangado, put some butter in the bottom of the pies, fill them, and being baked ice them, and scrape on sugar; Make them according to these forms.

To make Chewits of Salmon.

Mince a rand of salmon with a good fresh water eel, being boned, flayed, and seasoned with pepper, salt, nutmeg cinamon, beaten ginger, caraway-seed, rose-water, butter, verjuyce, sugar, and orange-peel minced mingle all together with some slic't dates, and currans, put butter in the bottom, fill the pies, close them up, bake them, and ice them.

To make a Lumber Pye of Salmon.

Mince a rand, jole, or tail with a good fat fresh eel seasoned in all points as beforesaid, put five or six yolks of eggs to it with one or two whites, make it into balls or rouls, with some hard eggs in quarters, put some butter in the pye, lay on the rouls, and on them large mace, dates in halves, slic't lemon, grapes, or barber-ries, & butter, close it up, bake it, and ice it; being baked, cut up the cover, fry some sage-leaves in batter, in clarified butter, and stick them in the rouls, cut the cover, and lay it on the plate about the pie, or mingle it with an eel cut into dice work, liquor it with verjuyce, sugar, and butter.

To boil Bace, Mullet, Gurnet, Rochet, Wivers, &c.

Take a mullet, draw it, wash it, and boil it in fair water and salt, with the scales on, either splatted or whole, but first let the liquor boil, being finely boiled, dish it upon a clean scowred dish, put carved sippets round about it, and lay the white side uppermost, garnish it with slic't lemon, large mace, lemon-peel, and barber-ries, then make a lear or sauce with beaten butter, a little water, slices of lemon, juyce of grapes or orange, strained with the yolks of two or three eggs.

To souce Mullets or Bace.

Draw them & boil them with the scales, but first wash them clean, & lay them in a dish with some salt, cast upon them some slic't ginger, & large mace, put some wine vinegar to them, and two or three cloves; then set on the fire a kettle with as much wine as water, when the pan boils put in the fish and some salt; boil it with a soft fire, & being finely boiled and whole, take them up with a false bottom and 2 wires all together. If you will jelly them, boil down the liquor to a jelly with a piece of ising-glass; being boil'd to a jelly, pour it on the fish, spices and all into an earthen flat bottomed pan, cover it up close, and when you dish the fish, serve it with some of the jelly on it, garnish the dish with slic't ginger and mace, and serve with it in saucers wine vinegar, minc't fennil and slic't ginger; garnish the dish with green fennil and flowers, and parsley on the fish.

To marinate Mullets or Bace.

Scale the mullets, draw them, and scrape off the slime, wash & dry them with a clean cloth, flour them and fry them in the best sallet oyl you can get, fry them in a frying pan or in a preserving pan, but first before you put in the fish to fry, make the oyl very hot, fry them not too much, but crisp and stiff; being clear, white, and fine fryed, lay them by in an earthen pan or charger till they be all fry'd, lay them in a large flat bottom'd pan that they may lie by one another, and upon one another at length, and pack them close; then make pickle for them with as much wine vinegar as will cover them the breadth of a finger, boil in it a pipkin with salt, bay-leaves, sprigs or tops of rosemary, sweet marjoram, time, savory, and parsley, a quarter of a handful of each, and whole pepper; give these things a warm or two on the fire, pour it on the fish, and cover it close hot; then slice 3 or 4 lemons being par'd, save the peels, and put them to the fish, strow the slices of lemon over the fish with the peels, and keep them close covered for your use. If this fish were barrel'd up, it would keep as long as sturgeon, put half wine vinegar, and half white-wine, the liquor not boil'd, nor no herbs in the liquor, but fry'd bay-leaves, slic't nutmegs, whole cloves, large mace, whole pepper, and slic't ginger; pack the fishes close, and once a month turn the head of the vessel downward; will keep half a year without barrelling.

Marinate these fishes following as the mullet; *viz*, Bace, Soals, Plaice, Flounders, Dabs, Pike, Carp, Bream, Pearch, Tench, Wivers, Trouts, Smelts, Gudgeons, Mackarel, Turbut, Holly-bur, Gurnet, Roachet, Conger, Oysters, Scollops, Cockles, Lobsters, Prawns, Crawfish, Muscles, Snails, Mushrooms, Welks, Frogs.

To marinate Bace, Mullet, Gurnet, or Rochet otherways.

Take a gallon of vinegar, a quart of fair water, a good handful of bay-leaves, as much of rosemary, and a quarter of a pound of pepper beaten, put these together, and let them boil softly, season it with a little salt, then fry your fish in special good sallet oyl, being well clarifi'd, the fish being fryed put them in an earthen vessel or barrel, lay the bay-leaves, and rosemary between every layer of the fish, and pour the broth upon it, when it is cold close up the vessel; thus you may use it to serve hot or cold, and when you dish it to serve, garnish it with slic't lemon, the peel and barberries.

To broil Mullet, Bace, or Bream.

Take a mullet; draw it, and wash it clean, broil it with the scales on, or without scales, and lay it in a dish with some good sallet oyl, wine vinegar, salt, some sprigs of rosemary, time, and parsley, then heat the gridiron, and lay on the fish, broil it on a soft fire, on the embers, and baste it with the sauce it was steep'd in, being broiled serve it in a clean warm dish with the sauce it was steeped in, the herbs on it, and about the dish, cast on salt, and so serve it with slices of orange, lemon, or barberries.

Or broil it in butter and vinegar with herbs as above-said, and make sauce with beaten butter and vinegar.

Or beaten butter and juyce of lemon and orange.

Sometimes for change, with grape verjuyce, juyce of sorrel, beaten butter and the herbs.

To fry Mullets.

Scale, draw, and scotch them, wash them clean, wipe them dry and flour them, fry them in clarified butter, and being fried, put them in a dish, put to them some claret wine, slic't ginger, grated nutmeg, an anchove, salt, and some sweet butter beat up thick, give the fish a warm with a minced lemon, and dish it, but first rub the dish with a clove of garlick.

The least Mullets are the best to fry.

To bake a Mullet or Bace.

Scale, garbidge, wash and dry the Mullet very well, then lard it with a salt eel, season it, and make a pudding for it with grated bread, sweet herbs, and some fresh eel minced, put also the yolks of hard eggs, an anchove wash'd & minc'd very small, some nutmeg, & salt, fill the belly or not fill it at all, but cut it into quarters or three of a side, and season them with nutmeg, ginger, and pepper, lay them in your pie, and make balls and lay them upon the pieces of Mullet, then put on some capers, prawns, or cockles, yolks of eggs minced, butter, large mace, and barberries, close it up, and being bak'd cut up the lid, and stick it full of cuts of paste, lozenges, or other pretty garnish, fill it up with beaten butter, and garnish it with slic't lemon.

Or you may bake it in a patty pan with better paste than that which is made for pyes.

This is a very good way for tench or bream.

SECTION XVI.

OR,

THE FOURTH SECTION FOR DRESSING OF FISH.

Shewing the exactest ways of dressing Turbut, Plaice, Flounders, and Lampry.

To boil Turbut to eat hot.

Draw and wash them clean, then boil them in white wine and water, as much of the one as of the other with some large mace, a few cloves, salt, slic't ginger, a bundle of time and rosemary fast bound up; when the pan boils put in the fish, scum it as it boils, and being half boil'd, put in some lemon-peel; being through boiled, serve it in this broth, with the spices, herbs, and slic't lemon on it; or dish it on sippets with the foresaid garnish, and serve it with beaten butter.

Turbut otherways calvered.

Draw the turbut, wash it clean, and boil it in half wine and half water, salt, and vinegar; when the pan boils put in the fish, with some slic't onions, large mace, a clove or two, some slic't ginger, whole pepper, and a bundle of sweet herbs, as time, rosemary, and a bay-leaf or two; scotch the fish on the white side very thick overthwart only one way, before you put it a boiling; being half boiled, put in some lemon or orange peel; and being through boil'd, serve it with the spices, herbs, some of the liquor, onions, and slic't lemon.

Or serve it with beaten butter, slic't lemon, herbs, spices, onions and barberries. Thus also you may dress holyburt.

To boil Turbut or Holyburt otherways.

Boil it in fair water and salt, being drawn and washed clean, when the pan boils put in the fish and scum it; being well boil'd dish it, and pour on it some stew'd oysters and slic't lemon; run it over with beaten butter beat up thick with juyce of oranges, pour it over all, then cut sippets, and stick it with fryed bread.

Otherways.

Serve them with beaten butter, vinegar, and barberries, and sippets about the dish.

To souce Turbut or Holyburt otherways.

Take and draw the fish, wash it clean from the blood and slime, and when the pan boils put in the fish in fair water and salt, boil it very leisurely, scum it, and season it pretty savory of the salt, boil it well with no more water then will cover it. If you intend to keep it long, boil it in as much water as white-wine, some wine vinegar, slic't ginger, large mace, two or three cloves, and some lemon-peel; being boil'd and cold, put in a slic't lemon or two, take up the fish, and keep it in an earthen pan close covered, boil these fishes in no more liquor than will cover them, boil them on a soft fire simering.

To stew Turbut or Holyburt.

Take it and cut it in slices, then fry it, and being half fryed put it in a stew-pan or deep dish, then put to it some claret, grated nutmeg, three or four slices of an orange, a little wine-vinegar, and sweet butter, stew it well, dish it, and run it over with beaten butter, slic't lemon or orange, and orange or lemon-peel.

To fry Turburt or Hollyburt.

Cut the fish into thin slices, hack it with the knife, and it will be ribbid, then fry it almost brown with butter, take it up, draining all the butter from it, then the pan being clean, put it in again with claret, slic't ginger, nutmeg, anchove, salt, and saffron beat, fry it till it be half consumed, then put in a piece of butter, shaking it well together with a minced lemon, and rub the dish with a clove of garlick.

To hash turbut, make a farc't meat of it, to rost or broil it, use in all points as you do sturgeon, and marinate it as you do carp.

The best way to calver Flounders.

Take them alive, draw and scotch them very thick on the white side, then have a pan of white-wine and wine vinegar over the fire with all manner of spices, as large mace, salt, cloves, slic't ginger, some great onions slic't, the tops of rosemary, time, sweet marjoram, pick'd parsley, and winter savory, when the pan boils put in the flounders, and no more liquor than will cover them; cover the pan close, and boil them up quick, serve them hot or cold with slic't lemon, the spices and herbs on them and lemon peel.

Broil flounders as you do bace and mullet, souce them as pike, marinate, and dress them in stoffado as carp, and bake them as oysters.

Otherways.

To boil Plaice hot to butter.

Draw them, and wash them clean, then boil them in fair water and salt, when the pan boils put them in being very new, boil them up quick with a lemon-peel; dish them upon fine sippets round about them, slic't lemon on them, the peel and some barberries, beat up some butter very thick with some juyce of lemon and nutmeg grated, and run it over them hot.

Otherways.

Boil them in white-wine vinegar, large mace, a clove or two, and slic't ginger; being boil'd serve them in beaten butter, with the juyce of sorrel, strained bread, slic't lemon, barberries, grapes, or gooseberries.

To stew Plaice.

Take and draw them, wash them clean, and put them in a dish, stew-pan or pipkin, with some claret or white wine, butter, some sweet herbs, nutmeg, pepper, an onion and salt; being finely stewed, serve them with beaten butter on carved sippets, and slic't lemon.

Otherways.

Draw, wash, and scotch them, then fry them not too much; being fried, put them in a dish or stew-pan, put to them some claret wine, grated nutmeg, wine vinegar, butter, pepper, and salt, stew them together with some slices of orange.

To bake a Lampry.

Draw it, and split the back on the inside from the mouth to the end of the tail, take out the string in the back, flay her and truss her round, parboil it and season it with nutmeg, pepper, and salt, put some butter in the bottom of the pie, and lay on the lampry with two or three good big onions, a few whole cloves and butter, close it up and baste it over with yolks of eggs, and beer or saffron water, bake it, and being baked, fill it up with clarified butter, stop it up with butter in the vent hole, and put in some claret wine, but that will not keep long.

To bake a Lampry otherways with an Eel.

Flay it, splat it, and take out the garbidg, then have a good fat eel, flay it, draw it, and bone it, wipe them dry from the slime, and season them with pepper, salt, and nutmeg, cut them in equal pieces as may conveniently lye in a square or round pye, lay butter in the bottom, and three or four good whole onions, then lay a layer of eels over the butter, and on that lay a lampry, then another of eel, thus do till the pye be full, and on the top of all put some whole cloves and butter, close it up and bake it being basted over with saffron water, yolks of eggs, and beer, and being baked and cold, fill it up with beaten butter. Make your pies according to these forms.

To bake a Lampry in the Italian Fashion to eat hot.

Flay it, and season it with nutmeg, pepper, salt, cinamon, and ginger, fill the pie either with Lampry cut in pieces or whole, put to it raisins, currans, prunes, dryed cherries, dates, and butter, close it up, and bake it, being baked liquor it with strained almonds, grape verjuyce, sugar, sweet herbs chop't and boil'd all together, serve it with juyce of orange, white wine, cinamon, and the blood of the lampry, and ice it, thus you may also do lampurns baked for hot.

To bake a Lampry otherways in Patty-pan or dish.

Take a lampry, roast it in pieces, being drawn and flayed, baste it with butter, and being roasted and cold, put it into a dish with paste or puff paste; put butter to it, being first seasoned with pepper, nutmeg, cinamon, ginger, and salt, seasoned lightly, some sweet herbs chopped, grated bisket bread, currans, dates, or slic't lemon, close it up and bake it, being baked liquor it with butter, white-wine, or sack, and sugar.

SECTION XVII.

OR,

THE FIFTH SECTION OF F I S H.

Shewing the best way to Dress Eels, Conger, Lump, and Soals.

To boil Eels to be eaten hot.

Draw them, flay them, and wipe them clean, then put them in a posnet or stew-pan, cut them three inches long, and put to them some white-wine, white-wine vinegar, a little fair water, salt, large mace, and a good big onion stew the foresaid together with a little butter; being finely stewed and tender, dish them on carved sippets, or on slices of French bread, and serve them with boil'd currans boil'd by themselves, slic't lemon, barberries, and scrape on sugar.

Otherways.

Draw and flay them, cut them into pieces, and boil them in a little fair water, white-wine, an anchove, some oyster-liquor, large mace, two or three cloves bruised, salt, spinage, sorrel, and parsley grosly minced with a little onion and pepper, dish them upon fine carved sippets; then broth them with a little of that broth, and beat up a lear with some good butter, the yolk of an egg or two, and the rinde and slices of a lemon.

To stew Eels.

Flay them, cut them into pieces, and put them into a skillet with butter, verjuyce, and fair water as much as will cover them, some large mace, pepper, a quarter of a pound of currans, two or three onions, three or four spoonfuls of yeast, and a bundle of sweet herbs, stew all these together till the fish be very tender, then dish them, and put to the broth a quarter of a pound of butter, a little salt, and sugar, pour it on the fish, sippet it, and serve it hot.

To stew Eels in an Oven.

Cut them in pieces, being drawn and flayed, then season them with pepper, salt, and a few sweet herbs chopped small, put them into an earthen pot, and set them up on end, put to them four or five cloves of garlick, and two or three spoonfulls of fair water, bake them, and serve them on sippets.

To stew Eels otherways to be eaten hot.

Draw the eels, flay them, and cut them into pieces three inches long, then put them into a broad mouthed pipkin with as much white-wine and water as will cover them put to them some stripped tyme, sweet marjoram, savory, picked parsley, and large mace, stew them well together and serve them on fine sippets, stick bay-leaves round the dish garnish the meat with slic't lemon, and the dish with fine grated manchet.

To stew whole Eels to be eaten hot.

Take three good eels, draw, flay them, and truss them round, (or in pieces,) then have a quart of white-wine, three half pints of wine-vinegar, a quart of water, some salt, and a handful of rosemary and tyme bound up hard, when the liquor boils put in the eels with some whole pepper, and large mace; being boil'd, serve them with some of the broth, beat up thick with some good butter and slic't lemon, dish them on sippets with some grapes, barberries, or gooseberries.

Otherways.

Take three good eels, draw, flay, and scotch them with your knife, truss them round, or cut them in pieces, and fry them in clarified butter, then stew them between two dishes, put to them some two or three spoonfuls of claret or white-wine, some sweet butter, two or three slices of an orange, some salt, and slic't nutmeg; stew all well together, dish them, pour on the sauce, and run it over with beaten butter, and slices of fresh orange, and put fine sippets round the dish.

To dress Eels in Stoffado.

Take two good eels, draw, flay them, and cut them in pieces three inches long, put to them half as much claret wine as will cover them, or white-wine, wine-vinegar, or elder-vinegar, some whole cloves, large mace, gross pepper, slic't ginger, salt, four or five cloves of garlick, being put into a pipkin that will contain it, put to them also three or four sprigs of sweet herbs, as rosemary, tyme, or sweet marjoram; 2 or 3 bay leaves, and some parsley; cover up the pipkin, and paste the cover, then stew it in an oven, in one hour it will be baked, serve it hot for dinner or supper on fine sippets of French bread, and the spices upon it, the herbs, slic't lemon, and lemon-peel, and run it over with beaten butter.

To souce Eels in Collars.

Take a good large silver eel, flay it (or not) take out the back bone, and wash and wipe away the blood with a dry cloth, then season it with beaten nutmeg and salt, cut off the head and roul in the tail; being seasoned in the in side, bind it up in a fine white cloth close and streight; then have a large skillet or pipkin, put in it some fair water and white wine, of each a like quantity, and some salt, when it boils put in the eel; being boil'd tender take it up, and let it cool, when it is almost cold keep it in sauce for your use in a pipkin close covered, and when you will serve it take it out of the cloth, pare it, and dish it in a clean dish or plate, with a sprig of rosemary in the middle of the Collar: Garnish the dish with jelly, barberries and lemon.

If you will have it jelly, put in a piece of ising-glass after the eel is taken up, and boil the liquor down to a jelly.

To jelly Eels otherways.

Flay an eel, and cut it into rouls, wash it clean from the blood, and boil it in a dish with some white-wine, and white-wine vinegar, as much water as wine and vinegar, and no more of the liquor than will just cover it; being tender boil'd with a little salt, take it up and boil down the liquor with a piece of ising-glass, a blade of mace, a little juyce of orange and sugar; then the eel being dished, run the clearest of the jelly over it.

To souce Eels otherways in Collars.

Take two fair eels, flay them, and part them down the back, take out the back-bone, then take tyme, parsley, & sweet marjoram, mince them small, and mingle them with nutmeg, ginger, pepper, and salt; then strow it on the inside of the eels, then roul them up like a collar of brawn, and put them in a clean cloth, bind the ends of the cloth, and boil them tender with vinegar, white-wine, salt, and water, but let the liquor boil before you put in the Eels.

To souce Eels otherways in a Collar or Roll.

Take a large great eel, and scowr it with a handful of salt, then split it down the back, take out the back bone and the guts, wipe out the blood clean, and season the eel with pepper, nutmeg, salt, and some sweet herbs minced and strowed upon it, roul it up, and bind it up close with packthred like a collar of brawn, boil it in water, salt, vinegar, and two or three blades of mace, boil it half an hour; and being boil'd, put to it a slic't lemon, and keep it in the same liquor; when you serve it, serve it in a collar or cut it out in round slices, lay six or seven in a dish, and garnish it in the dish with parsley and barberries, or serve with it vinegar in saucers.

To souce Eels otherways cut in pieces, or whole.

Take two or three great eels, scowr them in salt, draw them and wash them clean, cut them in equal pieces three inches long, and scotch them cross on both sides, put them in a dish with wine-vinegar, and salt; then have a kettle over the fire with fair water and a bundle of sweet herbs 2 or three great onions, and some large mace; when the kettle boils put in the eels, wine, vinegar, and salt; being finely boil'd and tender, drain them from the liquor and when they are cold take some of the broth and a pint of white wine, boil it up with some saffron beaten to powder, or it will not colour the wine; then take out the spices of the liquor where it was boiled and put it in the last broth made for it, leave out the onions and herbs of the first broth, and keep it in the last.

To make a Hash of Eels.

Take a good large eel or two, flay, draw, and wash them, bone and mince them, then season them with cloves and mace, mix with them some good large oysters, a whole onion, salt, a little white-wine, and an anchove, stew them upon a soft fire, and serve them on fine carved sippets, garnish them with some slic't orange and run them over with beaten butter thickned with the yolk of an egg or two, some grated nutmeg, and juyce of orange.

To make a Spitch-Cock, or broil'd Eels.

Take a good large eel, splat it down the back, and joynt the back-bone; being drawn, and the blood washed out, leave on the skin, and cut it in four pieces equally, salt them, and bast them with butter, or oyl and vinegar; broil them on a soft fire, and being finely broil'd, serve them in a clean dish, with beaten butter and juyce of lemon, or beaten butter, and vinegar, with sprigs of rosemary round about them.

To broil salt Eels.

Take a salt eel and boil it tender, being flayed and trust round with scuers, boil it tender on a soft fire, then broil it brown, and serve it in a clean dish with two or three great onions boil'd whole and tender, and then broil'd brown; serve them on the eel with oyl and mustard in saucers.

To roast an Eel.

Cut it three inches long, being first flayed and drawn, split it, put it on a small spit, & roast it, set a dish under it to save the gravy, and roast it fine and brown, then make sauce with the gravy, a little vinegar, salt, pepper, a clove or two, and a little grated parmisan, or old *English* cheese, or a little botargo grated; the eel being roasted, blow the fat off the gravy, and put to it a piece of sweet butter, shaking it well together with some salt, put it in a clean dish, lay the eel on it, and some slices of oranges.

To roast Eels otherways.

Take a good large silver eel, draw it, and flay it in pieces of four inches long, spit it on a small spit with some bay-leaves, or large sage leaves between each piece spit it cross ways, and roast it; being roasted, serve it with beaten butter, beaten with juyce of oranges, lemons, or elder vinegar, and beaten nutmeg, or serve it with venison sauce, and dredge it with beaten caraway-seed, cinamon, flour, or grated bread.

To bake Eels in Pye, Dish or Patty-pan.

Take good fresh water eels, draw, and flay them, cut them in pieces, and season them with pepper, salt, and nutmeg, lay them in a pye with some prunes, currans, grapes, gooseberries, or barberries, large mace, slic't dates and butter, close it up and bake it, being baked, liquor it with white-wine, sugar, and butter, and ice it.

If you bake it in a dish in paste, bake it in cold butter paste, rost the eel, & let it be cold, season it with nutmeg pepper, ginger, cinamon, and salt, put butter on the paste, and lay on the eel with a few sweet herbs chopped, and grated bisket-bread, grapes, currans, dates, large mace, and butter, close it up and bake it, liquor it, and ice it.

Otherways.

Take good fresh water eels; flay and draw them, season them with nutmeg, pepper, and salt, being cut in pieces, lay them in the pie, and put to them some two or three onions in quaters, some butter, large mace, grapes, barberries or gooseberries, close them up and bake them; being baked liquor them with beaten butter, beat up thick with the yolks of two eggs, and slices of an orange.

Sometimes you may bake them with a minced onion, some raisins of the sun, and season them with some ginger, pepper, and salt.

To bake Eels otherways.

Take half a douzen good eels, flay them and take out the bones, mince them and season them with nutmeg, pepper, and salt, lay some butter in the pye, and lay a lay of Eel, and a lay of watred salt Eel, cut into great lard as big as your finger, lay a lay of it, and another of minced eel, thus lay six or seven lays, and on the top lay on some whole cloves, slic't nutmeg, butter, and some slices of salt eel, close it up and bake it, being baked fill it up with some clarified butter, and close the vent. Make your pye round according to this form.

To bake Eels with Tenches in a round or square Pie to eat cold.

Take four good large eels, flayed and boned, and six good large tenches, scale, splat, and bone them, cut off the heads and fins, as also of the eels; cut both eels, and tenches a handful long, & season them with pepper, salt and nutmeg; then lay some butter in the bottom of the pie, lay a lay of eels, and then a lay of tench, thus do five or six layings, lay on the top large mace, & whole cloves and on that butter, close it up and bake it; being baked and cold, fill it up with clarified butter.

Or you may bake them whole, and lay them round in the pye, being flayed, boned, and seasoned as the former, bake them as you do a lampry, with two or three onions in the middle.

To make minced Pies of an Eel.

Take a fresh eel, flay it and cut off the fish from the bone, mince it small, and pare two or three wardens or pears, mince of them as much as of the eel, or oysters, temper and season them together with ginger, pepper, cloves, mace, salt, a little sanders, some currans, raisins, prunes, dates, verjuyce, butter, and rose-water.

Minced Eel Pyes otherways.

Take a good fresh water eel flay, draw, and parboil it, then mince the fish being taken from the bones, mince also some pippins, wardens, figs, some great raisins of the sun, season them with cloves, mace, pepper, salt, sugar, saffron, prunes, currans, dates on the top, whole raisins, and butter, make pies according to these forms; fill them, close them up and bake them, being baked, liquor them with grape verjuyce, slic't lemon, butter, sugar, and white-wine.

Other minced Eel Pyes.

Take 2 or three good large eels, being cleans'd, mince them & season them with cloves, mace, pepper, nutmeg, salt, and a good big onion in the bottom of your pye, some sweet herbs chopped, and onions, put some goosberries and butter to it, and fill your pie, close it up and bake it, being baked, liquor it with butter and verjuyce, or strong fish broth, butter, and saffron.

Otherways.

Mince some wardens or pears, figs, raisins, prunes, and season them as above-said with some spices, but no onions nor herbs, put to them goosberries, saffron, slic't dates, sugar, verjuyce, rose-water, and butter; then make pyes according to these forms, fill them and bake them, being baked, liquor them with white batter, white-wine and sugar, and ice them.

To boil Conger to be eaten hot.

Take a piece of conger being scalded and wash'd from the blood and slime, lay it in vinegar & salt, with a slice or two of lemon, and some large mace, slic't ginger, and two or three cloves, then set some liquor a boiling in a pan or kettle, as much wine and water as will cover it when the liquor boils put in the fish, with the spices, and salt, and when it is boil'd put in the lemon, and serve the fish on fine carved sippets; then make a lear or sauce with beaten butter, beat with juyce of oranges or lemons, serve it with slic't lemon on it, slic't ginger and barberries; and garnish it with the same.

To stew Conger.

Take a piece of conger, and cut it into pieces as big as a hens egg, put them in a stew-pan or two deep dishes with some large mace, salt, pepper, slic't nut-meg, some white-wine, wine vinegar, as much water, butter, and slic't ginger, stew these well together, and serve them on sippets with slic't orange, lemon, and bar-berries, and run them over with beaten butter.

To marinate Conger.

Scald and draw it, cut it into pieces, and fry it in the best sallet oyl you can get; being fried put it in a little barrel that will contain it; then have some fryed bay-leaves, large mace, slic't ginger, and a few whole cloves, lay these between the fish, put to it white-wine, vinegar, and salt, close up the head, and keep it for your use.

To souce Conger.

Take a good fat conger, draw it at two several, vents or holes, being first scalded and the fins shaved off, cut it into three or four pieces, then have a pan of fair water, and make it boil, put in the fish, with a good quantity of salt, and let it boil very softly half an hour: being tender boil'd, set it by for your use for present spending; but to keep it long, boil it with as much wine as water, and a quart of white-wine vinegar.

To souce Conger in Collars like Brawn.

Take the fore part of a conger from the gills, splat it, and take out the bone, being first flayed and scalded, then have a good large eel or two, flay'd also and boned, seasoned in the inside with minced nutmeg, mace, and salt, seasoned and cold with the eel in the inside, bind it up hard in a clean cloth, boil it in fair water, white-wine and salt.

To roast Conger.

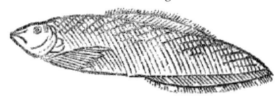

Take a good fat conger, draw it, wash it, and scrape off the slime, cut off the fins, and spit it like an S. draw it with rosemary and time, put some beaten nutmeg in his belly, salt, some stripped time, and some great oysters parboil'd, roast it with the skin on, and save the gravy for the sauce, boil'd up with a little claret-wine, beaten butter, wine vinegar, and an anchove or two, the fat blown off, and beat up thick with some sweet butter, two or three slices of an orange, and elder vinegar.

Or roast it in short pieces, and spit it with bay-leaves between, stuck with rosemary. Or make venison sauce, and instead of roasting it on a spit, roast it in an oven.

To broil Conger.

Take a good fat conger being scalded and cut into pieces; salt them, and broil them raw; or you may broil them being first boiled and basted with butter, or steeped in oyl and vinegar, broil them raw, and serve them with the same sauce you steeped them in, bast them with rosemary, time, and parsley, and serve them with the sprigs of those herbs about them, either in beaten butter, vinegar, or oyl and vinegar, and the foresaid herbs: or broil the pieces splatted like a spitch-cock of an eel, with the skin on it.

To fry Conger.

Being scalded, and the fins shaved off, splat it, cut it into rouls round the conger, flour it, and fry it in clarified butter crisp, sauce it with butter beaten with vinegar, juyce of orange or lemon, and serve it with fryed parsley, fryed ellicksanders, or clary in butter.

To bake Conger in Pasty proportion.

In Pye Proportion.

Bake it any way of the sturgeon, as you may see in the next Section, to be eaten either hot or cold, and make your pies according to these forms.

To stew a Lump.

Take it either flayed (or not) and boil it, being splated in a dish with some white-wine, a large mace or two, salt, and a whole onion, stew them well together, and dish them on fine sippets, run it over with some beaten butter, beat up with two or three slices of an orange, and some of the gravy of the fish, run it over the lump, and garnish the meat with slic't lemon, grapes, barberries, or gooseberries.

To bake a Lump.

Take a lump, and cut it into pieces, skin and all, or flay it, and part it in two pieces of a side, season it with nutmeg, pepper, and salt, and lay it in the pye, lay on it a bay-leaf or two, three or four blades of large mace, the slices of an orange, gooseberries, grapes, barberries, and butter, close it up and bake it, being baked liquor it with beaten butter.

Thus you make bake it in a dish, pye, or patty-pan.

To boil Soals.

Draw and flay them, then boil them in vinegar, salt, white-wine and mace, but let the liquor boil before you put them in; being finely boil'd, take them up and dish them in a clean dish on fine carved sippets, garnish the fish with large mace, slic't lemon, gooseberries, grapes, or barberries, and beat up some butter thick with juyce of oranges, white-wine, or grape verjuyce and run it over the fish. Sometimes you may put some stew'd oysters on them.

Otherways.

Take the soals, flay and draw them, and scotch one side with your knife, lay them in a dish, & pour on them some vinegar and salt, let them lie in it half an hour, in the mean time set on the fire some water, white-wine, six cloves of garlick, and a faggot of sweet herbs; then put the fish into the boiling liquor, and the vinegar and salt where they were in steep; being boiled, take them up and drain them very well, then beat up sweet butter very thick, and mix with it some anchoves minced small, and dissolved in the butter, pour it on the fish being dished, and strow on a little grated nutmeg, and minced orange mixt in the butter.

To stew Soals.

Being flayed and scotched, draw them and half fry them, then take some claret wine, and put to it some salt, grated ginger, and a little garlick, boil this sauce in a dish, when it boils put the soals therein, and when they are sufficiently stewed upon their backs, lay the two halves open on the one side and on the other; then lay anchoves finely washed and boned all along, and on the anchoves slices of butter, then turn the two sides over again, and let them stew till they be ready to be eaten, then take them out of the sauce, and lay them on a clean dish, pour some of the liquor wherein they were stewed upon them, and squeeze on an orange.

Otherways.

Draw, flay, and scotch them, then flour them and half fry them in clarified butter, put them in a clean pewter dish, and put to them three or four spoonfuls of claret wine, two of wine vinegar, two ounces of sweet butter, two or three slices of an orange, a little grated nutmeg, and a little salt; stew them together close covered, and being well stewed dish them up in a clean dish, lay some sliced lemon on them, and some beaten butter, with juyce of oranges.

To dress Soals otherways.

Take a pair of Soals, lard them with water'd salt Salmon, then lay them on a pye-plate, and cut your lard all of an equall length, on each side lear it but short; then flour the Soals, and fry them in the best ale you can get; when they are fryed lay them on a warm dish, and put to them anchove sauce made of some of the gravy in the pan, and two or three anchoves, grated nutmeg, a little oyl or butter, and an onion sliced small, give it a warm, and pour it on them with some juyce, and two or three slices of orange.

To souce Soals.

Take them very new, and scotch them on the upper or white side very thick, not too deep, then have white-wine, wine vinegar, cloves, mace, sliced ginger, and salt, set it over the fire to boil in a kettle fit for it; then take parsley, tyme, sage, rosemary, sweet marjoram, and winter savory, the tops of all these herbs picked, in little branches, and some great onions sliced, when it boils put in all the foresaid materials with no more liquor than will just cover them, cover them close in boiling, and boil them very quick, being cold dish them in a fair dish, and serve them with sliced lemon, and lemon-peels about them and on them.

Otherways.

Draw them and wash them clean, then have a pint of fair water with as much white-wine, some wine vinegar & salt; when the pan or kettle boils, put in the soals with a clove or two, slic't ginger, and some large mace; being boil'd and cold, serve them with the spices, some of the gravy they were boil'd in, slic't lemon, and lemon-peel.

To jelly Soals.

Take three tenches, 2 carps, and four pearches, scale them and wash out the blood clean, then take out all the fat, and to every pound of fish take a pint of fair spring-water or more, set the fish a boiling in a clean pipkin or pot, and when it boils scum it, and put in some ising-glass, boil it till one fourth part be wasted, then take it off and strain it through a strong canvas cloth, set it to cool, and being cold, divide it into three or four several pipkins, as much in the one as in the other, take off the bottom and the top, and to every quart of broth put a quart of white-wine, a pound and a half of refined sugar, two nutmegs, 2 races of ginger, 2 pieces of whole cinamon, a grain of musk, and 8 whites of eggs, stir them together with a rowling-pin, and equally divide it into the several pipkins amongst the jellies, set them a stewing upon a soft charcoal fire, when it boils up, run it through the jelly-bags, and pour it upon the soals.

To roast Soals.

Draw them, flay off the black skin, and dry them with a clean cloth, season them lightly with nutmeg, salt, and some sweet herbs chopped small, put them in a dish with some claret-wine and two or three anchoves the space of half an hour, being first larded with small lard of a good fresh eel, then spit them, roast them and set the wine under them, baste them with butter, and being roasted, dish them round the dish; then boil up the gravy under them with three or four slices of an orange, pour on the sauce, and lay on some slices of lemon.

Marinate, broil, fry and bake Soals according as you do Carps, as you may see in the thirteenth Section.

SECTION XVIII.

OR,

THE SIXTH SECTION OF FISH.

The A-la-mode ways of Dressing and Ordering of Sturgeon.

To boil Sturgeon to serve hot.

Take a rand, wash off the blood, and lay it in vinegar and salt, with the slice of a lemon, some large mace, slic't ginger, and two or three cloves, then set on a pan of fair water, put in some salt, and when it boils put in the fish, with a pint of white-wine, a pint of wine vinegar, and the foresaid spices, but not the lemon; being finely boil'd, dish it on sippets, and sauce it with beaten butter, and juyce of orange beaten together, or juyce of lemon, large mace, slic't ginger, and barberries, and garnish the dish with the same.

Otherways.

Take a rand and cut it in square pieces as big as a hens egg, stew them in a broad mouthed pipkin with two or three good big onions, fome large mace, two or three cloves, pepper, salt, some slic't nutmeg, a bay-leaf or two some white-wine and water, butter, and a race of slic't ginger, stew them well together, and serve them on sippets of French bread, run them over with beaten butter, slic't lemon and barberries, and garnish the dish with the same.

Sturgeon buttered.

Boil a rand, tail, or jole in water and salt, boil it tender, and serve it with beaten butter and slic't lemon.

To make a hot Hash of Sturgeon.

Take a rand, wash it out of the blood, and take off the scales, and skin, mince the meat very small, and season it with beaten mace, pepper, salt, and some sweet herbs minced small, stew all in an earthen pipkin with two or three big whole onions, butter, and white-wine; being finely stewed, serve it on sippets with beaten butter, minced lemon, and boil'd chesnuts.

To make a cold Hash of Sturgeon.

Take a rand of sturgeon being fresh and new, bake it whole in an earthen pan dry, and close it up with a piece of course paste; being baked and cold slice it into little slices as small as a three pence, and dish them in a fine clean dish, lay them round the bottom of it, and strow on them pepper, salt, a minced onion, a minced lemon, oyl, vinegar, and barberries.

To marinate a whole Sturgeon in rands and joles.

Take a sturgeon fresh taken, cut it in joles and rands, wash off the blood, and wipe the pieces dry from the blood and slime, flour them, & fry them in a large kettle in four gallons of rape oyl clarified, being fryed fine and crisp, put it into great chargers, frayes, or bowls; then have 2 firkins, and being cold, pack it in them as you do boil'd sturgeon that is kept in pickle, then make the sauce or pickle of 2 gallons of white-wine, and three gallons of white-wine vinegar; put to them six good handfuls of salt, 3 in each vessel, a quarter of a pound large mace, six ounces of whole pepper, and three ounces of slic't ginger, close it up in good sound vessels, and when you serve it, serve it in some of its own pickle, the spices on it, and slic't lemon.

To make a farc't meat of Sturgeon.

Mince it raw with a good fat eel, and being fine minced, season it with cloves, mace, pepper, and salt, mince some sweet herbs and put to it, and make your farcings in the forms of balls, pears, stars, or dolphins; if you please stuff carrots or turnips with it.

To dress a whole Sturgeon in Stoffado cut into Rands and Joles to eat hot or cold.

Take a sturgeon, draw it, and part it in two halves from the tail to the head, cut it into rands and joles a foot long or more, then wash off the blood and slime, and steep it in wine-vinegar, and white-wine, as much as will cover it, or less, put to it eight ounces of slic't ginger, six ounces of large mace, four ounces of whole cloves, half a pound of whole pepper, salt, and a pound of slic't nutmegs, let these steep in the foresaid liquor six hours, then put them into broad earthen pans flat bottom'd, and bake them with this liquor and spices, cover them with paper, it will ask four or five hours baking; being baked serve them in a large dish in joles or rands, with large slices of French bread in the bottom of the dish, steep them well with the foresaid broth they were baked in, some of the spices on them, some slic't lemon, barberries, grapes, or gooseberries, and lemon peel, with some of the same broth, beaten butter, juyce of lemons and oranges, and the yolks of eggs beat up thick.

If to eat cold, barrel it up close with this liquor and spices, fill it up with white-wine or sack; and head it up close, it will keep a year very well, when you serve it, serve it with slic't lemon, and bay-leaves about it.

To souce Sturgeon to keep all the year.

Take a Sturgeon, draw it, and part it down the back in equal sides and rands, put it in a tub into water and salt, and wash it from the blood and slime, bind it up with tape or packthred, and boil it in a vessel that will contain it, in water, vinegar, and salt, boil it not too tender; being finely boil'd take it up, and being pretty cold, lay it on a clean flasket or tray till it be through cold, then pack it up close.

To souce Sturgeon in two good strong sweet Firkins.

If the Sturgeon be nine foot in length, 2 firkins will serve it, the vessels being very well filled and packed close, put into it eight handfuls of salt, six gallons of white wine, and four gallons of white wine vinegar, close on the heads strong and sure, and once a month turn it on the other end.

To broil Sturgeon, or toast it against the fire.

Broil or toast a rand or jole of sturgeon that comes new out of the sea or river, (or any piece) and either broil it in a whole rand, or slices an inch thick, salt them, and steep them in oyl-olive and wine vinegar, broil them on a soft fire, and baste them with the sauce it was steeped in, with branches of rosemary, tyme, and pars-ley; being finely broiled, serve it in a clean dish with some of the sauce it was bast-ed with, and some of the branches of rosemary; or baste it with butter, and serve it with butter and vinegar, being either beaten with slic't lemon, or juyce of oranges.

Otherways.

Broil it on white paper, either with butter or sallet oyl, if you broil it in oyl, be-ing broil'd, put to it on the paper some oyl, vinegar, pepper, and branches or slices of orange. If broil'd in butter, some beaten butter, with lemon, claret, and nutmeg.

To fry Sturgeon.

Take a rand of fresh sturgeon, and cut it into slices of half an inch thick, hack it, and being fried, it will look as if it were ribbed, fry it brown with clarified butter; then take it up, make the pan clean, and put it in again with some claret wine, an anchove, salt, and beaten saffron; fry it till half be consumed, and then put in a piece of butter, some grated nutmeg, grated ginger, and some minced lemon; gar-nish the dish with lemon, dish it, and run jelly first rubbed with a clove of garlick.

To jelly Sturgeon.

Season a whole rand with pepper, nutmeg, and salt, bake it dry in an earthen pan, and being baked and cold, slice it into thin slices, dish it in a clean dish, the dish being on it.

To roast Sturgeon.

Take a rand of fresh sturgeon, wipe it very dry, and cut it in pieces as big as a goose-egg, season them with nutmeg, pepper, and salt, and stick each piece with two or 3 cloves, draw them with rosemary, & spit them thorow the skin, and put some bay-leaves or sage-leaves between every piece; baste them with butter, and being roasted serve them on the gravy that droppeth from them, beaten butter, juyce of orange or vinegar, and grated nutmeg, serve also with it venison sauce in saucers.

To make Olines of Sturgeon stewed or roasted.

Take spinage, red sage, parsley, tyme, rosemary, sweet marjoram, and win-ter-savory, wash and chop them very small, and mingle them with some currans, grated bread, yolks of hard eggs chopped small, some beaten mace, nutmeg, cina-mon and salt; then have a rand of fresh sturgeon, cut in thin broad pieces, & hackt with the back of a chopping knife laid on a smooth pie-plate, strow on the minced herbs with the other materials, and roul them up in a roul, stew them in a dish in the oven, with a little white-wine or wine-vinegar, some of the farcing under them, and some sugar; being baked, make a lear with some of the gravy, and slices of oranges and lemons.

To make Olines of Sturgeon otherways.

Take a rand of sturgeon being new, cut it in fine thin slices, & hack them with the back of a knife, then make a compound of minced herbs, as tyme, savory, sweet marjoram, violet-leaves, strawberry leaves, spinage, mints, sorrel, endive and sage; mince these herbs very fine with a few scallions, some yolks of hard eggs, currans, cinamon, nutmegs, sugar, rosewater, and salt, mingle all together, and strow on the compound herbs on the hacked olines, roul them up, and make pies according to these forms, put butter in the bottom of them, and lay the olines on it; being full, lay on some raisins, prunes, large mace, dates, slic't lemon, some gooseberries, grapes, or barberries, and butter, close them up and bake them, being baked, liquor them with butter, white-wine, and sugar, ice them, and serve them up hot.

To bake Sturgeon in Joles and Rands dry in Earthen Pans, and being baked and cold, pickled and barreld up, to serve hot or cold.

Take a sturgeon fresh and new, part him down from head to tail, and cut it into rands and joles, cast it into fair water and salt, wash off the slime and blood, and put it into broad earthen pans, being first stuffed with penniroyal, or other sweet herbs; stick it with cloves and rosemary, and bake it in pans dry, (or a little white-wine to save the pans from breaking) then take white or claret wine and make a pickle, half as much wine vinegar, some whole pepper, large mace, slic't nutmegs, and six or seven handfuls of salt; being baked and cold, pack and barrel it up close, and fill it up with this pickle raw, head it up close, and when you serve it, serve it with some of the liquor and slic't lemon.

To bake Sturgeon Pies to eat cold.

Take a fresh jole of sturgeon, scale it, and wash off the slime, wipe it dry, and lard it with a good salt eel, seasoned with nutmeg, and pepper, cut the lard as big as your finger, and being well larded, season the jole or rand with the foresaid spices and salt, lay it in a square pie in fine or course paste, and put some whole cloves on it, some slic't nutmeg, slic't ginger, and good store of butter, close it up, and bake it, being baked fill it up with clarified butter.

To bake Sturgeon otherways with Salmon.

Take a rand of sturgeon, cut it into large thick slices, & 2 rands of fresh salmon in thick slices as broad as the sturgeon, season it with the same seasoning as the former, with spices and butter, close it up and bake it; being baked, fill it up with clarified butter. Make your sturgeon pyes or pasties according to these forms.

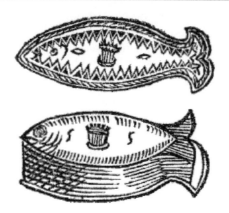

To make a Sturgeon Pye to eat cold otherways.

Take a rand of sturgeon, flay it and wipe it with a dry cloth, and not wash it, cut it into large slices; then have carps, tenches, or a good large eel flayed and boned, your tenches and carps scaled, boned, and wiped dry, season your sturgeon and the other fishes with pepper, nutmeg, and salt, put butter in the bottom of the pie, and lay a lay of sturgeon, and on that a lay of carps, then a lay of sturgeon, and a lay of eels, next a lay of sturgeon, and a lay of tench, and a lay of sturgeon above that; lay on it some slic't ginger, slic't nutmeg, and some whole cloves, put on butter, close it up, and bake it, being baked liquor it with clarified butter. Or bake it in pots as you do venison, and it will keep long.

Otherways.

Take a rand of sturgeon, flay it, and mince it very fine, season it with pepper, cloves, mace, and salt; then have a good fresh fat eel or 2 flayed and boned, cut it into lard as big as your finger, and lay some in the bottom of the pye, some butter on it, and some of the minced meat or sturgeon, and so lard and meat till you have filled the pye, lay over all some slices of sturgeon, sliced nutmeg, sliced ginger, and butter, close it up and bake it, being baked fill it up with clarified butter. If to eat hot, give it but half the seasoning, and make your pyes according to these forms.

To bake sturgeon Pies to be eaten hot.

Flay off the scales and skin of a rand, cut it in pieces as big as a walnut, & season it lightly with pepper, nutmeg, and salt; lay butter in the bottom of the pye, put in the sturgeon, and put to it a good big onion or two whole, some large mace, whole cloves, slic't ginger, some large oysters, slic't lemon, gooseberries, grapes, or barberries, and butter, close it up and bake it, being bak'd, fill it up with beaten butter, beaten with white-wine or claret, and juyce or slices of lemon or orange.

To this pye in Winter, you may use prunes, raisins, or currans, and liquor it with butter, verjuyce, and sugar, and in Summer, pease boil'd and put in the pye, being baked, and leave out fruit.

Otherways.

Cut a rand of sturgeon into pieces as big as a hens egg, cleanse it, and season them with pepper, salt, ginger, and nutmeg, then make a pye and lay some butter in the bottom of it, then the pieces of sturgeon, and two or three bay-leaves, some large mace, three or four whole cloves, some blanched chesnuts, gooseberries, grapes, or barberries, and butter, close it up and bake it, and being baked, liquor it with beaten butter, and the blood of the sturgeon boil'd together with a little claret-wine.

To bake Sturgeon Pyes in dice work to be eaten hot.

Take a pound of sturgeon, a pound of a fresh fat eel, a pound of carp, a pound of turbut, a pound of mullet, scaled, cleans'd, and bon'd, a tench, and a lobster, cut all the fishes into the form of dice, and mingle with them a quart of prawns, season them all together with pepper, nutmeg & salt, mingle some cockles among them, boil'd artichocks, fresh salmon, and asparagus all cut into dice-work. Then make pyes according to these forms, lay butter in the bottom of them, then the meat being well mingled together, next lay on some gooseberries, grapes, or barberries, slic't oranges or lemons, and put butter on it, with yolks of hard eggs and pistaches, close it up and bake it, and being baked liquor it with good sweet butter, white-wine, or juyce of oranges.

To make minced Pyes of Sturgeon.

Flay a rand of it, and mince it with a good fresh water eel, being flay'd and bon'd, then mince some sweet herbs with an onion, season it with cloves, mace, pepper, nutmeg and salt, mingle amongst it some grapes, gooseberries, or barberries, and fill the pye, having first put some butter in the bottom of it, lay on the meat, and more butter on the top, close it up, bake it, and serve it up hot.

Otherways.

Mince a rand of fresh sturgeon, or the fattest part of it very small, then mince a little spinage, violet leaves, strawberry leaves, sorrel, parsley, sage, savory, marjoram, and time, mingle them with the meat, some grated manchet, currans, nutmeg, salt, cinamon, cream, eggs, sugar, and butter, fill the pye, close it up, and bake it, being baked ice it.

Minced Pyes of Sturgeon otherways.

Flay a rand of sturgeon, and lard it with a good fat salt eel, roast it in pieces, and save the gravy, being roasted mince it small, but save some to cut into dice-work, also some of the eels in the same form, mingle it amongst the rest with some beaten pepper, salt, nutmeg, some gooseberries, grapes, or barberries, put butter in the bottom of the pye, close it up and bake it, being baked liquor it with gravy, juyce of orange, nutmeg, and butter.

Sometimes add to it currans, sweet herbs, and saffron, and liquor it with ver-juyce, sugar, butter, and yolks of eggs.

To make Chewits of Sturgeon, according to these Forms.

Mince a rand of sturgeon the fattest part, and season it with pepper, salt, nut-meg, cinamon, ginger, caraway-seed, rose-water, butter, sugar, and orange peel minced, mingle all together with some slic't dates, and currans, and fill your pyes.

To make a Lumber Pye of Sturgeon.

Mince a rand of sturgeon with some of the fattest of the belly, or a good fat fresh eel, being minced, season it with pepper, nutmeg, salt, cinamon, ginger, cara-ways, slic't dates, four or eight raw eggs, and the yolks of six hard eggs in quarters, mingle all together, and make them into balls or rolls, fill the pye, and lay on them some slic't dates, large mace, slic't lemon, grapes, gooseberries, or barberries, and butter, close it up, and bake it, being bak'd liquor it with butter, white-wine, and sugar.

Or only add some grated bread, some of the meat cut into dice-work, & some rose-water, bak'd in all points as the former, being baked cut up the cover, and stick it with balls, with fryed sage-leaves in batter; liquor it as aforesaid, and lay on it a cut cover, scrape on sugar.

To make an Olive Pye of Sturgeon in the Italian fashion.

Make slices of sturgeon, hack them, and lard them with salt salmon, or salt eel, then make a composition of some of the sturgeon cut into dice-work, some fresh eel, dry'd cherries, prunes taken from the stones, grapes, some mushrooms & oysters; season the foresaid things all together in a dish or tray, with some pepper, nutmeg, and salt, roul them in the slices of the hacked sturgeon with the larded side outmost, lay them in the pye with the butter under them; being filled lay on it some oysters, blanched chesnuts, mushrooms, cockles, pine-apple-seeds, grapes, gooseberries, and more butter, close it up, bake it, and then liquor it with butter, verjuyce, and sugar, serve it up hot.

To bake Sturgeon to be eaten hot with divers farcings or stuffings.

Take a rand and cut it into small pieces as big as a walnut, mince it with fresh eel, some sweet herbs, a few green onions, pennyroyal, grated bread, nutmeg, pepper, and salt, currans, gooseberries, and eggs; mingle all together, and make it into balls, fill the pye with the whole meat and the balls, and lay on them some large mace, barberries, chesnuts, yolks of hard eggs, and butter; fill the pye, and bake it, being baked, liquor it with butter and grape-verjuyce.

Or mince some sturgeon, grated parmisan, or good Holland cheese, mince the sturgeon, and fresh eel together, being fine minced put some currans to it, nutmeg, pepper, and cloves beaten, some sweet herbs minced small, some salt, saffron, and raw yolks of eggs.

Other stuffings or Puddings.

Grated bread, nutmeg, pepper, sweet herbs minced very fine, four or five yolks of hard eggs minced very small, two or three raw eggs, cream, currans, grapes, barberries and sugar, mix them all together, and lay them on the Sturgeon in the pye, close it up and bake it, and liquor it with butter, white-wine, sugar, the yolk of an egg, and then ice it.

To make an Olio of Sturgeon with other Fishes.

Take some sturgeon and mince it with a fresh eel, put to it some sweet herbs minc't small, some grated bread, yolks of eggs, salt, nutmeg, pepper, some gooseberries, grapes or barberries, and make it into little balls or rolls. Then have fresh fish scal'd, washed, dryed, and parted into equal pieces, season them with pepper, nutmeg, salt, and set them by; then make ready shell-fish, and season them as the other fishes lightly with the same spices. Then make ready roots, as potatoes, skirrets, artichocks and chesnuts, boil them, cleanse them, and season them with the former spices. Next have yolks of hard eggs, large mace, barberries, grapes, or gooseberries, and butter, make your pye, and put butter in the bottom of it, mix them all together, and fill the pye, then put in two or three bay-leaves, and a few whole cloves, mix the minced balls among the other meat and roots; then lay on the top some large mace, potatoes, barberries, grapes, or gooseberries, chesnuts, pistaches and butter, close it up and bake it, fill it up with beaten butter, beaten with the juyce of oranges, dish and cut up the cover, and put all over it slic't lemons, and sometimes to the lear the yolk of an egg or two.

To make minced Herring Pies.

Take salt herrings being watered, crush them between your hands, and you shall loose the fish from the skin, take off the skin whole, and lay them in a dish; then have a pound of almond paste ready, mince the herrings, and stamp them with the almond paste, two of the milts or rows, five or six dates, some grated manchet, sugar, sack, rose-water, and saffron, make the composition somewhat stiff, and fill the skins, put butter in the bottom of your pye, lay on the herring, and on them dates, gooseberries, currans, barberries, and butter, close it up and bake it, being baked liquor it with butter, verjuyce, and sugar.

Make minced pyes of any meat, as you may see in page 232, in the dishes of minced pyes you may use those forms for any kind of minced pies, either of flesh, fish, or fowl, which I have particularized in some places of my Book.

Otherways.

Bone them, and mince them being finely cleansed with 2 or three pleasant pears, raisins of the sun, some currans, dates, sugar, cinamon, ginger, nutmeg, pepper, and butter, mingle all together, fill your pies, and being baked, liquor them with verjuyce, claret, or white-wine.

To make minced Pies of Ling, Stock-fish, Harberdine, &c.

Being boil'd take it from the skin and bones, and mince it with some pippins, season it with nutmeg, cinamon, ginger, pepper, caraway-seed, currans, minced raisins, rose-water, minced lemon-peel, sugar, slic't dates, white-wine, verjuyce, and butter, fill your pyes, bake them, and ice them.

Otherways.

Mince them with yolks of hard eggs, mince also all manner of good pot-herbs, mix them together, and season them with the seasoning aforesaid, then liquor it with butter, verjuyce, sugar, and beaten cinamon, and then ice them; making them according to these forms.

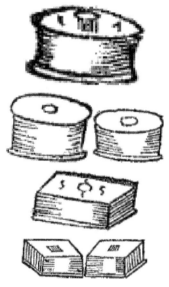

SECTION XIX.

OR,

THE SEVENTH SECTION OF FISH.

Shewing the exactest Ways of Dressing all manner of Shell-Fish.

To stew oysters in the French Way.

Take oysters, open them and parboil them in their own liquor, the quantity of three pints or a pottle; being parboil'd, wash them in warm water clean from the dregs, beard them and put them in a pipkin with a little white wine, & some of the liquor they were parboil'd in, a whole onion, some salt, and pepper, and stew them till they be half done; then put them and their liquor into a frying-pan, fry them a pretty while, put to them a good piece of sweet butter, and fry them a therein so much longer, then have ten or twelve yolks of eggs dissolved with some vinegar, wherein you must put in some minced parsley, and some grated nutmeg, put these ingredients into the oysters, shake them in the frying-pan a warm or two, and serve them up.

To stew Oysters otherways.

Take a pottle of large great oysters, parboil them in their own liquor, then wash them in warm water from the dregs, & put them in a pipkin with a good big onion or two, and five or six blades of large mace, a little whole pepper, a slic't nutmeg, a quarter of a pint of white wine, as much wine-vinegar, a quarter of a pound of sweet butter, and a little salt, stew them finely together on a soft fire the space of half an hour, then dish them on sippets of French bread, slic't lemon on them, and barberries, run them over with beaten butter, and garnish the dish with dryed manchet grated and searsed.

To stew Oysters otherways.

Take a pottle of large great oysters, parboil them in their own liquor, then wash them in warm water, wipe them dry, and pull away the fins, flour them and fry them in clarifi'd butter fine and white, then take them up, and put them in a large dish with some white or claret wine, a little vinegar, a quarter of a pound of sweet butter, some grated nutmeg, large mace, salt, and two or three slices of an orange, stew them two or three warms, then serve them in a large clean scowred dish, pour the sauce on them, and run them over with beaten butter, slic't lemon or orange, and sippets round the dish.

Otherways.

Take a pottle of great oysters, and stew them in their own liquor; then take them up, wash them in warm water, take off the fins, and put them in a pipkin with some of their own liquor, a pint of white-wine, a little wine vinegar, six large maces, 2 or three whole onions, a race of ginger slic't, a whole nutmeg slic't, twelve whole pepper corns, salt, a quarter of a pound of sweet butter, and a little faggot of sweet herbs; stew all these together very well, then drain them through a cullender, and dish them on fine carved sippets; then take some of the liquor they were stewed in; beat it up thick with a minced lemon, and half a pound of butter, pour it on the oysters being dished, and garnish the dish and the oysters with grapes, grated bread, slic't lemon, and barberries.

Or thus.

Boil great oysters in their shells brown, and dry, but burn them not, then take them out and put them in a pipkin with some good sweet butter, the juice of two or three oranges, a little pepper, and grated nutmeg, give them a warm, and dish them in a fair scowred dish with carved sippets, and garnish it with dryed, grated, searsed fine manchet.

To make Oyster Pottage.

Take some boil'd pease, strain them and put them in a pipkin with some capers, some sweet herbs finely chopped, some salt, and butter; then have some great oysters fryed with sweet herbs, and grosly chopped, put them to the strained pease, stew them together, serve them on a clean scowred dish on fine carved fippets, and garnish the dish with grated bread.

Otherways.

Take a quart of great oysters, parboil them in their own liquor, and stew them in a pipkin with some capers, large mace, a faggot of sweet herbs, salt, and butter, being finely stewed, serve them on slices of dryed *French* bread, round the oysters slic't lemon, and on the pottage boil'd spinage, minced, and buttered, but first pour on the broth.

To make a Hash of Oysters.

Take three quarts of great oysters, parboil them, and save their liquor, then mince 2 quarts of them very fine, and put them a stewing in a pipkin with a half pint of white wine, a good big onion or two, some large mace, a grated nutmeg, some chesnuts, and pistaches, and three or 4 spoonfuls of wine-vinegar, a quarter of a pound of good sweet butter, some oyster liquor, pepper, salt, and a faggot of sweet herbs; stew the foresaid together upon a soft fire the space of half an hour, then take the other oysters, and season them with pepper, salt and nutmeg, fry them in batter made of fine flour, egg, salt, and cream, make one half of it green with juyce of spinage, and sweet herbs chopped small, dip them in these batters, and fry them in clarified butter, being fried keep them warm in an oven; then have a fine clean large dish, lay slices of French bread all over the bottom of the dish, scald and steep the bread with some gravy of the hash, or oyster-liquor, & white wine boil'd together; dish the hash all over the slices of bread, lay on that the fryed oysters, chesnuts, and pistaches; then beat up a lear or sauce of butter, juyce of lemon or oranges, five or six, a little white-wine, the yolks of 3 or 4 eggs, and pour on this sauce over the hash with some slic't lemon, and lemon-peel; garnish the dish with grated bread, being dryed and searsed, some pistaches, chesnuts, carved lemons, & fryed oysters.

Sometimes you may use mushrooms boild in water, salt, sweet herbs—large mace, cloves, bayleaves, two or three cloves of garlick, then take them up, dip them in batter & fry them brown, make sauce for them with claret, and the juyce of two or three oranges, salt, butter, the juyce of horse-raddish roots beaten and strained, grated nutmeg, and pepper, beat them up thick with the yolks of two or three eggs, do this sauce in a frying-pan, shake them well together, and pour it on the hash with the mushrooms.

To marinate great oysters to be eaten hot.

Take three quarts of great oysters ready opened, parboil them in their own liquor, then take them out and wash them in warm water, wipe them dry and flour them, fry them crisp in a frying-pan with three pints of sweet sallet oyl, put them in a dish, and set them before the fire, or in a warm oven; then make sauce with white wine; wine-vinegar, four or five blades of large mace, two or three slic't nutmegs, two races of slic't ginger, some twenty cloves, twice as much of whole pepper, and some salt; boil all the foresaid spices in a pipkin, with a quart of white wine, a pint of wine vinegar, rosemary, tyme, winter savory, sweet marjoram, bay leaves, sage, and parsley, the tops of all these herbs about an inch long; then take three or four good lemons, slic't dish up the oysters in a clean scowred dish, pour on the broth, herbs, and spices on them, lay on the slic't lemons, and run it over with some of the oyl they were fried in, and serve them up hot. Or fry them in clarified butter.

Oysters in Stoffado.

Parboil a pottle or three quarts of great Oysters, save the liquor and wash the oysters in warm water, then after steep them in white-wine, wine-vinegar, slic't nutmeg, large mace, whole pepper, salt, and cloves; give them a warm on the fire, set them off and let them steep two or three hours; then take them out, wipe them dry, dip them in batter made of fine flour, yolks of eggs, some cream and salt, fry them, and being fryed keep them warm, then take some of the spices liquor, some of the oysters-liquor, and some butter, beat these things up thick with the slices of an orange or two, and two or three yolks of eggs; then dish the fryed oysters in a fine clean dish on a chafing-dish of coals, run on the sauce over them with the spices, slic't orange, and barberries, and garnish the dish with searsed manchet.

To Jelly Oysters.

Take ten flounders, two small pikes or plaice, and 4 ounces of ising glass; being finely cleansed, boil them in a pipkin in a pottle of fair spring-water, and a pottle of white-wine, with some large mace, and slic't ginger; boil them to a jelly, and strain it through a strainer into a bason or deep dish; being cold pare off the top and bottom and put it in a pipkin, with the juyce of six or seven great lemons to a pottle of this broth, three pound of fine sugar beaten in a dish with the whites of twelve eggs rubbed all together with a rouling-pin, and put amongst the jelly, being melted, but not too hot, set the pipkin on a soft fire to stew, put in it a grain of musk, and as much ambergriece well rubbed, let it stew half an hour on the embers, then broil it up, and let it run through your jelly-bag; then stew the oysters in white wine, oyster-liquor, juyce of orange, mace, slic't nutmeg, whole pepper, some salt, and sugar; dish them in a fine clean dish with some preserved barberries, large mace, or pomegranat kernels, and run the jelly over them in the dish, garnish the dish with carved lemons, large mace, and preserved barberries.

To pickle Oysters.

Take eight quarts of oysters, and parboil them in their own liquor, then take them out, wash them in warm water and wipe them dry, then take the liquor they were parboil'd in, and clear it from the grounds into a large pipkin or skillet, put to it a pottle of good white-wine, a quart of wine vinegar, some large mace, whole pepper, and a good quantity of salt, set it over the fire, boil it leisurely, scum it clean, and being well boil'd put the liquor into eight barrels of a quart a piece, being cold, put in the oyster, and close up the head.

Otherways.

Take eight quarts of the fairest oysters that can be gotten, fresh and new, at the full of the Moon, parboil them in their own liquor, then wipe them dry with a clean cloth, clear the liquor from the dregs, and put the oysters in a well season'd barrel that will but just hold them, then boil the oyster liquor with a quart of white-wine, a pint of wine-vinegar, eight or ten blades of large mace, an ounce of whole pepper, four ounces of white salt, four races of slic't ginger, and twenty cloves, boil these ingredients four or five warms, and being cold, put them to the oysters, close up the barrel, and keep it for your use.

When you serve them, serve them in a fine clean dish with bay-leaves round about them, barberries, slic't lemon, and slic't orange.

To souce Oysters to serve hot or cold.

Take a gallon of great oysters ready opened, parboil them in their own liquor, and being well parboil'd, put them into a cullender, and save the liquor; then wash the oysters in warm water from the grounds & grit, set them by, and make a pickle for them with a pint of white-wine, & half a pint of wine vinegar, put it in a pipkin with some large mace, slic't nutmegs, slic't ginger, whole pepper, three or four cloves, and some salt, give it four or five warms and put in the oysters into the warm pickle with two slic't lemons, and lemon-peels; cover the pipkin close to keep in the spirits, spices, and liquor.

To roast Oysters.

Strain the liquor from the oysters, wash them very clean and give them a scald in boiling liquor or water; then cut small lard of a fat salt eel, & lard them with a very small larding-prick, spit them on a small spit for that service; then beat two or three yolks of eggs with a little grated bread, or nutmeg, salt, and a little rosemary & tyme minced very small; when the oysters are hot at the fire, baste them continually with these ingredients, laying them pretty warm at the fire. For the sauce boil a little white-wine, oyster-liquor, a sprig of tyme, grated bread, and salt, beat it up thick with butter, and rub the dish with a clove of garlick.

To roast Oysters otherways.

Take two quarts of large great oysters, and parboil them in there own liquor, then take them out, wash them from the dregs, and wipe them dry on a clean cloth; then haue slices of a fat salt eel, as thick as a half crown peice, season the oysters with nutmeg, and salt, spit them on a fine small wooden spit for that purpose, spit first a sage leafe, then a slice of eel, and then an oyster, thus do till they be all spitted, and bind them to another spit with packthread, baste them with yolks of eggs, grated bread and stripped time, and lay them to a warm fire with here and there a clove in them; being finely roasted make sauce with the gravy, that drops from them, blow off the fat, and put to it some claret wine, the juyce of an orange, grated nutmeg, and a little butter, beat it up thick together with some of the oyster-liquor, and serve them on this sauce with slices of orange.

Otherways.

Take the greatest oysters you can get, being opened parboil them in their own liquor, save the liquor, & wash the oysters in some water, wipe them dry, & being cold lard them with eight or ten lardons through each oyster, the lard being first seasoned with cloves, pepper, & nutmeg, beaten very small; being larded, spit them upon two wooden scuers, bind them to an iron spit and rost them, baste them with anchove sauce made of some of the oyster-liquor, let them drip in it, and being enough bread them with the crust of a roul grated, then dish them, blow the fat off the gravy, put it to the oysters, and wring on them the juyce of a lemon.

To broil Oysters.

Take great oysters and set them on a gridiron with the heads downwards, put them up an end, and broil them dry, brown, and hard, then put two or three of them in a shell with some melted butter, set them on the gridiron till they be finely stewed, then dish them on a plate, and fill them up with good butter only melted, or beaten with juyce of orange, pepper them lightly, and serve them up hot.

To broil Oysters otherways upon paper.

Broil them on a gridiron as before, then take them out of the shells into a dish, and chuse out the fairest, then have a sheet of white paper made like a dripping pan, set it on the gridiron, and run it over with clarified butter, lay on some sage leaves, some fine thin slices of a fat fresh eel, being parboil'd, and some oysters, stew them on the hot embers, and being finely broil'd, serve them on a dish and a plate in the paper they are boil'd in, and put to them beaten butter, juyce of orange, and slices of lemon.

To broil large Oysters otherways.

Take a pottle of great oysters opened & parboil them in there own liquor, being done, pour them in to a cullender, and save the liquor, then wash the oysters in warm water from the grounds, wipe them with a clean cloth, beard them, and put them in a pipkin, put to them large mace, two great onions, some butter, some of their own liquor, some white-wine, wine vinegar, and salt; stew them together very well, then set some of the largest shells, on a gridiron, put 2 or 3 in a shell, with some of the liquor out of the pipkin, broil them on a soft fire, and being broil'd, set them on a dish and plate, and fill them up with beaten butter.

Sometimes you may bread them in the broiling.

To fry Oysters.

Take two quarts of great Oysters being parboil'd in their own liquor, and washed in warm water, bread them, dry them, and flour them, fry them in clarified butter crisp and white, then have butter'd prawns or shrimps, butter'd with cream and sweet butter, lay them in the bottom of a clean dish, and lay the fryed oysters round about them, run them over with beaten butter, juyce of oranges, bay-leaves stuck round the Oysters, and slices of oranges or lemons.

Otherways.

Strain the liquor from the oysters, wash them, and parboil them in a kettle, then dry them and roul them in flour, or make a batter with eggs, flour, a little cream, and salt, roul them in it, and fry them in butter. For the sauce, boil the juyce of two or three oranges, some of their own liquor, a slic't nutmeg, and claret; being boil'd a little, put in a piece of butter, beating it up thick, then warm the dish, rub it with a clove of garlick, dish the oysters, and garnish them with slices of orange.

To bake Oysters.

Parboil your oysters in their own liquor, then take them out and wash them in warm water from the dregs dry them and season them with pepper, nutmeg, yolks of hard eggs, and salt; the pye being made, put a few currans in the bottom, and lay on the oysters, with some slic't dates in halves, some large mace, slic't lemon, barberries and butter, close it up and bake it, then liquor it with white-wine, sugar, and butter; or in place of white-wine, use verjuyce.

The Forms of Oyster Pyes.

To bake Oysters otherways.

Season them with pepper, salt, and nutmegs, the same quantity as beforesaid, and the same quantity oysters, two or three whole onions, neither currans nor sugar, but add to it in all respects else; as slic't nutmeg on them, large mace, hard eggs in halves, barberries, and butter, liquor it with beaten nutmeg, white-wine, and juyce of oranges.

Otherways, for change, in the seasoning put to them chopped tyme, hard eggs, some anchoves, and the foresaid spices.

Or bake them in Florentines, or patty-pans, and give them the same seasoning as you do the pies.

Or take large oysters, broil them dry and brown in the shells, and season them with former spices, bottoms of boil'd artichocks, pickled mushrooms, and no onions, but all things else as the former, liquor them with beaten butter, juyce of orange, and some claret wine.

Otherways.

Being parboil'd in their own liquor, season them with a little salt, sweet herbs minced small one spoonful, fill the pie, and put into it three or four blades of large mace, a slic't lemon, and on flesh days a good handful of marrow rouled in yolks of eggs and butter, close it up and bake it, make liquor for it with two nutmegs grated, a little pepper, butter, verjuyce, and sugar.

To make an Oyster Pye otherways.

Take a pottle of oysters, being parboil'd in their own liquor, beard and dry them, then season them with large mace, whole pepper, a little beaten ginger, salt, butter, and marrow, then close it up and bake it, and being baked, make a lear with white wine the oyster liquor, and one onion, or rub the ladle with garlick you beat it up with all; it being boil'd, put in a pound of butter, with a minced lemon, a faggot of sweet herbs, and being boil'd put in the liquor.

To make minced Pies or Chewits of Oysters.

Take three quarts of great oysters ready opened and parboil'd in their own liquor, then wash them in warm water from the dregs, dry them and mince them very fine, season them lightly with nutmeg, pepper, salt, cloves, mace, cinamon, caraway-seed, some minced, rasins of the sun, slic't dates, sugar, currans, and half a pint of white wine, mingle all together, and put butter in the bottoms of the pies, fill them up and bake them.

To bake Oysters otherways.

Season them with pepper, salt, nutmeg, and sweet herbs strowed on them in the pie, large mace, barberries, butter, and a whole onion or two, for liquor a little white wine, and wine-vinegar, beat it up thick with butter, and liquor the pie, cut it up, and lay on a slic't lemon, let not the lemon boil in it, and serve it hot.

Otherways.

Season them as before with pepper, nutmeg, and salt, being bearded, but first fry them in clarified butter, then take them up and season them, lay them in the pie being cold, put butter to them and large mace, close it up and bake it; then make liquor with a little claret wine and juyce of oranges, beat it thick with butter, and a little wine vinegar, liquor the pie, lay on some slices of orange, and set it again into the oven a little while.

To bake Oysters otherways.

Take great oysters, beard them, and season them with grated nutmeg, salt, and some sweet herbs minc'd small, lay them in the pye with a small quantity of the sweet herbs strowed on them, some twenty whole corns of pepper, slic't ginger, a whole onion or two, large mace, and some butter, close it up and bake it, and make liquor with white-wine, some of their own liquor, and a minced lemon, and beat it up thick.

Otherways.

Broil great oysters dry in the shells, then take them out, and season them with great nutmeg, pepper, and salt, lay them in the pye, and strow on them the yolks of two hard eggs minced, some stripp'd tyme, some capers, large mace, and butter; close it up, and make liquor with claret wine, wine vinegar, butter, and juyce of oranges, and beat it up thick, and liquor the pye, set it again into the oven a little while, and serve it hot.

To make a made Dish of Oysters and other Compounds.

Take oysters, cockles, prawns, craw-fish, and shrimps, being finely cleans'd from the grit, season them with nutmeg, pepper, and salt, next have chesnuts roasted, and blanch't, skerrets boil'd, blanched and seasoned; then have a dish or patty-pan ready with a sheet of cool butter paste, lay some butter on it, then the fishes, and on them the skirrets, chesnuts, pistaches, slic't lemon, large mace, barberries, and butter; close it up and bake it, and being baked, fill it up with beaten butter, beat with juyce of oranges, and some white-wine, or beaten butter with a little wine-vinegar, verjuyce, or juyce of green grapes, or a little good fresh fish broth, cut it up and liquor it, lay on the cover or cut it into four or five pieces, lay it round the dish, and serve it hot.

To make cool Butter-Paste for this Dish.

Take to every peck of flour five pound of butter, and the whites of six eggs, work it well together dry, then put cold water to it; this paste is good only for patty-pans and pasties.

To make Paste for Oyster-Pies.

The paste for thin bak't meats must be made with boiling liquor, put to every peck of flour two pound of butter, but let the butter boil in the liquor first.

To fry Mushrooms.

Blanch them & wash them clean if they be large, quarter them, and boil them with water, salt, vinegar, sweet herbs, large mace, cloves, bay-leaves, and two or three cloves of garlick, then take them up, dry them, dip them in batter and fry them in clarifi'd butter till they be brown, make sauce for them with claret-wine, the juice of two or three oranges, salt, butter, the juyce of horse-raddish roots beaten and strained, slic't nutmeg, and pepper; put these into a frying pan with the yolks of two or 3 eggs dissolved with some mutton gravy, beat and shake them well together in the pan that they curdle not; then dish the mushrooms on a dish, being first rubbed with a clove of garlick, and garnish it with oranges, and lemons.

To dress Mushrooms in the Italian Fashion.

Take mushrooms, peel & wash them, and boil them in a skillet with water and salt, but first let the liquor boil with sweet herbs, parsley, and a crust of bread, being boil'd, drain them from the water, and fry them in sweet sallet oyl; being fried serve them in a dish with oyl, vinegar, pepper, and fryed parsley. Or fry them in clarified butter.

To stew Mushrooms.

Peel them, and put them in a clean dish, strow salt on them, and put an onion to them, some sweet herbs, large mace, pepper, butter, salt, and two or three cloves, being tender stewed on a soft fire, put to them some grated bread, and a little white wine, stew them a little more and dish them (but first rub the dish with a clove of garlick) sippet them, lay slic't orange on them, and run them over with beaten butter.

To stew Mushrooms otherways.

Take them fresh gathered, and cut off the end of the stalk, and as you peel them put them in a dish with white wine; after they have laid half an hour, drain them from the wine, and put them between 2 silver dishes, and set them on a soft fire without any liquor, & when they have stewed a while pour away the liquor that comes from them; then put your mushrooms into another clean dish with a sprig of time, a whole onion, 4 or five corns of whole pepper, two or three cloves, a piece of an orange, a little salt, and a piece of good butter, & some pure gravy of mutton, cover them, and set them on a gentle fire, so let them stew softly till they be enough and very tender; when you dish them, blow off the fat from them, and take out the time, spice, and orange from them, then wring in the juyce of a lemon, and a little nutmeg among the mushrooms, toss them two or three times, and put them in a clean dish, and serve them hot to the table.

To dress Champignions in fricase, or Mushrooms, which is all one thing; they are called also Fungi, commonly in English Toad Stools.

Dress your Champignions, as in the foregoing Chapter, and being stewed put away the liquor, put them into a frying-pan with a piece of butter, some tyme, sweet marjoram, and a piece of an onion minced all together very fine, with a little salt also and beaten pepper, and fry them, and being finely fried, make a lear or sauce with three or four eggs dissolved with some claret-wine, and the juyce of two or three oranges, grated nutmeg, and the gravy of a leg of mutton, and shake them together in a pan with two or three tosses, dish them, and garnish the dish with orange and lemon, and rub the dish first with a clove of garlick, or none.

To broil Mushrooms.

Take the biggest and the reddest, peel them, and season them with some sweet herbs, pepper, and salt, broil them on a dripping-pan of paper, and fill it full, put some oyl into it, and lay it on a gridiron, boil it on a soft fire, turn them often, and serve them with oyl and vinegar.

Or broil them with butter, and serve them with beaten butter, and juyce of orange.

To stew Cockles being taken out of the shells.

Wash them well with vinegar, broil or broth them before you take them out of the shells, then put them in a dish with a little claret, vinegar, a handful of capers, mace, pepper, a little grated bread, minced tyme, salt, and the yolks of two or three hard eggs minced, stew all together till you think them enough; then put in a good piece of butter, shake them well together, heat the dish, rub it with a clove of garlick, and put two or three toasts of white bread in the bottom, laying the meat on them. Craw-fish, prawns, or shrimps, are excellent good the same way being taken out of their shells, and make variety of garnish with the shells.

To stew Cockles otherways.

Stew them with claret wine, capers, rose or elder vinegar, wine vinegar, large mace, gross pepper, grated bread, minced tyme, the yolks of hard eggs minced, and butter: stew them well together. Thus you may stew scollops, but leave out capers.

To stew Scollops.

Boil them very well in white wine, fair water, and salt, take them out of the shells, and stew them with some of the liquor elder vinegar, two or three cloves, some large mace, and some sweet herbs chopped small; being well stewed together, dish four or five of them in scollop shells and beaten butter, with the juyce of two or three oranges.

To stew Muscles.

Wash them clean, and boil them in water, or beer and salt; then take them out of the shells, and beard them from gravel and stones, fry them in clarified butter, and being fryed put away some of the butter, and put to them a sauce made of some of their own liquor, some sweet herbs chopped, a little white-wine, nutmeg, three or four yolks of eggs dissolved in wine vinegar, salt, and some sliced orange; give these materials a warm or two in the frying-pan, make the sauce pretty thick, and dish them in the scollop shells.

To fry Muscles.

Take as much water as will cover them, set it a boiling, and when it boils put in the muscles, being clean washed, put some salt to them, and being boil'd take them out of the shells, and beard them from the stones, moss, and gravel, wash them in warm water, wipe them dry, flour them and fry them crisp, serve them with beaten butter, juyce of orange, and fryed parsley, or fryed sage dipped in batter, fryed ellicksander leaves, and slic't orange.

To make a Muscle Pye.

Take a peck of muscles, wash them clean, and set them a boiling in a kettle of fair water, (but first let the water boil) then put them into it, give them a warm, and as soon as they are opened, take them out of the shells, stone them, and mince them with some sweet herbs, some leeks, pepper, and nutmeg; mince six hard eggs and put to them, put some butter in the pye, close it up and bake it, being baked liquor it with some butter, white wine, and slices of orange.

To stew Prawns, Shrimps, or Craw-Fish.

Being boil'd and picked, stew them in white wine, sweet butter, nutmeg, and salt, dish them in scollop shells, and run them over with beaten butter, and juyce of orange or lemon.

Otherways, stew them in butter and cream, and serve them in scollop shells.

To stew Lobsters.

Take claret-wine vinegar, nutmeg, salt, and butter, stew them down some what dry, and dish them in a scollop-shell, run them over with butter and slic't lemon.

Otherways, cut it into dice-work, and warm it with white-wine and butter, put it in a pipkin with claret wine or grape verjuyce, and grated manchet, and fill the scollop-shells.

Otherways.

Being boil'd, take out the meat, break it small, but break the shells as little as you can, then put the meat into a pipkin with claret-wine, wine-vinegar, slic't nutmeg, a little salt, and some butter; stew all these together softly an hour, being stewed almost dry, put to it a little more butter, and stir it well together; then lay very thin toasts in a clean dish, and lay the meat on them. Or you may put the meat in the shells, and garnish the dish about with the legs, and lay the body or barrel over the meat with some sliced lemon, and rare coloured flowers being in summer, or pickled in winter. Crabs are good the same way, only add to them the juyce of two or three oranges, a little pepper, and grated bread.

To stew Lobsters otherways.

Take the meat out of the shells, slice it, and fry it in clarified butter, (the Lobsters being first boil'd and cold), then put the meat in a pipkin with some claret wine, some good sweet butter, grated nutmeg, salt, and 2 or three slices of an orange; let it stew leisurely half an hour, and dish it up on fine carved sippets in a clean dish, with sliced orange on it, and the juyce of another, and run it over with beaten butter.

To hash Lobsters.

Take them out of the shells, mince them small, and put them in a pipkin with some claret wine, salt, sweet butter, grated nutmeg, slic't oranges, & some pistaches; being finely stewed, serve them on sippets, dish them, and run them over with beaten butter, slic't oranges, some cuts of paste, or lozenges of puff-paste.

To boil Lobsters to eat cold the common way.

Take them alive or dead, lay them in cold water to make the claws tuff, and keep them from breaking off; then have a kettle over the fire with fair water, put in it as much bay-salt, as will make it a good strong brine, when it boils scum it, and put in the Lobsters, let them boil leisurely the space of half an hour or more according to the bigness of them, being well boil'd take them up, wash them, and then wipe them with beer and butter; and keep them for your use.

To keep Lobsters a quarter of a year very good.

Take them being boil'd as aforesaid, wrap them in course rags having been steeped in brine, and bury them in a cellar in some sea-sand pretty deep.

To farce a Lobster.

Take a lobster being half boil'd, take the meat out of the shells, and mince it small with a good fresh eel, season it with cloves & mace beaten, some sweet herbs minced small and mingled amongst the meat, yolks of eggs, gooseberries, grapes, or barberries, and sometimes boil'd artichocks cut into dice-work, or boil'd aspragus, and some almond-paste mingled with the rest, fill the lobster shells, claws, tail, and body, and bake it in a blote oven, make sauce with the gravy and whitewine, and beat up the sauce or lear with good sweet butter, a grated nutmeg, juyce of oranges, and an anchove, and rub the dish with a clove of garlick.

To this farcing you may sometime add almond paste currans, sugar, gooseberries, and make balls to lay about the lobsters, or serve it with venison sauce.

To marinate Lobsters.

Take lobsters out of the shells being half boil'd, then take the tails and lard them with a salt eel (or not lard them) part the tails into two halves the longest way, and fry them in sweet sallet oyl, or clarified butter; being finely fryed, put them into a dish or pipkin, and set them by; then make sauce with white wine, and white wine vinegar, four or five blades of large mace, three or four slic't nutmegs, two races of ginger slic't, some ten or twelve cloves twice as much of whole pepper, and salt, boil them altogether with rosemary, tyme, winter-savory, sweet marjoram, bay-leaves, sage, and parsley, the tops of all these herbs about an inch long; then take three or four lemons and slice them, dish up the lobsters on a clean dish, and pour the broth, herbs and spices on the fish, lay on the lemons, run it over with some of the oyl or butter they were fryed in, and serve them up hot.

To broil Lobsters.

Being boil'd lay them on a gridiron, or toast them against the fire, and baste them with vinegar and butter, or butter only, broil them leisurely, and being broil'd serve them with butter and vinegar beat up thick with slic't lemon and nutmeg.

Otherways.

Broil them, the tail being parted in two halves long ways, also the claws cracked and broil'd; broil the barrel whole being salted, baste it with sweet herbs, as tyme, rosemary, parsley, and savory, being broil'd dish it, and serve it with butter and vinegar.

To broil Lobsters on paper.

Slice the tails round, and also the claws in long slices, then butter a dripping-pan made of the paper, lay it on a gridiron, and put some slices of lobster seasoned with nutmeg and salt, and slices of a fresh eel, some sageleaves, tops of rosemary, two or three cloves, and sometimes some bay-leaves or sweet herbs chopped; broil them on the embers, and being finely broil'd serve them on a dish and a plate in the same dripping-pan, put to them beaten butter, juyce of oranges, and slices of lemon.

To roast Lobsters.

Take a lobster and spit it raw on a small spit, bind the claws and tail with packthred, baste it with butter, vinegar, and sprigs of rosemary, and salt it in the roasting.

Otherways.

Half boil them, take them out of the shells, and lard them with small lard made of a salt eel, lard the claws and tails, and spit the meat on a small spit, with some slices of the eel, and sage or bay leaves between, stick in the fish here and there a clove or two, and some sprigs of rosemary; roast the barrel of the lobsters whole, and baste them with sweet butter, make sauce with claret wine, the gravy of the lobsters, juyce of oranges, an anchove or two, and sweet butter beat up thick with the core of a lemon, and grated nutmeg.

Otherways.

Half boil them, and take the meat out of the tail, and claws as whole as can be, & stick it with cloves and tops of rosemary; then spit the barrels of the lobsters by themselves, the tails and claws by themselves, and between them a sage or bay-leaf; baste them with sweet butter, and dredg them with grated bread, yolks of eggs, and some grated nutmeg. Then make sauce with claret wine, vinegar, pepper, the gravy of the meat, some salt, slices of oranges, grated nutmeg, and some beaten butter; then dish the barrels of the lobsters round the dish, the claws and tails in the middle, and put to it the sauce.

Otherways.

Make a farcing in the barrels of the lobsters with the meat in them, some almond-paste, nutmeg, tyme, sweet marjoram, yolks of raw eggs, salt, and some pistaches, and serve them with venison sauce.

To fry Lobsters.

Being boil'd take the meat out of the shells, and slice it long ways, flour it, and fry it in clarified butter, fine, white, and crisp; or in place of flouring it in batter, with eggs, flour, salt, and cream, roul them in it and fry them, being fryed make a sauce with the juyce of oranges, claret wine, and grated nutmeg, beaten up thick

with some good sweet butter, then warm the dish and rub it with a clove of garlick, dish the lobsters, garnish it with slices of oranges or lemons, and pour on the
sauce.

To bake Lobsters to be eaten hot.

Being boil'd and cold, take the meat out of the shells, and season it lightly with
nutmeg, pepper, salt, cinamon, and ginger; then lay it in a pye made according to
the following form, and lay on it some dates in halves, large mace, slic't lemons,
barberries, yolks of hard eggs and butter, close it up and bake it, and being baked
liquor it with white-wine, butter, and sugar, and ice it. On flesh days put marrow
to it.

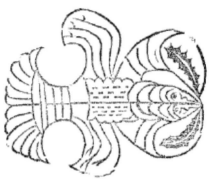

Otherways.

Take the meat out of the shells being boil'd and cold, and lard it with a salt eel
or salt salmon, seasoning it with beaten nutmeg, pepper, and salt; then make the
pye, put some butter in the bottom, and lay on it some slices of a fresh eel, and on
that a layer of lobsters, put to it a few whole cloves, and thus make two or three
layers, last of all slices of fresh eel, some whole cloves and butter, close up the pye,
and being baked, fill it up with clarified butter.

If you bake it these ways to eat hot, season it lightly, and put in some large
mace; liquor it with claret wine, beaten butter, and slices of orange.

Otherways.

Take four lobsters being boil'd, and some good fat conger raw, cut some of it
into square pieces as broad as your hand, then take the meat of the lobsters, and
slice the tails in two halves or two pieces long wayes, as also the claws, season both
with pepper, nutmeg and salt then make the pie, put butter in the bottom, lay on
the slices, of conger, and then a layer of lobsters; thus do three or four times till the
pie be full, then lay on a few whole cloves, and some butter; close it up and bake
it, being baked liquor it with butter and white-wine, or only clarified butter. Make
your pyes according to these forms.

If to eat hot season it lightly, and being baked liquor it with butter, white-wine, slic't lemon, gooseberries, grapes, or barberries.

To pickle Lobsters.

Boil them in vinegar, white-wine, and salt, being boiled take them up and lay them by, then have some bay-leaves, rosemary tops, winter-savory, tyme, large mace, and whole pepper: boil these foresaid materials all together in the liquor with the lobsters, and some whole cloves; being boil'd, barrel them up in a vessel that will but just contain them, and pack them close, pour the liquor to them, herbs spices, and some lemon peels, close up the head of the kegg or firkin; and keep them for your use; when you serve them, serve them with spices, herbs, peels, and some of the liquor or pickle.

To jelly Lobsters, Craw-fish, or Prawns.

Take a tench being new, draw out the garnish at the gills, and cut out all the gills, it will boil the whiter, then set on as much clear water aswil conveniently boil it, season it with salt, wine-vinegar, five or six bay-leaves large mace, three or four whole cloves, and a faggot of sweet herbs bound up hard together: so soon as this preparative boils, put in the tench being clean wiped, do not scale it, being boil'd take it up and wash off all the loose scales, then strain the liquor through a jelly-bag, and put to it a piece of ising-glass being first washed and steeped for the purpose, boil it very cleanly, and run it through a jelly-bag; then having the fish taken out of the shells, lay them in a large clean dish, lay the lobsters in slices, and the craw fish and prawns whole, and run this jelly over them. You may make this jelly of divers colours, as you may see in the Section of Jellies, page 202.

Garnish the dish of Jellies with lemon-peels cut in branches, long slices as you fancy, barberries, and fine coloured flowers.

Or lard the lobsters with salt eel, or stick it with candied oranges, green citterns, or preserved barberries, and make the jelly sweet.

To stew Crabs.

Being boil'd take the meat out of the bodies or barrels, and save the great claws, and the small legs whole to garnish the dish, strain the meat with some claret wine, grated bread, wine-vinegar, nutmeg, a little salt, and a piece of butter; stew them together an hour on a soft fire in a pipkin, and being stewed almost dry, put in some beaten butter with juyce of oranges beaten up thick; then dish the shells being washed and finely cleansed, the claws and little legs round about them, put the meat into the shells, and so serve them.

Sometimes you may use yolks of eggs strained with butter.

To stew Crabs otherways.

Being boil'd take the meat out of the shells, and put it in a pipkin with some claret wine, and wine vinegar, minced tyme, pepper, grated bread, salt, the yolks of two or three hard eggs strained or minced very small, some sweet butter, capers, and some large mace; stew it finely, rub the shells with a clove or two of garlick, and dish them as is shown before.

Otherways.

Take the meat out of the bodies, and put it in a pipkin with some cinamon, wine vinegar, butter, and beaten ginger, stew them and serve them as the former, dished with the legs about them.

Sometimes you may add sugar to them, parboil'd grapes, gooseberries, or barberries, and in place of vinegar, juyce of oranges, and run them over with beaten butter.

To butter Crabs.

The Crabs being boil'd, take the meat out of the bodies, and strain it with the yolks of three or four hard eggs, beaten cinamon, sugar, claret-wine, and wine-vinegar, stew the meat in a pipkin with some good sweet butter the space of a quarter of an hour, and serve them as the former.

Otherways.

Being boil'd, take the meat out of the shells, as also out of the great claws, cut it into dice-work, & put both the meats into a pipkin, together with some white wine, juyce of oranges, nutmeg, and some slices of oranges, stew it two or three warms on the fire, and the shells being finely cleansed and dried, put the meat into them, and lay the legs round about them in a clean dish.

To make a Hash of Crabs.

Take two crabs being boil'd, take out the meat of the claws, and cut it into dice-work, mix it with the meat of the body, then have some pine-apple seed, and some pistaches or artichock-bottoms, boil'd, blanched, and cut into dice-work, or some asparagus boil'd and cut half an inch long; stew all these together with some claret wine, vinegar, grated nutmeg, salt, sweet butter, and the slices of an orange; being finely stewed, dish it on sippets, cuts, or lozenges of puff paste, and garnish it with fritters of arms, slic't lemon carved, barberries, grapes, or gooseberries, and run it over with beaten butter, and yolks of eggs beaten up thick together.

To farce a Crab.

Take a boil'd crab, take the meat out of the shell, and mince the claws with a good fresh eel, season it with cloves, mace, some sweet herbs chopped, and salt, mingle all together with some yolks of eggs, some grapes, gooseberries, or barberres, and sometimes boil'd artichocks in dice-work, or boil'd asparagus, some almond-paste, the meat of the body of the crab, and some grated bread, fill the shells with this compound, & make some into balls, bake them in a dish with some butter and white wine in a soft oven; being baked, serve them in a clean dish with a sauce made of beaten butter, large mace, scalded grapes, gooseberries, or barberries, or some slic't orange or lemon and some yolks of raw eggs dissolved with some white-wine or claret, and beat up thick with butter; brew it well together, pour it on the fish, and lay on some slic't lemon, stick the balls with some pistaches, slic't almonds, pine-apple-seed, or some pretty cuts in paste.

To broil Crabs in Oyl or Butter.

Take Crabs being boil'd in water and salt, steep them in oyl and vinegar, and broil them on a gridiron on a soft fire of embers, in the broiling baste them with some rosemary branches, and being broil'd serve them with the sauces they were boil'd with, oyl and vinegar, or beaten butter, vinegar, and the rosemary branches they were basted with.

To fry Crabs.

Take the meat out of the great claws being first boiled, flour and fry them, and take the meat out of the body strain half of it for sauce, and the other half to fry, and mix it with grated bread, almond paste, nutmeg, salt, and yolks of eggs, fry it in clarified butter, being first dipped in batter, put in a spoonful at a time; then make sauce with wine-vinegar, butter, or juyce of orange, and grated nutmeg, beat up the butter thick, and put some of the meat that was strained into the sauce, warm it and put it in a clean dish, lay the meat on the sauce, slices of orange over all, and run it over with beaten butter, fryed parsley, round the dish brim, and the little legs round the meat.

Otherways.

Being boil'd and cold, take the meat out of the claws, flour and fry them, then take the meat out of the body, butter it with butter vinegar, and pepper, and put it in a clean dish, put the fryed crab round about it, and run it over with beaten butter, juyce and slices of orange, and lay on it sage leaves fryed in batter, or fryed parsley.

To bake Crabs in Pye, Dish, or Patty pan.

Take four or five crabs being boil'd, take the meat out of the shell and claws as whole as you can, season it with nutmeg and salt lightly; then strain the meat that came out of the body, shells, with a little claret-wine, some cinamon, ginger, juyce of orange and butter, make the pie, dish, or patty pan, lay butter in the bottom, then the meat of the claws, some pistaches, asparagus, some bottoms of artichocks, yolks of hard eggs, large mace, grapes, gooseberries or barberries, dates of slic't orange, and butter, close it up and bake it, being baked, liquor it with the meat out of the body.

Otherways.

Mince them with a tench or fresh eel, and season it with sweet herbs minced small, beaten nutmeg, pepper, and salt, lightly season, and mingle the meat that was in the bodies of the crabs with the other seasoned fishes; mingle also with this foresaid meat some boil'd or roasted chesnuts, or artichocks, asparagus boil'd and cut an inch long, pistaches, or pine-apple-seed, and grapes, gooseberries or barberries, fill the pie, dish, or patty-pan, close it up and bake it, being baked, liquor it with juyce of oranges, some claret wine, good butter beat up thick, and the yolks of two or three eggs; fill up the pie, lay slices of an orange on it and stick in some lozenges of puff-paste, or branches of short paste.

To make minced Pies of a Crab.

Being boil'd, mince the legs, and strain the meat in the body with two or three yolks of eggs, mince also some sweet herbs and put to it some almond-paste or grated bread, a minced onion, some fat eel cut like little dice, or some fat belly of salmon; mingle it all together, and put it in a pie made according to this form, season it with nutmeg, pepper, salt, currans, and barberries, grapes, or gooseberries, mingle also some butter, and fill your pie, bake it, and being baked, liquor it with beaten butter and white wine. Or with butter, sugar, cinamon, sweet herbs chopped, and verjuyce.

To dress Tortoise.

Cast off the head, feet, and tail, and boil it in water, wine, and salt, being boil'd, pull the shell asunder, and pick the meat from the skins, and the gall from the liver, save the eggswhole if a female, and stew the eggs, meat and liver in a dish with some grated nutmeg, a little sweet herbs minced small, and some sweet butter, stew it up, and serve it on fine sippets, cover the meat with the upper shell of the tortoise, and slices or juyce of orange.

Or stew them in a pipkin with some butter, whitewine some of the broth, a whole onion or two, tyme, parsley, winter savory, and rosemary minc't, being finely stewed serve them on sippets, or put them in the shells, being cleansed; or make a fricase in a frying-pan with 3 or four yolks of eggs and some of the shells amongst them, and dress them as aforesaid.

To dress Snails.

Take shell snails, and having water boil'd, put them in, then pick them out of the shells with a great pin into a bason, cast salt to them, scour the slime from them, and after wash them in two or three waters; being clean scowred, dry them with a clean cloth; then have rosemary, tyme, parsley, winter-savory, and pepper very small, put them into a deep bason or pipkin, put to them some salt, and good sallet oyl, mingle all together, then have the shells finely cleansed, fill them, and set them on a gridiron, broil them upon the embers softly, and being broil'd, dish four or five dozen in a dish, fill them up with oyl, and serve them hot.

To stew Snails.

Being well scowred and cleansed as aforesaid, put to them some claret wine and vinegar, a handful of capers, mace, pepper, grated bread, a little minced tyme, salt, and the yolks of two or 3 hard eggs minced; let all these stew together till you think it be enough, then put in a good piece of butter, shaking it together, heat the dish, and rub it with a clove of garlick, put them on fine sippets of French bread, pour on the snails, and some barberries, or slic't lemons.

Otherways.

Being cleansed, fry them in oyl or clarified butter, with some slices of a fresh eel, and some fried sage leaves; stew them in a pipkin with some white-wine, butter, and pepper, and serve them on sippets with beaten butter, and juyce of oranges.

Otherways.

Being finely boil'd and cleansed, fry them in clarified butter; being fryed take them up, and put them in a pipkin, put to them some sweet butter chopped parsley, white or claret wine, some grated nutmeg, slices of orange, and a little salt; stew them well together, serve them on sippets; and then run them over with beaten butter, and slices of oranges.

To fry Snails.

Take shell snails in *January*, *February*, or, *March*, when they be closed up, boil them in a skillet of boiling water, and when they be tender boil'd, take them out of the shell with a pin, cleanse them from the slime, flour them, and fry them; being fryed, serve them in a clean dish, with butter, vinegar, fryed parsley, fryed onions, or ellicksander leaves fryed, or served with beaten butter, and juyce of orange, or oyl, vinegar, and slic't lemon.

Otherways.

Fry them in oyl and butter, being finely cleansed, and serve them with butter, vinegar, and pepper, or oyl, vinegar, and pepper.

To make a Hash of Snails.

Being boil'd and cleansed, mince them small, put them in a pipkin with some sweet herbs minced, the yolks of hard eggs, some whole capers, nutmeg, pepper, salt, some pistaches, and butter, or oyl; being stewed the space of half an hour on a soft fire; then have some fried toasts of French bread, lay some in the bottom, and some round the meat in the dish.

To dress Snails in a Pottage.

Wash them very well in many waters, then put them in an earthen pan, or a wide dish, put as much water as will cover them, and set your dish on some caols; when they boil take them out of the shells, and scowr them with water and salt three or four times, then put them in a pipkin with water and salt, and let them boil a little, then take them out of the water, and put them in a dish with some excellent sallet oyl; when the oyl boils put in three or four slic't onions, and fry them, put the snails to them, and stew them well together, then put the oyl snails and onions all together in a pipkin of a fit size for them, and put as much warm water to them as will make a pottage, with some salt, and so let them stew three or four hours, then mince tyme, parsley, pennyroyal, and the like herbs; when they are minced, beat them to green sauce in a mortar, put in some crumbs of bread soakt with that broth or pottage, some saffron and beaten cloves; put all in to the snails, and give them a warm or 2, and when you serve them up, squeeze in the juyce of a lemon, put in a little vinegar, and a clove of garlick amongst the herbs, and beat them in it; serve them up in a dish with sippets in the bottom of it.

This pottage is very nourishing, and excellent good against a Consumption.

To bake Snails.

Being boil'd and scowred, season them with nutmeg, pepper, and salt, put them into a pie with some marrow, large mace, a raw chicken cut in pieces, some little bits of lard and bacon, the bones out, sweet herbs chopped, slic't lemon, or orange and butter; being full, close it up and bake it, and liquor it with butter and white-wine.

To bake Frogs.

Being flayed, take the hind legs, cut off the feet, and season them with nutmeg, pepper, and salt, put them in a pye with some sweet herbs chopped small, large mace, slic't lemon, gooseberries, grapes, or barberries, pieces of skirrets, artichocks, potatoes, or parsnips, and marrow; close it up and bake it; being baked, liquor it with butter, and juyce of orange, or grape-verjuyce.

SECTION XX.

To make all manner of Pottages for Fish-Days.

French Barley Pottage.

CLeanse the barley from dust, and put it in boiling milk, being boil'd down, put in large mace, cream, sugar, and a little salt, boil it pretty thick, then serve it in a dish, scrape sugar on it, and trim the dish sides.

Otherways.

Boil it in fair water, scum it, and being almost boil'd, put to it some saffron, or disolved yolks of eggs.

To make Gruel Pottage the best way for service.

Pick your oatmeal, and boil it whole on a stewing fire; being tender boil'd, strain it through a strainer, then put it into a clean pipkin with fair boiling water, make it pretty thick of the strained oatmeal, and put to it some picked raisins of the sun well washed, some large mace, salt, and a little bundle of sweet herbs, with a little rose-water and saffron; set it a stewing on a fire of charcoal, boil it with sugar till the fruit be well allom'd, then put to it butter and the yolks of three or four eggs strained.

Otherways.

Good herbs and oatmel chopped, put them into boiling liquor in a pipkin, pot, or skillet, with some salt, and being boil'd put to it butter.

Otherways.

With a bundle of sweet herbs and oatmeal chopped, some onions and salt, seasoned as before with butter.

To make Furmety.

Take wheat and wet it, then beat it in a sack with a wash beetle, being finely hulled and cleansed from the dust and hulls, boil it over night, and let it soak on a soft fire all night; then next morning take as much as will serve the turn, put it in a pipkin, pan, or skillet, and put it a boiling in cream or milk, with mace, salt, whole cinamon, and saffron, or yolks of eggs, boil it thick and serve it in a clean scowred dish, scrape on sugar, and trim the dish.

To make Rice Pottage.

Pick the rice and dust it clean, then wash it, and boil it in water or milk; being boil'd down, put to it some cream, large mace, whole cinamon, salt, and sugar; boil it on a soft stewing fire, and serve it in a fair deep dish, or a standing silver piece.

Otherways.

Boil'd rice strained with almond milk, and seasoned as the former.

Milk Pottage.

Boil whole oatmel, being cleanly picked, boil it in a pipkin or pot, but first let the water boil; being well boil'd and tender, put in milk or cream, with salt, and fresh butter, &c.

Ellicksander Pottage.

Chop ellicksanders and oatmeal together, being picked and washed, then set on a pipkin with fair water, and when it boils, put in your herbs, oatmeal, and salt, boil it on a soft fire, and make it not too thick, being almost boil'd put in some butter.

Pease Pottage.

Take green pease being shelled and cleansed, put them in a pipkin of fair boiling water; when they be boil'd and tender, take and strain some of them, and thicken the rest, put to them a bundle of sweet herbs, or sweet herbs chopped, salt, and butter; being through boil'd dish them, and serve them in a deep clean dish with salt and sippets about them.

Otherways.

Put them into a pipkin or skillet of boiling milk or cream, put to them two or three sprigs of mint, and salt; being fine and tender boil'd, thick them with a little milk and flour.

Dry or old Pease Pottage.

Take the choicest pease, (that some call seed way pease) commonly they be a little worm eaten, (those are the best boiling pease) pick and wash them, and put them in boiling liquor in a pot or pipkin; being tender boil'd take out some of them, strain them, and set them by for your use; then season the rest with salt, a bundle of mint and butter, let them stew leisurely, and put to them some pepper.

Strained Pease Pottage.

Take the former strained pease-pottage, put to them salt, large mace, a bundle of sweet herbs, and some pickled capers; stew them well together, then serve them in a deep dish clean scowred, with thin slices of bread in the bottom, and graced manchet to garnish it.

An excellent stewed Broth for Fish-Day.

Set a boiling some fair water in a pipkin, then strain some oatmeal and put to it, with large mace, whole cinamon, salt, a bundle of sweet herbs, some strained and whole prunes, and some raisins of the sun; being well stewed on a soft fire, and pretty thick, put in some claret-wine and sugar, serve it in a clear scowred deep dish or standing piece, and scrape on sugar.

Onion Pottage.

Fry good store of slic't onions, then have a pipkin of boiling liquor over the fire, when the liquor boils put in the fryed onions, butter and all, with pepper and salt; being well stewed together, serve it on sops of French bread or pine-molet.

Almond Pottage.

Take a pound of almond-paste, and strain it with some new milk; then have a pottle of cream boiling in a pipkin or skillet, put in the milk; and almonds with some mace, salt, and sugar; serve it in a clean dish on sippets of French bread, and scrape on sugar.

Otherways.

Strain them with fair water, and boil them with mace, salt, and sugar, (or none) add two or three yolks of eggs dissolved, or saffron; and serve it as before.

Almond Caudle.

Strain half a pound of almonds being blanched and stamped, strain them with a pint of good ale, then boil it with slices of fine manchet, large mace, and sugar; being almost boil'd put in three or four spoonfuls of sack.

Oatmeal Caudle.

Boil ale, scum it, and put in strained oatmeal, mace, sugar, and diced bread, boil it well, and put in two or three spoonfuls of sack, white-wine or claret.

Egg Caudle.

Boil ale or beer, scum it, and put to it two or three blades of large mace, some sliced manchet and sugar; then dissolve four or five yolks of eggs with some sack, claret or white-wine, and put it into the rest with a little grated nutmeg; give it a warm, and serve it.

Sugar, or Honey Sops.

Boil beer or ale, scum it, and put to it slices of fine manchet, large mace, sugar, or honey; sometimes currans, and boil all well together.

To make an Alebury.

Boil beer or ale, scum it, and put in some mace, and a bottom of a manchet, boil it well, then put in some sugar.

Buttered Beer.

Take beer or ale and boil it, then scum it, and put to it some liquorish and anniseeds, boil them well together; then have in a clean flaggon or quart pot some yolks of eggs well beaten with some of the foresaid beer, and some good butter; strain your butter'd beer, put it in the flaggon, and brew it with the butter and eggs.

Buttered Beer or Ale otherways.

Boil beer or ale and scum it, then have six eggs, whites and all, and beat them in a flaggon or quart pot with the shells, some butter, sugar, and nutmeg, put them together, and being well brewed, drink it when you go to bed.

Otherways.

Take three pints of beer or ale, put five yolks of eggs to it, strain them together, and set it in a pewter pot to the fire, put to it half a pound of sugar, a penniworth of beaten nutmeg, as much beaten cloves, half an ounce of beaten ginger, and bread it.

Panado's.

Boil fair water in a skillet, put to it grated bread or cakes, good store of currans, mace and whole cinamon: being almost boil'd and indifferent thick, put in some sack or white wine, sugar, some strained yolks of eggs.

Otherways with slic't bread, water, currans, and mace, and being well boil'd, put to it some sugar, white-wine, and butter.

To make a Compound Posset of Sack, Claret, White-Wine, Ale, Beer, or Juyce of Oranges, &c.

Take twenty yolks of eggs with a little cream, strain them, and set them by; then have a clean scowred skillet, and put into it a pottle of good sweet cream, and a good quantity of whole cinamon, set it a boiling on a soft charcoal fire, and stir it continually; the cream having a good taste of the cinamon, put in the strained eggs and cream into your skillet, stir them together, and give them a warm, then have some sack in a deep bason or posset-pot, good store of fine sugar, and some sliced nutmeg; the sack and sugar being warm, take out the cinamon, and pour your eggs and cream very high in to the bason, that it may spatter in it, then strow on loaf sugar.

To make a Posset simple.

Boil your milk in a clean scowred skillet, and when it boils take it off, and warm in the pot, bowl, or bason some sack, claret, beer, ale, or juyce of orange; pour it into the drink, but let not your milk be too hot, for it will make the curd hard, then sugar it.

Otherways.

Beat a good quantity of sorrel, and strain it with any of the foresaid liquors, or simply of it self, then boil some milk in a clean scowred skillet, being boil'd, take it off and let it cool, then put it to your drink, but not too hot, for it will make the curd tuff.

Possets of Herbs otherways.

Take a fair scowred skillet, put in some milk into it, and some rosemary, the rosemary being well boil'd in it, take it out and have some ale or beer in a pot, put to it the milk and sugar, (or none.)

Thus of tyme, carduus, cammomile, mint, or marigold flowers.

To make French Puffs.

Take spinage, tyme, parsley, endive, savory and marjoram, chop or mince them small; then have twenty eggs beaten with the herbs, that the eggs may be green, some nutmeg, ginger, cinamon, and salt; then cut a lemon in slices, and dip it in batter, fry it, and put a spoonful on every slice of lemon, fry it finely in clarified butter, and being fryed, strow on sack, or claret, and sugar.

Soops or butter'd Meats of Spinage.

Take fine young spinage, pick and wash it clean; then have a skillet or pan of fair liquor on the fire, and when it boils, put in the spinage, give it a warm or two, and take it out into a cullender, let it drain, then mince it small, and put it in a pipkin with some slic't dates, butter, white-wine, beaten cinamon, salt, sugar, and some boil'd currans; stew them well together, and dish them on sippets finely carved, and about it hard eggs in halves or quarters, not too hard boil'd, and scrape on sugar.

Soops of Carrots.

Being boil'd, cleanse, stamp, and season them in all points as before; thus also potatoes, skirrets, parsnips, turnips, Virginia artichocks, onions, or beets, or fry any of the foresaid roots being boil'd and cleansed, or peeled, and floured, and serve them with beaten butter and sugar.

Soops of Artichocks, Potatoes, Skirrets, or Parsnips.

Being boil'd and cleansed, put to them yolks of hard eggs, dates, mace, cinamon, butter, sugar, white-wine, salt, slic't lemon, grapes gooseberries, or barberries; stew them together whole, and being finely stewed, serve them on carved sippets in a clean scowred dish, and run it over with beaten butter and scraped sugar.

To butter Onions.

Being peeled, put them into boiling liquor, and when they are boil'd, drain them in a cullender, and butter them whole with some boil'd currans, butter, sugar, and beaten cinamon, serve them on fine sippets, scrape on sugar, and run them over with beaten butter.

Otherways.

Take apples and onions, mince the onions and slice the apples, put them in a pot, but more apples, than onions, and bake them with houshold bread, close up the pot with paste or paper; when you use them, butter them with butter, sugar, and boil'd currans, serve them on sippets, and scrape on sugar and cinamon.

Buttered Sparagus.

Take two hundred of sparagus, scrape the roots clean and wash them, then take the heads of an hundred and lay them even, bind them hard up into a bundle, and so likewise of the other hundred; then have a large skillet of fair water, when it boils put them in, and boil them up quick with some salt; being boil'd drain them, and serve them with beaten butter and salt about the dish, or butter and vinegar.

Buttered Colliflowers.

Have a skillet of fair water, and when it boils put in the whole tops of the colliflowers, the root being cut away, put some salt to it; and being fine and tender boiled dish it whole in a dish, with carved sippets round about it, and serve it with beaten butter and water, or juyce of orange and lemon.

Otherways.

Put them into boiling milk, boil them tender, and put to them a little mace and salt; being finely boil'd, serve them on carved sippets, the yolk of an egg or two, some boil'd raisins of the sun, beaten butter, and sugar.

To butter Quinces.

Roast or boil them, then strain them with sugar and cinamon, put some butter to them, warm them together, and serve them on fine carved sippets.

To butter Rice.

Pick the rice and sift it, and when the liquor boils, put it in and scum it, boil it not too much, then drain it, butter it, and serve it on fine carved sippets, and scraping sugar only, or sugar and cinamon.

Butter wheat, and French barley, as you do rice, but hull your wheat and barley, wet the wheat and beat it in a sack with a wash-beetle, fan it, and being clean hulled, boil it all night on a soft fire very tender.

To butter Gourds, Pumpions, Cucumbers or Muskmelons.

Cut them into pieces, and pare and cleanse them; then have a boiling pan of water, and when it boils put in the pumpions, &c. with some salt, being boil'd, drain them well from the water, butter them, and serve them on sippets with pepper.

Otherways.

Bake them in an oven, and take out the seed at the top, fill them with onions, slic't apples, butter, and salt, butter them, and serve them on sippets.

Otherways.

Fry them in slices, being cleans'd & peel'd, either floured or in batter; being fried, serve them with beaten butter, and vinegar, or beaten butter and juyce of orange, or butter beaten with a little water, and served in a clean dish with fryed parsley, elliksanders, apples, slic't onions fryed, or sweet herbs.

To make buttered Loaves.

Season a pottle of flour with cloves, mace, and pepper, half a pound of sweet butter melted, and half a pint of ale-yeast or barm mix't with warm milk from the cow and three or four eggs to temper all together, make it as soft as manchet paste, and make it up into little manchets as big as an egg, cut and prick them, and put them on a paper, bake them like manchet, with the oven open, they will ask an hours baking; being baked melt in a great dish a pound of sweet butter, and put rose-water in it, draw your loaves, and pare away the crust then slit them in three toasts, and put them in melted butter, turn them over and over in the butter, then take a warm dish, and put in the bottom pieces, and strow on sugar in a good thickness, then put in the middle pieces, and sugar them likewise, then set on the tops and scrape on sugar, and serve five or six in a dish. If you be not ready to send them in, set them in the oven again, and cover them with a paper to keep them from drying.

To boil French Beans or Lupins.

First take away the tops of the cods and the strings, then have a pan or skillet of fair water boiling on the fire, when it boils put them in with some salt, and boil them up quick; being boil'd serve them with beaten butter in a fair scowred dish, and salt about it.

To boil Garden Beans.

Being shelled and cleansed, put them into boiling liquor with some salt, boil them up quick, and being boiled drain away the liquor and butter them, dish them in a dish like a cross, and serve them with pepper and salt on the dish side.

Thus also green pease, haslers, broom-buds, or any kind of pulse.

SECTION XXI.

The exactest Ways for the Dressing of Eggs.

To make Omlets divers Ways.
The First Way.

 B Reak six, eight, or ten eggs more or less, beat them together in a dish, and put salt to them; then put some butter a melting in a frying pan, and fry it more or less, according to your discretion, only on one side or bottom.

You may sometimes make it green with juyce of spinage and sorrel beat with the eggs, or serve it with green sauce, a little vinegar and sugar boil'd together, and served up on a dish with the Omlet.

The Second Way.

Take twelve eggs, and put to them some grated white bread finely searsed, parsley minced very small, some sugar beaten fine, and fry it well on both sides.

The Third Way.

Fry toasts of manchet, and put the eggs to them being beaten and seasoned with salt, and some fryed; pour the butter and fryed parsley over all.

The Fourth Way.

Take three or four pippins, cut them in round slices, and fry them with a quarter of a pound of butter, when the apples are fryed, pour on them six or seven eggs beaten with a little salt, and being finely fryed, dish it on a plate-dish, or dish, and strow on sugar.

The Fifth Way.

Mix with the eggs pine-kernels, currans, and pieces of preserved lemons, being fried, roul it up like a pudding, and sprinkle it with rose-water, cinamon water, and strow on fine sugar.

The Sixth Way.

Beat the eggs, and put to them a little cream, a little grated bread, a little preserved lemon-peel minced or grated very small, and use it as the former.

The Seventh Way.

Take a quarter of a pound of interlarded bacon, take it from the rinde, cut it into dice-work, fry it, and being fried, put in some seven or eight beaten eggs with some salt, fry them, and serve them with some grape-verjuyce.

The Eighth Way.

With minced bacon among the eggs fried and beaten together, or with thin slices of interlarded bacon, and fryed slices of bread.

The Ninth way.

Made with eggs and a little cream.

The Tenth Way.

Mince herbs small, as lettice, bugloss, or borrage, sorrel, and mallows, put currans to them, salt, and nutmeg, beat all these amongst the herbs, and fry them with sweet butter, and serve it with cinamon and sugar, or fried parsley only; put the eggs to it in the pan.

The Eleventh Way.

Mince some parsley very small being short and fine picked, beat it amongst the eggs, and fry it. Or fry the parsley being grosly cut, beat the eggs, and pour it on.

The Twelfth Way.

Mince leeks very small, beat them with the eggs and some salt, and fry them.

The Thirteenth Way.

Take endive that is very white, cut it grosly, fry it with nutmeg, and put the eggs to it, or boil it being fried, and serve it with sugar.

The Fourteenth Way.

Slice cheese very thin, beat it with the eggs, and a little salt, then melt some butter in the pan, and fry it.

The Fifteenth Way.

Take six or eight eggs, beat them with salt, and make a stuffing, with some pine kernels, currans, sweet herbs, some minced fresh fish, or some of the milts of carps that have been fried or boiled in good liquor, and some mushrooms half boiled and sliced; mingle all together with some yolks or whites of eggs raw, and fill up great cucumbers therewith being cored, fill them up with the foresaid fars- ing, pare them, and bake them in a dish, or stew them between two deep basons or deep dishes; put some butter to them, some strong broth of fish, or fair water, some verjuyce or vinegar, and some grated nutmeg, and serve them on a dish with sippets.

The Sixteenth Way, according to the Turkish Mode.

Take the flesh of a hinder part of a hare, or any other venison and mince it small with a little fat bacon, some pistaches or pine-apple kernels, almonds, Span- ish or hazle nuts peeled, Spanish chesnuts or French chesnuts roasted and peeled, or some crusts of bread cut in slices, and rosted like unto chesnuts; season this minced stuff with salt, spices, and some sweet herbs; if the flesh be raw, add thereunto butter and marrow, or good sweet suet minced small and melted in a skillet, pour it into the seasoned meat that is minced, and fry it, then melt some butter in a skillet or pan, and make an omlet thereof; when it is half fried, put to the minced meat, and take the omlet out of the frying-pan with a skimmer, break it not, and put it in a dish that the minced meat may appear uppermost, put some gravy on the minced meat, and some grated nutmeg, stick some sippets of fryed manchet on it, and slices of lemon. Roast meat is the best for this purpose.

The Seventeenth Way.

Take the kidneys of a loin of veal after it hath been well roasted, mince it together with its fat, and season it with salt, spices, and some time, or other sweet herbs, add thereunto some fried bread, some boil'd mushrooms or some pistaches, make an omlet, and being half fried, put the minced meat on it.

Fry them well together, and serve it up with some grated nutmeg and sugar.

The Eighteenth Way.

Take a carp or some other fish, bone it very well, and add to it some milts of carps, season them with pepper and salt, or with other spices; add some mushrooms, and mince them all together, put to them some apple-kernels, some currans, and preserved lemons in pieces shred very small: fry them in a frying-pan or tart-pan, with some butter, and being fryed make an omlet. Being half fried, put the fried fish on it, and dish them on a plate, rowl it round, cut it at both ends, and spread them abroad, grate some sugar on it, and sprinkle on rose-water.

The Nineteenth Way.

Mince all kind of sweet herbs, and the yolks of hard eggs together, some currans, and some mushrooms half boil'd, being all minced cover them over, fry them as the former, and strow sugar and cinamon on it.

The Twentieth Way.

Take young and tender sparagus, break or cut them in small pieces, and half fry them brown in butter, put into them eggs beaten with salt, and thus make your omlet.

Or boil them in water and salt, then fry them in sweet butter, put the eggs to them, and make an omlet, dish it, and put a drop or two of vinegar, or verjuyce on it.

Sometimes take mushrooms, being stewed make an omlet, and sprinkle it with the broth of the mushrooms, and grated nutmeg.

The one and Twentieth Way.

Slice some apples and onions, fry them, but not too much, and beat some six or eight eggs with some salt, put them to the apples and onions, and make an omlet, being fried, make sauce with vinegar or grape-verjuyce, butter, sugar, and mustard.

To dress hard Eggs divers ways.

The First Way.

Put some butter into a dish, with some vinegar or verjuyce, and salt; the butter being melted, put in two or three yolks of hard eggs, dissolve them on the butter and verjuice for the sauce; then have hard eggs, part them in halves or quarters, lay them in the sauce, and grate some nutmeg over them, or the crust of white-bread.

The Second Way.

Fry some parsley, some minced leeks, and young onions, when you have fried them pour them into a dish, season them with salt and pepper, and put to them hard eggs cut in halves, put some mustard to them, and dish the eggs, mix the sauce well together, and pour it hot on the eggs.

The Third Way.

The eggs being boil'd hard, cut them in two, or fry them in butter with flour and milk or wine; being fried, put them in a dish, put to them salt, vinegar, and juyce of lemon, make a sweet sauce for it with some sugar, juyce of lemon, and beaten cinamon.

The Fourth Way.

Cut hard eggs in twain, and season them with a white sauce made in a frying-pan with the yolks of raw eggs; verjuyce and white-wine dissolved together, and some salt, a few spices, and some sweet herbs, and pour this sauce over the eggs.

The Fifth Way in the Portugal Fashion.

Fry some parsley small minced, some onions or leeks in fresh butter, being half fried, put into them hard eggs cut into rounds, a handful of mushrooms well picked, washed and slic't, and salt, fry all together, and being almost fried, put some vinegar to them, dish them, and grate nutmeg on them, sippet them, and on the sippets slic't lemons.

The Sixth Way.

Take sweet herbs, as purslain, lettice, borrage, sorrel, parsley, chervil & tyme, being well picked and washed mince them very small, and season them with cloves, pepper, salt, minced mushrooms, and some grated cheese, put to them some grated nutmeg, crusts of manchet, some currans, pine-kernels, and yolks of hard eggs in quarters, mingle all together, fill the whites, and stew them in a dish, strow over the stuff being fryed with some butter, pour the fried farce over the whites being dished, and grate some nutmeg, and crusts of manchet.

Or fry sorrel, and put it over the eggs.

To butter a Dish of Eggs.

Take twenty eggs more or less, whites and yolks as you please, break them into a silver dish, with some salt, and set them on a quick charcoal fire, stir them with a silver spoon, and being finely buttered put to them the juyce of three or four oranges, sugar, grated nutmeg, and sometimes beaten cinamon, being thus drest, strain them at the first, or afterward being buttered.

To make a Bisk of Eggs.

Take a good big dish, lay a lay of slices of cheese between two lays of toasted cheat bread, put on them some clear mutton broth, green or dry pease broth, or any other clear pottage that is seasoned with butter and salt, cast on some chopped parsley grosly minced, and upon that some poached eggs.

Or dress this dish whole or in pieces, lay between some carps, milts fried, boil'd, or stewed, as you do oysters, stewed and fried gudgeons, smelts, or oysters, some fried and stewed capers, mushrooms, and such like junkets.

Sometimes you may use currans, boil'd or stewed prunes, and put to the fore-said mixture, with some whole cloves, nutmegs, mace, ginger, some white-wine, verjuyce, or green sauce, some grated nutmeg over all, and some carved lemon.

Eggs in Moon shine.

Break them in a dish upon some butter and oyl melted or cold, strow on them a little salt, and set them on a chafing dish of coals make not the yolks too hard, and in the doing cover them, and make a sauce for them of an onion cut into round slices, and fried in sweet oyl or butter, then put to them verjuyce, grated nutmeg, a little salt, and so serve them.

Eggs in Moon shine otherways.

Take the best oyl you can get, and set it over the fire on a silver dish, being very hot, break in the eggs, and before the yolks of the eggs do become very hard, take them up and dish them in a clean dish; then make the sauce of fryed onions in round slices, fryed in oyl or sweet butter, salt, and some grated nutmeg.

Otherways.

Make a sirrup of rose-water, sugar, sack, or white-wine, make it in a dish and break the yolks of the eggs as whole as you can, put them in the boiling sirrup with some ambergriece, turn them and keep them one from the other, make them hard, and serve them in a little dish with sugar and cinamon.

Otherways.

Take a quarter of a pound of good fresh butter, balm it on the bottom of a fine clean dish, then break some eight or ten eggs upon it, sprinkle them with a little salt, and set them on a soft fire till the whites and yolks be pretty clear and stiff, but not too hard, serve them hot, and put on them the juyce of oranges and lemons.

Or before you break them put to the butter sprigs of rosemary, juyce of orange, and sugar; being baked on the embers, serve them with sugar and beaten cinamon, and in place of orange, verjuyce.

Eggs otherways.

Fry them whole in clarified butter with sprigs of rosemary under, fry them not too hard, and serve them with fried parsley on them, vinegar, butter, and pepper.

To dress Eggs in the Spanish Fashion, called, wivos me quidos[6].

Take twenty eggs fresh and new and strain them with a quarter of a pint of sack, claret, or white-wine, a quarter of sugar, some grated nutmeg, and salt; beat them together with the juyce of an orange, and put to them a little musk (or none) set them over the fire, and stir them continually till they be a little thick, (but not too much) serve them with scraping sugar being put in a clean warm dish, on fine toasts of manchet soaked in juyce of orange and sugar, or in claret, sugar, or white-wine, and shake the eggs with orange, comfits, or muskedines red and white.

To dress Eggs in the Portugal Fashion.

Strain the yolks of twenty eggs, and beat them very well in a dish, put to them some musk and rose-water made of fine sugar, boil'd thick in a clean skillet, put in the eggs, and stew them on a soft fire; being finely stewed, dish them on a French plate in a clean dish, scrape on sugar, and trim the dish with your finger.

Otherways.

Take twenty yolks of eggs, or as many whites, put them severally into two dishes, take out the cocks tread, and beat them severally the space of an hour; then have a sirrup made in two several skillets, with half a pound a piece of double refined sugar, and a little musk and ambergriece bound up close in a fine rag, set them a stewing on a soft fire till they be enough on both sides, then dish them on a silver plate, and shake them with preserved pistaches, muskedines white and red, and green citron slic't.

Put into the whites the juyce of spinage to make them green.

To dress Eggs called in French A-la-Hugenotte, or, the Protestant-way.

Break twenty eggs, beat them together, and put to them the pure gravy of a leg of mutton or the gravy of roast beef, stir and beat them well together over a chafing-dish of coals with a little salt, add to them also juyce of orange and lemon, or grape verjuyce; then put in some mushrooms well boil'd and seasoned. Observe as soon as your eggs are well mixed with the gravy and the other ingredients, then take them off from the fire, keeping them covered a while, then serve them with some grated nutmeg over them.

Sometimes to make them the more pleasing and toothsome, strow some powdered ambergriece, and fine loaf sugar scraped into them, and so serve them.

To dress Eggs in Fashion of a Tansie.

Take twenty yolks of eggs, and strain them on flesh days with about half a pint of gravy, on fish days with cream and milk, and salt, and four mackerooms small grated, as much bisket, some rose-water, a little sack or claret, and a quarter of a pound of sugar, put these things to them with a piece of butter as big as a walnut, and set them on a chafing-dish with some preserved citron or lemon grated, or cut into small pieces or little bits and some pounded pistaches; being well buttered dish it on a plate, and brown it with a hot fire-shovel, strow on fine sugar, and stick

---

[6] The Index has the obviously wrong "wivos qme uidos", but "me quidos" may also be an error. One possibility is "huevos ('wivos') quemados".

it with preserved lemon-peel in thin slices.

Eggs and almonds.

Take twenty eggs and strain them with half a pound of almond-paste, and almost half a pint of sack, sugar, nutmeg, and rose-water, set them on the fire, and when they be enough, dish them on a hot dish without toast, stick them with blanched and slic't almond, and wafers, scrape on fine sugar, and trim the dish with your finger.

To broil Eggs.

Take an oven peel, heat it red hot, and blow off the dust, break the eggs on it, and put them into a hot oven, or brown them on the top with a red hot fire shovel; being finely broil'd, put them into a clean dish, with some gravy, a little grated nutmeg, and elder vinegar; or pepper, vinegar, juyce of orange, and grated nutmeg on them.

To dress poached Eggs.

Take a dozen of new laid eggs, and the meat of 4 or five partridges or any roast poultrey, mince it as small as you can, and season it with a few beaten cloves, mace, and nutmeg, put them into a silver dish with a ladle full or 2 of pure mutton gravy, and 2 or three anchoves dissolved, then set it a stewing on a chafing dish of coals; being half stewed, as it boils put in the eggs one by one, and as you break them, put by most of the whites, and with one end of your egg shell put in the yolks round in order amongst the meat, let them stew till the eggs be enough, then put in a little grated nutmeg, and the juice of a couple of oranges, put not in the seeds, wipe the dish, and garnish it with four or five whole onions boiled and broil'd.

Otherways.

The eggs being poached, put them into a dish, strow salt on them, and grate on cheese which will give them a good relish.

Otherways.

Being poached and dished, strow on them a little salt, scrape on sugar, and sprinkle them with rose-water, verjuyce, juyce of lemon, or orange, a little cinamon water, or fine beaten cinamon.

Otherways to poach Eggs.

Take as many as you please, break them into a dish and put to them some sweet butter, being melted, some salt, sugar, and a little grated nutmeg, give them a cullet in the dish, &c.

Otherways.

Poach them, and put green sauce to them, let them stand a while upon the fire, then season them with salt, and a little grated nutmeg.

Or make a sauce with beaten butter, and juyce of grapes mixt with ipocras, pour it on the eggs, and scrape on sugar.

Otherways.

Poach them either in water, milk, wine, sack, or clear verjuyce, and serve them with vinegar in saucers.

Or make broth for them, and serve them on fine carved sippets, make the broth with washed currans, large mace, fair water, butter, white wine, and sugar, vinegar, juyce of orange, and whole cinamon; being dished run them over with beaten butter, the slices of an orange, and fine scraped sugar.

Or make sauce with beaten almonds, strained with verjuyce, sugar beaten, butter, and large mace, boiled and dished as the former.

Or almond milk and sugar.

A grand farc't Dish of Eggs.

Take twenty hard eggs, being blanched, part them in halves long ways, take out the yolks and save the whites, mince the yolks, or stamp them amongst some march pane paste, a few sweet herbs chopt small, & mingled amongst sugar, cinamon, and some currans well washed, fill again the whites with this farcing, and set them by.

Then have candied oranges or lemons, filled with march-pane paste, and sugar, and set them by also.

Then have the tops of boil'd sparagus, mix them with a batter made of flour, salt, and fair water, & set them by.

Next boil'd chesnuts and pistaches, and set them by.

Then have skirrets boil'd, peeled, and laid in batter.

Then have prawns boil'd and picked, and set by in batter also, oysters parboil'd and cockles, eels cut in pieces being flayed, and yolks of hard eggs.

Next have green quodling stuff, mixt with bisket bread and eggs, fry them in little cakes, and set them by also.

Then have artichocks and potatoes ready to fry in batter, being boil'd and cleansed also.

Then have balls of parmisan, as big as a walnut, made up and dipped in batter, and some balls of almond paste.

These aforesaid being finely fryed in clarified butter, and muskefied, mix them in a great charger one amongst another, and make a sauce of strained grape verjuyce, or white-wine, yolks of eggs, cream, beaten butter, cinamon and sugar, set them in an oven to warm; the sauce being boil'd up, pour it over all, and set it again in the oven, ice it with fine sugar, and so serve it.

Otherways.

Boil ten eggs hard, and part them in halves long ways, take out the yolks, mince them, and put to them some sweet herbs minc'd small, some boil'd currans, salt, sugar, cinamon, the yolks of two or three raw eggs, and some almond paste, (or none) mix all together, and fill again the whites, then lay them in a dish on some butter with the yolks downwards, or in a patty-pan, bake them, and make sauce of verjuyce & sugar, strained with the yolk of an egg and cinamon, give it a walm, and put to it some beaten butter; being dished, serve them with fine carved sippets, slic't orange, and sugar.

To make a great compound Egg, as big as twenty Eggs.

Take twenty eggs, part the whites from the yolks, and strain the whites by them selves, and the yolks by themselves; then have two bladders, boil the yolks in one bladder, fast bound up as round as a ball, being boil'd hard, put it in another bladder, and the whites round about it, bind it up round like the former, and being boil'd it will be a perfect egg. This serves for grand sallets.

Or you may add to these yolks of eggs, musk, and ambergriece, candied pistaches, grated bisket-bread, and sugar, and to the whites, almond-paste, musk, juyce of oranges, and beaten ginger, and serve it with butter, almond milk, sugar, and juyce of oranges.

To butter Eggs upon toasts.

Take twenty eggs, beat them in a dish with some salt and put butter to them; then have two large rouls or fine manchets, cut them into toasts, & toast them against the fire with a pound of fine sweet butter; being finely buttered, lay the toasts in a fair clean scowred dish, put the eggs on the toasts, and garnish the dish with pepper and salt. Otherways, half boil them in the shells, then butter them, and serve them on toasts, or toasts about them.

To these eggs sometimes use musk and ambergriece, and no pepper.

Otherways.

Take twenty eggs, and strain them whites and all with a little salt; then have a skillet with a pound of clarified butter, warm on the fire, then fry a good thick toast of fine manchet as round as the skillet, and an inch thick, the toast being finely fryed, put the eggs on it into the skillet, to fry on the manchet, but not too hard; being finely fried put it on a trencher-plate with the eggs uppermost, and salt about the dish.

An excellent way to butter Eggs.

Take twenty yolks of new laid or fresh eggs, put them into a dish with as many spoonfuls of jelly, or mutton gravy without fat, put to it a quarter of a pound of sugar, 2 ounces of preserved lemon-peel either grated or cut into thin slices or very little bits, with some salt, and four spoonfuls of rose-water, stir them together on the coals, and being butter'd dish them, put some musk on them with some fine sugar; you may as well eat these eggs cold as hot, with a little cinamon-water, or without.

Otherways.

Dress them with claret, white-wine, sack, or juyce of oranges, nutmeg, fine sugar, & a little salt, beat them well together in a fine clean dish, with carved sippets, and candied pistaches stuck in them.

Eggs buttered in the Polonian fashion.

Take twelve eggs, and beat them in a dish, then have steeped bread in gravy or broth, beat them together in a mortar, with some salt, and put it to the eggs, then put a little preserv'd lemon peel into it, either small shred or cut into slices, put some butter into it, butter them as the former, and serve them on fine sippets.

Or with cream, eggs, salt, preserved lemon-peels grated or in slices.

Or grated cheese in buttered eggs and salt.

Otherways.

Boil herbs, as spinage, sage, sweet marjoram, and endive, butter the eggs amongst them with some salt, and grated nutmeg.

Or dress them with sugar, orange juyce, salt, beaten cinamon, and grated nutmeg, strain the eggs with the juyce of oranges, and let the juyce serve instead of butter; being well soaked, put some more juyce over them and sugar.

To make minced Pies of Eggs according to these forms.

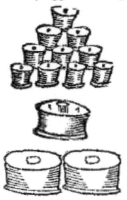

Boil them hard, then mince them and mix them with cinamon, raw currans, carraway-seed, sugar, and dates, minced lemon peel, verjuyce, rose-water, butter, and salt; fill your pie or pies, close them, and bake them, being baked, liquor them with white-wine, butter, and sugar, and ice them.

Eggs or Quelque shose.

Break forty eggs, and beat them together with some salt, fry them at four times, half, or but of one side; before you take them out of the pan, make a composition or compound of hard eggs, and sweet herbs minced, some boil'd currans, beaten cinamon, almond-paste, sugar, and juyce of orange, strow all over these omlets, roul them up like a wafer, and so of the rest, put them in a dish with some white-wine, sugar, and juyce of lemon; then warm and ice them in an oven, with beaten butter and fine sugar.

Otherways.

Set on a skillet, either full of milk, wine, water, verjuyce, or sack, make the liquor boil, then have twenty eggs beaten together with salt, and some sweet herbs chopped, run them through a cullender into the boiling liquor, or put them in by spoonfuls or all together; being not too hard boil'd, take them up and dish them with beaten butter, juice of orange, lemon, or grape-verjuyce, and beaten butter.

Blanch Manchet in a frying-Pan.

Take six eggs, a quart of cream, a penny manchet grated, nutmeg grated, two spoonfuls of rose-water, and 2 ounces of sugar, beat it up like a pudding, and fry it as you fry a tansie; being fryed turn it out on a plate, quarter it, and put on the juyce of an orange and sugar.

Quelque shose otherways.

Take ten eggs, and beat them in a dish with a penny manchet grated, a pint of cream, some beaten cloves mace, boil'd currans, some rose-water, salt, and sugar; beat all together, and fry it either in a whole form of a tansie, or by spoonfuls in little cakes, being finely fried, serve them on a plate with juyce of orange and scraping sugar.

Other Fricase or Quelque shose.

Take twenty eggs, and strain them with a quart of cream, some nutmeg, salt, rose-water, and a little sugar, then have sweet butter in a clean frying-pan, and put in some pieces of pippins cut as thick as a half crown piece round the apple being cored; when they are finely fried, put in half the eggs, fry them a little, and then pour on the rest or other half, fry it at two times, stir the last, dish the first on a plate, and put the other on it with juyce of orange and sugar.

Other Fricase of Eggs.

Beat a dozen of eggs with cream, sugar, nutmeg, mace, and rose-water, then have two or three pippins or other good apples, cut in round slices through core and all, put them in a frying-pan, and fry them with sweet butter; when they be enough, take them up and fry half the eggs and cream in other fresh butter, stir it like a tansie, and being enough put it out into a dish, put in the other half of the eggs and cream, lay the apples round the pan, and the other eggs fried before, uppermost; being finely fried, dish it on a plate, and put to it the juyce of an orange and sugar.

SECTION XXII.

The best Ways for the Dressing of Artichocks.

To stew Artichocks.

 The artichocks being boil'd, take out the core, and take off all the leaves, cut the bottoms into quarters splitting them in the middle; then have a flat stewing-pan or dish with manchet toasts in it, lay the artichocks on them, then the marrow of two bones, five or six large maces, half a pound of preserved plumbs, with the sirrup, verjuyce, and sugar; if the sirrup do not make them sweet enough, let all these stew together 2 hours, if you stew them in a dish, serve them up in it, not stirring them, only laying on some preserves which are fresh, as barberries, and such like, sippet it, and serve it up.

Instead of preserved, if you have none, stew ordinary plumbs which will be cheaper, and do nigh as well.

To fry Artichocks.

Boil and sever all from the bottoms, then slice them in the midst, quarter them, dip them in batter, and fry them in butter. For the sauce take verjuyce, butter, and sugar, with the juyce of an orange, lay marrow on them, garnish them with oranges, and serve them up.

To fry young Artichocks otherways.

Take young artichocks or suckets, pare off all the outside as you pare an apple, and boil them tender, then take them up, and split them through the midst, do not take out the core, but lay the split side downward on a dry cloth to drain out the water; then mix a little flour with two or three yolks of eggs, beaten ginger, nutmeg & verjuyce, make it into batter and roul them well in it, then get some clarified butter, make it hot and fry them in it till they be brown. Make sauce with yolks of eggs, verjuyce or white-wine, cinamon, ginger, sugar, and a good piece of butter, keep it stirring upon the fire till it be thick, then dish them on white-bread toasts, put the caudle on them, and serve them up.

SECTION XXIII.

Shewing the best way of making Diet for the Sick.

To make a Broth for a Sick body.

Take a leg of veal, and set it a boiling in a gallon of fair water, scum it clean, and when you have so done put in three quarters of a pound of currans, half a pound of prunes, a handful of borrage, as much mint, and as much harts-tongue; let them seeth together till all the strength be sodden out of the flesh, then strain it as clean as you can. If you think the party be in any heat, put in violet leaves and succory.

To stew a Cock against a Consumption.

Cut him in six pieces, and wash him clean, then take prunes, currans, dates, raisins, sugar, three or four leaves of gold, cinamon, ginger, nutmeg, and some maiden hair, cut very small; put all these foresaid things into a flaggon with a pint of muskadine, and boil them in a great brass pot of half a bushel; stop the mouth of the flaggon with a piece of paste, and let it boil the space of twelve hours; being well stewed, strain the liquor, and give it to the party to drink cold, two or three spoonfuls in the morning fasting, and it shall help him. *This is an approved Medicine.*

Otherways.

Take a good fleshy cock, draw him and cut him to pieces, wash away the blood clean, and take away the lights that lie at his back, wash it in white-wine, and no water, then put the pieces in a flaggon, and put to it two or three blades of large mace, a leaf of gold, ambergriece, some dates, and raisins of the Sun; close up the flaggon with a piece of paste, and set it in a pot a boiling six hours; keep the pot filled up continually, with hot water; being boil'd strain it, and when it is cold give of it to the weak party the bigness of a hazelnut.

Stewed Pullets against a Consumption.

Take two pullets being finely cleansed, cut them to pieces, and put them in a narrow mouthed pitcher pot well glazed, stop the mouth of it with a piece of paste and set it a boiling in a good deep brass pot or vessel of water, boil it eight hours, keep it continually boiling, and still filled up with warm water; being well stewed, strain it, and blow off the fat; when you give it to the party, give it warm with the yolk of an egg, dissolved with the juyce of an orange.

To distill a Pig good against a Consumption.

Take a pig, flay it and cast away the guts; then take the liver, lungs, and all the entrails, and wipe all with a clean cloth; then put it into a Still with a pound of dates, the stones taken out, and sliced into thin slices, a pound of sugar, and an ounce of large mace. If the party be hot in the stomach, then take these cool herbs, as violet leaves, strawberry leaves, and half a handful of bugloss, still them with a soft fire as you do roses, and let the party take of it every morning and evening in any drink or broth he pleases.

You may sometimes add raisins and cloves.

To make Broth good against a Consumption.

Take a cock and a knuckle of veal, being well soaked from the blood, boil them in an earthen pipkin of five quarts, with raisins of the sun, a few prunes, succory, lang de-beef roots, fennel roots, parsley, a little anniseed, a pint of white-wine, hyssop, violet leaves, strawberry-leaves, bind all the foresaid roots, and herbs, a little quantity of each in a bundle, boil it leisurely, scum it, and when it is boil'd strain it through a strainer of strong canvas, when you use it, drink it as often as you please blood-warm.

Sometimes in the broth, or of any of the meats aforesaid, use mace, raisins of the sun, a little balm, endive, fennel and parsley roots.

Sometimes sorrel, violet leaves, spinage, endive, succory, sage, a little hyssop, raisins of the sun, prunes, a little saffron, and the yolk of an egg, strained with verjuyce or white-wine.

Otherways.

Fennil-roots, colts foot, agrimony, betony, large mace, white sander slic't in thin slices the weight of six pence, made with a chicken and a crust of manchet, take it morning and evening.

Otherways.

Violet leaves, wild tansie, succory-roots, large mace, raisins, and damask prunes boil'd with a chicken and a crust of bread.

Sometimes broth made of a chop of mutton, veal, or chicken, French barley, raisins, currans, capers, succory root, parsley roots, fennil-roots, balm, borrage, bugloss, endive, tamarisk, harts-horn, ivory, yellow sanders, and fumitory, put to these all (or some) in a moderate quantity.

Otherways, a sprig of rosemary, violet-leaves, tyme, mace, succory, raisins, and a crust of bread.

To make a Paste for a Consumption.

Take the brawn of a roasted capon, the brawn of two partridges, two rails, two quails, and twelve sparrows all roasted; take the brawns from the bones, and beat them in a stone mortar with two ounces, of the pith of roast veal, a quarter of a pound of pistaches, half a dram of ambergriece, a grain of musk, and a pound of white sugar-candy beaten fine; beat all these in a mortar to a perfect paste, now and then putting in a spoonful of goats milk, also two or three grains of bezoar;

when you have beaten all to a perfect paste, make it into little round cakes, and bake them on a sheet of white paper.

To make a Jelly for a Consumption of the Lungs.

Take half a pound of ising glass, as much harts-horn, an ounce of cinamon, an ounce of nutmegs, a few cloves, a pound of sugar, a stick of liquoras, four blades of large mace, a pound of prunes, an ounce of ginger, a little red sanders, and as much rubarb as will lie on a six pence, boil the foresaid in a gallon of water, and a pint of claret till a pint be wasted or boil'd away, boil them on a soft fire close covered, and slice all your spices very thin.

An excellent Water for a Consumption.

Take a pint of new milk, and a pint of good red wine, the yolks of twenty four new laid eggs raw, and dissolved in the foresaid liquors; then have as much fine slic't manchet as will drink up all this liquor, put it into a fair rose-still with a soft fire, and being distilled, take this water in all drinks and pottages the sick party shall eat, or the quantity of a spoonful at a draught in beer, in one month it will recover any Consumption.

Other drink for a Consumption.

Take a gallon of running water of ale measure, put to it an ounce of cinamon, an ounce of cloves, an ounce of mace, and a dram of acter-roots, boil this liquor till it come to three quarts, and let the party daily drink of it till he mends.

To make an excellent Broth or Drink for a Sick Body.

Take a good fleshy capon, take the flesh from the bones, or chop it in pieces very small, and not wash it; then put them in a rose still with slics of lemon-peel, wood-sorrel, or other herbs according to the *Physitians* direction; being distilled, give it to the weak party to drink.

Or soak them in malmsey and some capon broth before you distill them.

To make a strong Broth for a Sick Party.

Roast a leg of mutton, save the gravy, and being roasted prick it, and press out the gravy with a wooden press; put all the gravy into a silver porrenger or piece, with the juyce of an orange and sugar, warm it on the coals, and give it the weak party.

Thus you may do a roast or boil'd capon, partridge, pheasant, or chicken, take the flesh from the bones, and stamp it in a stone or wooden mortar, with some crumbs of fine manchet, strained with capon broth, or without bread, and put the yolk of an egg, juyce of orange, lemon, or grape verjuyce and sugar.

To make China Broth.

Take an ounce of China thin slic't, put it in a pipkin of fair water, with a little veal or chicken, stopped close in pipkin, let it stand 4 and twenty hours on the embers but not boil; then put to it colts foot, scabious-maiden-hair, violet leaves half a handful, candied eringo, and 2 or 3 marsh mallows, boil them on a soft fire till the third part be wasted, then put in a crust of manchet, a little mace, a few raisins of the sun stoned, and let it boil a while longer. Take of this broth every morning half a pint for a month, then leave it a month, & use it again.

China Broth otherways.

Take 2 ounces of China root thin sliced, and half an ounce of long pepper bruised; then take of balm, tyme, sage, marjoram, nepe, and smalk, of each two slices, clary, a hanful of cowslips, a pint of cowslip water, and 3 blades of mace; put all into a new and well glazed pipkin of 4 quarts, & as much fair water as will fill the pipkin, close it up with paste and let it on the embers to warm, but not to boil; let it stand thus soaking 4 and twenty hours; then take it off, and put to it a good big cock chickens, calves foot, a knuckle of mutton, and a little salt; stew all with a gentle fire to a pottle, scum it very clean & being boil'd strain the clearest from the dregs & drink of it every morning half a pint blood-warm.

To make Almond Milk against a hot Disease.

Boil half a pound of French barley in 3 several waters, keep the last water to make your milk of, then stamp half a pound of almonds with a little of the same water to keep them from oyling; being finely beaten, strain it whith the rest of the barley water, put some hard sugar to it, boil it a little, and give it the party warm.

An excellent Restorative for a weak back.

Take clary, dates, the pith of an oxe, and chop them together, put some cream to them, eggs, grated bread, and a little white saunders, temper them all together fry them, and eat it in the morning fasting.

Otherways, take the leaves of clary and nepe, fry them with yolks of eggs, and eat them to break fast.

SECTION XXIV.

Excellent Ways for Feeding of Poultrey.

To feed Chickens.

IF you will have fat crammed chickens, coop them up when the dam hath forsaken them, the best cramming for them is wheat-meal and milk made into dough the crams steeped in milk, and so thrust down their throats; but in any case let the crams be small and well wet, for fear you choak them. Fourteen days will feed a chicken sufficiently.

To feed Capons.

Either at the barn doors with scraps of corn and chavings of pulse, or else in pens in the house, by cramming them, which is the most dainty. The best way to cram a capon (setting all strange inventions apart) is to take barley meal, reasonably sifted, and mixing it with new milk, make it into good stiff dough; than make it into long crams thickest in the middle, & small at both ends, then wetting them in luke-warm milk, giue the capon a full gorge thereof three times a day morning noon, and night, and he will in a fortnight or three weeks be as fat as any man need to eat.

The ordering of Goslings.

After they are hatched you shall keep them in the house ten or twelve days, and feed them with curds, scalded chippins, or barley meal in milk knodden and broken, also ground malt is exceeding good, or any bran that is scalded in water, milk, or tappings of drink. After they have got a little strength, you may let them go abroad with a keeper five or six hours in a day, and let the dam at her leisure entice them into the water; then bring them in, and put them up, and thus order them till they be able to defend themselves from vermine. After a gosling is a month or six weeks old you may put it up to feed for a green goose, & it will be perfectly fed in another month following; and to feed them, there is no better meat then skeg oats boil'd, and given plenty thereof thrice a day, morning, noon, and night, with good store of milk, or milk and water mixt together to drink.

For fatting of elder Geese.

For elder geese which are five or six months old, having been in the stubble fields after harvest, and got into good flesh, you shall then choose out such geese as you would feed, and put them in several Pens which are close and dark, and there feed them thrice a day with good store of oats, or spelted beans, and give them to drink water and barly meal mixt together, which must evermore stand before them. This will in three weeks feed a goose so fat as is needfull.

The fatting of Ducklings.

You may make them fat in three weeks giving them any kind of pulse or grain, and good store of water.

Fatting of Swans and Cygnets.

For Swans and their feeding, where they build their nests, you shall suffer them to remain undisturbed, and it will be sufficient because they can better order themselves in that business than any man.

Feed your Cygnets in all sorts as you feed your Geese, and they will be through fat in seven or eight weeks. If you will have them sooner fat, you shall feed them in some pond hedged, or placed in for that purpose.

Of fatting Turkies.

For the fatting of turkies sodden barley is excellent, or sodden oats for the first fortnight, and then for another fortnight cram them in all sorts as you cram your capon, and they will be fat beyond measure. Now for their infirmities, when they are at liberty, they are so good *Physitians* for themselves, that they will never trouble their owners; but being coopt up you must cure them as you do pullets. Their eggs are exceeding wholesome to eat, and restore nature decayed wonderfully.

Having a little dry ground where they may sit and prune themselves, place two troughs, one full of barley and water, and the other full of old dried malt wherein they may feed at their pleasure. Thus doing, they will be fat in less than a month: but you must turn his walks daily.

Of nourishing and fatting Herns, Puets, Gulls, and Bitterns.

Herns are nourished for two causes, either for Noblemens sports, to make trains for the entering their hawks, or else to furnish the table at great feasts; the manner of bringing them up with the least charge, is to take them out of their nests before they can flie, and put them into a large high barn, where there is many high cross beams for them to pearch on; then to have on the flour divers square boards with rings in them, and between every board which should be two yards square, to place round shallow tubs full of water, then to the boards you shall tye great gobbits of dogs flesh, cut from the bones, according to the number which you feed, and be sure to keep the house sweet, and shift the water often, only the house must be made so, that it may rain in now and then, in which the hern will take much delight; but if you feed her for the dish, then you shall feed them with livers, and the entrals of beasts, and such like cut in great gobbits.

To feed Codwits, Knots, Gray-Plovers, or Curlews.

Take fine chilter-wheat, and give them water thrice a day, morning, noon, and night; which will be very effectual; but if you intend to have them extraordinary crammed fowl, then you shall take the finest drest wheat-meal, and mixing it with milk, make it into paste, and ever as you knead it, sprinkle into the grains of small chilter-wheat, till the paste be fully mixt therewith; then make little small crams thereof, and dipping them in water, give to every fowl according to his bigness, and let his gorge be well filled: do thus as oft as you shall find their gorges empty, and in one fortnight they will be fed beyond measure, and with these crams you may feed any fowl of what kind or nature soever.

Otherways.

Feed them with good wheat and water, give them thrice a day, morning, noon, and night; if you will have them very fat & crammed fowl, take fine wheat meal & mix it with milk, & make it into paste, and as you knead it, put in some corns of wheat sprinkled in amongst the paste till the paste be fully mixt therewith; then make little small crams thereof, and dipping them in water, give to every fowl according to his bigness, and that his gorge be well filled: do thus as oft as you shall find their gorges empty, and in one fortnight they will be fed very fat; with these crams you may feed any fowl of what kind or nature soever.

To feed Black-Birds Thrushes, Felfares, or any small Birds whatsoever.

Being taken old and wild, it is good to have some of their kinds tame to mix among them, and then putting them into great cages of three or four yards square, to have divers troughs placed therein, some filled with haws, some with hemp seed, and some with water, that the tame teaching the wild to eat, and the wild finding such change and alteration of food, they will in twelve or fourteen days grow exceeding fat, and fit for the kitchen.

To feed Olines.

Put them into a fine room where they may have air, give them water, and feed them with white bread boiled in good milk, and in one week or ten days they will be extraordinary fat.

To feed Pewets.

Feed them in a place where they may have the air, set them good store of water, and feed them with sheeps lungs cut small into little bits, give it them on boards, and sometimes feed them with shrimps where they are near the sea, and in one fortnight they will be fat if they be followed with meat. Then two or three days before you spend them give them cheese curd to purge them.

The feedings of Pheasant, Partridge, Quails, and Wheat Ears.

Feed them with good wheat and water, this given them thrice a day, morning noon, and night, will do it very effectually; but if you intend to have them extraordinary crammed fowl, then take the finest drest wheatmeal, mix it with milk, and make into paste, ever as you knead it, sprinkle in the grains of corns of wheat, till the paste be full mixt there with; then make little small crams, dip them in water, and give to every fowl according to his bigness, that his gorge be well filled; do thus as often as you shall find his gorge empty, and in one fortnight they will be fed beyond measure. Thus you may feed turtle Doves.

FINIS.

INDEX

Lector House believes that a society develops through a two-fold approach of continuous learning and adaptation, which is derived from the study of classic literary works spread across the historic timeline of literature records. Therefore, we aim at reviving, repairing and redeveloping all those inaccessible or damaged but historically as well as culturally important literature across subjects so that the future generations may have an opportunity to study and learn from past works to embark upon a journey of creating a better future.

This book is a result of an effort made by Lector House towards making a contribution to the preservation and repair of original ancient works which might hold historical significance to the approach of continuous learning across subjects.

HAPPY READING & LEARNING!

LECTOR HOUSE LLP
E-MAIL: lectorpublishing@gmail.com

9 789353 426217

9 789353 426217